Living in a digital world
Demystifying technology
by Mark C Baker

General

First published 2018

Edition 1, version 1.06

Soft cover -   ISBN-10:   1540697517   ISBN-13:   978-1540697516
Hard cover - n/a   ISBN-13:   979-8498499345

Copyright © 2018 by Mark C Baker

All rights reserved. No part of this publication may be reproduced or transmitted in any form or by any means, electronic or mechanical, including photocopy, recording, or any information storage and retrieval system, without prior permission in writing from the author, except in the case of brief quotations embodied in critical reviews and certain other noncommercial uses permitted by copyright law.

Use the contact details at educationvision.co.uk for permission requests (scan QR Code below for link).

Printed by Kindle Direct Publishing

Available from Amazon.com and other retail outlets

Cover design: Mark C Baker

For *Mark C Baker* webpages, scan the QR Code (below) or see: **educationvision.co.uk/books.html**

Mark C Baker webpages

By the same author

- *UK Canals 1: The Kennet and Avon Canal in pictures*
- *UK Canals 2: Wildlife of the Kennet and Avon Canal*
- *UK Canals 3: Weird and wonderful canal photographs*
- *UK Canals 4: The Erewash Canal in context*
- *Pandemic diary: Newbury in a time of crisis*
- *Pandemic diary 2: Newbury emerges from lockdown*

Trademarks

Macintosh and Mac OS are trademarks of Apple Inc., registered in the U.S.A. and other countries.

Microsoft and Windows are either registered trademarks of Microsoft Corporation in the United States and/or other countries.

Google and YouTube are registered trademarks of Google LLC.

QR Code is a registered trademark of DENSO WAVE INCORPORATED.

Raspberry Pi is a trademark of the Raspberry Pi Foundation.

All other brand or product names mentioned in this book are the trademarks or registered trademarks of their respective holders.

Contents (summary)

Contents..5

Dedication..13

Author..14

Acknowledgements...14

Preface...15

Introduction...17

1: Input, process, output......................................23

2: Digital devices and data...................................43

3: Algorithms and software..................................91

4: Computer networks and the internet.............149

5: How some stuff works....................................187

6: Some technology issues.................................259

Appendix A: SI prefixes - kilo, mega, giga.........291

Appendix B: Computing timeline.......................293

Appendix C: Failed IT projects..........................299

Sources..305

Glossary...315

Index..321

Contents

Dedication..13

Author..14

Acknowledgements...14

Preface...15
    Navigating through the book..15

Introduction..17
A brief history of computers..18

Digital natives and digital immigrants..20

Introduction: Key learning points..22

1: Input, process, output..23
The Black Box Model..23

Key inputs and outputs of two example systems..............................27
    Supermarket checkout..27
    Booking a flight using an online travel agent............................28

Hardware - input, output, storage...28

Self test..31

Looking inside the black box - basic computer architecture................32

Interfaces..36

Types of computer..37

Raspberry Pi..39

Supercomputers..40

Self test..41

Chapter 1: Key learning points...42

2: Digital devices and data............................43

Analogue vs Digital..43
What makes a digital device, "digital"?...................................44
Digitising data..46
    Digitising temperature readings...................................46
    Digitising sound..49
    Digitising text...50
Self test...52
    Representing pictures with numbers.............................53
    Compressing image files..54
Self test...57
    A selection of image formats.......................................59
Example visual degradation due to JPEG compression................60
Data vs Information...64
Metadata and images...65
    Scanners..66
The discovery of zero...67
Alternative number systems..67
The easy introduction to binary...68
Self test...70
Bits, bytes and words...71
The nature of digital signals..72
Error detection..74
    Parity checks..74
    Redundancy..76
    Check digits..76
    International Article Numbers (EAN).............................78
Error correction...81

Colour and grey-scale images..81
Different types of number..84
    Positive integers..84
    Negative numbers - two's complement..85
    Real numbers - representing fractions...86
Self test...88
    Real numbers - scientific notation..89
    Real numbers - floating point representation......................................89
Chapter 2: Key learning points..90

3: Algorithms and software..............................91

Algorithms...91
Computer programs..95
Types of software...95
UEFI/Basic input output system or BIOS..96
Operating system (OS)...96
Application software or apps..97
Utility software...98
    Disc fragmentation...98
    File renaming..100
Programming languages...101
Self test...104
Some example algorithms..105
    Variables...105
    Arrays...105
    Selection Sort...105
    j = j + 1...108
    Pseudocode..109
    Exchange or Bubble Sort..113

Measuring the efficiency of sorting algorithms..114
Atomic data types..115
Data structures..115
Using pointers to maintain an ordered list...116
Self test...119
Linear search algorithm...120
Binary search algorithm...120
A selection of application software..121
Office suite...121
Word processor...123
Spreadsheet..123
Presentation graphics..125
Desktop publisher...127
Database..129
Graphics software..134
Web browser..141
Mobile device apps...142
Beware the 'ware words!..144
Self test...146
Chapter 3: Key learning points..147

4: Computer networks and the internet...........149

What is a computer network?..149
Network hardware..151
Ethernet..153
The Internet..153
Global brain?...153
Internet services..155
Self test...156

Internet governance...158
History of the internet..158
The World Wide Web (WWW)..161
The deep, dark web...161
Web versions..163
Markup Languages...165
HTML - The language of the web..165
Putting pages on the World Wide Web 173
XML and the SVG graphics format...175
Streaming...177
Web caching..179
Internet search engines...179
Internet snapshot...180

Self test..182

Chapter 4: Key learning points...184

5: How some stuff works..............................187

Handshaking..187

Universal Serial Bus (USB)...189

Solid state memory..192
Types of solid state memory...193
How flash memory works...195
Solid state drives or SSD...197

Self test..198

Magnetic backing storage..199
Magnetic tape..199
Floppy discs...199
Hard disc drives...202
Deleting and recovering files..204

- How a hard disc drive works...205
- Drive letters...205
- Where is my data stored?..205

Self test..208
Optical media...209
- Compact disc (CD)..209

Radio-frequency identification (RFID)...210
Barcodes..212
- The anatomy of an EAN barcode..212
- 2-D barcodes..216
- QR Codes..217
- Uses of QR Codes...220
- Types of barcode reader...222
- An example barcode reader..222

Communications..223
- Mobile telephony..224
- Smartphones..227
- Satellite communications...232
- The inverse square law..233
- Satellite navigation systems..233

Artificial intelligence..234
- Why is AI so difficult?...239

Bitcoin and other cryptocurrencies..242
- What is money?..243
- Public key cryptography...246
- How does bitcoin work?...248
- Is bitcoin a real currency?..251
- Other applications of blockchain technology...252

Self test..254

Chapter 5: Key learning points...256

6: Some technology issues............................259

The pace of technological change...259
Online safety..261
Digital footprint...269
    Cookies..271
    To link or not to link? That is the question..............................272
    The Internet Archive and the Wayback Machine.....................273
    Digital footprint - what is at stake?..274
    The snooper's charter..274
    The right to be forgotten and the GDPR....................................275
Technical tools that support online safety......................................276
    Firewall..276
    Anti-malware / Anti-virus software..277
    Parental controls and filtering..278
    Encrypting devices including laptops, smartphones and flash memory drives..278
    Device tracking and disabling...279
    Virtual Private Network (VPN)...279
    Proxy server..280
War and peace and fake news..280
The vision thing..285
Self test...287
Chapter 6: Key learning points..289

Appendix A: SI prefixes - kilo, mega, giga............291
IEC binary (bi) prefixes............292

Appendix B: Computing timeline............293

Appendix C: Failed IT projects............299

Some failed IT projects - UK Government and related bodies............299
Project: London Ambulance Computer Aided Dispatch System, 1992............299
Project: NHS National Program for IT, 2002............300
Project: Department for Transport Shared Services Centre, 2005............300
Project: Defence Information Infrastructure, 2005............300
Project: Common Agricultural Policy Delivery Programme, 2014............301

Some failed IT projects - worldwide............301
Project: State of Washington License Application Mitigation Project, begun 1990, USA............301
Project: FoxMeyer Drugs ERP Program 1993 - 1996, USA............301
Project: National Firearm Registration System, 1997, Canada............302
Project: Sainsbury's Warehouse Automation, 2003, UK............302
Project: Queensland Health Payroll and Rostering System, 2006, Australia...303

Manifesto for Agile Software Development............303
Principles behind the Agile Manifesto............304

Sources............305

Glossary............315

Index............321

Dedication

This book is dedicated to Trevor and Chris Pedley and their daughter, Rebecca.

Trevor was an energetic and very supportive head of department, who was largely responsible for my decision to change subjects and take up the teaching of computing/ICT. I am also very grateful for his carefully considered reviews of the content of this book, as writing progressed.

My thanks are also due to Chris for her ongoing support and encouragement and to both of them for their friendship over the years.

I am very grateful to Rebecca, who gave much crucial guidance with regard to publishing. This was invaluable in getting the project off the ground and as part of the final review.

Author

Mark C Baker is founder and director of Education Vision Consultancy Ltd, which he established to continue a long career in education. This began in the classroom and continued with advisory/consultancy roles with a commercial company, local authority and then Becta, the government agency that led the national drive to ensure the effective and innovative use of technology throughout learning.

In common with many computing/ICT teachers of his generation, Mark began teaching other subjects (mathematics, physics and photography), moving over mid-career. He has always enjoyed finding ways of making important ideas and concepts as accessible as possible to the widest possible audience. Following the completion of a master's degree in computer science, he also wrote software to use in school, that sold internationally as shareware. Programs included the word puzzle creator Crosswords for Teachers and Sorting for Teachers, which allowed the in-depth study of sorting algorithms. He is a qualified teacher of the deaf.

Mark is an enthusiastic photographer (he is responsible for most of the photographs and all of the diagrams in the book) and he volunteers regularly with the Canal and River Trust on the Kennet and Avon Canal. He lives in Newbury, Berkshire in the south of England.

Website: educationvision.co.uk

Twitter: @EducationVision

Acknowledgements

My thanks are due to the following.

Williams F1 for providing photographs of their FW08B test car (Chapter 5).

Katie John and **Jon Tarrant** for their contributions to a review of the Becta hazard matrix. Katie also had the idea of developing a benefits matrix (Chapter 6).

Derrick and/or **Patrick** (@DPRK_News) for allowing a selection of their tweets to be reproduced (Chapter 6).

Thomas Ng for his considered feedback and many conversations about technology and education.

Preface

This book is designed to explain some of the fundamentals of digital technology and help readers to reach a working understanding of devices such as computers and mobile phones, software (programs, apps) and the internet. If you are tired of treating all the digital devices that surround us as magical black boxes and would like to build an understanding of how they operate, then this is the book for you.

Initially written to build up the background knowledge and confidence of non-specialist teachers who now have to teach computing to children, it will appeal to a wider audience who would like a better understanding of the digital world. It will also make interesting background reading for students and pupils starting introductory technology courses.

An improved understanding of digital technology, including its limitations and constraints, should allow us to have a more informed debate about what we want from it and how we want to use it. We should be aspiring to be driving developments in technology, instead of being driven by them.

I have spent much of my career in education dealing with areas that are considered "difficult". It has been my experience that whilst some learners can lack confidence, it is rare that people are incapable of understanding – it all comes down to how the information is structured and presented. However there are people who like to maintain a degree of mystery around technology, as this protects their position as "experts" and the weapon of choice for many of these is specialist jargon. Terms like bits, bytes, caches, CPU, interfaces and double data rate synchronous dynamic random access memory are carelessly thrown about, creating a frightening web of seemingly impenetrable complexity.

In reality things are much more straightforward, especially at the level likely to be of interest to most people. Whilst it is true that some of the mathematics that lies behind things like file compression and 3-D graphics can be truly mind-bending, it is only specialists working in these areas that need to understand this in detail. Much of computing involves elegant simplicity.

Navigating through the book
This book was intended to be something readers can dip in and out of. I have tried to avoid making the understanding of sections dependent on reading earlier material, so far as is possible. However, there are themes and concepts that build and are reinforced as the book progresses.

The text includes short self tests with answers to allow readers to check and consolidate their learning. Occasional practical tasks are suggested that offer the opportunity to deepen understanding and explore further.

Each chapter ends with a list of key learning points and a word cloud diagram (below) that represents the vocabulary used.

Title

In some places diagrams and/or text have been added as an insert, that interrupts the flow of the text. To aid clarity where this might not be obvious, the section begins with a grey dotted line on either side of the title. If the insert lasts for *more* than one page, the line is shown *above* the title and there is a similar line at the end.

Mark C Baker, 2018

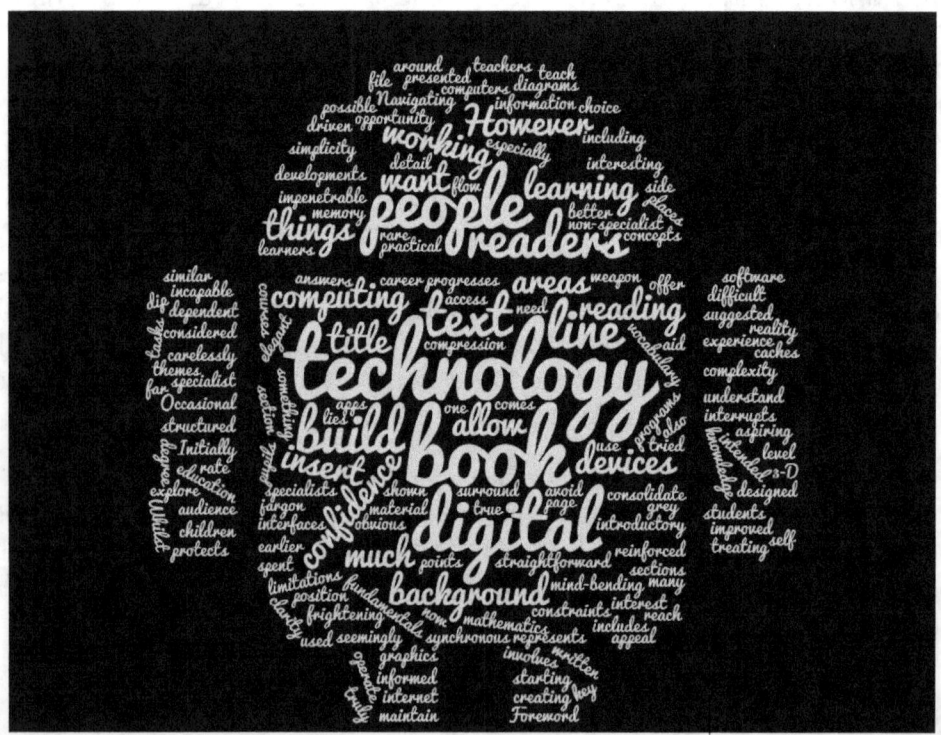

Note: The word cloud diagram above was produced by pasting all the text from the preface into a tool hosted at http://www.wordclouds.com. The size of each word is based on how often it is used, with the largest words being the ones that are used the most. It is a simple, yet engaging, text analysis tool. Similar word clouds can be found at the end of each chapter.

1 0 1 1 0 0 0 1 0 0 1 1 1 0 1 1 0 1 0 1 1 0 0 1 0 0 0

Introduction

A digital device is one that uses a computer to control its operations. It may be a readily recognised computer, such as a desktop, laptop, or tablet computer or it may be a device that incorporates a **microcontroller**, such as a microwave oven, digital camera, washing machine or TV remote control. Microcontrollers are small computers on a single integrated circuit or "chip", often referred to as a "system on a chip" and abbreviated to **SoC**. They have become ubiquitous, being used in all sorts of modern devices; domestic, commercial and industrial. We live in a world that is increasingly dominated by digital devices.

Computing devices work by processing data made up of zeros and ones and so the emphasis is usually on simplicity. Computers cannot do horribly complex things. They do very simple things, like adding numbers together, comparing two numbers to see which one is bigger and moving a number from one part of the computer to another.

Because computing devices can only do simple things there is often a lovely elegance to the ways in which people get them to produce something useful. Think of some of the superb models that have been produced using children's construction bricks. Each brick is incredibly simple and in relation to the final model, very small. Yet, when put together with imagination it is possible to produce something outstanding – perhaps a model of the Eiffel Tower, a polar bear, a life-size dinosaur, a full-size automobile or a reproduction of Times Square in New York City. Models can contain tens of thousands, hundreds of thousands, even millions of individual bricks.

Computer programs are very similar. Writing computer programs is how a programmer can tell a computer how it should behave in different circumstances. Each one is made up of a structured set of programming statements. Each statement is an instruction telling the computer to do something very simple and in relation to the final program, it is very small indeed. Large programs can contain many thousands or millions of programming statements that took hundreds or thousands of hours to write. Crafted with imagination you can end up with an incredibly lifelike computer game, a social media website, a flight simulator for training pilots or general purpose software like a spreadsheet, that can be used by people in all walks of life to make repetitive calculations in whatever way they want, with great speed and accuracy.

That is what computing devices do; they carry out simple operations at great speed and with incredible accuracy and these operations can be put together to build fantastically flexible tools, according to whatever needs that have been identified.

A brief history of computers

The word "computer" was originally used to describe a person who carried out calculations and it was only in the 20th Century that it was increasingly used to describe calculating machines instead.

Early general calculating devices included abacuses and there were specialised calculating devices too, for example to calculate astronomical positions. Some of these date back thousands of years, however modern electronic computing can be thought of as beginning in the 1940s. It was given significant boosts by the invention of the transistor in 1947, followed soon after by the first integrated circuits, which combined multiple transistors and other electronic components on a single semiconductor chip, the forerunners of the now ubiquitous microcontrollers. These replaced the glass vacuum tubes used in the early computers, which took up a great deal of space and consumed a lot of electrical power.

Glass vacuum tube "valves", the forerunners of semiconductor diodes, transistors and other electronic components.

The drive to develop computers came from the need to perform very large numbers of calculations quickly and accurately. The exploits of the Bletchley Park code breakers in hacking the German Enigma coding machines in the 1940s have been well documented. Another military application was the production of comprehensive firing and bombing tables from 1914 onwards. However, there were also non-military tasks where manual data processing was proving increasingly unsatisfactory because it was too slow and too expensive.

From 1870 onwards, the processing needs of the US census drove the development of new automated methods. The final results of the 1880 census were not available until 1887, just 3 years before the next census was due! Herman Hollerith, a former Census Office employee, invented a counting machine that used punched cards, each one representing the census data of a single individual. These were used to help process the 1890 census. The work was completed well ahead of schedule and significantly under budget. The company that Hollerith founded went on to become International Business Machines, better known today as IBM. The US Census Bureau continued to be at the forefront of computing technology as late as the 1950s, when they were the first civilian government agency to install an electronic computer (UNIVAC - Universal Automatic Computer).

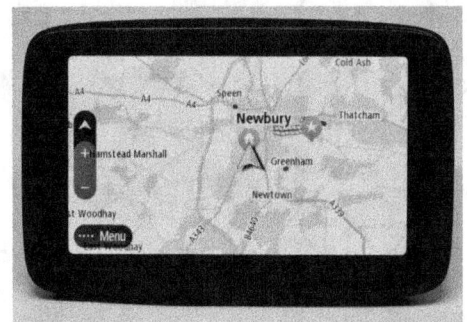

Digital device: Vehicle satellite navigation system

Today we are dependent on the large-scale data processing capabilities of electronic computers to maintain bank accounts, allow credit and debit cards to function, book travel tickets, supply water and power, make online purchases, operate social media websites, control telephone networks, ease traffic flows on congested roads, keep aircraft safe in the air and a myriad of other applications. Yet go back to the 1930s and computers as we know them today were barely a gleam in the eye of one or two theoreticians, such as Englishman Alan Turing and American John von Neumann. By the 1960s computers could only be feasibly operated by large organisations, with some smaller organisations renting time on them. Today there are perhaps 2 billion personal computers in the world and another 6 or 8 billion internet connected devices, such as smartphones, tablets and, increasingly, everyday items such as smart TVs and home heating controls, the so-called "internet of things".

The pace of change has been rapid and accelerating, leading to the coining of the phrase "The Information Revolution". We have come so far in such a short span of time, it is hard to know where the world will be in twenty or thirty years, but no doubt some of the ideas that are currently in the realms of fantasy and science fiction will have come to pass, made possible by digital technology...

Digital natives and digital immigrants

In his 2001 paper[1], Marc Prensky uses the terms **digital natives** and **digital immigrants**, to highlight the differences between those in the younger generations who grew up in a world where they were fully immersed in digital technology and those in the older generations who have grown up in a predominantly non-digital world. He saw the younger generations as being "native speakers" of digital language, having been steeped in a range of digital technology - video games, the internet, email, smartphones and computers.

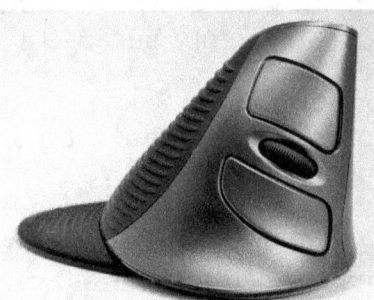

Digital device: Ergonomic wireless mouse

Older people tended to "speak digital" with a heavy immigrant accent. They might print out emails and documents rather than just deal with them on screen, or worse still, get a PA or admin assistant to print these out on their behalf. They might call someone to their desk to see an interesting website, rather than simply send them the URL (web address). They might talk about "giving someone a ring" when thinking of calling them on the phone, which to a younger person might sound more like an intention to propose marriage! And what does it mean "to dial a phone number"?

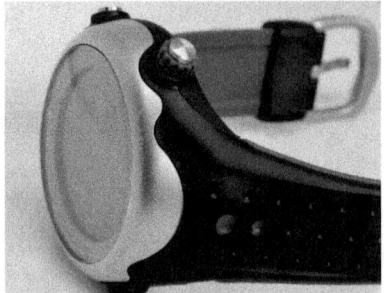

Digital device: Sport watch, with altimeter, compass and temperature sensor

These are relatively superficial differences, but they serve to illustrate the cultural divide that Prensky saw between the natives and the immigrants. His message was clear, educators in particular, ignored this divide at their peril. They needed to embrace new technologies if they really wanted to fully engage all their learners.

This idea caught on and became influential and whilst thinking has moved on and become more nuanced, it does help to illustrate how the pace of technological change affects the generations in different ways.

Perhaps we should refer instead to digital orphans, those who grew up without digital parents to guide and nurture their learning about the digital world, or is this taking the metaphor too far?

Digital device: Remote control

---

[1] Digital Natives, Digital Immigrants by Marc Prensky. From On the Horizon (NCB University Press, Vol. 9 No. 5, October 2001)

Living in a digital world - Introduction

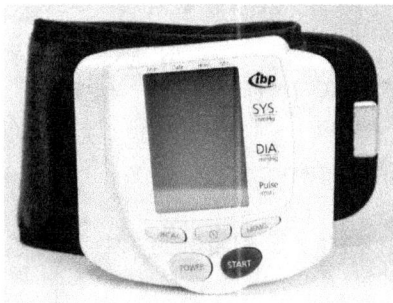

Digital device: Wrist blood pressure monitor

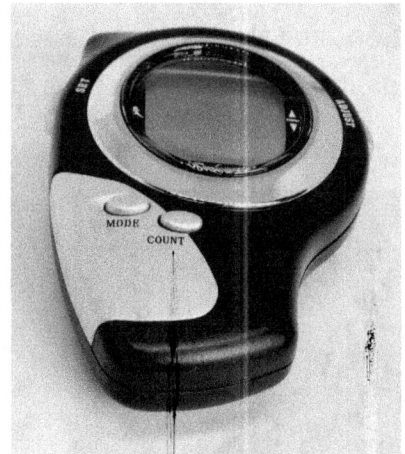

Digital device: Pedometer

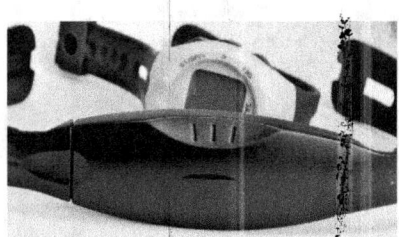

Digital device: Sport watch with heart rate monitor

One issue with the digital natives/digital immigrants idea is that whilst it highlights some important generational differences, it possibly encourages the view that all young people are simply more technologically savvy than their elders. My personal experience is that youngsters can flatter to deceive. Certainly they have plenty of time to learn how to use various digital devices and may well become the family experts when it comes to interconnecting certain equipment and accessing their favourite TV programmes, video games and websites and communicating with their friends.

However, whilst they may display more expertise and confidence than their parents, this expertise might be very narrow, limited to social media, computer games and communications. Their wider understanding might be quite poor, depending on the quality of education they have received in this area. Young people, unless they have been well taught, often fail to understand, for example, how their use of technology may be putting themselves at risk. It takes time and guidance to develop good hazard awareness, their youth and relative naivety count against them. And yet their technical skills can appear so impressive at first sight, especially if we lack confidence in our own technical abilities. It is important not to be dazzled by this!

Given the incredible pace of technological change in the increasingly digitally dominated modern world, it is to be expected that many people will feel that they have been left behind. With little or no understanding of some of the key ideas that underpin digital technology, it is hardly surprising if people conclude that the digital world is a very complex, alien place that they will never be able to come to terms with.

This book aims to show that this is far from the situation by shining a light into some of the deep, dark corners. Instead of complexity there is often a surprising and elegant simplicity. Building an understanding of the basic concepts and ideas that drive the digital world is well within the grasp of the average reader. I invite you to join me on a journey of discovery.

Introduction: Key learning points

- Digital devices include all computers and all devices incorporating a microcontroller.
- Digital devices work by processing 2-state data, which can be represented by zeros and ones.
- Computing is built on doing very simple things with great speed and accuracy.
- The development of modern computing began in the 1940s and has been driven by the need to process large volumes of data efficiently.
- Modern society is becoming increasingly dependent on digital devices.
- The basic concepts that underpin much of modern digital technology can be understood by the average reader.

1: Input, process, output

The Black Box Model

At a simple level, digital devices can be described using the Black Box Model.

This input-process-output model is known as the Black Box Model because the output(s) that are wanted can be decided on, together with the input(s) that will be needed in order to achieve the desired output(s), without having to worry about the detailed processing. This takes place within a "magical" black box.

Each digital device receives data as input. This could come from the user of the device typing something in, speaking an instruction, clicking on a link or a button. The data could come from another device, such as a scanner or a temperature sensor or it could be downloaded from the internet.

The device then processes this data in some way using **software** (computer program or **application** (sometimes abbreviated to **app**)).

It will then produce some sort of output, often via a screen, but other outputs are possible, such as sound, vibrating (phone) or activating a switch.

From this follows the normal order in which computer solutions are designed. Firstly, what is wanted from the solution must be specified precisely (output). This is used to work out the input that will be needed. Finally, the processing that will be required to turn the input into the desired output, must be designed.

When using a microwave oven, the user will **input** what the oven should do by using some combination of a touchpad, dials and buttons to select power settings and times. Suppose a user wants to have the defrost setting for 3 minutes. Part of the **processing** will involve storing this command in a temporary memory location.

When START is pressed (another **input**) the microwave retrieves the command from memory (**processing**) and sets the power setting to DEFROST before turning on the oven light, turntable and magnetron (this creates the microwaves). These are all forms of **output**. It also starts a timer to measure the 3 minute interval (**processing**) whilst displaying a count-down clock, showing how much time is left (**output**). At the end of the 3 minutes, it then turns the light, turntable and magnetron off, beeps and displays the message "OPEN DOOR" (all **outputs**).

Consider a more involved example. Suppose a simple fire alarm system is being designed, where bells are sounded throughout a building if a smoke detector is triggered. At the same time, a display on the alarm panel shows a light to indicate which smoke detector has gone off and a text message is sent to alert the on-call member of the site maintenance team.

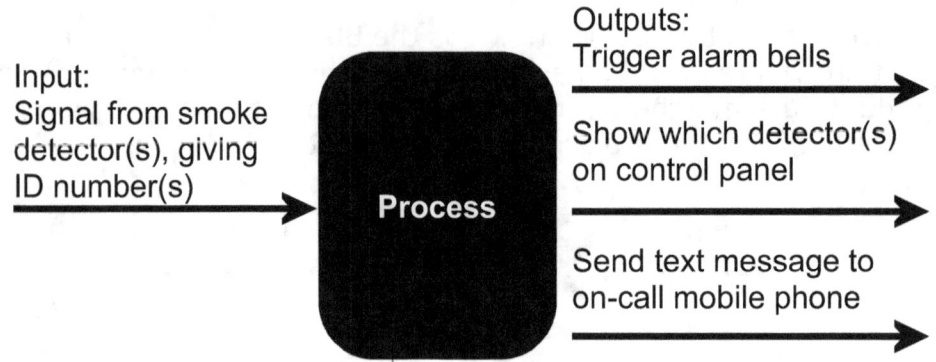

Outputs required
- All alarm bells triggered simultaneously.
- Switch on the correct alarm control panel light(s) to show which smoke detector(s) have been triggered.
- Send a generic text message to the on-call mobile phone, stating that a smoke detector has been triggered and giving its location.

Inputs required
- Signal from any triggered smoke detectors, giving their identification numbers.

Processing needed to produce the desired outputs
- Look up the mobile phone number currently recorded for the on-call member of staff.
- Look up the standard text message for use when a smoke detector is triggered.
- Look up the location(s) of the smoke detector(s) that have been triggered.
- Create a text message combining the standard text, the ID number(s) of the detector(s) and their location(s).
- Work out which light(s) on the alarm display panel need to be turned on, to show which smoke detector(s) have gone off.

The phrase "look up" is used repeatedly above. This is information that will have been entered into the alarm system software as part of the initial setting up when the alarm system was installed and amended whenever necessary, for example if the on-call mobile phone number changes. There is likely to be default standard text message wording that can either be used as is, amended to suit the user or changed completely. Each smoke detector in the system will have had its ID number and location logged during installation and then saved electronically using the alarm system software.

This is a very basic example and clearly a real alarm system is likely to be much more complex. For example, you will want to be able to manually override the alarm system and turn it off in case a fault develops that leaves all the alarms sounding for no reason. You might want to be able to limit who can do this and require the use of a special key or a PIN number before disabling the system. When running a fire drill or alarm test you will want to be able to turn the alarms on and off manually. You may want to be able to isolate a single faulty smoke detector, until it can be repaired or replaced. You may want the system to be able to check itself for faults and report back appropriately, probably via warning lights on the display panel. The fire detection system may be combined with an intruder detection system and/or a water sprinkler system where other types of sensor form part of the system. If a site consists of several buildings, you might want a system that covers the whole site and only evacuates the building where a detector has been triggered. And so on...

As you define more realistic functions, the complexity quickly grows and describing exactly what you want to happen under all possible scenarios becomes more difficult and errors become more likely. One reason for faults or bugs in a digital system is that a particular set of circumstances was not anticipated by the design team and therefore the system did not behave appropriately when those circumstances all happened together. The system lacked the correct rules to process those particular circumstances.

Systems and software engineers typically use **decomposition** to help them deal with the complexity of real-world demands. This means starting with the whole problem/system and progressively breaking it down into smaller and smaller pieces, until you reach a level where you can start working on the detail, without being overwhelmed by the size and complexity of the project.

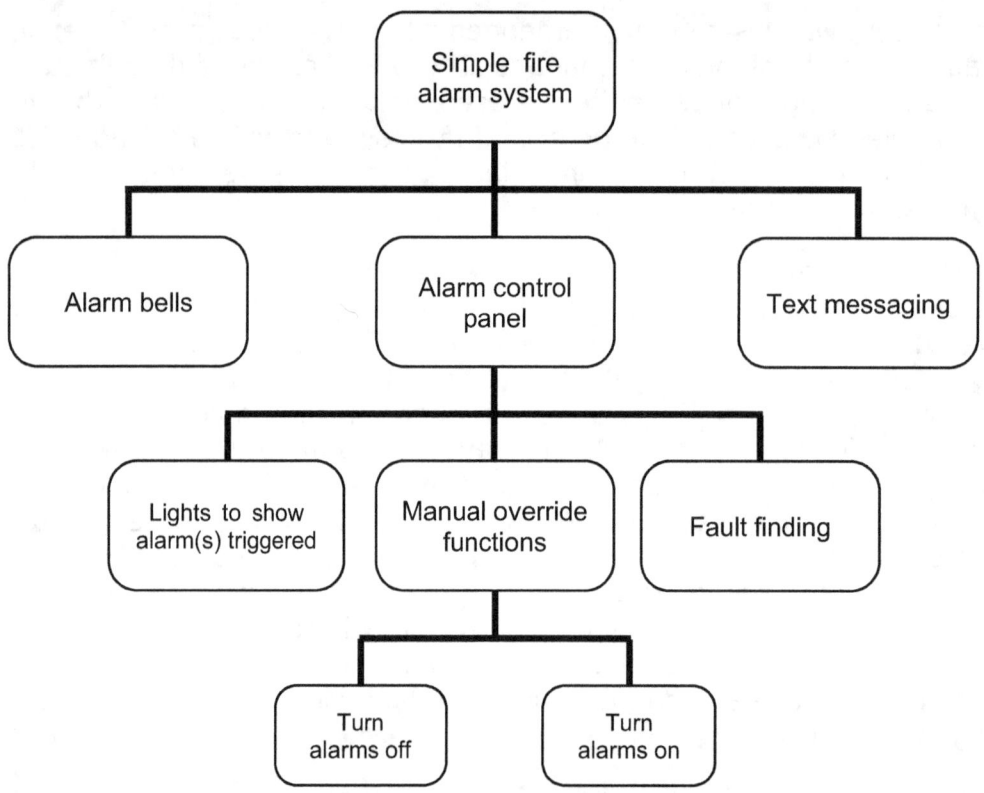

For an alarm system, you could start with a tree diagram.

At the top level is the whole fire alarm system. This can be broken down into three key components, the alarm bells, the alarm control panel and the text messaging function.

Each of these can be broken down further, for example the control panel has been broken down into the display lights, the manual override functions and fault finding.

Each of these can also be broken down. The manual override functions are shown as breaking down into turning sounding alarms off and, when no smoke sensors have been triggered, manually turning the alarms on. Eventually a point is reached where each box on the diagram relates to something small enough that designers and programmers can start thinking in detail about what they need to do, in particular the hardware (equipment) they need to specify and the programming code that needs to be written.

Systems will usually be designed and built by teams, so this kind of diagram and accompanying documentation help with communicating how everything is intended to work and make it possible for different groups within the team to look after different aspects. There might be one team dealing with the alarm bells, another looking at the control panel, whilst a third works on the text messaging.

Problems can occur because those designing and building a system do not fully understand the needs of the people who will be using the system. For a system to be successful, everyone needs to be really clear about what is required from it, i.e. the **output**. Traditional system design started with a systems analysis phase, where a comprehensive requirements specification was drawn up, following an in-depth investigation of exactly what was needed.

However, this can lead to another problem, especially with large projects that will take a long time to complete. The requirements often change once the project has begun. Some very large projects have been cancelled after incurring significant costs over many months or years, because changes to what is needed cannot be delivered at a sensible price and the system as originally specified is no longer useful. Some of these projects have been complete write-offs, delivering nothing of value.

Example project failures include the London Ambulance Computer Aided Dispatch System (UK, 1992), the FoxMeyer Drugs ERP Program (USA, 1993), the National Firearm registration system (Canada, 1997) and the Queensland Health payroll and rostering system (Australia, 2006). Details of these and some other failed projects, can be found in Appendix C.

The future of IT projects

In response to these and other high profile project failures, software engineers have developed more flexible development methods, commonly referred to as agile software development. These take a more incremental approach where large systems are built in a series of small steps, evolving and adapting as they progress. This reduces the complexity that has to be dealt with at any one time and makes it easier to modify systems in the face of changing priorities.

Key inputs and outputs of two example systems

Supermarket checkout
Key outputs

- Display the total amount the customer has to pay
- Print an itemised bill for the customer
- If a payment card has been used, obtain a payment authorisation from the card provider and print out a card payment receipt for the customer
- Update the supermarket's stock database

Key inputs

- Checkout operator to indicate via the keypad when starting a new customer and when all their shopping has been scanned

- Product code of each item purchased, either read automatically by a barcode scanner or typed in via the keypad
- Use this code to look up the product's price and description from the supermarket's stock database
- If a payment card is to be used, read the necessary details from the card, customer to enter their PIN (personal identification number) if appropriate

Additional data will need to be input if the customer has a store loyalty card or wants to part-pay using vouchers or coupons.

Booking a flight using an online travel agent
Key outputs

- Flight ticket
- Payment authorisation
- Customer invoice
- Confirmation for airline with all flight and passenger details
- New or updated customer database record, including their contact details and details of the flight purchased

Key inputs

- Details of the chosen flight, such as airline, flight number, date, destination, class of ticket
- Number of people travelling and whether they are adults or children
- Seat availability, provided by the airline's flight database
- Passenger details if they do not have these currently recorded with the travel agent, including name and contact details
- List of any extras or upgrades purchased and any special requirements
- Payment card details

Hardware - input, output, storage

Computer **hardware** is equipment; something with a physical form, something you can reach out and touch. A computer case and its contents are hardware, so too are keyboards, monitors and scanners. Whereas computer **software** are the programs that run on a computer; in contrast they are intangible, made up of instructions that can be copied into the memory of a computer and then run.

It follows from the Black Box Model that there must be ways of getting data and instructions from a user, onto a computer, in a form that the computer can understand. The data can then be processed. There also must be means of taking the results of that processing and presenting them in a form that a user can understand or make use of.

Hardware is typically classified as being for either **input**, **output** or **storage**, depending on its purpose.

Input devices are used to transfer data into a computer and include keyboards, mice, microphones, scanners, sensors and cameras. Take a selfie using the camera on a laptop or phone and the visual data that makes up the photograph will be transferred onto the device. The photograph can then be stored, edited or sent to friends. Typing inputs text and clicking with a mouse or tapping a touchscreen are two ways of getting instructions into a device so that it knows what the user would like to do.

Output devices present the results of the work done by a computer, the most obvious output device being a computer monitor or screen. Other examples include speakers, headphones, printers, buzzers and bells.

Storage devices are such an important part of computer systems that they are classified as a group in their own right. They allow data and software to be stored indefinitely once a computer has been switched off, when everything in its working memory is lost. Most, like the ubiquitous hard disc drives and USB flash drives, can have data saved onto them as output from a computer or can input data or programs stored on the drive onto a computer. They are therefore capable of acting as both **input AND output** devices, but that problem is neatly sidestepped by classifying them as storage devices. Other storage devices include memory card readers, tape drives and CD/DVD drives.

Aside from storage devices there are a few other hybrid input/output devices. Smartphone screens not only display information (output), but they are also touch-sensitive, allowing users to press buttons and click on links (input). Game controllers are primarily input devices and often have various input controls, such as joysticks and buttons. However some also produce output, for example a controller being used for a car racing game may vibrate when a crash occurs. The vibration is produced by turning on a motor that has been unbalanced by the addition of a small weight and this is a type of output.

So how would you classify a CD or DVD disc that contained one or more programs? Is this hardware or software? The disc is hardware, since it has a physical form. The programs that are stored on the disc are software. However, this conundrum is easily skirted by using the term **media** or **storage media** when describing items such as CDs, DVDs, tapes, memory cards and if we go back in time far enough, floppy discs, paper tape and punched cards.

And finally... devices that are not physically part of the main computer case are called **peripherals** as they are located around the periphery of the computer. They may be input, output or storage devices. Keyboards, mice, printers, external hard disc drives and scanners are all examples of peripherals. Peripherals either provide input to a computer, take output from a computer or do both.

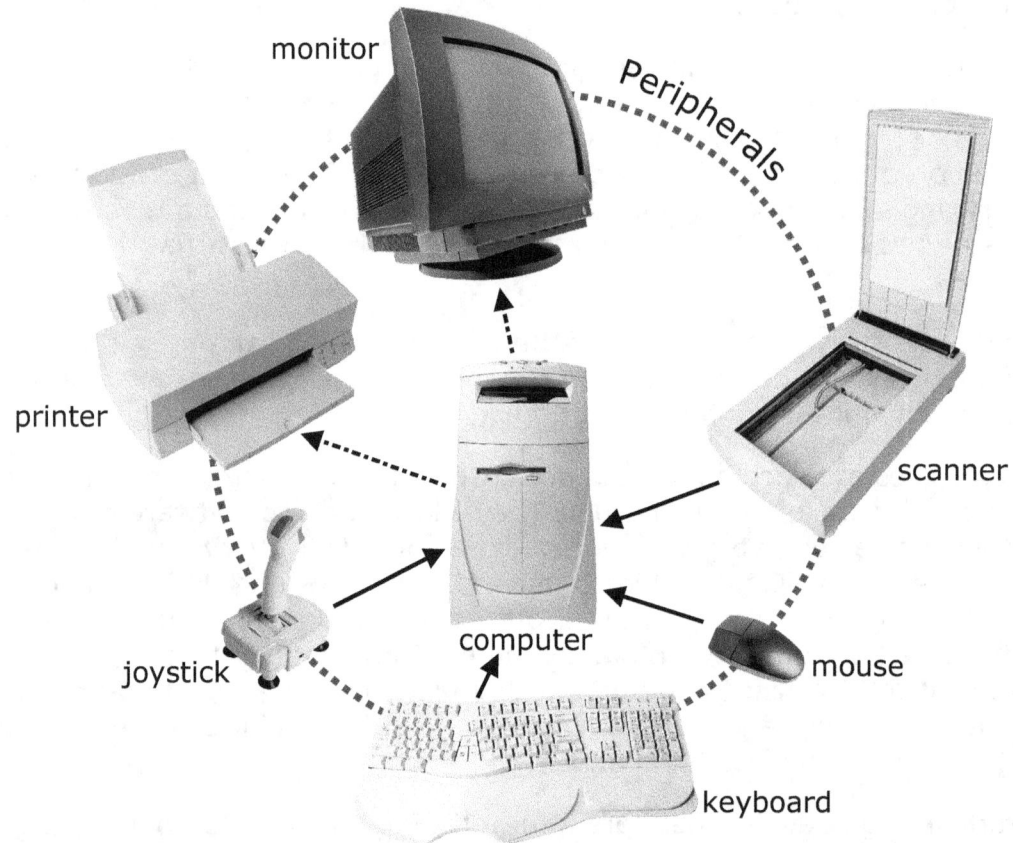

The diagram (above) shows a computer surrounded by a selection of peripherals. The arrows show the direction of the principal information flows. An arrow pointing from a device to the computer shows that it is an **input** device, whereas an arrow pointing from the computer to the device indicates that it is an **output** device.

Living in a digital world - Chapter 1: Input, process, output

Self test

For each of the devices below, find as many words as you can from the box on the right that can be used to describe them. The first one has been done for you.

1. **Keyboard**   *hardware, input, peripheral*
2. Mouse
3. Printer
4. External hard disc drive
5. Internal hard disc drive
6. Monitor
7. USB memory drive
8. Touch screen for a desktop computer
9. Speakers
10. Word processing program

```
input              software
storage            peripheral
output             input & output
        hardware
```

Answers:

1. Keyboard *hardware, input, peripheral*
2. Mouse *hardware, input, peripheral*
3. Printer *hardware, output, peripheral*
4. External hard disc drive *hardware, storage, peripheral*
5. Internal hard disc drive *hardware, storage*
6. Monitor *hardware, output, peripheral*
7. USB memory drive *hardware, storage, peripheral*
8. Touch screen for a desktop computer *hardware, input & output, peripheral*
9. Speakers *hardware, output, peripheral*
10. Word processing program *software*

Looking inside the black box - basic computer architecture

The early computers needed to be extensively rewired for each task that they had to undertake, a very time-consuming process. In 1945 both John von Neumann and Alan Turing independently suggested a computer where both the data AND the program were stored in the computer's working memory. The program would be run by fetching the instructions to a central processing unit one at a time, where they would be decoded and executed.

Now the computer was controlled not by how it was wired, but by the program that was held in its memory, which made it much easier to re-program. This was a huge leap forwards in computer design and it became known as stored program or von Neumann architecture.

The central processing unit (or CPU/processor) forms the working heart of a computer and it includes two key units. The control unit decodes each instruction and supervises its execution. The arithmetic and logic unit carries out all the required calculations and logic operations. See the diagram below.

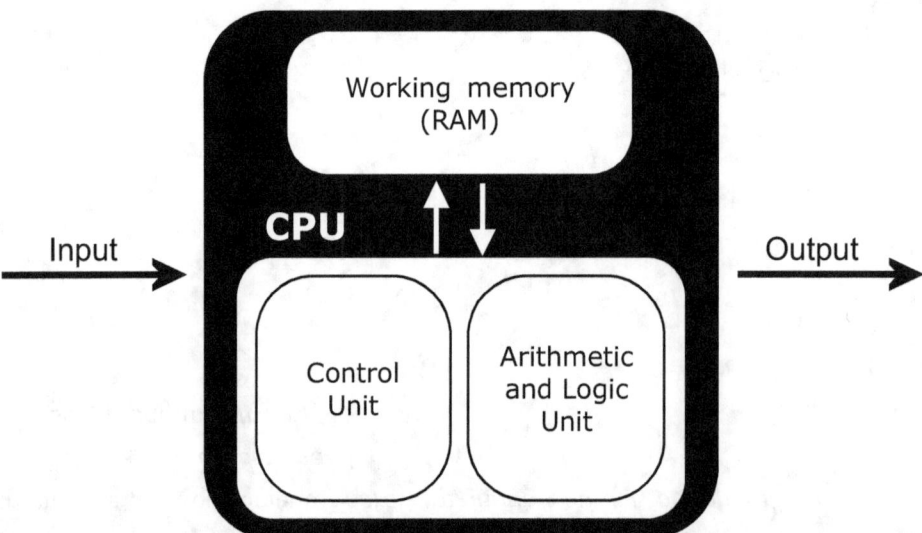

So what would you expect to find if you took the lid off a typical desktop computer? Clearly there must be a CPU; one of the largest, if not **the** largest chip, usually square shaped. It is mounted on a large printed circuit board containing most of the essential computer electronics, called the **motherboard**. There will be working memory or **RAM**, usually in the form of plug-in memory modules - rectangular printed circuit boards covered with memory chips. These are mounted on long, thin sockets, that make it easy to add additional memory, either by plugging in additional modules, or replacing those already there with ones of a higher capacity.

The computer will need electrical power, so there will be a socket for a mains lead and a transformer. Some kind of storage device will be needed to provide a permanent store for software and data, since the contents of the working memory is cleared every time the computer is turned off. Most personal computers use a hard disc drive for this, mounted internally within the computer's case. The heat generated by a computer when it is operating can cause reliability problems, so there is usually at least one fan to help provide cooling. Finally the computer will need the means to connect to various input, output and storage devices. For convenience, some of these will be mounted internally within the case. However most consumers do not want to have to open up their computers to add a new device, whilst some, like keyboards and mice, have to be external to allow them to be used. As a result, most devices are external, connecting to the computer by one of a small number of standard interfaces, such as the now ubiquitous USB (Universal Serial Bus) sockets.

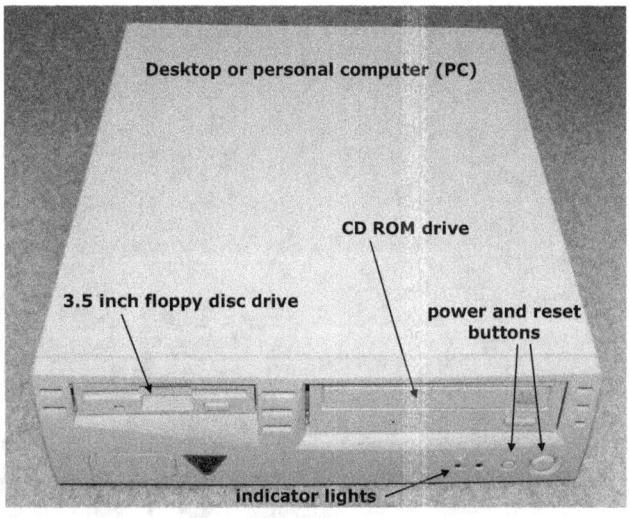

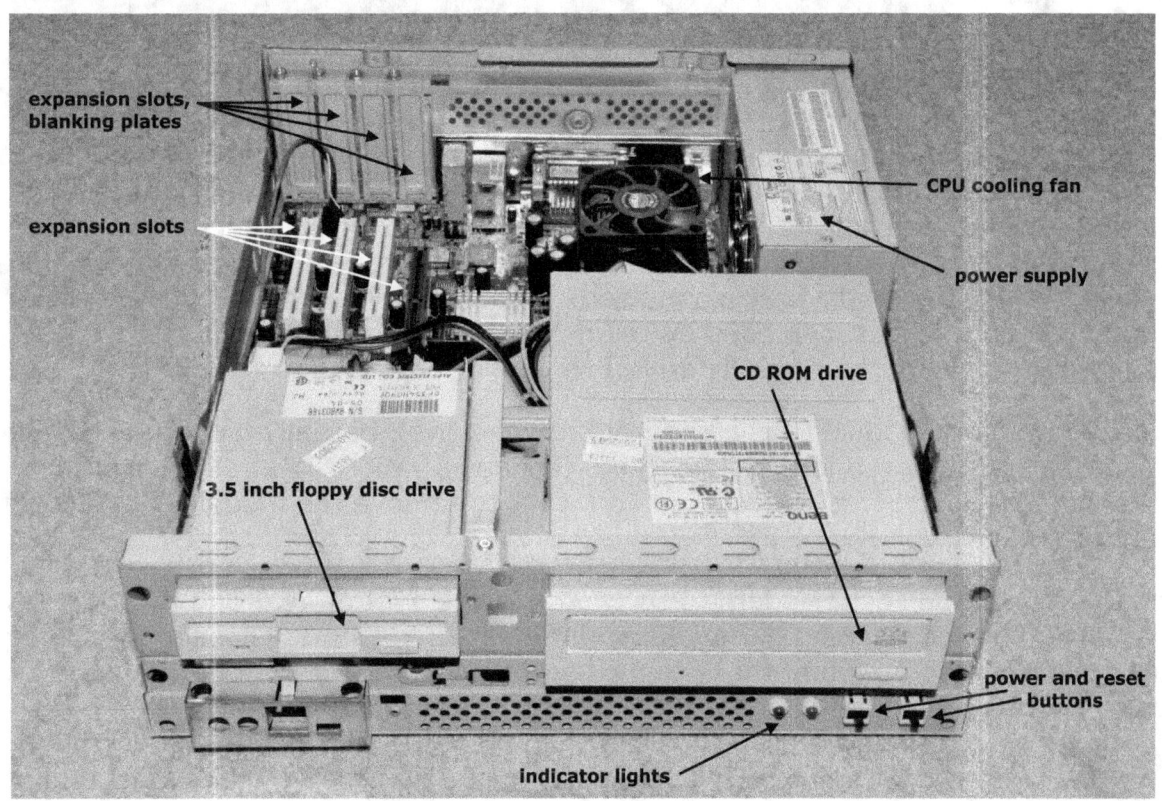

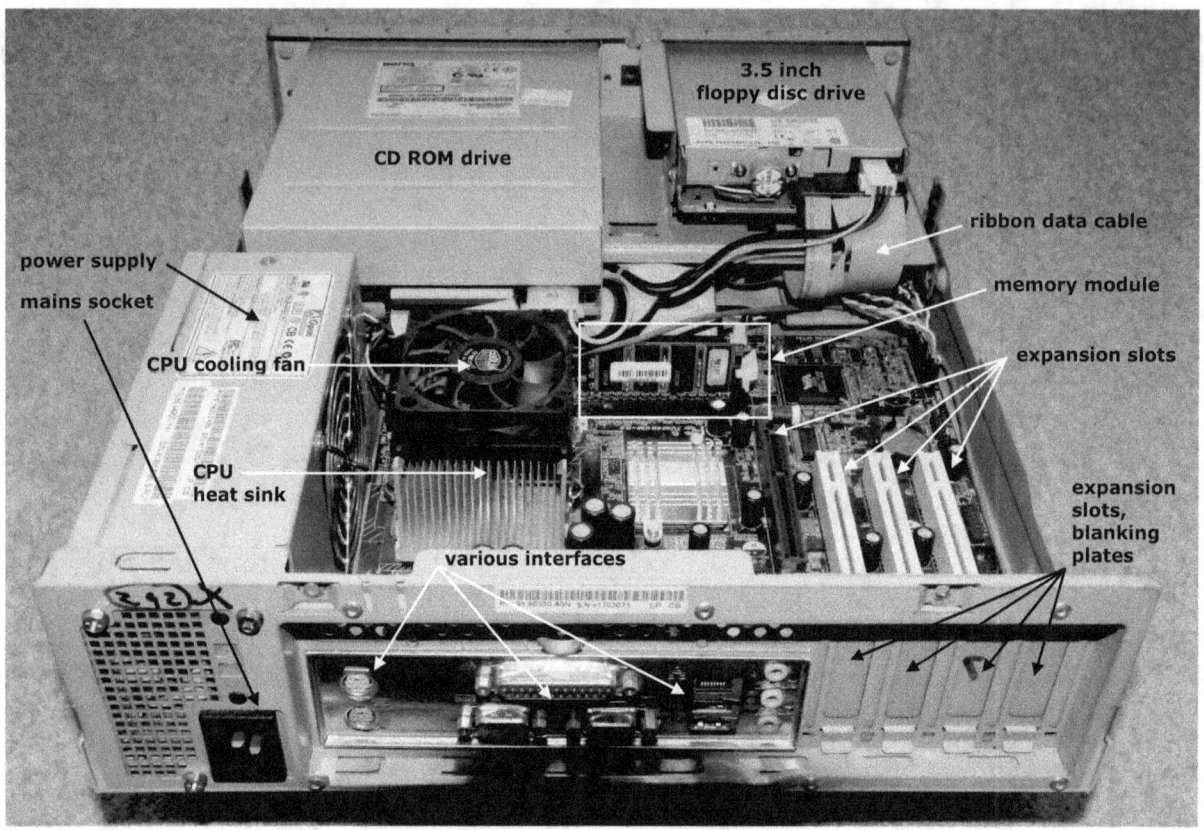

This computer dates from around the year 2000, so there are some older features such as the floppy disc drive. As well as two USB sockets at the back, there are also the older style PS/2 mouse, keyboard and general serial port connectors and a parallel printer port. These have been largely superceded by the USB interface. There is a network (Ethernet) socket, as well as sockets for speakers and a microphone. Underneath the long parallel printer port you can find a VGA graphics socket, to allow a monitor to be connected. These are still seen for legacy reasons, but have been largely superceded by the HDMI interface. The hard disc drive is mounted underneath the CD ROM drive and cannot be seen.

The long memory module (this computer only has one), partially hidden by the CPU cooling fan, is sitting upright in its socket. This has a white clip at either end that locks the module in place and, should you want to remove the module, helps to lift it out of the socket.

The CPU cannot be seen. Modern CPUs can generate a lot of heat and this one has been mounted underneath a large aluminium heat sink, with tall cooling fins. A fan had been mounted on top of these to further aid cooling. In addition, the power supply (large rectangular box, bottom left) has its own cooling fan.

The expansion slots allow additional interfaces to be added to the computer. Additional standard interfaces, such as more USB ports could be added. When a new, faster version of the USB interface is released, these faster ports could be added. Some specialist devices may require their own proprietary means of connecting to a computer and are supplied with their own interface card which must be fitted before the device can be used. However, the standard interfaces have become so easy to use and fast that this is becoming much less common.

To use an expansion slot the computer's cover would have to be taken off and one of the blanking plates removed. The expansion card can then be carefully inserted into the appropriate expansion slot and the computer cover replaced. The interface socket(s) can now be accessed through the hole previously covered by the blanking plate.

The photograph above gives a clearer view of the motherboard, mounted on the base of the computer case, with all its markings in white and a variety of electronic components soldered on. To the right of the CPU heat sink and its fan is a second, smaller heat sink (also square-shaped and made from aluminium), cooling another chip.

The Black Box Model can be further adapted to show how it applies to a typical computer, with a selection of input and output devices listed.

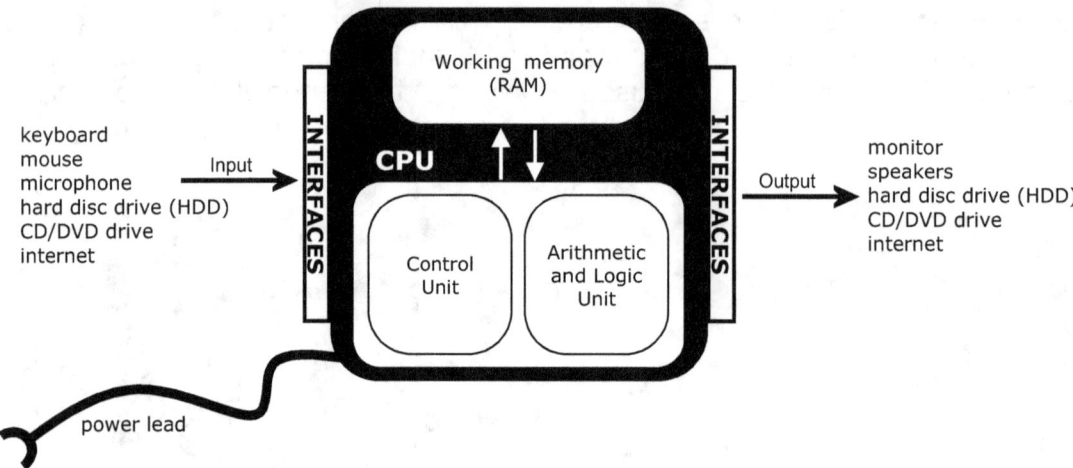

Interfaces

An interface forms the boundary between two different parts of a computer system and allows data to be passed from one to the other. The obvious physical parts of most interfaces are sockets and plugs that fit together. USB ports, SD card readers and HDMI ports are all types of interface. Interfaces take up much of the rear of a desktop computer's case. They typically extend along the back and sides of most laptop computers. The size of sockets constrains the level of miniaturisation that is possible and some interfaces offer reduced size options, such as the micro USB.

There may be specialised electronic components to allow the elements to connect, as well as specialised software, such as a printer driver. In effect an interface is providing a translation service, e.g. translating a document from a form that a computer can understand and work with, to a form that can be understood and processed by a particular printer.

An interface will include some or all of sockets, plugs and cables, specialised electronics and software.

Driven by a desire to be able to miniaturise devices (such as smartphones), as well as making it easier for users to connect difference devices, there has been a move to develop wireless links. Bluetooth is one such interface, using radio waves rather than cables to link two devices over short distances. These are typically less than 10m but can be up to 100m. Wi-Fi is another radio technology and it has a range of the order to tens of metres, typically up to 100m outdoors. It was designed to allow wire-free local area networking (linking) of computers. Near Field Communication (NFC) uses magnetic induction to connect over very short distances, typically much less than 20 cm. An NFC equipped smartphone, together with an appropriate app, can be used to make contactless payments. Two smartphones could use NFC to exchange data, such as photographs.

There also has to be an interface between a computer and its user. A user has to be able to tell a computer what he/she wants to do and enter any appropriate data. This must be converted into a form that the computer can work with efficiently. Then the results must then be presented in a human-friendly way, often visually, via a monitor. Head-up displays for pilots and 3-D immersion headsets provide alternatives, as do other types of output, such as sound. A great deal of thought goes into the design of the human-computer interface since the better it is, the easier it is to get things done and the more productive people can be. Human-computer interaction is a specialised area of study at some universities.

Types of computer

In the 1980s computers were categorised primarily by their physical size and there were three main types, mainframe, mini and microcomputers. Mainframe computers and their associated storage devices could fill a large room. They were very expensive to buy and to operate and typically supported many users, who communicated with the mainframe via terminals. These terminals had a keyboard and screen, but no local processing capability, all the work was done on the mainframe. The available processing power was shared amongst all the users, giving rise to the term "time-sharing". The terminals were connected either by cables or via the telephone network.

Microcomputers (which today we would refer to as desktop or personal computers) were at the other end of the scale. Relatively compact, they could fit on an office desk and became increasingly affordable as time went on. People could aspire to owning their own microcomputer, heralding the era of personal computer ownership.

In between came mini-computers, typically the size of a couple of filing cabinets. These were affordable to smaller organisations, such as university departments, and smaller companies.

Today, computers are categorised more for their function/use, although size can still be important! There was a time when a distinction was drawn between larger laptop computers and the smaller notebook computers, which had a footprint of a sheet of A4 paper or smaller. However all portable computers, with a hinged screen and built in keyboard tend to be referred to as laptops.

Tablet computers have been around for a long time, but there were problems with their usability, such as limited processing power, short battery life and weight. The release of Apple's first iPad in 2010 revitalised this format, which has become popular, particularly for mobile use and where there is a need for a relatively large screen.

However, tablet computers have been eclipsed for personal use by the smartphone. These devices, like tablets, demonstrate technology convergence, i.e. a single device that uses many different technologies. A typical smartphone can not only make and receive phone calls, but it allows internet access, the taking of videos and photographs, the sending and receiving of email and can use the phone's microphone and speaker as input and output devices. A GPS receiver coupled with appropriate software adds satellite navigation options. WiFi, Bluetooth and NFC capability allow wireless communication with other devices.

7-inch tablet computer in a protective case

Sensors usually include

- accelerometer to detect the phone's movements, such as shaking
- gyroscope which works with the accelerometer to detect rotation of the phone
- digital compass to find magnetic North
- light sensor so that the screen brightness can be automatically adjusted
- proximity sensor to automatically lock the screen to prevent unwanted touch commands when receiving a phone call with the device held near the ear

IBM developed a prototype smartphone in 1992. By 1994 Bell South had developed this idea and launched their Simon Personal Communicator, which could make and receive calls, send and receive emails and faxes (remember them?) and had other business oriented software, such as an address book, calendar, calculator and notepad. However most mobile phone users carried a separate PDA (personal data assistant) to provide these additional functions throughout the 1990s.

1999 saw the first widespread adoption of smartphones in Japan, although these did not achieve global success. Devices made by Blackberry and firmly aimed at the business community saw widespread adoption in the 2000s, reaching a peak in 2013. However it was Apple's release of its first iPhone in 2007 and Google's release of the Android operating system (the first Android phone was released in 2008) that ushered in the mass global adoption of this technology - well over 2 billion in use in 2014. It is estimated that there will be over 6 billion smartphones by 2020, representing 70% of the world's population.

Smartphone in a protective case

Raspberry Pi

The Raspberry Pi Foundation in the UK felt that [some[1]] children who grew up in the 1980s and had to program computers in order to use them, built up an intimate knowledge of how they worked. This is something they felt has since been lost and the Foundation wanted a way to re-ignite enthusiasm for computer science and computing. They came up with the Raspberry Pi, a credit card-sized computer that, when it was launched in 2012, cost around £30. It is cheap and small and therefore particularly well suited to hobbyists and those who need portable computer power for a range of design and make projects.

The Foundation has particularly targeted UK schools and those in developing countries. Various versions have followed the launch of the original Model B in 2012 and the range now includes the even smaller Zero, a mere 65mm by 30mm by 5mm, costing about £5 in 2017. The Zero W doubles the price and adds Bluetooth and Wi-Fi. The photograph below shows an original Model B in a clear plastic case.

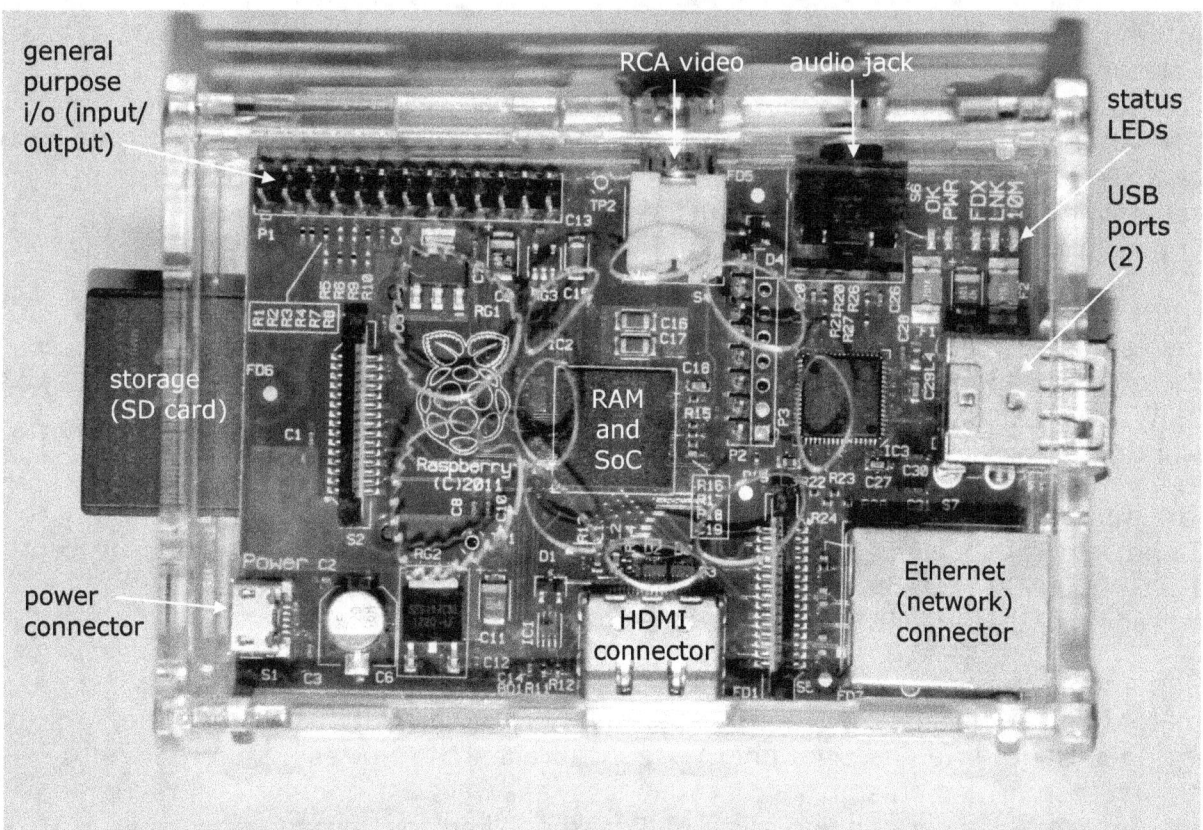

At first glance, the Raspberry Pi looks very different from the desktop computer seen earlier in this chapter. However, thinking about the Black Box model shows

---
[1] *my brackets*

that it contains exactly the same basic components. There is a CPU, RAM and long term storage (the CPU is part of a System on a Chip, SoC, mounted underneath the RAM chip. An SD card provides the long term storage). There are a series of interfaces for input, output and storage devices and a power connector. Add a touch screen and a SIM card holder, remove most of the bulkier interfaces and replace the power connector with a rechargeable battery and you are on your way to a smartphone. In fact, all computers will show a great deal of similarity as they all fit the simple **input-process-output** Black Box Model.

Supercomputers

Supercomputers sit at the apex of computer evolution. They have extreme data processing capabilities and breathtaking design specifications at the time of their construction. Their design, construction and operating costs far exceed those of everyday devices. They are very special pieces of hardware, for extreme applications.

Around 1960, Seymour Cray, an American then working for Control Data Corporation, decided to design a computer that would be by far the fastest computer in the world. Completed in 1964 the CDC 6000 was several times faster than the best of the competition and was given the title "Supercomputer". This term came to define the market segment for computers with prodigious processing capabilities, allowing work to be carried out that was previously considered impossible. The name "Cray" was synonymous with supercomputing for decades.

However, things have moved on and, as of November 2016, the title of world's fastest supercomputer was held by the Sunway TaihuLight, at the National Supercomputing Centre in Wuxi, China. It uses 40,960 processors, each containing 256 cores. Each core acts as a CPU, so processing is carried out by dividing the work up amongst the different cores, producing phenomenal processing power.

The numbers that surround supercomputers are always eye-watering. The Sunway TaihuLight is capable of 105,000,000,000,000,000 calculations per second. It has 1,310,000 GB (1.31PB or petabytes) of memory and 20,000,000 GB (20PB) of storage, costing around £220 million to build.

Supercomputers are needed wherever it is useful to run highly complex mathematical models, that require vast numbers of calculations to be made. This includes weather forecasting, pharmaceutical research (e.g. as an alternative to animal testing), oil prospecting, life sciences research, astronomy (e.g. recreating the Big Bang), understanding earthquakes, modelling the spread of disease, simulating nuclear explosions (as an alternative to real tests) and predicting climate change.

Living in a digital world - Chapter 1: Input, process, output

Self test

1. Describe the Black Box Model using just three words.

2. In traditional systems design, what needs to be specified first?

3. What is decomposition?

4. What is computer software?

5. Name the two key components of a CPU or processor.

6. In a microcomputer, what is the name given to the large printed circuit board that contains most of the essential computer electronics, including the CPU?

7. What is the acronym for a computer's working memory?

8. What is an interface?

9. Give another common term for a microcomputer.

Smartphone (rear) in a protective case

Answers:

1. Describe the Black Box Model using just three words.
   Input, process, output.

2. In traditional systems design, what needs to be specified first?
   The output required.

3. What is decomposition?
   Progressively breaking down a problem or system into smaller and smaller components.

4. What is computer software?
   Computer programs (also referred to as applications or apps).

5. Name the two key components of a CPU or processor.
   The control unit and the arithmetic and logic unit (ALU).

6. In a microcomputer, what is the name given to the large printed circuit board that contains most of the essential computer electronics, including the CPU?
   The motherboard.

7. What is the acronym for a computer's working memory?
   RAM

8. What is an interface?
   An interface is a boundary between two different parts of a computer system that allows data to be passed between them.

9. Give another common term for a microcomputer.
   Personal computer, PC or desktop computer.

Chapter 1: Key learning points

- Digital devices can be described using the Black Box Model (input, process, output).
- Decomposition is the process of breaking down a problem or proposed system into ever smaller parts to make it easier to deal with the complexity of the whole.
- Hardware can be classified as being for input, output or storage.
- The heart of a digital device is the CPU or processor.
- Interfaces handle the transfer of data from input devices to the processor and from the processor to output devices.
- There are many different types of computer, however they all share important similarities.

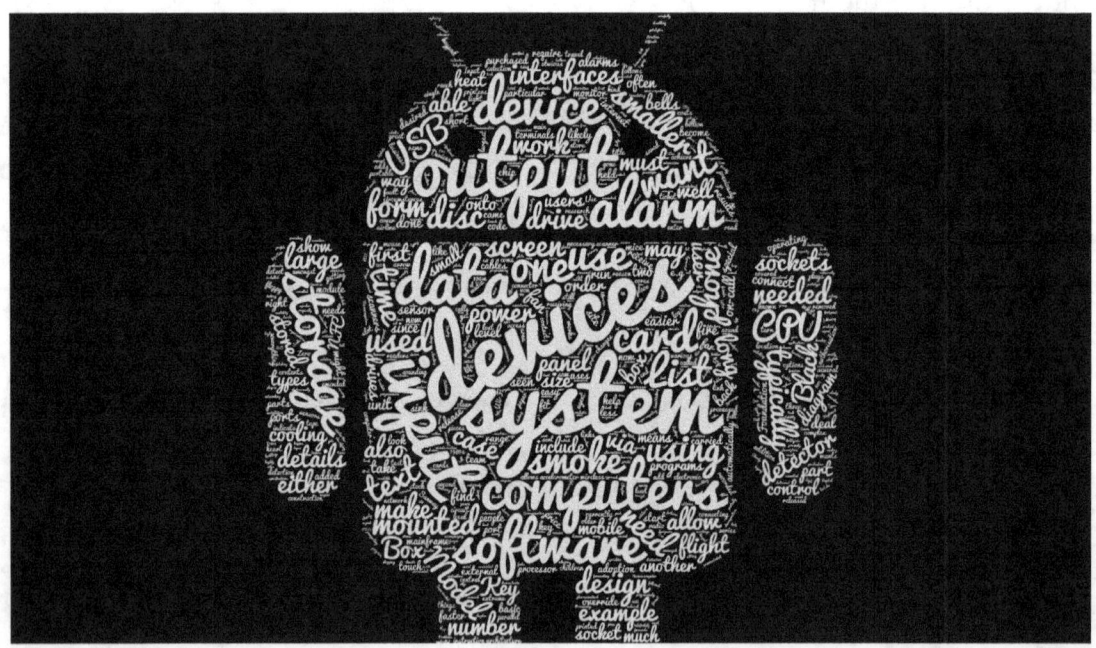

2: Digital devices and data

Chapter 1 explored how different digital devices are, in fact, all data processing devices. They take in data as input and process it in some way in order to produce useful output. If the processor or CPU can be described as the heart of a digital device, then data is its lifeblood.

Data could be the numbers that a computer is required to process. They could be readings from sensors (temperature, pressure, etc) for a system that has to respond to events that are happening around it, such as the control system for a chemical processing plant, power station or a domestic heating boiler. Data might come from an operator that wants to give instructions or alter the settings that the system is using. Data could be the text produced by a blogger for their next post or an author working on a novel. It could be the tune and lyrics of a new song or the design of a house, car or aircraft.

This chapter will look at the nature of that data and how the way that digital devices work can place limits and constraints on what we can do with data. The starting point is to look at two different types of data, analogue data and digital data.

Analogue vs Digital

Old Devices = Analogue, New Devices = Digital

The bald statements given above are an over-simplification, however it is a useful initial point to say that many older devices are analogue in nature, whilst many modern devices are digital.

The key point about analogue data is that it **varies continuously**. Think about the outside temperature. That will go through a continuous cycle, being generally warmer once the sun has risen and cooler after sunset. There will be changes as warmer and colder air masses move through the area and as the amount of cloud

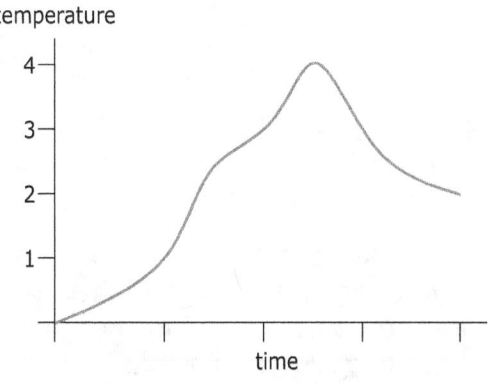

cover varies. A graphical representation of temperature would be some sort of continuous, curved line. Temperature is an analogue quantity.

Below are some analogue devices. Some, like the film cameras and dial telephone have strong associations with older technology. Others, like the mercury thermometer and the microphone, are still commonly used, although in all cases there are also equivalent digital devices available. These analogue devices depend on continuously variable physical properties, such as temperature, light intensity, and air pressure.

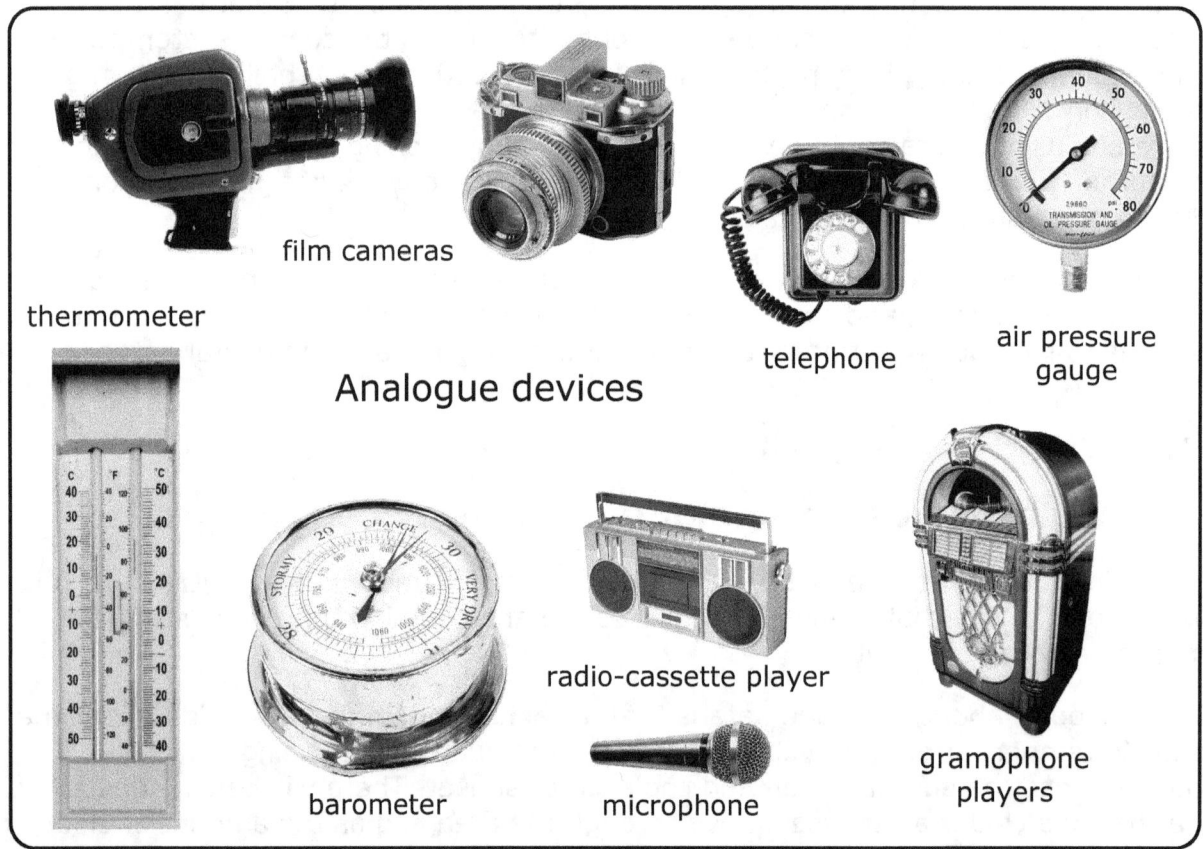

Analogue devices

What makes a digital device, "digital"?

A digital device is defined as a device which uses discrete, numerable data and processes for all its operations. Which is a fancy way of saying that it uses numbers for everything.

I encourage you to pause for a moment and think about the implications of that definition. **Everything** that you might do with a digital device (apart from using one to prop open a door) will have to be converted into numbers for the device to work on. Once that numerical data has been processed, it must then be converted from numbers into a useful form of output. This applies whether you are using a remote control to change channels on your television, a microwave oven to heat up a meal or a computer to do any of the myriad things that they are capable of, such as checking your bank balance, creating a poster, composing a song...

The world around us is mostly analogue, but for digital devices to function it must be reinterpreted in the form of numbers - real world analogue data has to be **digitised** before it can be input onto a digital device.

Digital devices

Cast your eye around the room you are currently in and do a quick count of all the digital devices that you can see. Remember to include all digital clocks and watches, digital cameras, all modern phones, many domestic appliances (certainly all those that can be set to follow different programs), all computing devices and peripherals, televisions, digital radios, PVRs, CD and DVD players, some room thermostats...

How many digital devices do you estimate you have in your entire home? The answer may surprise you!

Digitising data

Digitising temperature readings

Consider a situation where the outside temperature in degrees centigrade is being monitored during winter. This will fluctuate over time and suppose that the following pattern occurred.

This temperature pattern can be digitised (turned into numbers) by **sampling**, i.e. taking temperature measurements at regular intervals.

Suppose that the samples are being measured to the nearest whole degree.

For this illustration, it does not matter what the time intervals are.

You can see from the bottom graph that a total of five samples have been taken, represented by the five bars.

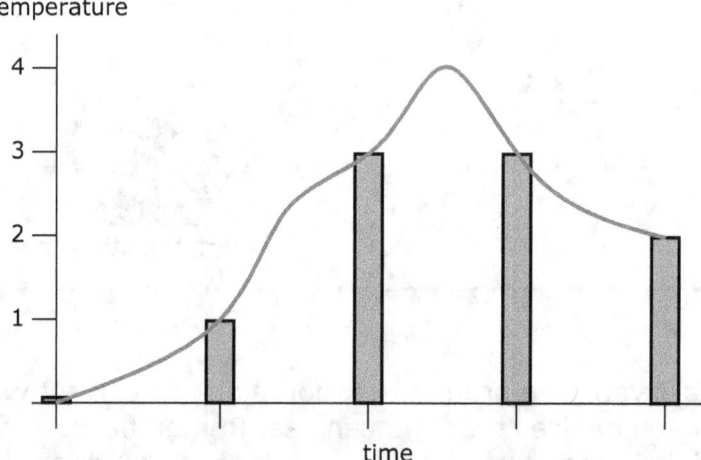

The temperatures recorded when each sample was taken were 0°C, 1°C, 3°C, 3°C, 2°C.

Therefore this temperature graph has been digitised as 0, 1, 3, 3, 2.

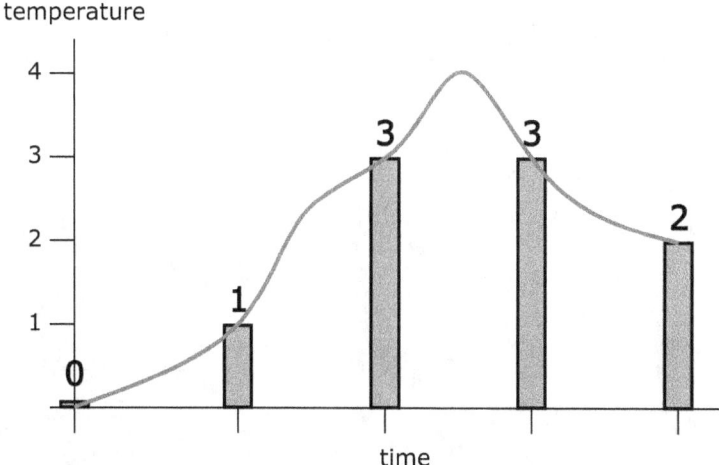

To reconstruct the original temperature graph, you would need to know how often the temperature samples were taken (the sampling rate) and the numbers 0, 1, 3, 3, 2.

This result can be seen in the middle graph.

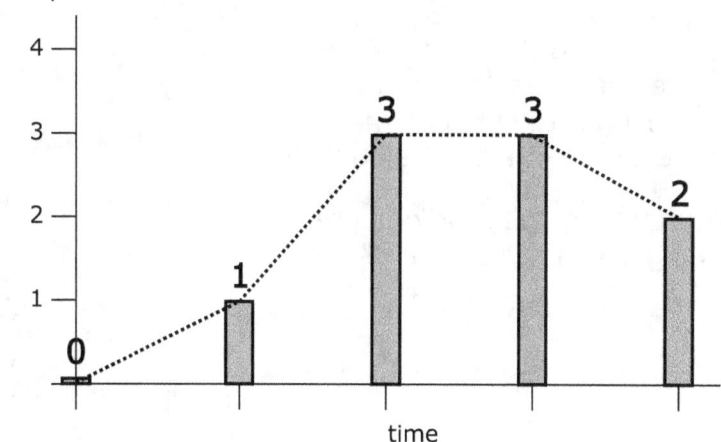

The digitised graph can been seen to follow the general shape of the actual temperature graph.

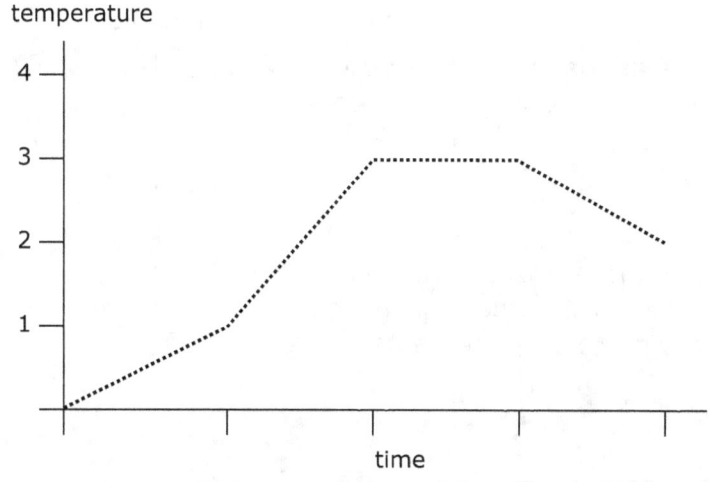

However, it is far from being a perfect replica of the original.

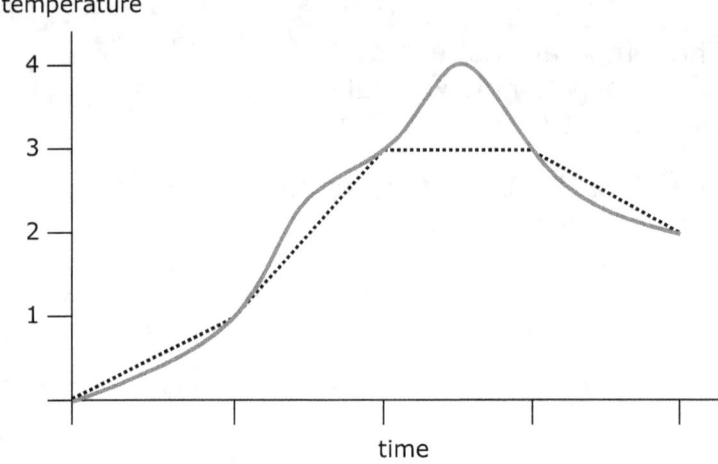

To get the digitised graph to look more like the actual graph, the sampling rate could be increased, for example it could be doubled.

Remember, the readings are being taken to the nearest degree.

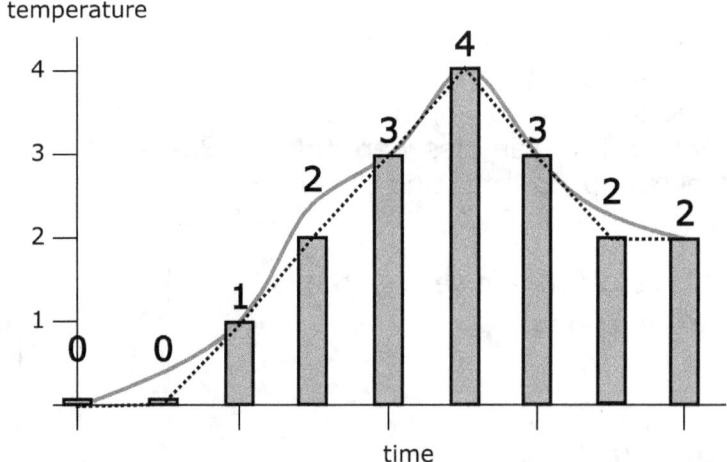

The digitised graph is now represented by the numbers
0, 0, 1, 2, 3, 4, 3, 2, 2
instead of
0, 1, 3, 3, 2

It is an improvement in accuracy, however it comes at the cost of having to store twice as many numbers.

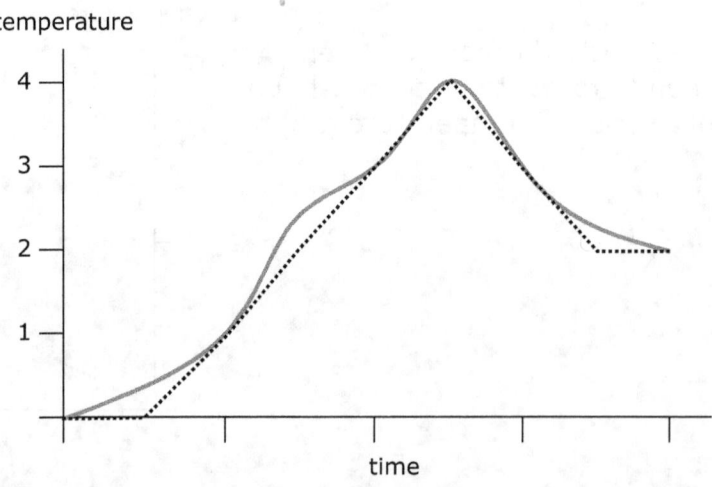

Another way to improve the accuracy of the digitised graph is to improve the level of accuracy with which the temperature readings are being made. Suppose that instead of being measured to the nearest degree, they were measured to the nearest 0.5 of a degree.

This version of the graph is digitised as
0, 0.5, 1, 2.5, 3, 4, 3, 2.5, 2

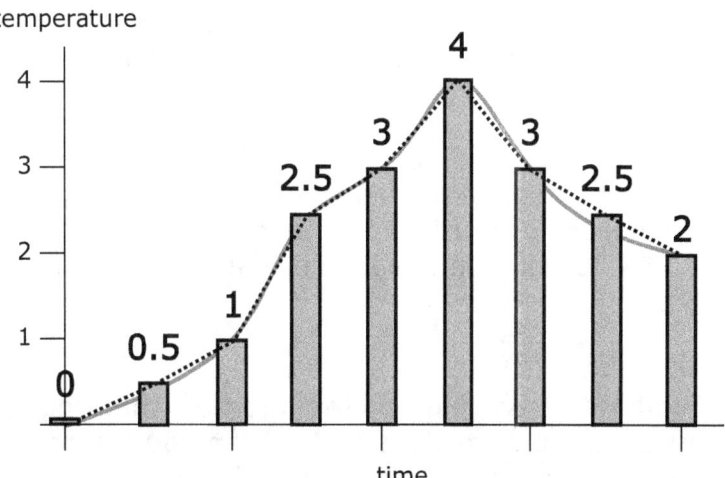

The digitised graph will never be a perfect representation of the actual temperature graph, but by increasing the sampling rate and measuring with finer and finer accuracy, the digitised graph can end up being very close indeed. From a practical standpoint there is clearly a balance to be struck between additional accuracy and the extra effort and storage cost required. A judgement has to be made as to what level of accuracy is required for a particular situation.

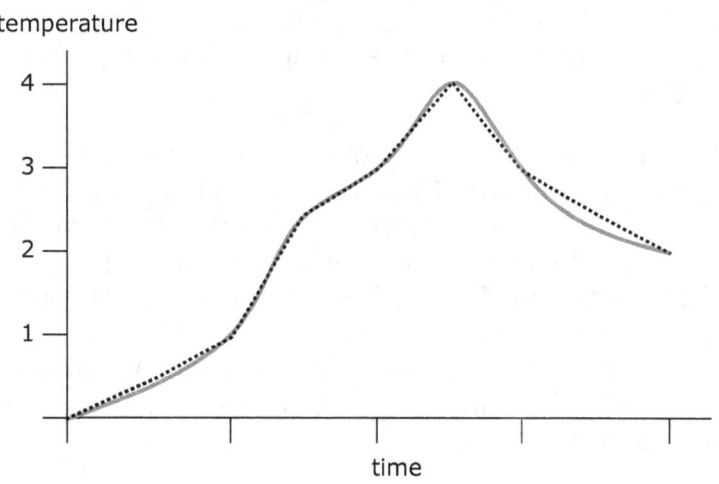

This example illustrates how real world analogue data can be digitised, so that it can be input onto a computer and processed. It also shows that whilst digitised data is never a perfect copy of the original analogue data, it can be made accurate enough that any differences are not important.

Digitising sound

Sound is digitised by sampling, in a similar way to that just described for temperature. When instruments are being played and people are singing, they produce sound waves which, when you are listening to a live performance, travel through the air to your ears. Here the pressure wave is converted into signals that are transmitted to your brain and you experience the sound.

When digitising sound, your ear is replaced by a microphone, which converts the sound pressure wave into an electrical signal. You can think of this varying in a similar way to the temperature graph. This electrical signal is then sampled.

A standard CD recording is sampled at a rate of 44,100 samples per second, for each of two (stereo) channels. This means 88,200 numbers have to be stored for each second of music. For a four minute track this makes a grand total of 21,168,000 numbers, which explains why music can take up so much storage space on a computer!

Digitising text

If you are researching on the internet, checking and responding to email or writing your next social media update, then you will be reading and/or typing text. I am currently writing this book using desktop publishing software and all these characters that I am typing must be converted to numbers before they can be accepted by the computer, displayed back to me on screen and periodically saved to the hard disc drive.

The standard way to digitise text is to use the ASCII code, which stands for the American Standard Code for Information Interchange. It was produced by what is now known as the American National Standards Institute, was first published in 1963 and has been widely adopted since. Initially it covered 128 different characters. The first 32 (i.e. 0 to 31) are non-printing characters, such as horizontal tab (9) and carriage return (13, what you get in a word processor if you press the ENTER key). 32 is a SPACE and various punctuation and other symbols follow. Codes 48 to 57 are the digits 0 to 9. Upper case letters start at 65 and lower case letters start at 97.

ASCII was designed for use in the USA, so the currency symbol is $ and it uses the standard English alphabet. Many countries have developed their own variants to incorporate non-English letters, accented letters and other currency symbols. For example, the Canadians developed a set that included French accented characters.

ASCII was later extended to cover 256 characters. This allowed the inclusion of some of the more common accented characters, additional mathematical symbols and some graphic characters (blocks and lines) so that simple graphics could be built using plain text.

However, many character sets were not part of ASCII and interest grew in developing a universal system. The Unicode Standard was first released in 1991 and currently defines over a million characters, character variations and symbol sets, all of which can be represented using UTF-8 encoding. The first 128 characters are identical to ASCII, maintaining compatibility, but UTF-8 goes on to cover most of the world's alphabets. The Unicode Standard is widely supported.

Encoding the phrase "Happy birthday to YOU!" would give the following.

Happy birthday to YOU!

72, 97, 112, 112, 121, **32**, 98, 105, 114, 116, 104, 100, 97, 121, **32**, 116, 111, **32**, 89, 79, 85, **33**

Simplified (reduced) ASCII table

Numbers, punctuation, etc.

#13 = Enter	#32 = Space	#33 = !	#44 = ,	#45 = -	#46 = .
#48 = 0	#49 = 1	#50 = 2	#51 = 3	#52 = 4	#53 = 5
#54 = 6	#55 = 7	#56 = 8	#57 = 9	#59 = ;	

Upper case letters

#65 = A	#66 = B	#67 = C	#68 = D	#69 = E	#70 = F
#71 = G	#72 = H	#73 = I	#74 = J	#75 = K	#76 = L
#77 = M	#78 = N	#79 = O	#80 = P	#81 = Q	#82 = R
#83 = S	#84 = T	#85 = U	#86 = V	#87 = W	#88 = X
#89 = Y	#90 = Z				

Lower case letters

#97 = a	#98 = b	#99 = c	#100 = d	#101 = e	#102 = f
#103 = g	#104 = h	#105 = i	#106 = j	#107 = k	#108 = l
#109 = m	#110 = n	#111 = o	#112 = p	#113 = q	#114 = r
#115 = s	#116 = t	#117 = u	#118 = v	#119 = w	#120 = x
#121 = y	#122 = z				

Self test

Using the reduced ASCII table (or searching for a full table online), answer the following questions.

1. What text is represented by these numbers?

a)

65, 116, 32, 104, 111, 109, 101, 32, 111, 110, 32 116, 104, 101, 32, 114, 97, 110, 103, 101 46

b)

66, 117, 116, 32, 73, 32, 100, 105, 100, 32, 105, 116, 32, 109, 121, 32, 119, 97, 121, 46, 46, 46

2. Convert this text into ASCII:

a) **Hit and run.**

b) **Tues 22nd - a red letter day.**

Practical task: Open up a simple text editor or word processor. Hold down the ALT key whilst typing in an ASCII code, e.g. ALT + 65 ('**A**'). Do not let go of the ALT key until you have finished typing the ASCII code. Does the corresponding character appear (this will work with some software, but not all)?

Answers:

1a. *At home on the range.*

1b. *But I did it my way...*

2a) **Hit and run.** Ans = 72, 105, 116, 32, 97, 110, 100, 32 114, 117, 110, 46

2b) **Tues 22nd - a red letter day.** Ans = 84, 117, 101, 115, 32, 50, 50, 110, 100, 32, 45, 32, 97, 32, 114, 101, 100, 32, 108, 101, 116, 116, 101, 114, 32, 100, 97, 121, 46

Representing pictures with numbers

The most simple way of digitising a graphic or photograph, is to use a bitmap. The image is divided into a grid of tiny picture elements or **pixels**. Consider a very simple situation where there is a graphic of a stick person, using only two colours, black and white. The graphic is rectangular, 12 pixels wide and 20 pixels high. Each pixel is "mapped" by giving it a number, that represents its colour. As there are only two colours, 0 can be used for black (what you get if you send zero signal to a screen) and 1 for white.

This is how the first five rows of pixels would be mapped.

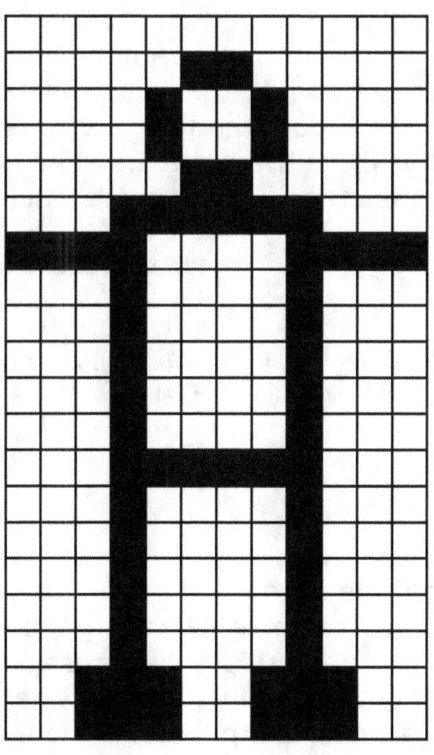

1, 1, 1, 1, 1, 1, 1, 1, 1, 1, 1, 1
1, 1, 1, 1, 1, 0, 0, 1, 1, 1, 1, 1
1, 1, 1, 1, 0, 1, 1, 0, 1, 1, 1, 1
1, 1, 1, 1, 0, 1, 1, 0, 1, 1, 1, 1
1, 1, 1, 1, 1, 0, 0, 1, 1, 1, 1, 1
(60 numbers so far, 1 per pixel)

The 1s and 0s follow the pattern of the stick person graphic and you can see that one number is needed for each pixel, making a total of 12 x 20 = 240 for the whole graphic. The first five rows require 60 numbers.

The graphic is quite crude and "blocky". To get a smoother, better looking image you need to use a much larger number of pixels, i.e. a **higher resolution**. As with the previous digitisation examples, higher resolution comes at a cost of having to store many more numbers in order to represent a picture.

At the time of writing, typical cameras take photographs with resolutions ranging between 5 and 35 **megapixels**, meaning between 5 and 35 million numbers would have to be stored for each photograph, if it was stored as a simple bitmap. Bitmaps have the advantage of being very simple for a computer to interpret and, for example, recreate on screen. However high resolution photographs and other graphics will take up very significant amounts of storage space and take a long time to transfer from a camera or over the internet.

Compressing image files

Bitmaps tend to be large and are often wasteful of precious computing resources. This is the case with the stick person graphic, but the bitmap could be significantly reduced in size if another way of organising the data was used and this is known as **file compression**.

The stick person graphic has large blocks of pixels that are all the same colour, especially white pixels, which make up the background. A new image format could be devised where numbers are used in pairs to describe the colour and how many of the pixels should be that colour. Just thinking about the first few rows of pixels, 12, 1 could be used to represent the top row where there are 12 white pixels. On the next row there are 5 white, 2 black then another 5 white pixels, and so on.

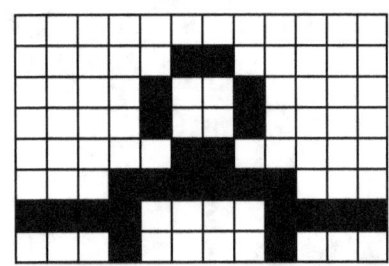

Pixel pattern
12 x 1
5 x 1, 2 x 0, 5 x 1
4 x 1, 1 x 0, 2 x 1, 1 x 0, 4 x 1
4 x 1, 1 x 0, 2 x 1, 1 x 0, 4 x 1
5 x 1, 2 x 0, 5 x 1

What needs to be stored
12, 1
5, 1, 2, 0, 5, 1
4, 1, 1, 0, 2, 1, 1, 0, 4, 1
4, 1, 1, 0, 2, 1, 1, 0, 4, 1
5, 1, 2, 0, 5, 1
(34 numbers instead of 60)

Using this method of representing the image (file format), the amount of data that would be needed to represent the first five rows of pixels has almost halved from 60 to 34 numbers. It is important to note that this nearly 50% compression has been achieved <u>without any loss of image information</u>, so the image quality remains the same. This is known, sensibly enough, as **lossless compression**. Note that if there were frequent changes from white to black and back again **more data** would be needed by this method than with the simple bitmap.

However, further compression is possible if the format is only going to be used for images made up of black and white pixels. Starting at the top, the first row is all white. The next row is all white until the first black pixel is reached. The following pixels are all black, until the next white pixel is reached, and so on. If it is assumed that each row starts with a white pixel, it is not necessary to keep specifying the colour, since it must always change from white, to black, to white, to black, etc.

There is also a flaw with the file format as it currently stands. A computer attempting to reproduce the graphic on screen would need to know where the end of each row of pixels is, so an end of line character needs to be added.

Assuming that the row always starts with a white pixel, the first row would be represented by 12, E (E being used as the end of line character).

5, 2, 5, E means that the next row has 5 white pixels followed by 2 black and 5 white.

12, E
5, 2, 5, E
4, 1, 2, 1, 4, E
4, 1, 2, 1, 4, E
5, 2, 5, E
(22 numbers instead of 60)

The first five rows of the graphic would be represented by

12, E, 5, 2, 5, E, 4, 1, 2, 1, 4, E, 4, 1, 2, 1, 4, E, 5, 2, 5, E

However, you will see that not all rows start with a white pixel. Oh dear, how can this be dealt with..?

Here is an an example of the importance of representing nothing with the number zero! The 7th line would be represented by:

0, 4, 4, 4, E

No whites, 4 black, 4 white and 4 black.

Occasionally then, an extra number (0) will be needed to show that a line starts with a black pixel, but significant compression has still been achieved. Note that in general, compressed images that have an identical image size will have **different** file sizes, as they will need different amounts of data. Using the scheme outlined above, images that have lots of rows starting with black pixels will have larger file sizes than those where most rows start with white pixels, because they will need lots of extra zeros. Images that have long runs of one colour, followed by long runs of the other will be highly compressed. The **amount of compression** that can be achieved depends on the **individual image**.

This image format can be further improved if all graphics are assumed to be rectangular. Instead of having lots of end-of-line E characters, the file format can start with two numbers to represent the width and the height of the image. The computer can then be left to work out what should appear on each row.

The 12, 20 at the beginning means that the graphic is 12 pixels wide and 20 pixels high. It starts with 17 white pixels, which means the whole of the first row plus 5 pixels of the second row. Then there are 2 black pixels followed by 9 white ones and so on. Only 15 numbers are needed to represent the first five rows plus the first 3 pixels of the next row (marked by the arrow). This compares with the simple bitmap format, which needs 63 numbers to represent the image up to the same point.

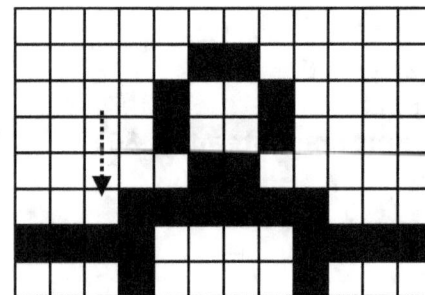

12, 20, 17, 2, 9, 1, 2, 1, 8, 1, 2, 1, 9, 2, 8

(15 numbers instead of 63)

For the improved format to work, there are certain rules that have to be followed, such as:

- The graphic is rectangular
- All pixels are black or white
- Start at the top left hand corner, then go row by row
- Assume the graphic starts with a white pixel
- The first two numbers give the width and height of the graphic

These details must be published, so that anyone writing software that might use the format, knows how to interpret the data. Even if a new image format is well received, it will take time for its adoption to spread. Existing programs will need to be updated to be able to make sense of the data and this could take years.

When an image file using the new format is opened, it will need to be processed according to the rules of the format, which will involve more work than interpreting a simple bitmap. Therefore compressed image files will need more processing to open and to save than a simple bitmap, so this aspect will take longer. However, there will be less data to load or save, which will result in some time being saved. Smaller, compressed files are cheaper to store as they take up less space and they can be transmitted more quickly over the internet as there is less data to transfer.

There are a lot of different image formats that have evolved over time and each will have its own strengths and shortcomings. Some are proprietary having been developed by one particular software company or another to support their own range of products. Others have been developed cooperatively, often through national or international standards organisations, usually to deal with particular perceived shortcomings of the other formats that are available.

Self test

1a. Code the smiley face graphic below, using 0 for black pixels and 1 for white pixels.

1b. What graphic do these numbers represent?

1, 1, 1, 1, 1, 1, 1, 1, 1, 1
1, 0, 0, 0, 0, 0, 0, 1, 1, 1
1, 0, 1, 1, 1, 1, 0, 0, 0, 1
1, 0, 1, 1, 1, 1, 0, 1, 0, 1
1, 0, 1, 1, 1, 1, 0, 0, 0, 1
1, 0, 1, 1, 1, 1, 0, 1, 1, 1
1, 1, 0, 1, 1, 0, 1, 1, 1, 1
1, 1, 1, 0, 0, 1, 1, 1, 1, 1
1, 0, 0, 0, 0, 0, 0, 1, 1, 1
1, 1, 1, 1, 1, 1, 1, 1, 1, 1

2a. Code the graphic below, row by row, assuming each line starts with a white pixel.

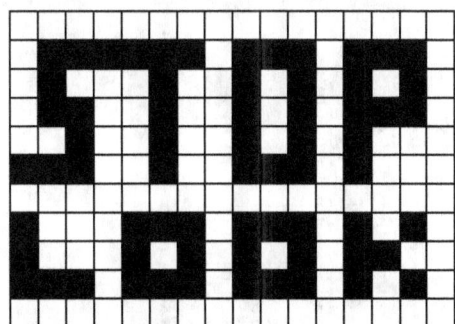

2b. What sport and what letter do these graphics represent?

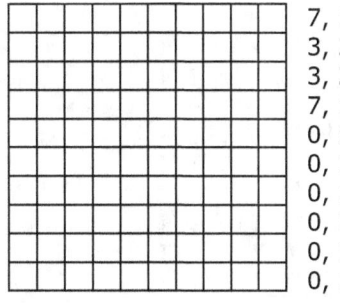

7, 1, 2
3, 2, 2, 1, 2
3, 2, 2, 1, 2
7, 1, 2
0, 5, 2, 1, 2
0, 1, 1, 1, 1, 1, 1, 3, 1
0, 1, 1, 1, 1, 1, 1, 3, 1
0, 1, 1, 1, 1, 1, 1, 3, 1
0, 1, 1, 1, 1, 1, 1, 3, 1
0, 1, 1, 1, 1, 1, 1, 3, 1

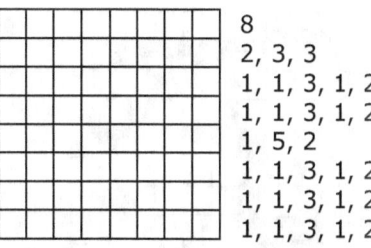

8
2, 3, 3
1, 1, 3, 1, 2
1, 1, 3, 1, 2
1, 5, 2
1, 1, 3, 1, 2
1, 1, 3, 1, 2
1, 1, 3, 1, 2

Living in a digital world - Chapter 2: Digital devices and data

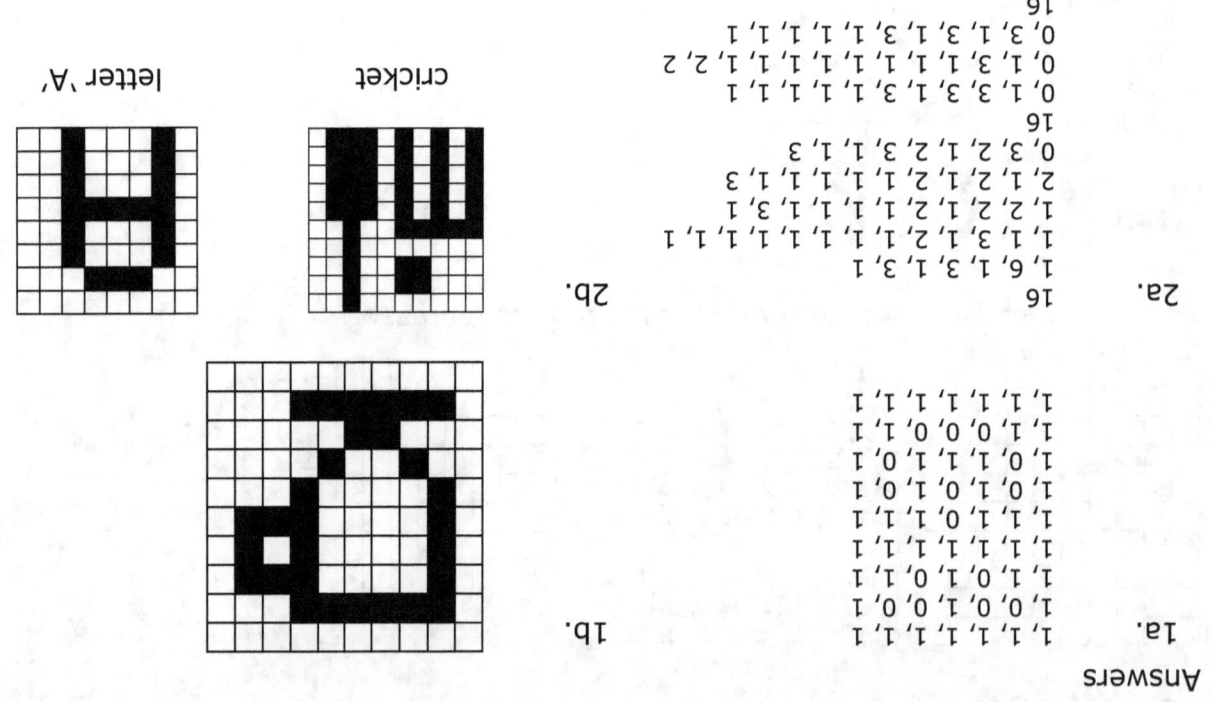

Answers

1a. 1, 1, 1, 1, 1, 1
1, 0, 0, 1, 0, 1
1, 1, 1, 1, 1, 1
1, 1, 0, 1, 1, 1
1, 0, 1, 0, 1, 1
1, 0, 1, 1, 0, 1
1, 0, 0, 0, 1, 1
1, 1, 1, 1, 1, 1

1b. (image: letter 'A')

2a. 16
1, 6, 1, 3, 3, 1
1, 1, 3, 1, 2, 1, 1, 1, 1, 1
1, 2, 2, 1, 2, 1, 1, 1, 1, 3, 1
2, 1, 2, 1, 2, 1, 1, 1, 1, 1, 3
0, 3, 2, 1, 2, 3, 1, 1, 3
16
0, 1, 3, 3, 1, 3, 1, 1, 1, 1
0, 1, 3, 1, 1, 1, 1, 1, 1, 2, 2
0, 3, 1, 3, 1, 3, 1, 1, 1, 1
16

2b. (image: cricket)

A selection of image formats

The use of a particular file format is indicated by the **filename extension**, a short addition (typically 3 characters) to a filename, following a full stop. For example, swan.jpg uses the JPEG format and duck.gif uses the GIF format.

Graphics Interchange Format or GIF (.gif)

The GIF format was developed by the internet company CompuServe and first published in 1987, followed by a revision in 1989.

This format is particularly efficient at representing clip art, logos, sprites and similar simple graphics that have areas of a single colour and use a limited range of colours throughout. Lossless compression is used, so the image quality will not degrade (see JPEG section below). A typical GIF file is limited to just 256 colours, which means there are much better options available for storing photographs, however it remains a popular web format for small graphics like buttons, arrows and logos. There is a way of using GIF files to represent a much bigger range of colours, but the resulting files are much larger than JPEGs, so there is no reason to use them for this purpose.

A particular feature of the GIF format is that it can also be used to store a stream of images in a single file, therefore supporting short animations. These can be viewed by opening them with a web browser, indeed collections of animated GIFs can be found on the internet.

Practical task: Find a GIF file by searching on a computer for "***.gif**". The * means *anything*, ***.gif** means any file that ends with **.gif**. You may be able to do this by opening a folder and using the search box. There should be many GIF files amongst the temporary files stored as a result of web browsing.

Open one of the GIF files in a simple text editor, like Notepad. Most of it will appear as complete gibberish. However, according to the standard, the first six characters should be either GIF87a or GIF89a to indicate which version of the format is going to follow. A semi-colon character (ASCII 59) is used to mark the end of the file.

JPEG (.jpg or .jpeg)

The Joint Photographic Experts Group (JPEG) is a joint committee of two international standards bodies, the ISO (International Standardization Organization) and the IEC (International Electrotechnical Commission). It continues to meet regularly to develop standards for the processing and compression of still images.

Example visual degradation due to JPEG compression

This photograph shows a section of the Stourbridge Canal at Wordsley in the West Midlands.

The original was 6048 x 4032 pixels, approximately 24 megapixels resolution, with a file size of 38.3 MB, using the Nikon raw image format (bitmap).

The first image was resized to 1024 x 683 pixels (700,000 pixels) and saved as a JPEG using a "highest quality" setting offered by an image editing program. It was also converted to monochrome. File size 603 kB.

The second image was saved in the same way, except this time the "good balance" setting was used, mid-way between "highest quality" and "highest compression ratio".

There is no perceptible loss of quality. File size 250kB, 2.4 times smaller than the first.

The third photograph was saved using the "highest compression ratio" setting and there is noticeable degradation of the image. The sky is starting to look 'blocky' and there is a ghosting effect noticeable along the edge of the bottle kiln (upper left). File size 143 kB, 4.2 times smaller than the first.

In this case the additional compression is not worth the significant loss in image quality.

Taking the third image from the previous page and zooming in on the sky, it is apparent that the JPEG compression algorithm has worked in square blocks, some of which have been coloured in a single shade of grey. Some of these blocks have been formed into longer rectangles or bands of a single shade of grey.

Zooming in still further and the blocks along the edge of the bottle kiln can be seen divided up into smaller bands. Some of the bands are horizontal, some are vertical.

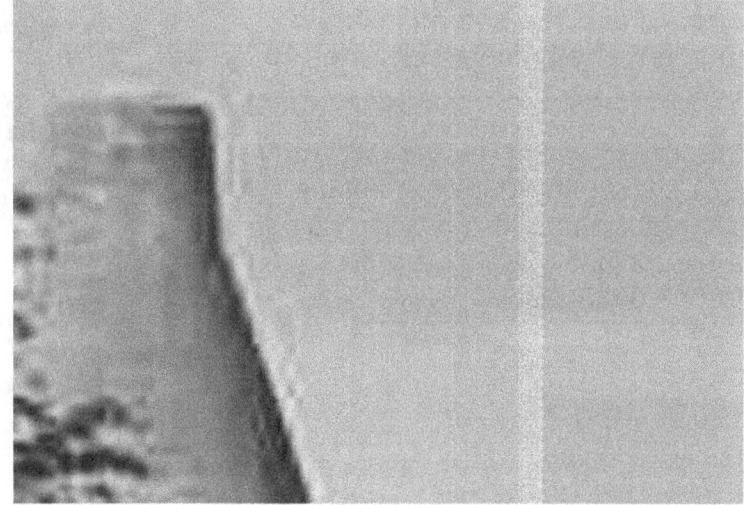

Similarly with the water, some blocks have a single shade, others are banded.

This image of two swans engaged in a territorial dispute, comes from a high resolution original. It was converted to monochrome and saved as a JPEG.

The picture was then cropped slightly along the left edge and saved again as a JPEG, using a medium quality setting.

This process was repeated ten times to simulate repeated editing and saving.

The first zoomed image shows the original and the second zoomed image is the final version after 10 edit-save cycles.

The final version (below) is clearly less sharp, showing that image degradation builds up when using a file format that incorporates lossy compression.

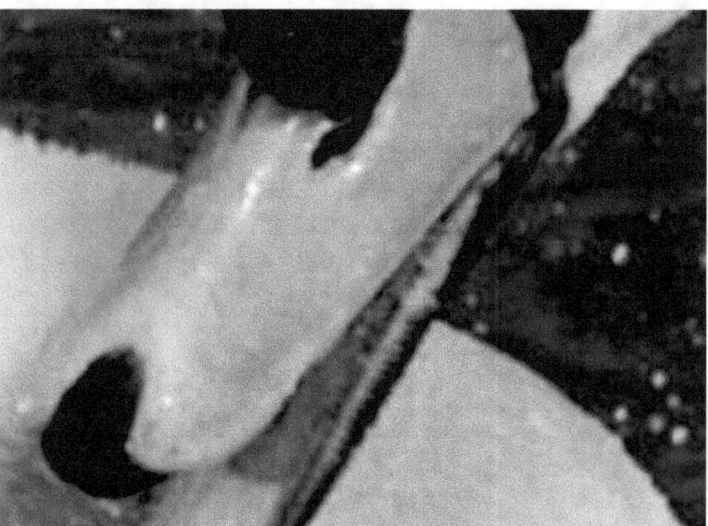

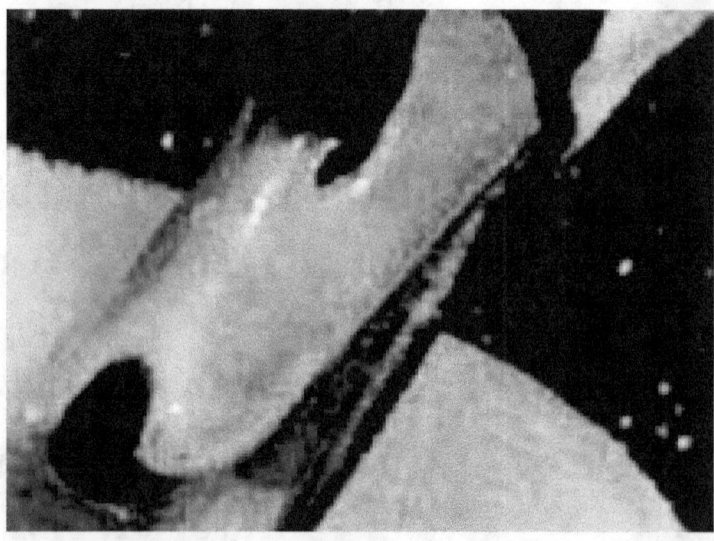

Work started on the JPEG standard in 1986 and it was first published in 1992, with the latest version dating from 1994. It is the most dominant still image format, being implemented on the vast majority of, if not all, digital cameras.

JPEG files use a type of **lossy compression**, which means that some data from the original image is discarded in order to achieve greater compression. When you save an image as a JPEG for the first time it is often not possible to perceive any loss of quality. However, if you repeatedly open, edit and re-save a JPEG image, the amount of lost data will build up and the image will **slowly degrade**.

Therefore it is preferable to use a lossless image format if you plan to significantly or repeatedly edit an image, especially if that will involve re-saving the file many times as the editing continues. If an important photograph has been taken with a camera that can only save images as JPEGs, it is good practice to always keep an original copy somewhere. If this is copied before editing starts then there will always be a top quality original to return to, should it be needed.

One useful aspect of the JPEG format (and common amongst those formats that use lossy compression) is that the degree of compression can be adjusted so that a user can choose an appropriate tradeoff between image quality and file size.

JPEGs can often achieve compression of around 10 to 1, with little perceptible loss in image quality.

Portable Network Graphics or PNG (.png)

The GIF format was very popular, particularly in the early days of the internet. However, around 1995 it was realised that this format used a data compression method that had been patented (these patents have since expired). It was also becoming increasingly common for computers to be able to display more than 256 colours.

Initially an ad-hoc group got together to produce the first draft of an alternative, non-patented, lossless, single image format. This led to the publication of an ISO/IEC standard in 2004. Animation was not included and although the same people produced a later format that would support animation, this is a niche area where, at the time of writing, GIFs still reign supreme!

Generally PNG files compress better (are smaller) than the corresponding GIF files, except for small images, where the GIF format is better.

PNG files also offer what is called an **alpha channel**. The alpha channel describes the levels of opacity of an image and makes it possible to have areas that are completely transparent, supporting, for example, irregular image cut-outs. The diagram of digital devices at the beginning of this chapter includes images that incorporate transparency, such as the mobile phone and remote control. Whereas the images of the washing machine and the tumble dryer do not include any transparency and are "normal" rectangular images. The PNG format has proved popular and is widely used.

Microsoft Windows Bitmap or BMP (.bmp)

This was developed as the standard bitmap format for devices using Microsoft's Windows operating system. It has become widely used and is supported by a wide range of software because it is simple and relatively well documented, as well as being free of any patents.

The first version of this format was a basic bitmap format with no compression available. Later versions introduced some compression options and features such as an alpha channel.

Most BMP files are relatively large, however where this is a problem, lossless data compression, such as ZIP, can often be very effective at producing a compressed version of the file.

Tagged Image File Format or TIFF (.tif or .tiff)

This bitmap image format is commonly used by graphic artists, photographers and the publishing industry, having been developed initially for use in desktop publishing. First released in 1986, it was most recently amended in 2002.

TIFF files can support a range of compression techniques, both lossy and lossless, however it is most common for it to be used as a lossless format. It is one of the most flexible and powerful image formats, but that also makes it relatively complex for software writers to include in their programs. This may result in it being left out or a limited range of the options available being offered.

The copyright on the TIFF specification is held by Adobe Systems.

Practical task: Load an image into some graphics/photo editing software. Use **Save As...** or **Export...** to save copies of the image using different file types/formats. Save them all to the same folder.

Open this folder and look at the size of each file and compare the amount of compression that each has achieved.

Data vs Information

In everyday language data and information are words that are often used interchangeably. However they have subtly different meanings which can be explained by considering the image digitising example that has just been covered.

Consider the final version (below).

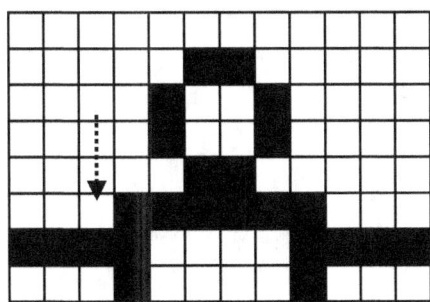

12, 20, 17, 2, 9, 1, 2, 1, 8, 1, 2, 1, 9, 2, 8

(15 numbers instead of 63)

In this case the **data** is **12, 20, 17, 2, 9, 1, 2, 1, 8, 1, 2, 1, 9, 2, 8**

Information is the *meaning* **given to this data.** In this case, the information is that the graphic is 12 pixels wide and 20 pixels high. Starting in the top left hand corner and going across the rows in turn, the graphic starts with 17 white pixels followed by 2 black, 9 white, 1 black, 2 white, and so on.

Metadata and images

Metadata is data about data. In the case of an image, it is extra data that is added to the image file to give further information about the picture. It can include **keyword tags** that help to describe what the image is about.

The picture of the water vole was taken from the towpath of the Kennet and Avon Canal in England, in April 2017. Appropriate keywords would include the following.

photograph, monochrome, england, united kingdom, uk, april, spring, 2017, outdoor, day, mammal, wildlife, water vole, eating, food, canal, kennet, avon, water

Cameras usually add metadata that list the camera settings when photographs are taken. This can include the shutter speed and aperture settings, the camera and lens that was used, the date and time it was taken, the ISO (sensitivity) setting, whether flash was used and many other pieces of information. If the camera has GPS capability it can also include the coordinates of where the picture was taken.

Cameras, as well as scanners and other imaging hardware, usually follow the **EXIF** (exchangeable image file format) standard. EXIF data is one form of metadata. Whilst EXIF data is added automatically by devices, it can also be edited using appropriate software, so that a photographer might choose to add their name as creator of the image and a copyright notice, as well as choosing the most appropriate keywords. Metadata makes it easier for automated software like internet search engines to find images appropriate for a given set of search terms. However, not all image file formats support the addition of metadata.

Tag	Name	Value
9004	Date Time Digitized	22/04/2017 12:06:47
9204	Exposure Bias Value	0
9205	Max Aperture Value	5 (F5.7)
9207	Metering Mode	Pattern
9208	Light Source	Unknown
9209	Flash	Not fired, compulsory flash mode
920a	Focal Length	300.0
927c	Maker Note	[33072 bytes] 78, 105, 107, 111, 11
.0001	Firmware Version	2.11
.0002	ISO Speed Used	1250
.0004	JPEG Quality	Raw
.0005	White Balance	Auto 1
.0007	Focus Mode	AF-A
.000b	White Balance Bias	0, 0
.000c	White Balance Coefficients	527/256, 411/256, 1.0, 1.0
.000d	Program Shift	0 EV
.000e	Exposure Difference	0 EV
.0013	ISO Speed Requested	1250
.0019	AE Bracket Compensation Applied	0 EV
.001b	Crop High Speed	0, 4992, 3280, 4992, 3280, 0, 0
.001c	Exposure Fine-Tuning	0 EV
.001d	Serial Number	7402487
.001e	Color Space	sRGB
.001f	Vibration Reduction Info	On
.0022	Active D-Lighting	Auto
.0023	Picture Control	[58 bytes] 48, 49, 48, 48, 83, 84, 65
.0024	World Time	UTC+0h no DST

Sample of the EXIF data attached to the water vole picture

The box shows a selection of the metadata from the photograph of the water vole.

Some of the terms will be familiar to hobby photographers. Some of the data is only relevant to specialists, for example a programmer wanting to use the available data to automatically improve how their software handles photographs.

Scanners

Scanners are devices that digitise printed and other flat media, such as photographic prints or film negatives. They do this by dividing the material into a fine grid and sampling each pixel, recording a value for the colour of each one.

At the time of writing, scanners designed for use in the home have typical resolutions ranging between 1200 and 9600 dots (pixels) per inch or dpi.

The images are saved in a standard format that is chosen by the user, with a selection of EXIF data added automatically, where the format allows this.

The discovery of zero

The number zero has a crucial role to play in the digital world but it was only invented/discovered relatively recently.

The Babylonians and Mayans both developed placeholder symbols independently. However, it was not until around 600 AD that a Hindu astronomer and mathematician called Brahmagupta not only had a symbol for zero, but developed mathematical operations that used zero. This is recognised as being the first time that zero was understood as being a number in its own right. Zero was introduced to Europe through the Moorish conquest of Spain, but it was not until the 17th Century that it was being widely used throughout Europe.

The invention of zero allowed the development of positional counting systems, such as the decimal or base ten system that is in common use today.

Consider the number **160**. The Romans would write this as CLX, the number being equal to the sum of the constituent parts, 100 + 50 + 10. There is no use of place value. In decimal, zero is the placeholder. It tells us that there are no units, but even more importantly, it also tells us that the 6 stands for 6 tens (or 60) and the 1 for 1 hundred. With the number **1600** the zeros are telling us that there is one thousand plus six hundreds. Combinations of only ten different digits are able to represent any number.

Alternative number systems

Having zero meant that number systems could be developed using any base number, not just ten.

Consider the place value headings in decimal (base ten). All number systems will need a units column, so that seems to be the best place to start. To get the value of the next column, just multiply by the base number, 10 and you get 1 x 10 = 10. For the next column, multiply by 10 again and you get 1 x 10 x 10 = 100. The next column is thousands, then ten thousands and so on. Just keep multiplying by the base number to get the value of the next column.

Base	Name	First three column headings, written in decimal			No. digits	Digits
ten	decimal	100	10	1 (units)	10	0 to 9
nine	nonary	81	9	1	9	0 to 8
eight	octal	64	8	1	8	0 to 7
seven	septenary	49	7	1	7	0 to 6
six	senary	36	6	1	6	0 to 5
five	quinary	25	5	1	5	0 to 4
four	quaternary	16	4	1	4	0 to 3
three	ternary	9	3	1	3	0 to 2
two	binary	4	2	1	2	0 and 1

Choosing another base number, say eight, exactly the same pattern is followed except that this time you multiply by eight, the new base number. The column headings are therefore 1, 8, 64, etc.

253 in base 10 can be written 253_{10} which means 2 x **100** + 5 x **10** + 3 x **1**

253_8 means 2 x **64** + 5 x **8** + 3 x **1** = 171_{10}

176_8 means 1 x **64** + 7 x **8** + 6 x **1** = 126_{10}

This is crucial for the development of electronic computing, because whilst digital devices are based entirely on numbers, base ten or decimal is not their natural counting system. It is likely that the only reason it has become the counting system of choice is because we humans have ten digits on the end of our arms and counting in tens follows naturally from our anatomy and counting on our fingers.

Electronic circuits naturally have two states, **on** and **off**. There either **is a voltage** or there is **no voltage**. The ideal number system would therefore be base two, better known as binary. Following the pattern already established, this number system has two digits, 0 and 1, that represent off and on. The place value column headings are 1, 2, 4, 8, 16, 32, 64, 128, 256... a series that is very familiar to computer scientists.

The easy introduction to binary

If the last section was beginning to make your head spin, rest assured that there is a very easy way to get a good feel for how the binary number system works. Remember, this is the number system that is used by all modern digital devices.

Binary cards

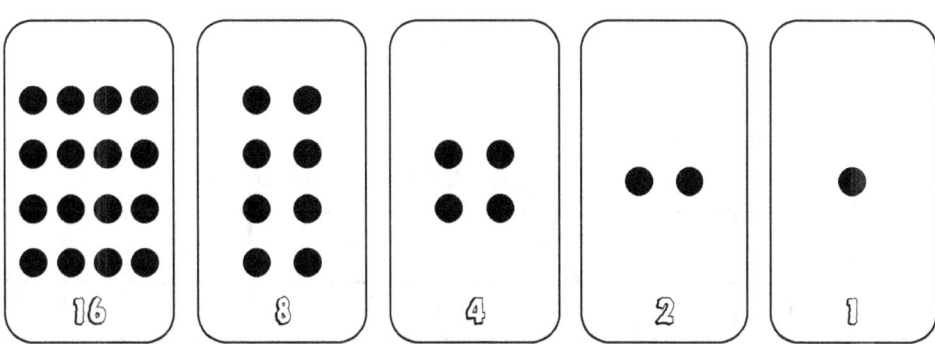

It requires a set of binary cards, an idea that I first came across in a booklet from New Zealand, **CS Unplugged**[1].

You do not need the numbers on the bottom if you are going to stick with five cards, but they come into their own if you want to expand the deck to include 32, 64, etc.

Once you have made a set of cards (or just tear up some pieces of paper), you can try using them to make different numbers. For example, can you make the decimal number 11? Start with all the cards face down.

Clearly you can do that by having the 8, 2 and 1 cards face up and keeping the 16 and 4 cards face down.

Try other numbers. What is the largest number you can make? Try counting from zero up to, say 30, using the cards. As you are counting, do you notice any patterns in the way in which you turn the cards over?

You are now exploring how binary works, quite possibly without knowing it! You may be completely focused on counting dots. But you also may have spotted that these cards represent the binary place value headings. Place the cards in the order shown in the diagram and turn over the cards that make 11_{10}. The face up cards can be replaced with a binary 1 and the face down cards with binary 0.

$01011_2 = 8_{10} + 2_{10} + 1_{10} = 11_{10}$

$10101_2 = 16_{10} + 4_{10} + 1_{10} = 21_{10}$

This chapter has shown how different types of data can be represented using numbers and how those numbers can be represented using just two digits, 0 and 1. If you could look inside the processor (CPU) of a digital device, down at a microscopic level, you would see streams of 0s and 1s flying about at ultra-high speed.

---

[1] CS Unplugged by Tim Bell, Ian H. Witten and Mike Fellows, adapted for classroom use by Robyn Adams and Jane McKenzie and revised in 2015 by Sam Jarman. At the time of writing, electronic copies could be downloaded free of charge from the csunplugged.org website. Printed copies were also available.

Self test

Fill in the table to show all the numbers in their decimal form AND their binary equivalents.

Decimal number	8-bit binary equivalent							
	128	64	32	16	8	4	2	1
3	0	0	0	0	0	0	1	1
14								
47								
88								
255								
	1	0	1	0	0	1	0	0
	0	1	1	0	0	0	1	1
	0	0	0	1	0	0	0	1
	1	0	0	0	1	1	1	0
	0	0	0	1	1	1	1	1

Extension: What is the easy way to spot if a binary number is odd or even?

Answers:

Decimal	8-bit binary equivalent							
	128	64	32	16	8	4	2	1
3	0	0	0	0	0	0	1	1
14	0	0	0	0	1	1	1	0
47	0	0	1	0	1	1	1	1
88	0	1	0	1	1	0	0	0
255	1	1	1	1	1	1	1	1
164	1	0	1	0	0	1	0	0
99	0	1	1	0	0	0	1	1
17	0	0	0	1	0	0	0	1
142	1	0	0	0	1	1	1	0
31	0	0	0	1	1	1	1	1

Extension: Odd numbers all end in a 1, even numbers end with 0.

> **Practical task:** Here are some ASCII codes written in binary. Can you spot the relationship between the upper and lower case letters?
>
> A = 65_{10} = 01000001   a = 97_{10} = 01100001
> B = 66_{10} = 01000010   b = 98_{10} = 01100010
> C = 67_{10} = 01000011   c = 99_{10} = 01100011
>
> How could a computer use this to check and see if a letter was upper case or not?
> What would be a quick way of changing a lower case letter to upper case?
>
> *If needed, see the hint on page 89.*

Bits, bytes and words

A single **B**inary dig**IT,** 0 or 1, is known as a **bit**. However, computers operate on groups of bits that are treated as a single unit and such a chunk of data is known as a **byte**.

Commonly a byte is taken as being made up of 8 bits, the number of bits you need to encode a single character. Storage figures are measured based in 8-bit bytes.

The extended ASCII set requires 256 numbers, which is what you get with 8 bits:

2 x 2 x 2 x 2 x 2 x 2 x 2 x 2 = 2^8 = 256, i.e. the numbers from 0 to 255.

A CPU uses registers for the temporary storage of data that is being worked on. The size of these registers is known as the **word** length.

Early desktop computers typically used an 8-bit word. This later became 16 bits as processors became more powerful. Currently most desktop and laptop computers have a word length of 32 or 64 bits.

When you are offered the choice between installing a 32-bit version or a 64-bit version of software, this is referring to the word length that the program is designed for. A 32-bit computer could only run the 32-bit version. A 64-bit computer will perform best with the 64-bit version, but could also run the 32-bit version. A 64-bit computer will operate faster and be able to use much more working memory than an equivalent 32-bit computer, in the same way that, in general, 32-bit computers were more powerful than the 16- and 8-bit predecessors.

The nature of digital signals

Data has to be passed around within a digital device and it will often have to be sent between two devices, either through a cable connection or via radio waves. Digital data consists only of zeros and ones and this means that digital signals are naturally more resilient than analogue signals.

Consider an analogue radio broadcast. There will be a continuously varying radio wave that is broadcast, which is represented in the graph below.

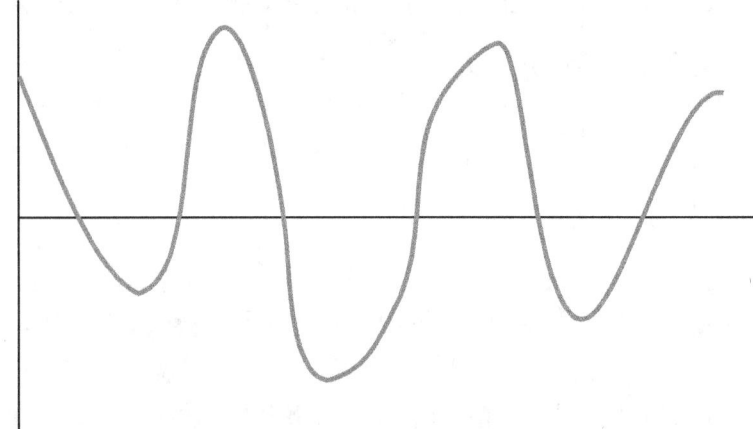

The closer that the received signal is to the original, the better the sound quality. However, radio signals can suffer from interference. Atmospheric effects, thunderstorms and nearby rogue electrical equipment, can all interfere with radio signals. Under poor reception conditions, the signal that is received might look more like this.

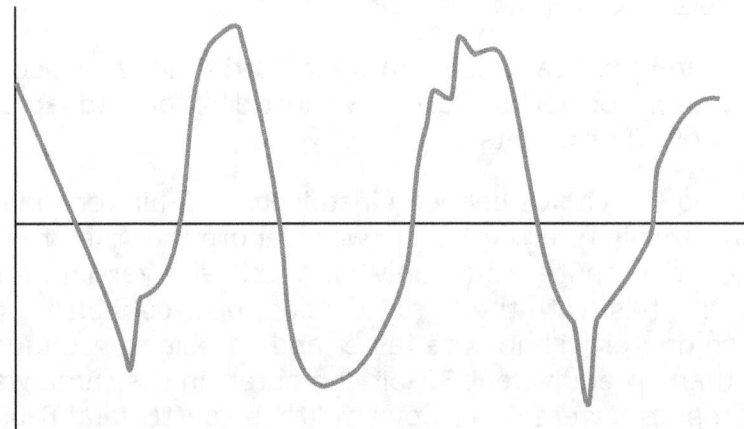

In this case the sound quality will be significantly degraded.

With a digital signal, all that you are transmitting is a series of zeros and ones. This is shown below.

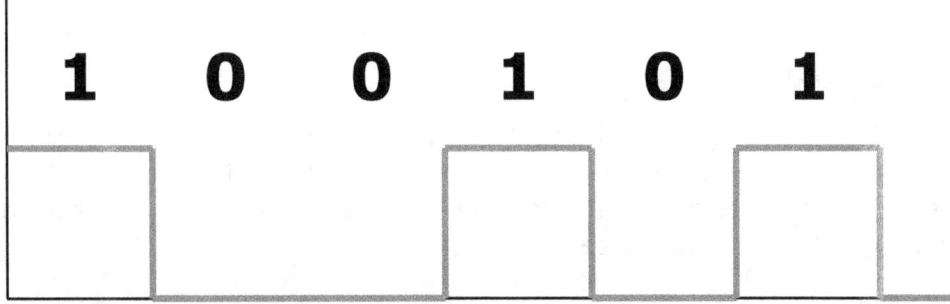

Consider a situation where the digital signal also suffers significant interference. The original signal is shown as a dotted line for comparison.

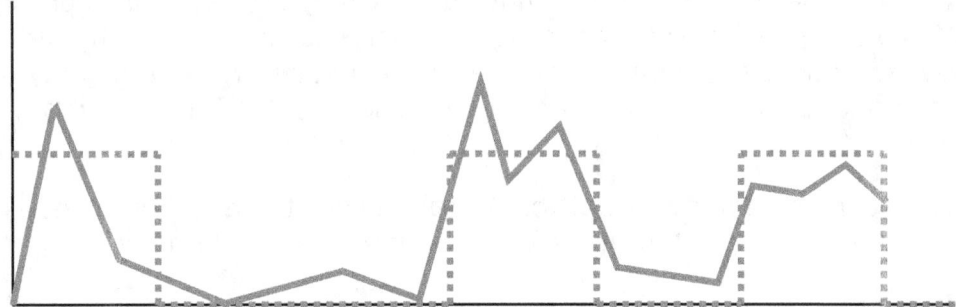

Providing the receiving device has enough information to tell which bits should be 1 and which should be 0 then the data will be received exactly as it was transmitted, with no loss of quality.

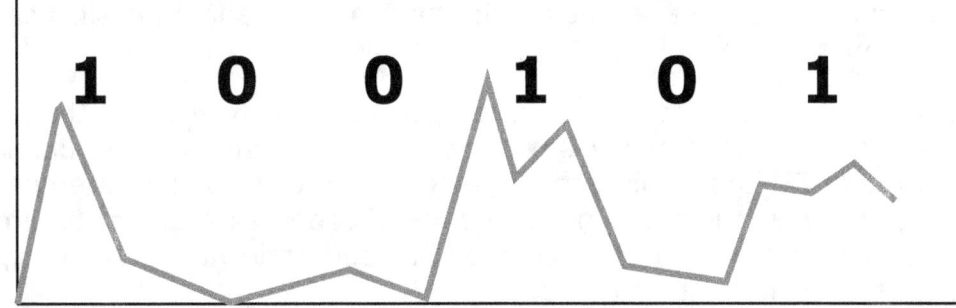

An analogue TV signal will degrade as reception conditions worsen, however it will remain watchable for much of this time, albeit at reduced quality. A digital signal will initially retain full quality as the signal starts to degrade. Small parts of the picture may then appear as blocks of one colour and fragments of the soundtrack may be lost. Any further degrading of the signal and the broadcast is lost completely. This rapid decline is sometimes called the digital cliff effect, as reception metaphorically "falls off a cliff"; it goes from full quality to nothing via a very short transition.

Error detection

Digital devices work at high speed and it is crucial that extremely high levels of accuracy are achieved as data is passed around, otherwise the potential exists to produce vast quantities of garbage. Electrical interference is one way that data transmissions can become corrupted.

Binary digits within a digital device are usually moved around in parallel, i.e. simultaneously. A wide thin ribbon cable made up of lots of individual wires side by side, is an obvious sign of parallel transmission. For many years personal computers would be equipped with a parallel printer port as standard, that allowed all 7 bits of a standard ASCII character to be transmitted together. If the physical properties of the wires (also any pins/sockets) carrying the different bits are slightly different, it is possible that errors can be introduced because the bits arrive at slightly different times. As computers work at higher and higher speeds, this becomes more of a problem.

It therefore becomes very important for digital devices to be able to check data automatically for errors, so that appropriate action can be taken.

Parity checks

This is probably the simplest method of error checking and it is based on the number of 1s being transmitted. Suppose that a computer is sending text data to a printer. The computer and printer would have to agree whether they were using odd parity or even parity. This could form part of an automated 'conversation' between the two devices (known as **handshaking**) when the computer tries to print or it could be a software setting within the computer and a physical switch setting on the printer.

Suppose data is going to be sent using **even parity**. This means that the printer will expect every byte that it receives will have an even number of 1s. Before it is transmitted, the ASCII codes for each character will have to be prepared using an additional bit, known as the parity bit. If the ASCII code has even parity already, the parity bit is set to zero. If the ASCII code has odd parity, then the parity bit is set to one, so that even parity is achieved.

On receiving the characters, the printer checks that each one has even parity. If any have odd parity then the printer knows that the data contains one or more errors. If the data is being received correctly, the parity bits can then be discarded and the text printed.

Suppose **Goodbye!** was going to be printed. Here are the characters, their ASCII codes and those codes in 7-bit binary.

Character	ASCII	64	32	16	8	4	2	1	1s
G	71	1	0	0	0	1	1	1	4
o	111	1	1	0	1	1	1	1	6
o	111	1	1	0	1	1	1	1	6
d	100	1	1	0	0	1	0	0	3
b	98	1	1	0	0	0	1	0	3
y	121	1	1	1	1	0	0	1	5
e	101	1	1	0	0	1	0	1	4
!	33	0	1	0	0	0	0	1	2

Three characters have odd parity, d, b, and y. Before sending to the printer these characters will be given parity bits of 1, the rest will have their parity bit set to 0.

Character	ASCII	64	32	16	8	4	2	1	Parity bit
G	71	1	0	0	0	1	1	1	0
o	111	1	1	0	1	1	1	1	0
o	111	1	1	0	1	1	1	1	0
d	100	1	1	0	0	1	0	0	1
b	98	1	1	0	0	0	1	0	1
y	121	1	1	1	1	0	0	1	1
e	101	1	1	0	0	1	0	1	0
!	33	0	1	0	0	0	0	1	0

The data in the above table is what is transmitted, starting with the character G, or **10001110**. Suppose that there is some electrical interference and the printer receives **11001110**. This byte has **odd parity**, the printer is expecting **even parity**, therefore it knows that an error has occurred.

This is a very simple system and it clearly cannot spot all errors. Suppose the G character had 2 bits changed and was received as **11101110**. This byte has the required even parity (six 1s), so the error would go undetected. Error checking methods all have their strengths and weaknesses. Parity is very simple to understand and the processing required is easy to do. It is likely to suffice for a simple application, such as sending text to a printer. In all likelihood if errors are being introduced, at least one of the changed characters is likely to fail the parity test, given the number of characters in a reasonably sized document, even if some errors are not spotted. Once an error is spotted, the printer can take a precautionary approach and request that all the data is re-transmitted.

Redundancy

The letters used to represent text contain more than the bare minimum of graphical information needed to read them. This can be seen by covering up part of a sentence.

HELLO, WHAT IS YOUR NAME?

About half of the phrase has been covered, yet it should still be possible to read "HELLO, WHAT IS YOUR NAME?", although you could be forgiven for missing out the comma. This clearly illustrates that there is more information contained in the text than the bare minimum required to read it. This additional information is redundant, it does not add anything to what you can read. However, it can be useful when the text is in poor condition - perhaps a tatty and stained piece of paper or really untidy handwriting. The additional redundant data can make up for the loss of data elsewhere.

The parity bits added to the characters "Goodbye!" before being sent to the printer are another example of redundant data. They do not change the characters being transmitted, they are simply used to help spot errors that might be introduced during transmission. Once the printer has received all the characters and checked that the parity is as expected, the parity bits can be ignored/thrown away.

Parity is a type of **redundancy check**.

Check digits

Since digital data is all numerical, another way of spotting errors is to take a chunk of data and carry out some sort of mathematical operation on it. The answer can then be added to the data and the data transmitted. On reception, the same mathematical operation is carried out. If the answer is different from the one appended prior to transmission, then there must be one or more errors in the data.

This is the principle behind check digits, another type of redundancy check. Bank card numbers commonly have a check digit added, using the Luhn Algorithm.

The Luhn Algorithm works as follows. Starting at the right-most digit, which is the check digit, double every second digit. Take these answers and add together the separate digits to get a total c_1. Add together all the remaining digits, not including the check digit, to get total c_2. Add c_1 and c_2 and multiply the result by 9. The last digit of the answer (i.e. in digit in the units column) is the check digit.

Example: Bank card number 9609 8433 7032 257**9** has a check digit of **9**. Does this fit the Luhn Algorithm?

Card number	9	6	0	9	8	4	3	3	7	0	3	2	2	5	7	9
Double every 2nd digit	18		0		16		6		14		6		4		14	
Add the separate digits	1 8	0	1 0	6	1 4	0 6	0 4	1 4								
Add the digits	9	6	0	9	7	4	6	3	5	0	6	2	4	5	5	

Instead of calculating c_1 and c_2 separately, you can just add up all the numbers in the *Add the digits* row.

You can see that the check digit calculated according to the Luhn Algorithm is **9**, which agrees with the check digit at the end of the number.

If the card number was read by a machine, or was typed into a website to make an online purchase and the check digit was calculated to be some other number, there must be an error in one or more of the digits. The card number would be rejected and would have to be read again or have its number re-typed.

$c_1 =$	42
$c_2 =$	29
$c_1 + c_2 =$	71
multiply by 9 =	639
check digit =	9

The Luhn Algorithm will detect any single-digit error, as well as almost all transpositions of adjacent digits. This is particularly important for situations where a number might be entered by hand, since one of the most common human data entry errors is to reverse two adjacent characters, be they letters or numbers. For example, you might type **48** instead of **84** or **97** instead of **79**. However, the Luhn Algorithm will not detect 09/90. Although it will detect most twin errors, it does not detect 22/55, 33/66 or 44/77. The check digit is the redundant data in this case.

> **Practical task:** Find a bank card and see if the card number fits the Luhn Algorithm. You can try other numbers, such as national ID numbers and bank account numbers.
>
> *Extension:* Make a spreadsheet to help calculate Luhn Algorithm check digits. Look for numbers that contain, e.g. two adjacent 3s. Swap these for 6s. The check digit should remain the same, showing that this error would **not** be spotted.

International Article Numbers (EAN)

International Article Numbers started life as European Article Numbers and are still known by the acronym EAN. If you have ever wondered how it is possible to scan an item at the supermarket checkout and have its description and price appear at the till and on your receipt, then it is all thanks to the humble EAN. It is a simple, yet elegant, solution to the problem that the products in shops come from many different suppliers and potentially, from anywhere in the world.

What is needed is the ability to give a product a unique code number. This will allow the product to be identified and can be encoded in the product barcode. When the barcode is scanned, the code number can be looked up on the store's database. The product should have been set up already and this is where the checkout automatically finds the price that the supermarket has set and the product description. Most of the time. When a particular product code cannot be found (perhaps it is a new product line and the store's database has not been updated with the product details) there is usually an annoying delay while the checkout assistant gets authorisation to carry out a manual override.

Initial organisation of EAN numbers

The key problem to overcome is how can you ensure that all products have unique EAN numbers? If two products have the same number, that has the potential to cause all sorts of confusion. When the EAN system was first set up it was very straightforward. Most EAN numbers follow the EAN-13 standard and are 13 digits long, made up of a 12-digit code plus a check digit.

The first two digits were an internationally agreed country number. The UK was allocated 50. When manufacturers from a particular country wanted to use EANs they applied to the appropriate national body. This ensured that no two manufacturers were allocated the same manufacturer code. Each manufacturer allocated product codes as it saw fit and was responsible for making sure that two products were never given the same product code. Finally, a check digit was added according to a set algorithm. Here is the EAN-13 number found on a loaf of bread.

By organising the EAN-13 numbers in this way, unique product numbers could be assigned that would be recognised in any country that signed up to the EAN system.

When the EAN system was introduced, there were already two popular barcode systems in use, the Universal Product Code (UPC, North America) and the Japanese Article Number (JAN). 12-digit UPC codes could be transformed into their EAN equivalent by prefixing the code with a zero. JAN numbers also transformed into EAN numbers when they were prefixed with 49.

The EAN system also incorporated other numbering standards. International Standard Book Numbers (ISBN) were prefixed 978 and International Standard Serial Numbers started with 977 (ISSN, magazines and periodicals).

EANs can have a 2-digit or 5-digit suffix added. A 2-digit suffix can be used for a monthly or weekly publication to show the issue number, for example week 12. A 5-digit suffix can be added to weighed products, such as fruit and vegetables or products from a delicatessen counter, to encode the price.

ISSN as EAN barcode, issue 12

The development of retail barcode standards

The first barcode standard was agreed in 1973 in the United States of America. The first product scanned in a supermarket is reported as being a packet of chewing gum, scanned in April 1974. The European Article Numbering Association launched in 1977 and built on what had already been established. This organisation has been since renamed as GS1.

GS1 is now a global member organisation that has moved beyond just barcode systems. It develops supply chain standards covering retail, healthcare, transport and logistics, however this still includes International Article Numbers.

The EAN system has worked very well, however one weakness was the allocation of 5 digits to all manufacturers (100,000 different codes, 00000-99999), whether they needed them or not. This resulted in a lot of unused numbers. As more countries and manufacturers wanted to join and the system started to run short of numbers to allocate, some reorganisation was necessary. Now the manufacturer code is of variable length, so if a manufacturer only expects to need a few product codes, they can be issued with a longer manufacturer code. This leaves less room for the product code, keeping some of the range for other users.

The first *three* digits are now used to identify the country where the manufacturer has joined GS1, this is known as the **GS1 Prefix**. Note that this prefix does **not** indicate the country of origin of the product. Moving from a 2- to 3-digit prefix means that smaller countries can be allocated a shorter range of numbers. Some countries have been allocated *more* than one number range to give them more

Selection of GS1 prefixes	
GS1 prefix	GS1 office/country
387	GS1 BIH (Bosnia-Herzegovina)
389	GS1 Montenegro
400 - 440	GS1 Germany
450 - 459 & 490 - 499	GS1 Japan
460 - 469	GS1 Russia
470	GS1 Kyrgyzstan
471	GS1 Taiwan
474	GS1 Estonia
475	GS1 Latvia

numbers to give out. The reorganisation has been done in such a way as to keep the validity of the pre-existing EAN numbers.

Not all prefixes have been allocated, leaving room for future growth.

The whole of the EAN system has now become a part of the GS1 Global Trade Item Number or GTIN standard. EAN-13 numbers are therefore sometimes referred to as GTIN-13 numbers.

EANs have a check digit appended. The algorithm has some similarity to the Luhn Algorithm seen earlier.

barcode digits, d	5	0	1	0	0	9	2	2	4	5	7	4	1
multiplier, m	1	3	1	3	1	3	1	3	1	3	1	3	
product, d x m	5	0	1	0	0	27	2	6	4	15	7	12	
EAN check digit algorithm							sum of products					79	
							subtract from nearest equal or higher multiple of 10					80-79	
							check digit					1	

This check digit algorithm will detect all single digit errors and 90% of transposition errors. It will not detect transposition errors where the difference in the adjacent digits is 5.

Shorter EAN-8 barcodes are available where packaging is too small to allow the use of a full 13-digit barcode.

EAN-8 barcodes that start with a 0 or a 2 encode what are known as restricted circulation numbers which are designed for use **within** an organisation. A supermarket may use these numbers for their own-brand products that are not sold by any other outlet. Restricted circulation numbers are also available for EAN-13 barcodes, using GS1 prefixes in the range 040-049.

The idea behind adding a check digit to a number as a way of spotting input/transmission errors can be extended to other data, such as an email message. The data that makes up the message can have some sort of mathematical process (known as a **hash function**) carried out on it with the resulting **hash value** being added to the data before the item is transmitted. When the data is received, the hash function is recalculated and compared with the received hash value.

> **Practical task:** Find some examples of grocery packaging and see if any have 13-digit product codes. Do the check digits fit the EAN-13 algorithm?
>
> *Extension:* Make a spreadsheet to help calculate EAN-13 check digits. Make up a valid EAN-13 number for a country of your choice, including a valid check digit.

Error correction

The simplest form of error correction is to use the addition of redundant data, such as parity bits, a check digit or hash value, to identify that errors have been introduced during data entry or transmission. The receiving device can then send an automatic repeat request to the transmitting device and have the data sent again.

However, it is possible to add more redundant data, to not only detect that errors have occurred, but also to enable the data to be corrected. The maximum number of errors that any scheme can correct will depend on the method chosen and the amount of error correction data that has been added. Error correction is widely used in digital broadcasting (radio and TV), where retransmission is not an option.

Colour and grey-scale images

Simple black and white images were discussed earlier in this chapter, but this type of graphic is not typical of what digital devices are used for. Images are normally either colour, or sometimes, grey-scale. With the latter, pixels can be black, white or various shades of grey. This means there has to be a way of representing the colour of each pixel, that goes beyond two values, 0 and 1.

A very common scheme, that matches the way monitors produce an image, is 24-bit RGB. RGB stands for **Red**, **Green**, **Blue**, the three colours that are used by monitors and televisions to produce a picture. The 24 bits are shared equally between the three colours, which means that each colour has 8 bits dedicated to it.

Remembering the binary place value headings, 8 bits gives us 1, 2, 4, 8, 16, 32, 64, 128. The largest number that can be represented with 8 bits is 11111111_2 or 255_{10}.

Red   can have any value from 0 to 255 (256 different shades)
Green can have any value from 0 to 255 (256 different shades)
Blue   can have any value from 0 to 255 (256 different shades)

The maximum number of different colours that can be represented by this scheme is therefore 256 x 256 x 256 = 16,777,216 (over 16 million colours). As the human eye can discriminate about 10 million colours, 24-bit colour is also known as **true colour**.

0, 0, 0 represents no red, no green and no blue. With a monitor, no light means **black**.

255, 255, 255 means full red, full green and full blue which is **white**.

255, 0, 0 is red   0, 255, 0 is green   0, 0, 255 is blue

25, 25, 25 is dark grey   200, 200, 200 is light grey

255, 255, 0 is yellow   0, 255, 255 is cyan (light blue) 255, 0, 255 is magenta

50, 100, 50 is a dark shade of green

It is common, especially in graphics software, but also elsewhere, to see colour controls that consist of three text boxes and possibly slider controls. You can either type in numbers, click the arrows or move the sliders to achieve the particular colour that you want.

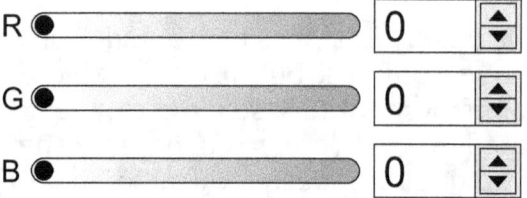

Using 24-bit colour means that each pixel requires 3 bytes of storage (3 x 8 = 24, one byte for each colour). A simple colour bitmap of a photograph taken by a 10 megapixel camera will therefore take up at least 10 million x 3 or 30 Mbytes of storage space. Many consumer 'point and shoot' cameras do not offer the option of saving images as a bitmap, preferring to take advantage of JPEG compression, which results in much smaller files.

There are colour models that use more than 24 bits. These allow more detail to be recorded, but at the cost of requiring much more data to be stored. Deep colour systems can represent a billion colours or more.

Since the human eye can only discern, typically, around 10 million colours, it might seem unnecessary to go beyond the 16 million colours of 24-bit true colour. However, use of true colour can lead to colour gradients, which should change imperceptibly from one shade to another, appearing to be made up of colour bands. This might occur where, for example, a wall is painted a uniform colour, but is unevenly lit. One end might be brightly lit and the other could be in shadow. Therefore the colour might change from a shade of blue to black. It can be very distracting if the wall appears banded, rather than there being a smooth, even, change of colour.

The RGB colour model is an additive model, the output is what you get from adding light of the three colours together in different amounts. There are other colour models. The CMYK (**c**yan, **m**agenta, **y**ellow and **k**ey or *black*) model is subtractive and is used in printing.

When looking at printed material light is seen that has been reflected. Some colours are absorbed (subtracted) and the observer sees the colours that are left. The colours used in four colour printing are cyan, magenta, yellow and black. Most colour inkjet and laser printers have ink or toner in these colours. Some early inkjet printers only used cyan, yellow and magenta, mixing all three to produce 'black'. However the resulting colour was a rather disappointing murky grey; having a separate black cartridge gives much better results.

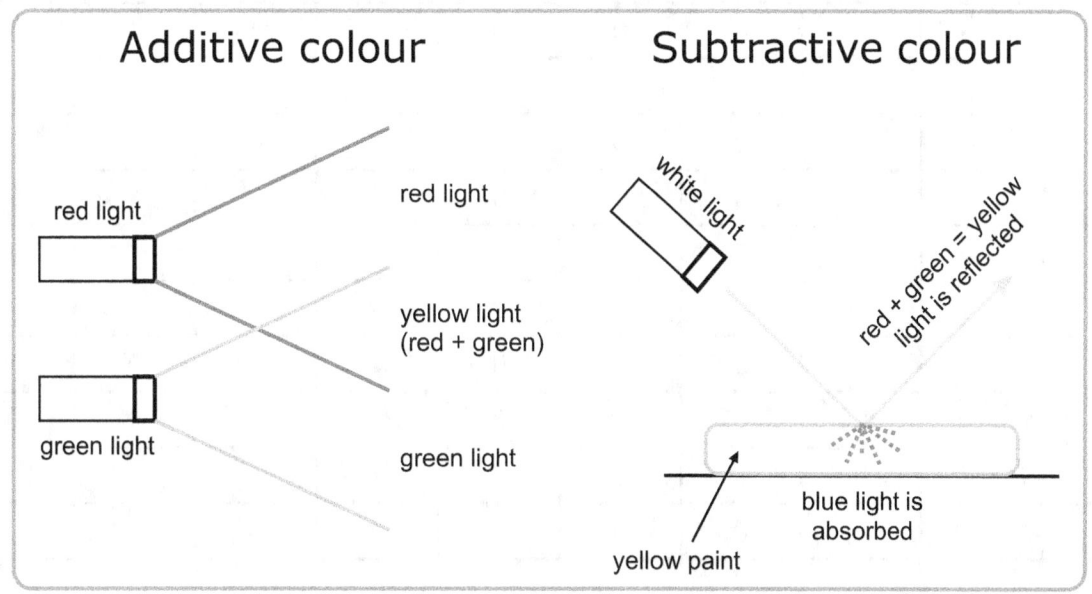

Different types of number

The introduction to binary looked at just one kind of number - positive whole numbers (positive integers). But there will be times where other numbers are needed, such as negative whole numbers (negative integers) and decimal (real) numbers. Computers represent numbers in different ways so that all of these types of number can be dealt with.

Positive integers

Counting from zero in binary gives the following, with some clear patterns.

Decimal number	8-bit binary equivalent							
	128	64	32	16	8	4	2	1
0	0	0	0	0	0	0	0	0
1	0	0	0	0	0	0	0	1
2	0	0	0	0	0	0	1	0
3	0	0	0	0	0	0	1	1
4	0	0	0	0	0	1	0	0
5	0	0	0	0	0	1	0	1
6	0	0	0	0	0	1	1	0
7	0	0	0	0	0	1	1	1
8	0	0	0	0	1	0	0	0
9	0	0	0	0	1	0	0	1
10	0	0	0	0	1	0	1	0
11	0	0	0	0	1	0	1	1
12	0	0	0	0	1	1	0	0
13	0	0	0	0	1	1	0	1
14	0	0	0	0	1	1	1	0
15	0	0	0	0	1	1	1	1
16...	0	0	0	1	0	0	0	0

Negative numbers - two's complement

The most common way of representing negative numbers is to use two's complement. The bit that has the largest numerical value, known as the most significant bit or MSB (i.e. the one farthest to the left), is made negative. Its place value is now -128, not 128.

Most significant bit ↓

Decimal number	Comment	8-bit two's complement							
		-128	64	32	16	8	4	2	1
127	Largest positive number	0	1	1	1	1	1	1	1
86	Arbitrary positive number	0	1	0	1	0	1	1	0
1	Smallest positive number	0	0	0	0	0	0	0	1
0	Zero	0	0	0	0	0	0	0	0
-1	Smallest negative number	1	1	1	1	1	1	1	1
-2	Arbitrary negative number	1	1	1	1	1	1	1	0
-3	Arbitrary negative number	1	1	1	1	1	1	0	1
-4	Arbitrary negative number	1	1	1	1	1	1	0	0
-64	Arbitrary negative number	1	1	0	0	0	0	0	0
-120	Arbitrary negative number	1	0	0	0	1	0	0	0
-128	Largest negative number	1	0	0	0	0	0	0	0

↑ Least significant bit

From the table it can be seen that positive numbers always start with zero and that negative numbers always start with 1.

$11111111 = -128 + 64 + 32 + 16 + 8 + 4 + 2 + 1 = -128 + 127 = -1_{10}$

Real numbers - representing fractions

Real numbers are those that can appear on a number line. In everyday terms, these are 'normal' numbers - whole numbers and fractions. For computers to be really useful, they need to be able to go beyond mere integers and be able to represent and process real numbers.

Thinking about place value will show how binary can be used to represent fractions. Starting with base ten/decimal, the familiar system that is based on the number ten, it is easy to see the place value patterns.

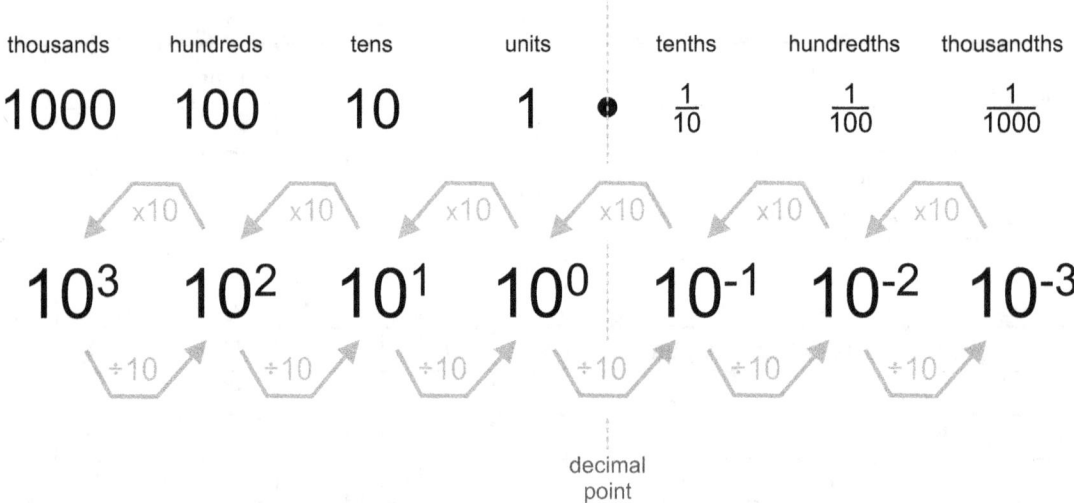

The same patterns apply to binary, except that this system is based on the number two.

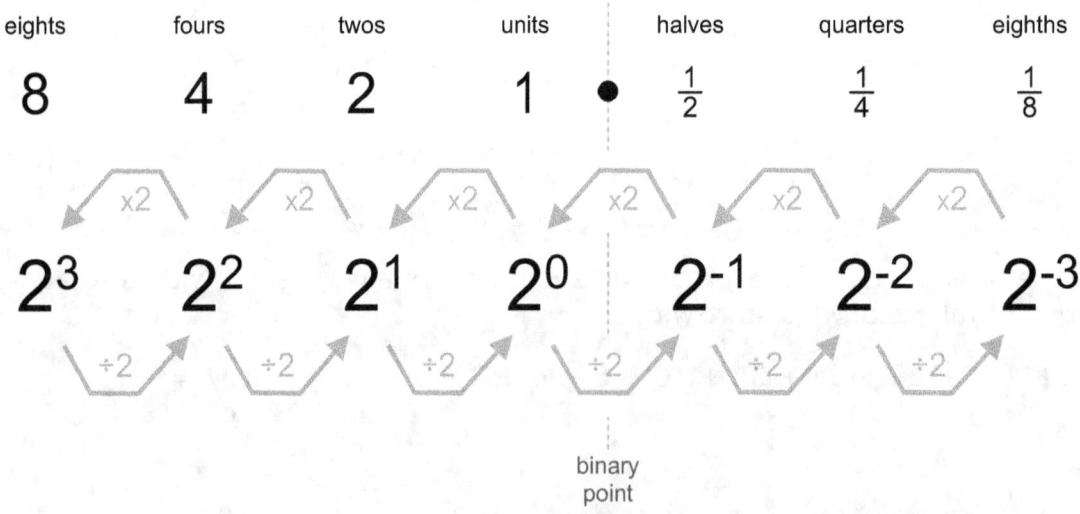

Taking an easy example, five and three-quarters or 5.75_{10} could be written as 101.11_2 i.e. $4 + 1 + 0.5 + 0.25$

The patterns seen above can be applied to all the different number bases, simply substitute the appropriate base number.

Some fractions cannot be shown exactly in decimal. One third is approximately 0.33333333..., you would have to continue to infinity to represent it exactly. One eleventh also has a recurring pattern, being 0.09090909...

The same happens with binary, but the more digits shown, the better the approximation. It does lead to small rounding errors sometimes; you might be expecting the answer to a calculation to be 3 but what you get is 2.9999999...

The following is a simple algorithm for converting decimal fractions that are less than one, to their binary equivalent.

Repeatedly multiply the fraction by two. Write down whether the digit to the left of the decimal point is 0 or 1. Discard any 1s before the next doubling. Continue until you are multiplying by 0, you are able to see a recurring pattern or you lose the will to continue. Write down the fraction from the **top**, as shown in the tables.

Fraction:	
0.625	
1.25	1
0.5	0
1	1
Result:	0.101

Fraction:	
0.6875	
1.375	1
0.75	0
1.5	1
1	1
Result:	0.1011

Fraction:	
0.775	
1.55	1
1.1	1
0.2	0
0.4	0
0.8	0
1.6	1
1.2	1
0.4	0
0.8	0
1.6	1
1.2	1
0.4	0
0.8	0
1.6	1
1.2	1
0.4	0
0.8	0
Result:	0.11000110011001100

$0.625_{10} = 0.101_2$

$0.6875_{10} = 0.1011_2$

$0.775_{10} = 0.11000\mathbf{1100}1100\mathbf{1100}11001100...$

The last example clearly has a recurring pattern, whereas the first two truncate nicely.

Self test

Complete this table showing some two's complement numbers and their decimal equivalents.

Decimal number	8-bit two's complement							
	-128	64	32	16	8	4	2	1
120								
	0	1	0	0	0	0	1	0
19								
-5								
	1	1	1	1	0	0	0	1
	1	1	0	1	1	0	0	0
-66								
	1	0	1	0	1	1	0	1
-100								
	1	0	0	0	0	0	0	1

Convert these decimal fractions to their binary equivalent.

a) 0.9375   b) 0.40625   c) 0.55   d) 0.1

Answers:

Decimal number	8-bit two's complement							
	-128	64	32	16	8	4	2	1
120	0	1	1	1	1	0	0	0
66	0	1	0	0	0	0	1	0
19	0	0	0	1	0	0	1	1
-5	1	1	1	1	1	0	1	1
-15	1	1	1	1	0	0	0	1
-40	1	1	0	1	1	0	0	0
-66	1	0	1	1	1	1	1	0
-83	1	0	1	0	1	1	0	1
-100	1	0	0	1	1	1	0	0
-127	1	0	0	0	0	0	0	1

a) 0.1111
b) 0.01101
c) 0.10001100110011001100...
d) 0.0001100110011001100...

Real numbers - scientific notation

Scientific notation, also known as standard form or standard index form, is a method for showing very large or very small numbers. Fill an 8 digit calculator with 9s to get 99999999 and then add 1 and the display will change to show **1 08**. This means **1** $\times 10^8$ or 100,000,000. Scientific notation allows an 8 digit calculator to display numbers up to 9.9999×10^{99}, many times greater than 99999999, which is the largest number that can be shown using normal representation.

4,375,000,000,000 would be represented as follows.

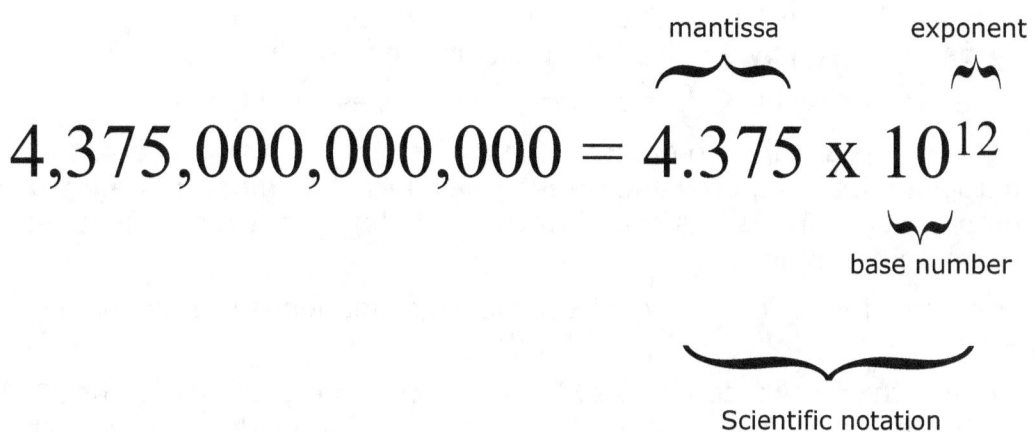

The number is now formed of two parts, a mantissa (decimal fraction) and an exponent (power of ten). The same principle can be applied to binary, where the base number would be two.

Real numbers - floating point representation

Floating point representation is the most common way of representing real numbers on a computer. The detail of how this is done is beyond the scope of this book, but it involves having a binary fractional mantissa and a binary exponent.

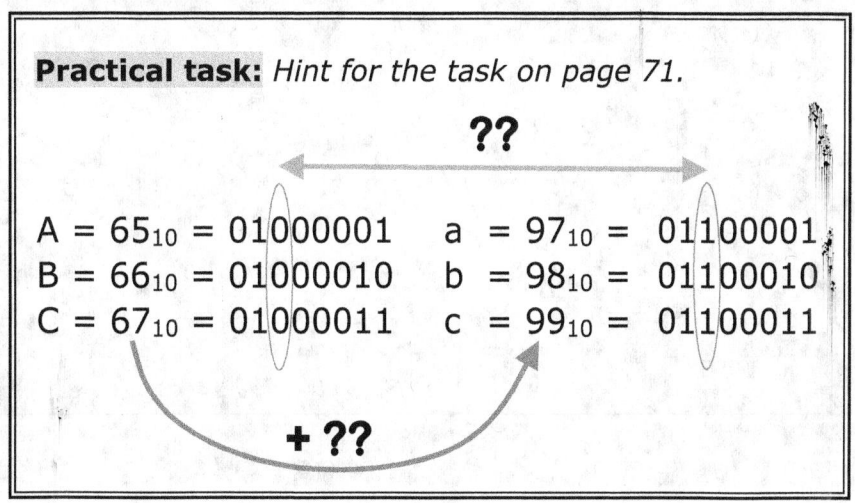

Chapter 2: Key learning points

- Data is the lifeblood of a digital device.
- Analogue data varies continuously. Digital data consists of discrete numbers.
- Many older devices are analogue in nature, many modern devices are digital.
- Digital devices use numbers for all their processing. Real world analogue data must be digitised (turned into numbers) before it can be processed by a digital device/computer.
- There are two types of data compression, lossless and lossy.
- Data can be saved using different file formats, which have different characteristics, strengths and weaknesses, including different degrees of data compression. Metadata is added to some file formats, which can assist with automated searching.
- Data and information are not the same - information is the meaning given to data.
- Binary is the natural counting system to use with digital devices because the two binary digits, 0 and 1 mirror the two states of an electronic circuit, off and on.
- Digital devices use various automated methods to spot errors that might have been introduced into data. A common method for spotting errors in single numbers is to add a check digit.
- Digital devices represent numbers using different types of binary (base two) representation. This includes binary integers, two's complement and floating point representation.

3: Algorithms and software

Algorithms

An algorithm is a set of steps or instructions to follow in order to complete a task or solve a problem.

Mathematical algorithms that you will probably have been taught at school include ones for carrying out long multiplication and division and algorithms are often thought about in a mathematical context. However algorithms come in many different forms.

Example algorithms can be seen in the diagram on the next page. The following are all types of algorithm.

- Recipe
- Science experiment method
- Knitting pattern
- Flat pack furniture assembly instructions
- Instructions explaining how to complete a tax or other official form
- Instructions posted in a hotel room explaining the actions to be taken in the event of a fire alarm being triggered
- Computer program

Algorithms can occur at different levels. The whole Scratch program for drawing a simple face (see diagram) is an algorithm. This algorithm contains smaller algorithms for drawing the different components of the face, such as the eyes and teeth.

There are many different types of algorithms found in computer programs, here are some common ones.

- Sorting algorithms - basic components of many computer programs, these allow data to be sorted in ascending or descending alphabetical or numerical order.
- File compression algorithms - for example, as used within popular file formats such as ZIP (lossless archive format), MP3 (lossy audio file format) and JPEG (lossy image file format).
- Rendering algorithms - for example, colouring a 3D virtual character in an animated movie based on the lighting conditions in a particular scene.
- Routing algorithms - to find the fastest driving route between two places.

Example algorithms

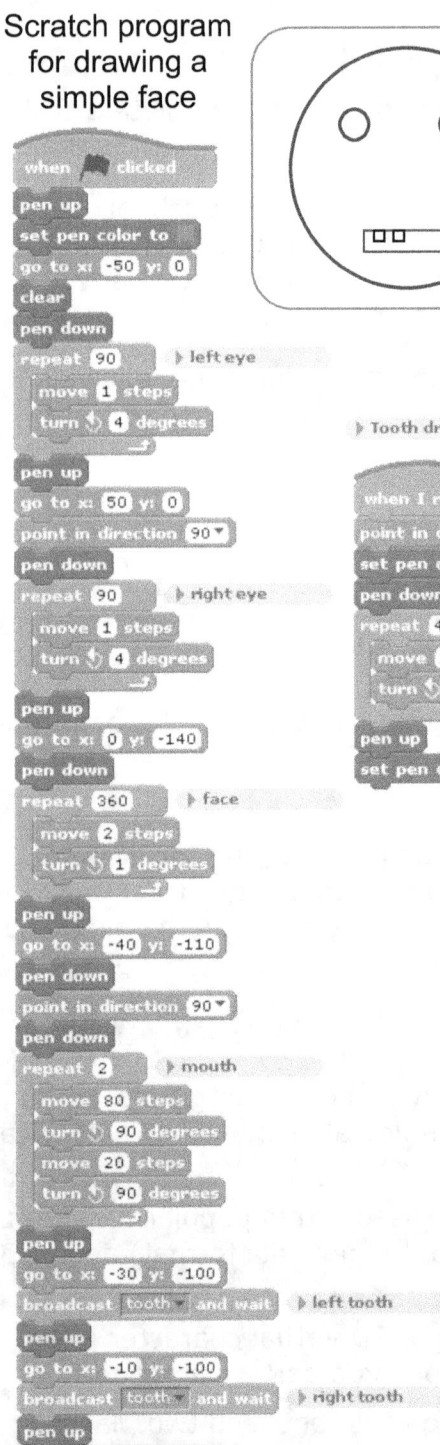

Scratch program for drawing a simple face

Method for making sloe gin

Place 400g of sloes in the freezer overnight.

Add the frozen sloes to 750ml gin, dividing the quantities between two bottles.

Keep the bottles for at least 2 months and preferably longer. Turn the bottles every day or so for the first two weeks, then approximately once a week thereafter.

When you are ready to bottle the sloe gin, make up a syrup using 200g sugar and 1 cup of water. Filter the steeped gin using a muslin bag or similar and mix with the syrup. Bottle.

Pictorial algorithm

Extract from a knitting pattern

Knit 20 (22, 24) stitches. Turn. Purl 10 stitches. Work 13 (13, 15) more rows stocking stitch (ending with k row) on these 10 stitches.

Pick up 7 (8, 9) stitches along side of instep. Knit across 10 (12, 14) stitches on needle.

Purl 17 (20, 23) stitches, then m1, p 10, m1, pick up 7 (8, 9) stitches along other side of instep. Purl 10 (12, 14). You should have 46 (52, 58) stitches.

K 1 row
P 1 row
K 1 row
P 1 row

K3, k2tog, knit to 5 stitches from end, k2tog, k3 (44, 50, 56 st)

P 1 row

K3, k2tog, knit to 5 stitches from end, k2tog, k3 (42, 48, 54 st)
P 1 row

Algorithms are made up of three basic structures, **sequence**, **selection** and **repetition**.

Sequence

Each instruction in an algorithm is carried out or **executed** in turn, unless modified by either of the two following structures. You start with the first instruction, then carry out the second, the third, the fourth, etc. When reading a computer program you generally start at the top and work your way down. With a recipe you also normally start at the top and work your way down. Sequence underpins all algorithms.

Selection

Often it is necessary to choose between two or more alternative routes through an algorithm. A very common programming selection structure is the IF statement, more fully described as the IF THEN, ELSE IF...ELSE IF, ELSE statement.

An algorithm for leaving the house might include this line.

IF it is raining take an umbrella **ELSE IF** it is snowing take a warm coat **ELSE IF** it is sunny take a sun hat **ELSE** take a light jacket.

Repetition

Repetition is a very common structure in algorithms. The Scratch face drawing program uses repetition to draw circles (face, eyes), squares (teeth) and a rectangle (mouth).

Here is another example of the essential simplicity of computing. Algorithms consist of just three types of structure; sequence, selection and repetition. The difficult part can be working out how you can achieve something useful using just these simple structures.

Automated processes may take each user through an algorithm one step at a time, such as when obtaining cash from an ATM (automated teller/hole in the wall machine), buying public transport tickets from a machine or paying for groceries at a supermarket self-checkout.

Algorithms can be described in different ways. These include text description (e.g. a recipe), a sequence of drawings/diagrams, a stack of programming instructions (e.g. a Scratch program) and shorthand codes (e.g. a knitting pattern). Another common way of representing an algorithm is to use a **flowchart**. These are often introduced by thinking about an everyday activity, such as leaving home. The example below highlights sections where sequence, selection and repetition have been used.

Algorithm for leaving home, shown as a flowchart

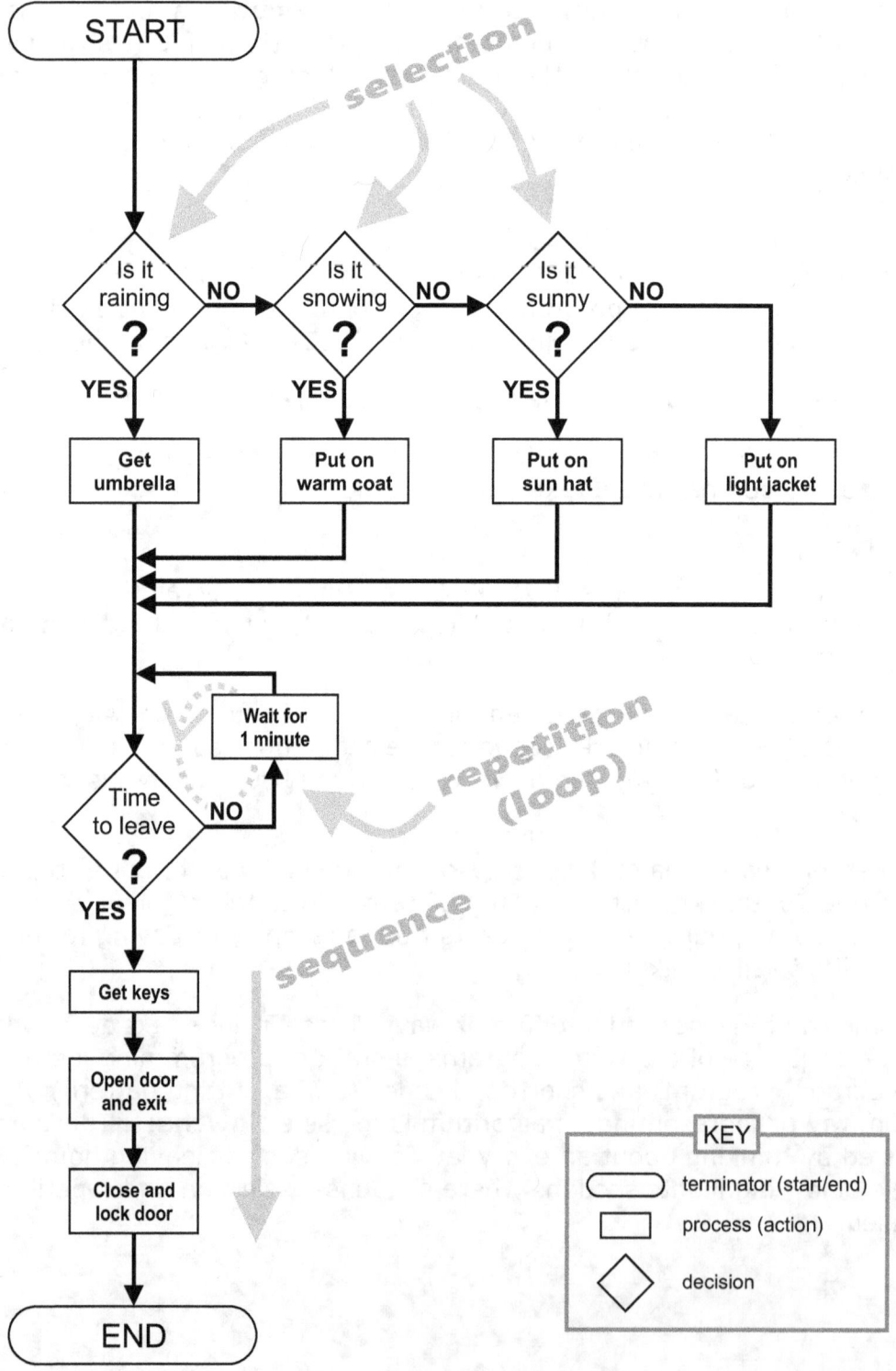

Computer programs

Computer programs, also called **software**, are the instructions that tell digital devices what to do and how to respond to different events. Software tells these devices how to process the data that has been input. It also forms an important part of many interfaces, helping to translate input data into a form that the computer can work with and preparing data for output by getting it into a form that the output devices can understand and work with.

A computer program is one type of algorithm. Break a computer program down and you will usually find that it is made up of many different, smaller algorithms. These smaller algorithms are often written as stand-alone modules that carry out a single task and may be re-used in different programs. The Scratch program had a tooth-drawing module that could be reused when drawing other cartoon-like characters.

Writing software is very labour intensive. Before advances in hardware can be taken advantage of, improved or new software may well be needed. As a result there is often a significant time lag before a new technology is fully exploited.

Types of software

Software is usually categorised by its function and can be thought of as working in layers. Here is a basic classification.

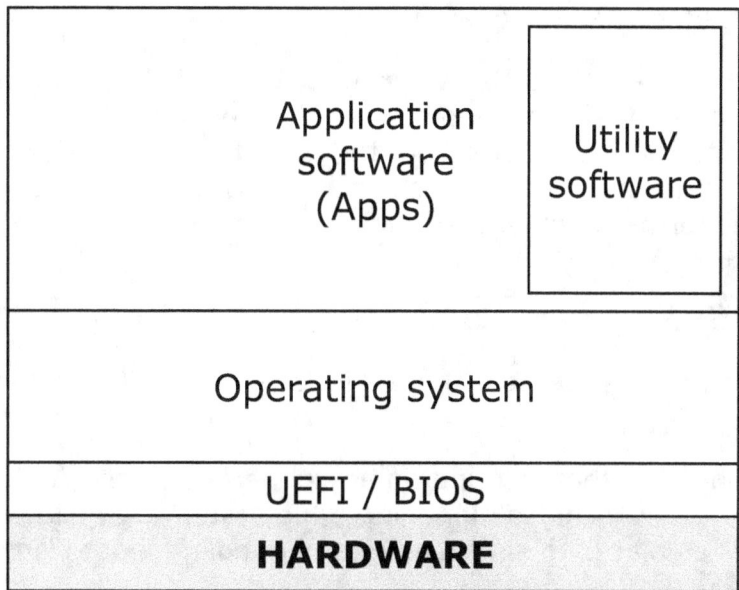

UEFI/Basic input output system or BIOS

When they are first switched on, computers and many other digital devices have to go through a process known as booting up, to initialise the hardware. That well known fix-all of turning a computer off, then on again, is often referred to as re-booting. The term comes from the phrase "pulling yourself up by your bootstraps", since the computer is bringing itself to life, from its dead, power-off, state.

With older computers, booting was controlled by **BIOS** (**Basic Input/Output System**) software, which was originally burned onto a **ROM** (read-only memory) chip that formed part of the motherboard. This meant that the BIOS software was permanent and would be retained after the computer was switched off. However, the only way to update the BIOS was to replace this chip, not usually a practical option. More recently flash memory chips have been used to store the BIOS, since these can be updated/reprogrammed, should improved versions of the BIOS for a particular device be released. This allows for any bugs (faults) to be fixed, any security concerns to be addressed, as well as other improvements to be made. However, making the BIOS re-programmable does make a computer vulnerable to a hacker planting malicious code that allows the device to be controlled remotely.

The first part of the boot-up process is to run a **power-on self-test** (POST), which checks the memory and any devices, such as hard disc drives, that are connected. It makes sure there are no hardware errors before the **bootstrap loader** is run.

The bootstrap loader finds the operating system and providing it is able to load and run, control can then be handed over to it.

In 2007 a new industry-devised **UEFI** (**Unified Extensible Firmware Interface**) specification was agreed. This tackled some of the technical limitations of BIOS, supporting larger hard drives, faster boot times and more security features. Computer manufacturers tend to still use the term BIOS, even though they are using UEFI, as the former acronym is widely understood.

Operating system (OS)

Examples of **operating systems** include Windows, Linux, iOS, Android and Mac OS X.

This is low level software that is found on any general purpose computer supporting the basic functions. This includes managing a file system that allows users to set up folders/directories as places to save files to and handling input from a keyboard and mouse.

They provide a **user interface** to allow users to interact with their computers and run different programs. The user interface may well be some form of graphical desktop, with icons and menus to allow selections to be made and actions to be chosen. Operating systems transfer programs in and out of memory, allocating space and monitoring how the available memory is being used. They also control communications with peripheral devices, such as monitors, hard disc drives and printers. They take care of **multi-tasking**, allowing more than one application to run simultaneously, preventing them from interfering with each other. Modern operating systems usually support the setting up of user accounts, protected by passwords, to aid security.

A computer's operating system provides a software platform on top of which a wide range of applications software can be run.

Application software or apps

When most people refer to computer software, they are talking about application software. These are programs that are designed to directly benefit an end user and can include general purpose software such as word processors, spreadsheets, graphic design programs and programming languages.

Office suites typically include a word processor, spreadsheet and presentation graphics programs packaged as a single product. A database and/or desk top publishing program may also be included. Personal information management is often covered, providing calendars, a contact manager and email software.

Software can have a very specific purpose such as web browsing, photo-editing and accountancy software. Restaurants often use specialist software to handle reservations, record orders, prepare bills and handle payments. Schools typically use a specialist information management system to support a range of functions, including pupil records, staff records and statutory reporting. Additional optional modules are usually available, for example to support behaviour monitoring, sanctions and rewards, payments from parents, timetabling, special needs and disabilities and so on.

Computer programs can be very large, sophisticated and offer a great many features and optional modules. They can also be very small and focused, which is typical of many of the apps designed for use on mobile devices.

Users normally buy and use computers in order to be able to run certain types of application software that are of interest to them. For most people, this is what owning a computer is all about.

With other digital devices, such as a microwave oven or washing machine, there might be just a single control program, that allows the device to function. Options are commonly offered and these are chosen by pressing buttons and turning dials or interacting with a touch screen.

Utility software

Examples include virus scanners, disc monitoring and defragmentation (defragging), file compression and file renaming.

Utility programs are a type of application software that are solely designed to improve the way in which a computer operates. They do this by helping to analyse, configure, optimise or maintain the computer.

Utility applications are often small programs that do one or two things very well. Although these are usually available as separate, stand-alone items, they are increasingly included as part of operating systems, where software companies are seeking to maintain or improve their competitive advantage. However this often triggers a competitive response from the utility writers, where they go on to offer additional features or improved ease of use.

Disc fragmentation

Data on a hard disc drive is saved in sectors or small sections of the surface of the discs or **platters** of which they are made. A sector is the smallest amount of space on the disc that a computer can access.

The algorithm that controls a hard disc drive will try to make best use of the space that is available. To reduce or eliminate the number of gaps on the disc, the algorithm will try to use all of the available sectors - a single file can be saved in non-contiguous sectors, i.e. they do not have to be physically next to each other. It can be seen from the disc fragmentation diagram that, over time, files can become increasingly fragmented, with a single file being potentially stored in several different areas, spread throughout the hard disc.

Fragmented files act as a drag on performance, since it takes longer to open and save files that are split up and not all together on the disc. A **disc defragger** is utility software that can be run periodically to reorganise how the data is stored. It attempts to rewrite all the individual files to contiguous sectors. Before running, defraggers will analyse how data is being stored on a disc to indicate to the user whether it would be useful carry out a defragmentation now, or would be better to wait.

Living in a digital world - Chapter 3: Algorithms and software

Disc fragmentation

A hard disc can be thought of as a series of sectors. A file will take up a minimum of one sector, usually more than one. Below represents a tiny part of a disc.

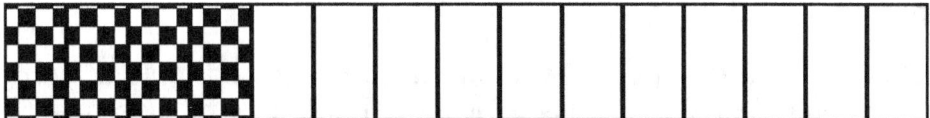

Suppose that the first file saved to a brand new disc is stored in the 1st four sectors.

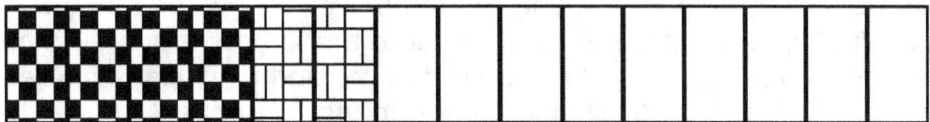

The next file takes up the next 2 sectors. At the moment it is easy for the computer to make efficient use of the space available on the hard disc.

The first file is reopened and some extra data added. When this is saved, it no longer fits within the first four sectors. The extra data is written to the 7th sector.

The second file is then deleted.

The next file takes up 5 sectors and this is saved in 2 fragments, to avoid leaving gaps.

More data is added to the first file, which is now spread across three fragments.

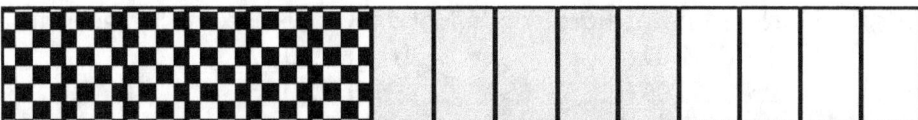

Defragging the disc reorganises the two files using contiguous sectors.

File renaming

Individual files can be easily renamed by using a computer's operating system. However, if there are a large number of files to be renamed, this quickly becomes an onerous task. File renaming utilities allow large batches of files to be renamed in a single operation.

It is possible to generate large numbers of files on a related topic when taking digital photographs. Cameras usually allocate generic, meaningless file names, such as DSC02965.jpg, DSC02966.jpg, DSC02967.jpg...

Suppose that a photographer took a large number of images of London. All the pictures showing Tower Bridge could be selected and a batch renaming utility run. The photographer would specify the required name and a special reserved character used to represent an automatically incrementing index number, say **#**.

By specifying the name "**Tower Bridge #**" and choosing a starting index number of 1, the selected batch would be renamed as Tower Bridge 1, Tower Bridge 2, Tower Bridge 3, and so on.

Some renaming utilities go further and allow a whole series of codes to add other elements to the file name, mostly selected from any metadata that may be included with the files. The photographer might select other shots showing the River Thames and using a more sophisticated utility, type in the following name.

%Y %M %D %N{3:001} River Thames

Suppose Y gives the year the photograph was taken, M the month and D the day. N is the index number and the numbers in curly brackets state that the index number will have 3 digits, starting at 001. This will then rename the chosen files to the following.

2017 02 16 001 River Thames
2017 02 16 002 River Thames
2017 02 16 003 River Thames
2017 02 16 004 River Thames
2017 02 16 005 River Thames, etc.

If you are wondering why the date has been added to the front of the filename in reverse order (compared with the normal UK date order), consider these numbers.

Reverse order	Normal date order	Normal date order, sorted numerically
2016 02 16	16 02 2016	01 02 2017
2016 02 25	25 02 2016	16 02 2016
2017 02 01	01 02 2017	16 02 2017
2017 02 16	16 02 2017	25 02 2016

When a date is written in reverse order, either as e.g. **2016 02 16** or as a single number **20160216**, files will appear in date order when the file names are sorted.

Add in the index number and when photographs, taken on different days, are stored in the same folder, (provided it has been sorted in filename order), all the images will appear in the order in which they were taken.

Adding a date to the front of a filename, in reverse order, is a useful way of organising files where that date is important. Not just for image files, but also documents like minutes of meetings, correspondence with the tax authorities and bank statements. File renaming utilities offer the opportunity to do this very quickly with large numbers of files.

Programming languages

Programming languages are a type of application software that allow users to write their own software, usually for bespoke requirements that cannot be dealt with using existing software.

Programming languages can also be classified using a layered model.

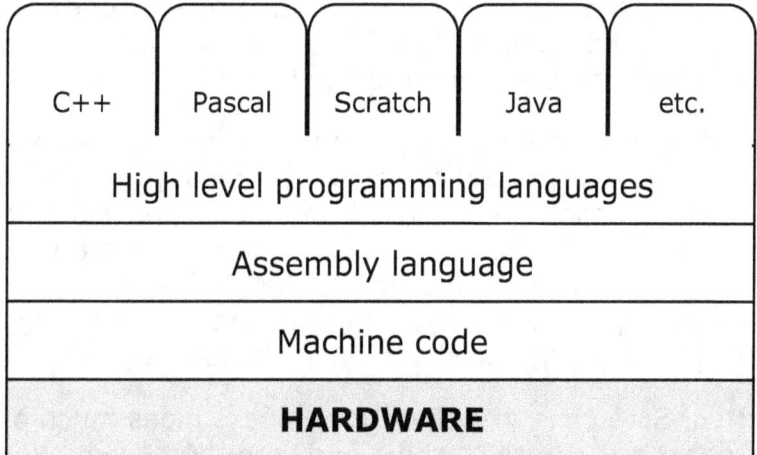

Every microprocessor has its own instruction set. An early example was the Intel 8085 microprocessor, which was launched in 1976 and continued to be produced into the 1990s. It was an 8-bit processor and had an instruction set of 80 different instructions. Each instruction was allocated a unique code number.

Machine code (also called machine language) programming uses these instruction codes directly, in binary. Machine code programs can be run by the microprocessor without any further translation. However, because everything is in binary, it is very difficult for human programmers to work with and is rarely used.

Assembly language is a step up from working directly in machine code. Instead of using binary, programs are written using simple mnemonics and numbers. A piece of software called an **assembler** converts each program into machine code so that it can be run on the microprocessor. However, you are usually programming using the microprocessor's instruction set directly, or something very close to it.

Intel 8085 instruction set	
Type of instruction	Number of instructions
Arithmetic	15
Logic	15
Control	6
Data transfer	16
Branching	28
Total	**80**

Both machine code and assembly language are described as **low level languages**, since both operate at or close to the level of the processor.

High level languages have been developed that are much easier for humans to work with, by combining various machine code instructions into single programming statements. Programs that have been written in a high level language need to be translated into machine code, before they can be run.

There are two types of translation software, **compilers** and **interpreters**. Both do a similar job, but a compiler will attempt to translate an entire program into machine code before attempting to run the resulting **object code**. Whereas an interpreter will go through a program one line at a time, convert each line into machine code, execute it and then go on to the next line.

Scratch is a high level, interpreted, programming language that was developed by MIT's[1] Lifelong Kindergarten Group for use as a teaching language for schools and young people. Bearing a close resemblance to an earlier teaching language, **Logo**, Scratch overcomes many of the hurdles experienced with traditional languages by young children and those new to programming. Instead of having to remember and type in instructions with great accuracy, programs are built by dragging and dropping individual programming blocks to form stacks.

The great strength of Scratch is that the use of blocks hides much of the complexity of programming that can frustrate learners and stop them from experiencing success. At the same time however, users can still learn lots of fundamental programming concepts, such as the use of sequence, selection and repetition to build algorithms, whilst successfully crafting creative programs.

Go back to the *Example algorithms* diagram to see a simple Scratch program for drawing a face. Below is a selection of Scratch programming blocks.

---

[1] MIT = Massachusetts Institute of Technology (USA)

Selection of Scratch programming blocks

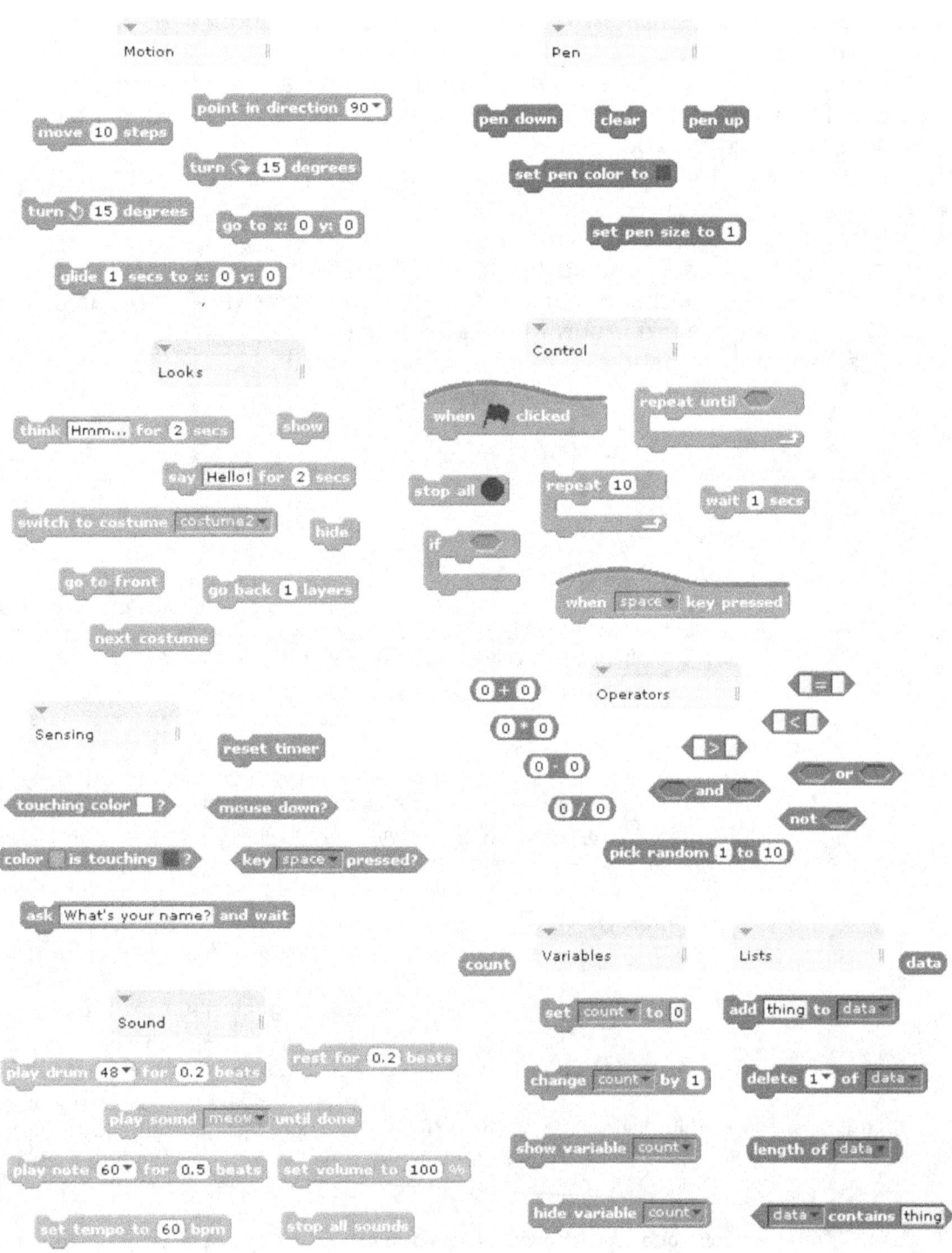

Living in a digital world - Chapter 3: Algorithms and software

Self test

1. Which of the following can be used to show an algorithm/explain how it works?
   Graph, flowchart, structured text, series of pictures, pseudocode, photograph
2. Which of the following are algorithms?
   Computer program, furniture assembly instructions, recipe, shopping list, directions for using a medicine or pharmaceutical product, calendar, method for carrying out a science experiment
3. What are the three basic structures that make up an algorithm?
4. What type of structure is an IF statement?
5. What is the role of UEFI/BIOS software?
6. Give an example of an operating system. What is its role?
7. Utility software is a specific type of what category of software? What is it for?
8. What type of software are programming languages?
9. What is a key characteristic of a high-level programming language?

Answers:

1. Which of the following can be used to show an algorithm/explain how it works?
   Graph, flowchart, structured text, series of pictures, pseudocode, photograph
   All except graph and photograph.
2. Which of the following are algorithms?
   Computer program, furniture assembly instructions, recipe, shopping list, directions for using a medicine or pharmaceutical product, calendar, method for carrying out a science experiment
   All except shopping list and calendar.
3. What are the three basic structures that make up an algorithm?
   Sequence, selection and repetition.
4. What type of structure is an IF statement?
   Selection
5. What is the role of UEFI/BIOS software?
   This software allows a computer to start up from its "dead", power-off state.
6. Give an example of an operating system. What is its role?
   For example, Microsoft Windows, macOS, Linux, Android or iOS. Operating systems support the basic functions of a computer including provision of the user interface.
7. Utility software is a specific type of what category of software? What is it for?
   Utility software is a type of application software. It aims to improve the operation of a digital device, by helping to analyse, configure, optimise or maintain it.
8. What type of software are programming languages?
   Programming languages are one type of application software
9. What is a key characteristic of a high-level programming language?
   Two key characteristics are: These are easier for humans to work with, but further away from the level of the computer. HLL programs must be translated into machine code (or object code) before they can run (or execute).

104

Some example algorithms

Variables

Computer programs use variables. Each one can be thought of as a box, container or memory location that can hold a single data item, typically a single number. Variables are given a name, which is normally a single word or letter. Their contents can vary, hence the term variable!

Suppose there are three variables in a sorting algorithm, called **j**, **k** and **small**. My program might start off with this:

k = 1
small = 1
j = 2

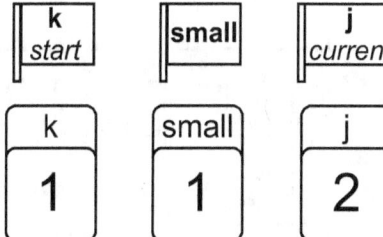

This would load the number 1 into variables **k** and **small** and the number 2 into variable **j**.

The flag markers will be used to help explain what the variables are being used for within the selection sort algorithm that follows.

Arrays

Arrays allow a programmer to collect lots of numbers within a single data structure, that can be used as a 'super-variable'. The simplest is a one-dimensional array that acts like a list. Suppose that the sorting algorithm below will be working with a set of eight numbers, using an array called **data**.

data[1] is the first item in the list, followed by data[2], data[3]...data[8]

Selection Sort

There are a number of sorting algorithms that can take a random set of numbers stored in an array and arrange them in ascending or descending order. This first example will look at using the selection sort algorithm to sort a set of eight numbers into ascending order.

The selection sort will make its first pass through the array, looking for the smallest number. This it will swap with whichever number is in data[1].

The next pass through the array will start at data[2], looking for the 2nd smallest number. This will be swapped with whichever number is in data[2].

This process of looking for the next smallest number will continue until all the numbers have been sorted correctly. It will take 7 passes through the data to sort a set of 8 numbers.

Suppose the data to be sorted is as follows.

data[1]	data[2]	data[3]	data[4]	data[5]	data[6]	data[7]	data[8]
27	63	1	72	64	58	14	9

⚑ k start   ⚑ j current

⚑ small

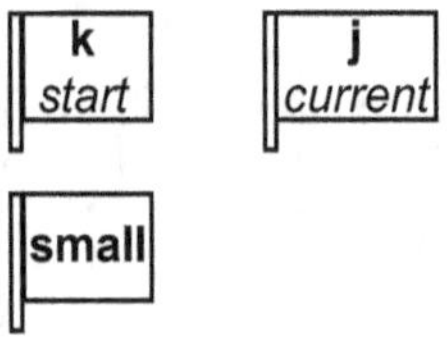

Remember that whilst a human could quickly scan the numbers and find the smallest one, a computer has to be given a process to carry out that will work with any set of 8 numbers.

The sorting algorithm will start at data[1], which is flagged as being both the start (k=1) and the smallest number found in the row so far (small=1). The first comparison will be between data[1] and data[2], so the current position is flagged (j=2).

data[1]	data[2]	data[3]	data[4]	data[5]	data[6]	data[7]	data[8]
27	63	1	72	64	58	14	9

⚑ k start   ...   ⚑ j current

⚑ small

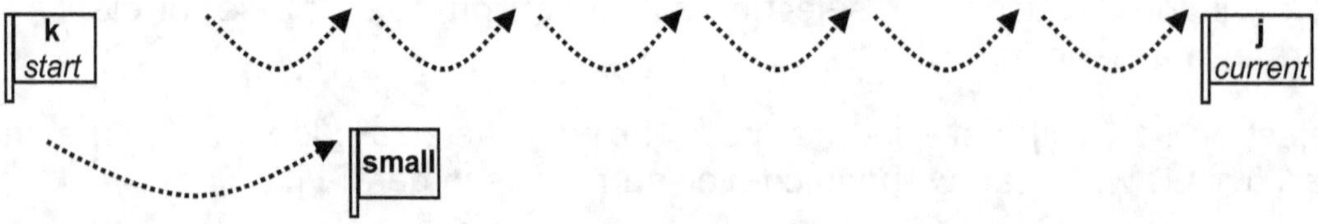

The first two positions are compared, since 63 is bigger than 27 the algorithm moves on to the next comparison (j=3). 1 is less than 27 so data[3] is now flagged as being the smallest number (small=3). The algorithm keeps going until it gets to the end of the row, but it does not find any number that is less than 1. Therefore the smallest number in the array is 1 and the contents of data[3] is swapped with data[1], i.e. 1 is swapped with 27.

data[1] has now been dealt with and correctly contains the smallest number in the array. The algorithm must now find the second smallest number so it repeats this process, but this time starting at data[2], so k=2.

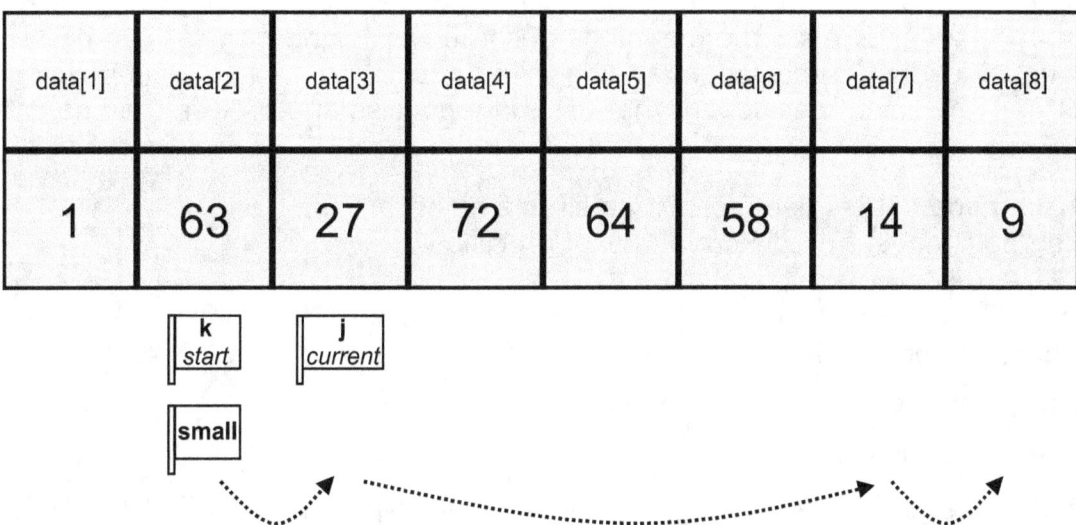

The starting number for the next pass is 63 and immediately a smaller number is found in data[3], so small = 3. 14 is less than 27, now small = 7. Finally, 9 is less than 14 so by the time the algorithm reaches the end of the 2nd pass, small = 8.

The number in the eighth position (small = 8) is swapped with the number in the starting position (k = 2), i.e. 9 and 63 are swapped. Now the first two elements, 1 and 9 are in their correctly sorted positions. The next pass starts at k=3 and so on. 14 and 27 are swapped on the next pass, then 27 and 72, 58 and 64, 63 and 64 and finally 64 and 72.

	data[1]	data[2]	data[3]	data[4]	data[5]	data[6]	data[7]	data[8]
Original data	27	63	1	72	64	58	14	9
1st pass	**1**	63	**27**	72	64	58	14	9
2nd pass	1	**9**	27	72	64	58	14	**63**
3rd pass	1	9	**14**	72	64	58	**27**	63
4th pass	1	9	14	**27**	64	58	**72**	63
5th pass	1	9	14	27	**58**	**64**	72	63
6th pass	1	9	14	27	58	**63**	72	**64**
7th pass	1	9	14	27	58	63	**64**	**72**

On each pass, this algorithm selects the next smallest number and puts it into the correct position.

There are problems with using a written explanation of algorithms. It has taken over two pages of text, including a carefully worked example, to try and explain the selection sort above. Also, the meanings of some words and phrases can be ambiguous, leading to misunderstandings. As a result, other ways of describing algorithms have been developed, that are more concise and precise than narrative text.

Many shampoo bottles used to carry a simple algorithm for washing hair that suffered from a lack of precision.

1. Wet hair
2. Apply shampoo to hair and scalp
3. Gently massage in
4. Rinse and repeat

If anyone was being pedantic and following this algorithm exactly, every time they got to step 4, they would go back to step 1 and start again. They would be stuck within a never-ending infinite loop!

The defect can be clearly seen from the flowchart, which is one way of describing algorithms more precisely. Clearly the intention was that the algorithm should be repeated just once, but the meaning was ambiguous.

$j = j + 1$

Statements like j=j+1 or k=k+1 are commonly seen in algorithms and programming. Mathematically they are a complete nonsense as a number can never be equal to itself plus 1. However, this type of statement is not being used as an equation. It is known as an **assignment**, because the "**j=**" is saying that a value is being assigned to, or given to, a variable called j.

j=j+1 means that you are adding one to the value of j or, to put it another way, you are incrementing j. This is commonly done with variables that are being used as counters, when counting how many times you are carrying out a particular action.

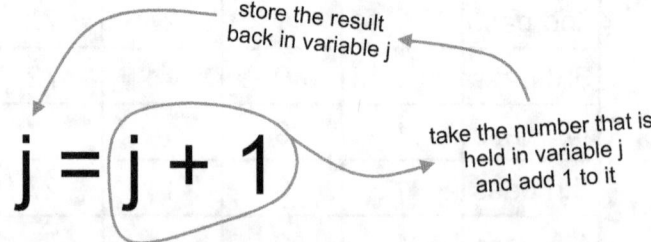

Look at the selection sort flowchart that follows and see if you can reconcile it with the worked example from earlier. As there are 8 numbers in the array to be sorted, n=8 throughout.

Pseudocode

Pseudocode is another way of describing algorithms precisely. It is written in a similar way to some programming languages, incorporating standard programming structures and variables, but is designed to be easier for humans to understand. There is no standard way of writing pseudocode, so different styles and conventions can be found. An individual's pseudocode style is often influenced by the programming language they feel most comfortable with.

Repetition - FOR...NEXT loops

The FOR...NEXT loop structure is commonly used where it is known before starting a loop, how many times the algorithm must go around it. As a result, it is often seen in pseudocode algorithms.

Suppose that I am writing an algorithm to make a cup of tea and I want to add three lumps of sugar. This could be written as follows.

for i = 1 to 3 do
⟶ Add one lump of sugar

The counter variable is **i** and it is going to count from one to three. The actions that are going to be carried out within the loop are shown indented, i.e. moved in from the left hand margin, as indicated by the arrow. In this case there is only one action within the loop. If there is more than one action to be carried out within the loop, these are shown at the same level of indenting. For example, a hair washing algorithm could be written as follows.

for k = 1 to 2 do
    begin
    Wet hair
    Apply shampoo to hair and scalp
    Gently massage in
    Rinse
    end

The **begin** and **end** statements are not strictly necessary, but they help to emphasise that the four statements they enclose are ALL within the loop.

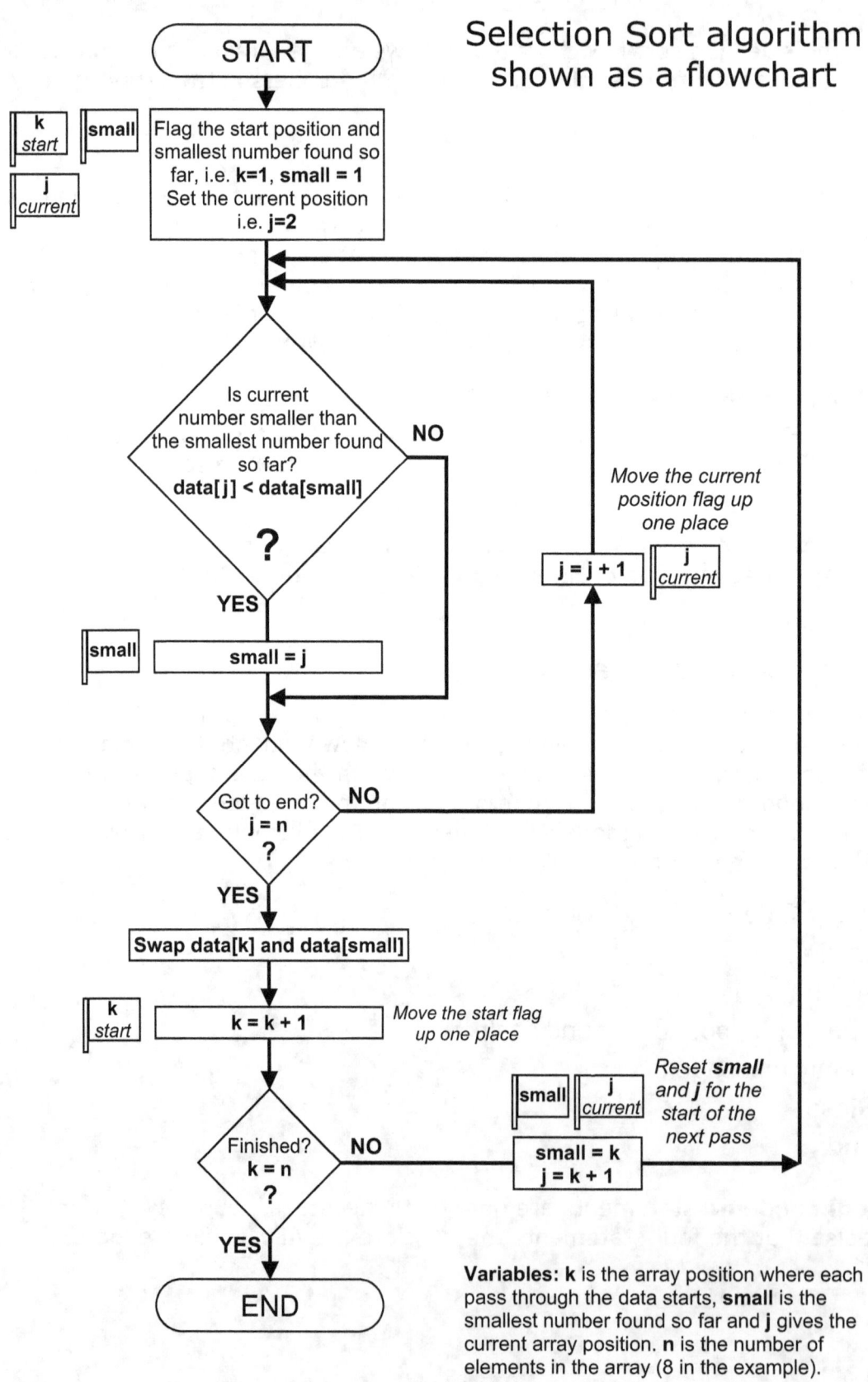

Selection Sort written as a pseudocode algorithm

The inner loop uses **j** as its counter and on the first pass this counts from 2 to 8, comparing the numbers found in those positions with 27, the first number in the array. On the second pass it counts from 3 to 8, then 4 to 8, 5 to 8, 6 to 8 and 7 to 8 for the final pass.

The outer loop uses **k** as its counter and this counts the 7 passes through the data that are needed to ensure that the array is fully sorted by the end.

A pseudocode selection sort algorithm is written below.

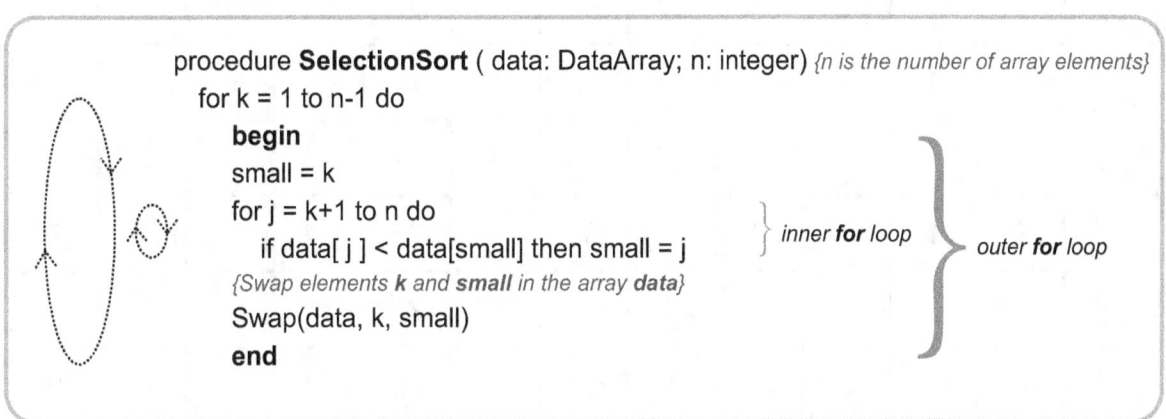

```
procedure SelectionSort ( data: DataArray; n: integer) {n is the number of array elements}
    for k = 1 to n-1 do
        begin
        small = k
        for j = k+1 to n do
            if data[ j ] < data[small] then small = j
        {Swap elements k and small in the array data}
        Swap(data, k, small)
        end
```

} inner **for** loop

} outer **for** loop

One advantage of using pseudocode is immediately clear; it is very concise, needing only 9 lines to unambiguously describe the algorithm. In fact, three of those lines could be left out (begin, end and the explanatory comments in *{curly brackets}*). It is also relatively straightforward to convert this algorithm to any programming language.

Dry running

Sometimes the only way to fully understand how an algorithm works is to pretend to be a computer and to work through it exactly as a computer would. It can be a long-winded, tedious process, but sometimes it just has to be done! Dry running can be used when debugging an algorithm that is not delivering the correct results, to identify exactly what is happening and locate any errors.

Dry running involves working through the algorithm line by line and recording the values of all the variables as they change. The following table dry runs the selection sort algorithm for the first two passes.

	n	k	small	j	data[1]	data[2]	data[3]	data[4]	data[5]	data[6]	data[7]	data[8]
Original data					**27**	**63**	**1**	**72**	**64**	**58**	**14**	**9**
1st pass	8	1	1	2	27	63	1	72	64	58	14	9
1st pass	8	1	3	3	27	63	1	72	64	58	14	9
1st pass	8	1	3	4	27	63	1	72	64	58	14	9
1st pass	8	1	3	5	27	63	1	72	64	58	14	9
1st pass	8	1	3	6	27	63	1	72	64	58	14	9
1st pass	8	1	3	7	27	63	1	72	64	58	14	9
1st pass	8	**1**	**3**	8	27 ⇔	63 ⇒	1	72	64	58	14	9
1st pass	8	1	3	8	**1**	63	**27**	72	64	58	14	9
2nd pass	8	2	2	3	1	63	27	72	64	58	14	9
2nd pass	8	2	3	3	1	63	27	72	64	58	14	9
2nd pass	8	2	3	4	1	63	27	72	64	58	14	9
2nd pass	8	2	3	5	1	63	27	72	64	58	14	9
2nd pass	8	2	6	6	1	63	27	72	64	58	14	9
2nd pass	8	2	7	7	1	63	27	72	64	58	14	9
2nd pass	8	**2**	**8**	8	1	63 ⇔	27	72	64	58	14	⇒ 9
2nd pass	8	2	8	8	1	**9**	27	72	64	58	14	**63**
3rd pass	8	3	3	4	1	9	27	72	64	58	14	63
etc...												

Dry running the selection sort algorithm

Exchange or Bubble Sort

The exchange sort is more popularly known as the bubble sort because on each pass the next biggest number 'bubbles up' to its correct position.

On the first pass, data[1] and data[2] are compared and if data[1] is bigger than data[2] the numbers are swapped. Next data[2] and data[3] are compared, then data[3] and data [4] and so on until the end of the array is reached.

The next pass repeats this process, although as the biggest number is now in data[8], this pass will finish with the comparison of data[6] and data[7].

	data[1]	data[2]	data[3]	data[4]	data[5]	data[6]	data[7]	data[8]
Original data	**27**	**63**	1	72	64	58	14	9
1st pass	**27**	**63**	1	72	64	58	14	9
1st pass	27	**63**	**1**	72	64	58	14	9
1st pass	27	1 ←→ 63		72	64	58	14	9
1st pass	27	1	**63**	**72**	64	58	14	9
1st pass	27	1	63	**72**	**64**	58	14	9
1st pass	27	1	63	64 ←→ 72		58	14	9
1st pass	27	1	63	64	**72**	**58**	14	9
1st pass	27	1	63	64	58 ←→ 72		14	9
1st pass	27	1	63	64	58	**72**	**14**	9
1st pass	27	1	63	64	58	14 ←→ 72		9
1st pass	27	1	63	64	58	14	**72**	**9**
1st pass	27	1	63	64	58	14	9 ←→ 72	
2nd pass	**27**	**1**	63	64	58	14	9	72
2nd pass	1 ←→ 27		63	64	58	14	9	72
2nd pass	1	27	**63**	64	58	14	9	72
etc...								

The exchange sort is not a very efficient algorithm, however one advantage is that it can be programmed to terminate promptly once all the numbers have been sorted, whereas the selection sort always goes through the same number of passes for any particular array.

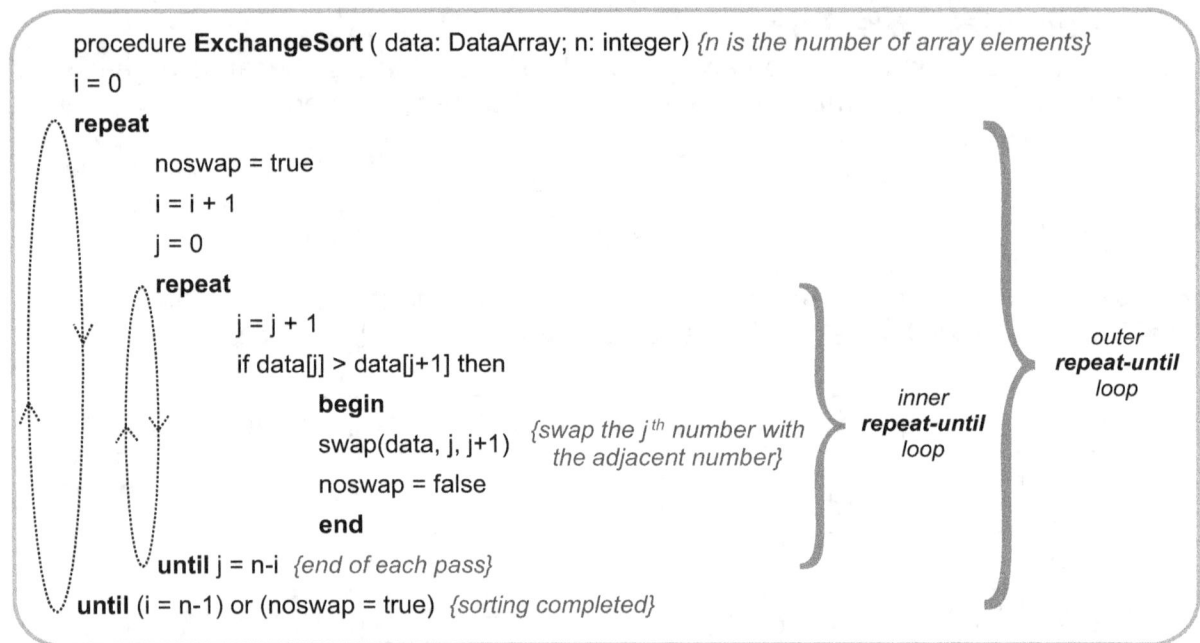

This version of the algorithm uses a **boolean variable**, **noswap** to record if an entire pass is made without swapping any numbers. Boolean variables can have just two possible values, **true** or **false**.

If an entire pass is made without swapping any numbers it means that the array is now sorted and the algorithm can be ended. If **noswap** is *true* when the algorithm reaches the outer **until**, then the algorithm terminates.

With this algorithm variable **i** is used to count the number of passes made. Variable **j** is used during each pass to count which array position has been reached.

Measuring the efficiency of sorting algorithms

Either the selection sort or the exchange sort algorithms would be perfectly acceptable for small-scale programming tasks. Both work and are relatively straightforward to program. However, neither of them are very efficient, the amount of work needed to sort an array increasing with the square of the number of items. In other words, double the number of items and the work needed goes up by four times. Treble the number of items and the work needed goes up by a factor of nine. With commercial scale applications, where you might be sorting thousands or millions of items, especially where speed of response is critical, choosing the right sorting algorithm can be a crucial part of system design.

It is possible to time how long it takes for an algorithm to complete a task, but whilst this might give a useful indication, computers will complete tasks at different speeds according to how powerful they are, what operating system they use, what other software they might be running and what other tasks they might be working on at the same time.

Another way of assessing the efficiency of an algorithm is to look at one or more key aspects. The two sorting algorithms illustrated involve comparing pairs of numbers many times. Therefore one useful metric would be how many comparisons are needed to sort arrays of different sizes. Another useful metric would be how many times data has to be moved (swapped) when sorting different arrays. This is especially important where you have to move large amounts of data around (see below).

Atomic data types
Atomic data types are those that cannot be broken down any further, such as the **integer** counter variables that were used in the sorting algorithms. Other atomic data types include **real number** variables, **boolean** (true/false) variables and **character** variables. The latter can contain a single text character (single number, single letter, single punctuation mark, etc).

Data structures
Data structures are combinations of one or more atomic data types. The **array** (list) of numbers used in the sorting algorithms examples is a data structure - eight integer variables grouped together.

A **string** variable is an array of characters which makes it easy to handle a single word or phrase, up to a maximum number of characters. The maximum length of a string is determined by the programming language that is being used.

The **record** data structure allows different data types to be grouped together, as specified by the programmer, usually describing or belonging to a single object. For example, a school will maintain a database that will include details of all their

Record

First name	Family name	Parent/carer	Phone	Year group on arrival
...				
Justin	Case	Mr & Mrs Case	07773 556 994	1
Felix	Cited	Mr & Mrs Smith	01136 444 295	1
Molly	Coddled	Mrs Coddled	01136 585 666	3
...				

Field

pupils. A pupil record will include their name, next of kin/key contact details, address, phone numbers and details about their academic history. These are known as **fields** and in this example, many will use string variables. However, other data types will be used, such as an integer to record the year group they joined on arrival at the school and date fields to record their data of birth and the date they joined the school.

The record for a single pupil is likely to include a great deal of information, in many fields. It may be necessary to produce lists of information using all pupils, sorted in various different ways - by family name, current class, date of birth and so on. Sorting pupil records using one of the algorithms already seen would not be sensible, since they require lots of swapping to be done. Moving large records around would require lots of work and would be slow, even for a computer.

Using pointers to maintain an ordered list

Where data is being stored using a record structure, there is the option to add one or more **pointer fields** to allow different ordered lists to be maintained. The example below uses a highly simplified employer database as a context. Like the pupil database mentioned previously, employer human resources databases are likely to include a great deal of information including contact details, employment history, training history, qualifications, payroll information and so on. Therefore it is better to leave the data alone and use pointers to order the data in different ways.

Suppose that the employer wants to be able to order the data according to family name (ascending alphabetical order) and age (descending age order, using date of birth).

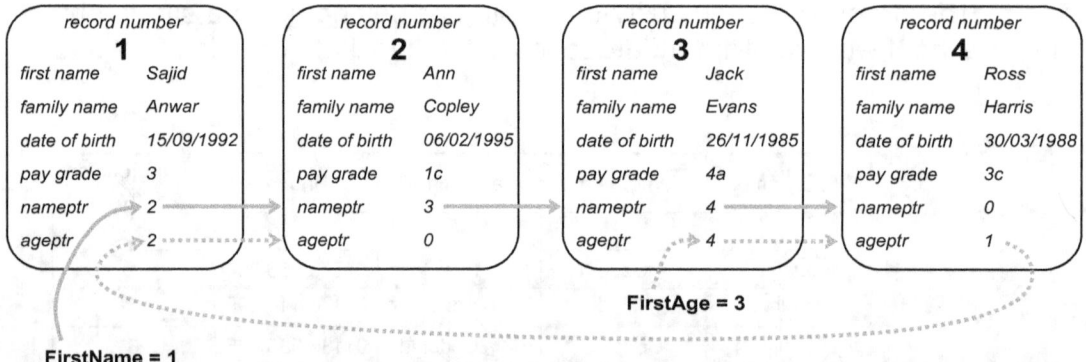

To maintain the list of employees in family name order, the record number of the first name in the list (Anwar) must be recorded. In this example **FirstName = 1**, in other words, the first record when the list is sorted in family name order is record number 1. The first four employee records have been created in name order, so the name pointer field **nameptr** of record 1 points to record 2. This record points to record 3, which points to record 4. In record 4 **nameptr = 0** to indicate that this is the end of the list. The solid grey arrows show how the pointers are used to give the correct order.

The oldest employee is Jack Evans, so **FirstAge = 3**. The next oldest employee is Ross Harris, record 4, then record 1. Record 2 is the youngest employee (Ann Copley) so in this record **ageptr = 0** since this is the end of this list. The dotted grey arrows show how the pointers indicate the correct order.

Suppose that a fifth employee, Coleen Dermott, is now added. All the existing records can remain saved in the same place as before and the new record can be saved in the first available space. **FirstAge** and some of the pointers must be updated to keep the correct ordering.

The diagram below shows how the **nameptr** fields are updated.

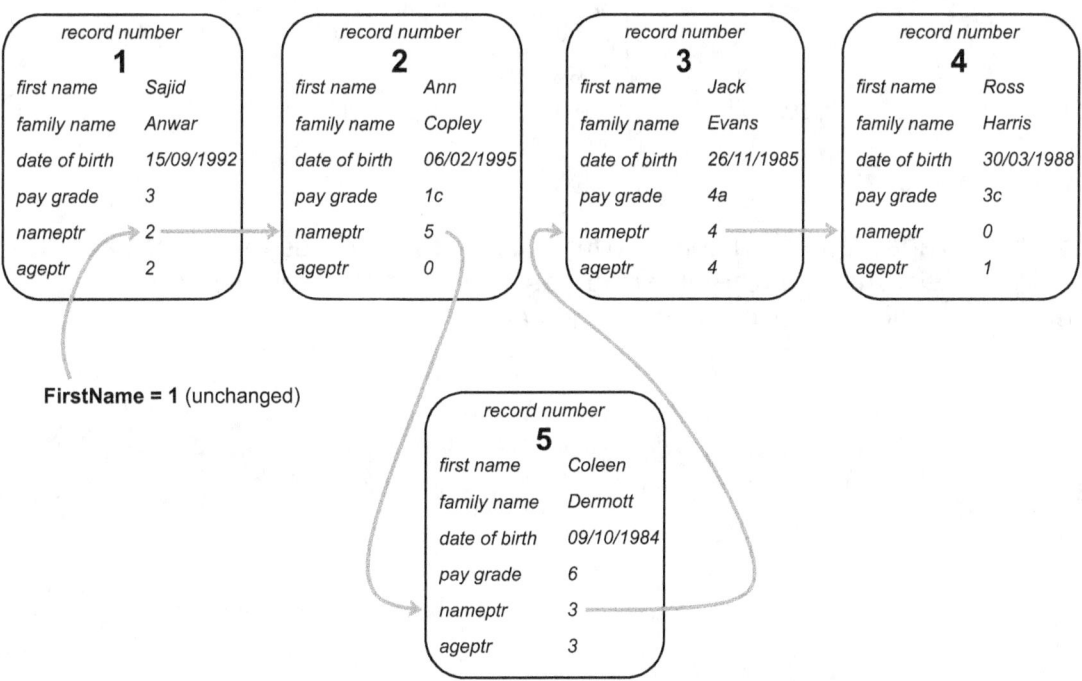

The diagram below shows how the **ageptr** fields are updated.

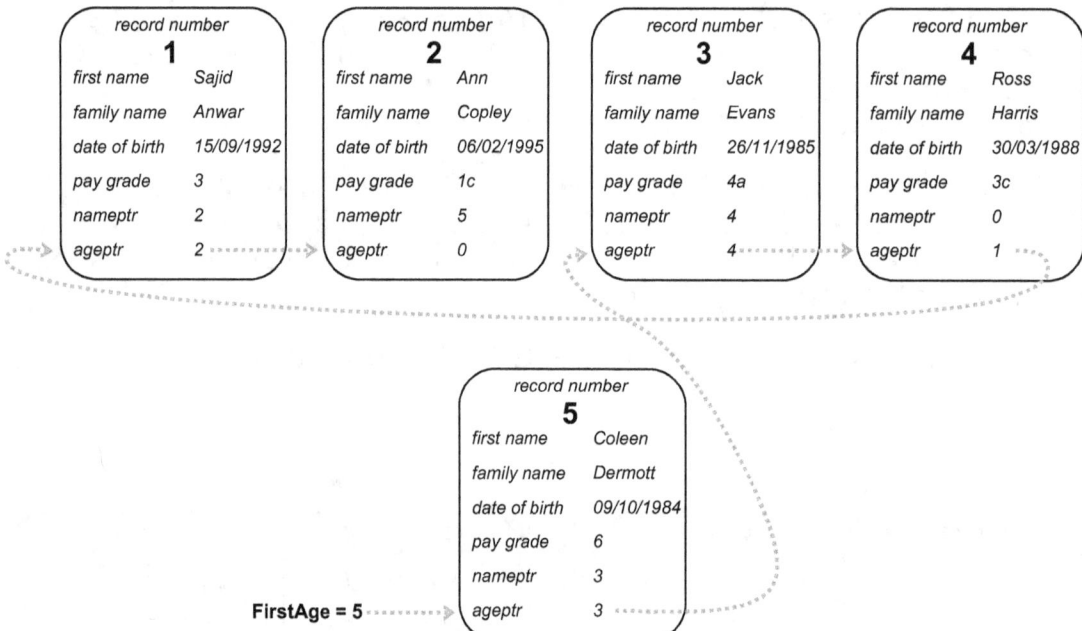

This could be regarded as "virtual sorting", since the records have not been physically sorted. Instead, the ordering has been achieved by using numeric pointers, that indicate which record comes next.

Self test

1. What is a variable?
2. What is a one dimensional array?
3. What does **count = count + 1** mean if seen in an algorithm?
4. Why is pseudocode such a good way of representing an algorithm?
5. When someone dry runs an algorithm, what are they doing?
6. How could you measure the efficiency of a sorting algorithm?
7. Name four atomic data types.
8. Name three data structures.
9. A _____ contains all the information on one particular student in a university database.
10. First name, phone number and date of birth are examples of _____ that would be found in this database.
11. Why might a series of records be ordered using pointer fields?

Answers:

1. A variable is a storage location or "box" that is given a name and can hold a single data item, e.g. a number.
2. A one dimensional array is a data structure that acts like a list, made up of more than one variable.
3. **count = count + 1** means that one is added to whatever the current value of **count** is.
4. Pseudocode is a good way of representing an algorithm because algorithms can be described unambiguously using relatively little text. Pseudocode is very precise and very concise.
5. When someone dry runs an algorithm, they are working through it, as a computer would, recording the values of all variables as they change.
6. The efficiency of a sorting algorithm can be measured by counting the number of comparisons and/or the number of exchanges made, with a range of data sets.
7. integer, real number, character, boolean
8. array, string, record
9. A *record* contains all the information on one particular student in a university database.
10. First name, phone number and date of birth are examples of *fields* that would be found in this database.
11. A series of records might be ordered using pointer fields because the records can be maintained in order without ever having to move where the records are stored. They can be kept in different orders by having more than one pointer field.

Linear search algorithm

Where records are stored in a database, such as a school pupil database or a company employee database, there will be a need to search for individual records in order to look up information on a person or to amend or add to what is already stored about them.

The most simple way of searching is simply to go through all the records in the order that they are stored, starting at the first record. This is called a linear search.

This is an inefficient way of searching, where there is a large number of records. If there were say, 1024 records and a very large number of searches were conducted for records known to be in the database, sometimes the one that was being looked for would be found straightaway. Sometimes it would not be found until the very last record was looked at. *On average*, though, 1024/2 or 512 record checks would be required for each search.

Binary search algorithm

A binary search is much more efficient, however it does require the data to be maintained in order. Searching for a particular name would require the data to be in alphabetical order.

Suppose that a search is being conducted for the name Aaronson. The binary search algorithm would start by looking at the middle record, number 512. Suppose the name found there is JONES. Since the data is sorted in alphabetical order, Aaronson must come before Jones, so records 512 to 1024 can immediately be eliminated and the "search space" is halved.

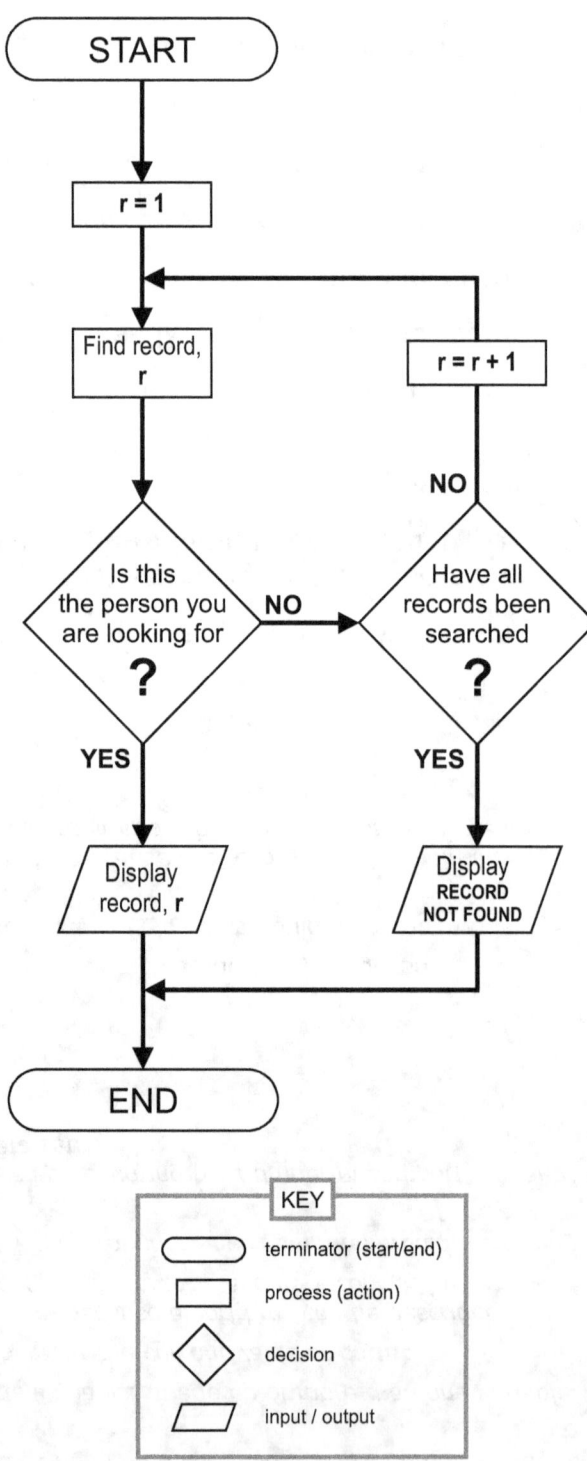

Linear search algorithm

Again the search algorithm goes to the new middle record, number 256. Suppose the name found there is FOWLER. Again the search space is halved as records 256 to 511 can be eliminated. This search pattern continues, going from record 512 to 256 to 128 to 64 to 32 to 16 to 8 to 4 to 2 to 1. Each record check reduces the search space by 50%.

Assuming the *worst case scenario* and that Aaronson is the first name in the database, it will only take **10** record checks to find it. This is over 50 times better than the *average* using the simple linear search. If there is no one with this name in the database, the binary search algorithm will still only require 10 record checks before it can give a **NOT FOUND** message, whereas the linear search will require 1024 record checks! These efficiencies become much greater as the number of records being searched increases - imagine searching a telephone directory covering the whole of the UK, which would contain millions of records. However, the much greater searching efficiency of the binary search comes at the cost of having to maintain the data in order.

A selection of application software

Most users will buy a computer in order to do certain jobs or tasks and there are normally one or two types of software that are the most appropriate to use for each task. It is important therefore to select a computer that is capable of running the desired software at an appropriate speed. As well as commercial software, produced for profit, there is a growing number of **open source** projects. This is software that is built collaboratively, using a published design and available to use free of charge.

There follows a list of some of the most widely used software applications.

Office suite
Examples: Microsoft Office, G Suite (Google), Word Perfect Office (Corel), iWork (Apple), LibreOffice (open source)

Office suites are incredibly popular, containing as they do the most widely used applications, especially for a work environment. Ferocious competition between software suppliers has seen many abandon this segment and the market is currently dominated by one supplier, with barely a handful of alternatives worth considering. Basic office suites contain three key applications, a word processor, a spreadsheet and presentation graphics software. In addition there are normally additional personal information management applications, covering things like contacts management/address book, calendars, email, task lists and so on. However, what is provided varies significantly, depending on the suite and the particular variant chosen. Some suppliers may add a database and/or desktop publisher, sometimes these are only available as part of a premium package.

Application software mind map

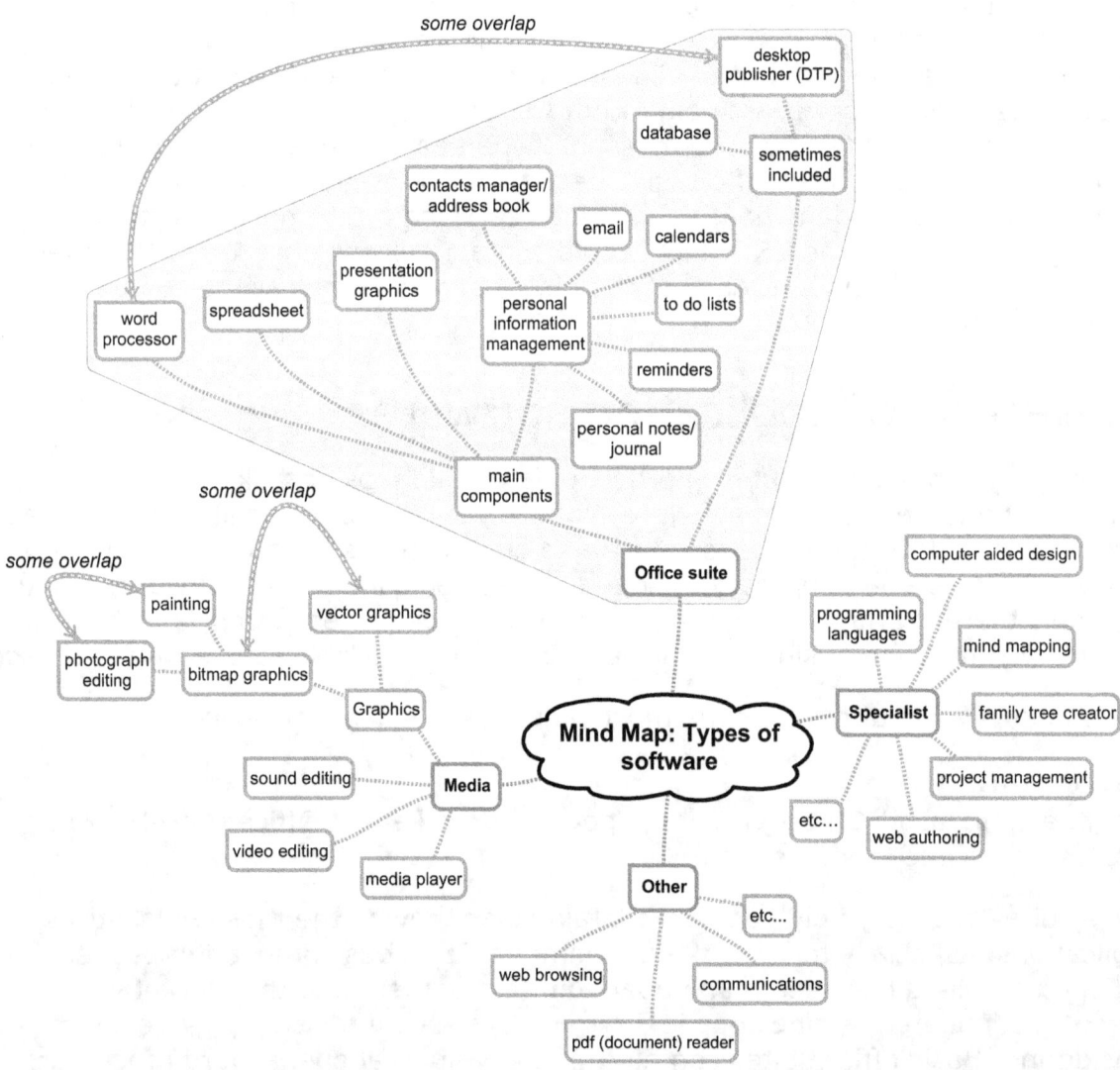

Word processor

Examples: Microsoft Word, Google Docs, Word Perfect (Corel), Pages (Apple), Writer (LibreOffice)

Probably the most widely used office application, word processors allow the creation, editing and viewing of text documents, such as letters, briefing documents, meeting minutes, simple notices and novels. These have evolved from being simple applications allowing users to enter, edit, save and print text, to complex software with a wide range of integrated tools. These may include spelling and grammar checkers, a word counter, table of contents and index creators as well as a range of drawing and layout tools. There is now significant overlap between word processors and desk top publishers and they can both be used for similar tasks. However desk top publishing (DTP) software is very much focused on layout, so tends to be the better tool for creating newspapers/newsletters/magazines, posters and books containing lots of graphical elements and pictures, whereas word processors tend to be better for documents containing mostly text.

Spreadsheet

Examples: Microsoft Excel, Sheets (Google), Quattro Pro (Corel), Numbers (Apple), Calc (LibreOffice)

In the early days of personal computers in the workplace, spreadsheets could well have claimed top spot for most important type of software and they are crucially important in many situations where there are large numbers of calculations to be carried out, such as accounting and budgeting and for the analysis of data collected as part of scientific experiments.

The concept is deceptively simple, with rows and columns of individual cells, looking like a giant table. Each cell can contain either a **number**, some **text** or a **formula**. It is the formulas that provide the magic of a spreadsheet. These combine the contents of other cells according to the formulas and display the results. Best of all, if a number is changed later, then all the formulas that use that number are automatically recalculated. This means that a spreadsheet can be a formidable mathematical modelling tool.

The example on the right shows a simple monthly home budgeting model.

Cell A1 contains the text **Money in** whilst cell B2 contains the number 1500, shown with currency formatting.

B5 looks as though it contains a number, whereas it actually contains a formula to add up all the sources of income, **B2+B3+B4**. The spreadsheet displays the answer to 1500+800+0 which is 2300.

	A	B
1	Money in	
2	Salary, spouse 1	£ 1,500.00
3	Salary, spouse 2	£ 800.00
4	Bar work	£ -
5	total	£ 2,300.00
6		
7	Money out	
8	Housing	£ 800.00
9	Utilities	£ 85.00
10	Transport	£ 250.00
11	Food	£ 200.00
12	Entertainment	£ 450.00
13	Miscellaneous	£ 200.00
14	total	£ 1,985.00
15		
16	Surplus (in - out)	£ 315.00

B14 sums all the outgoings using the formula **B8+B9+B10+B11+B12+B13**

B16 shows the net surplus (or deficit if it is negative) calculated by the formula **B5-B14**

If spouse 2 had their working hours reduced by their employer so that they were typically earning £770 per month and the monthly food bill rose to closer to £215, the appropriate entries in the table could be changed and the totals would be automatically recalculated.

	A	B	
1	**Money in**		
2	Salary, spouse 1	£	1,500.00
3	Salary, spouse 2	£	770.00
4	Bar work	£	200.00
5	*total*	£	2,470.00
6			
7	**Money out**		
8	*Housing*	£	1,020.00
9	Utilities	£	85.00
10	Transport	£	250.00
11	Food	£	215.00
12	Entertainment	£	400.00
13	Miscellaneous	£	200.00
14	*total*	£	2,170.00
15			
16	Surplus (in - out)	£	300.00

This sort of budget model has three possible uses. The amounts earned and spent last year could be entered to see how the surplus varied in order to **review** the past. Alternatively, the amounts that are currently being earned and spent could be entered to **monitor** the current state of the domestic finances. Finally, various alternative scenarios could be modelled to answer some *what-if* questions and **predict** what might happen in the future.

For instance, if the couple were interested in moving to a larger home, in a better area, they may want to investigate how much more they could afford to pay on housing, e.g. if spouse 2 took on some bar work in addition to their current part-time job. They could explore how much they might need to trim their spending (e.g. *Entertainment* = £400) and how much extra they would need to earn in order to be able to afford the sort of home that they would like. Would that leave them enough left over to deal with any unexpected costs? What would happen if spouse 2 wanted to give up work altogether? How would transport costs change if they used public transport and got rid of their car? If they could not stretch their budget for their choice of home, how much extra do they realistically think they *could* spend on housing? Calculating that figure would allow them to investigate the sort of home they could afford and whether the upgrade was worth the lifestyle changes.

Various alternatives could be tried out to help them to make a better quality decision. Clearly the example shown is very simple and a much more complex model could be developed taking lots more things into account. The spending categories could be broken down to show more detail. Entertainment could be broken down into eating out, cinema & theatre and *other*. Transport could be broken down into car costs and bus fares. Extra categories could be added for insurance and savings. This may be useful, but sometimes a very simple model is all that is needed to help show the likely implications of different courses of action.

The spreadsheet bug can bite and it is possible to spend a lot of time enthusiastically constructing spreadsheets. A good question to ask periodically is "Has using this spreadsheet led to better quality decisions being taken?" If not, then there has been little or no positive impact and the value of continuing to use the spreadsheet should be reviewed.

Sometimes spreadsheets of dubious value are presented in work situations, presumably in an attempt to justify the choice of a particular course of action or to try and bamboozle an audience into believing that a particular situation has been carefully considered. This prompted me to submit a suggestion for a new word to the Urban Dictionary website.

Bullsheet: *noun*

Definition: Spurious management information generated by the indiscriminate use of spreadsheets.

Example: On receipt of many rows and columns of numbers, superficially useful but using either poor data, untested formulas, unnecessary graphs, or just surplus to requirements, "Oh no! MORE bullsheet!".

However, thoughtfully constructed spreadsheets can save huge amounts of work and offer valuable additional information. This is potentially very powerful analytical software.

Sadly there has been some tedious teaching of spreadsheets in schools and some UK politicians have been happy to jump in and question why boring spreadsheets are being taught instead of something more up to date and exciting. It is important to differentiate between weak teaching and a poor curriculum choice. Spreadsheets are a key tool for the Information Age and fully deserve their place on the curriculum. The issue is to equip teachers with the vision, skills and confidence to open up their pupils to the possibilities of this amazing software.

Presentation graphics

Examples: Microsoft PowerPoint, Slides (Google), Presentations (Corel), Keynote (Apple), Impress (LibreOffice)

Presentation graphics software is mostly used to create slide shows to support presentations, usually combining text and graphics. Graphs and tables can be readily included, as can other media such as sound and video.

As with spreadsheets, the software is so compelling it can suffer from over-use, leading to the well-known "death by bullet point" endurance events/meetings. Used well, however, it supports presentations by helping to structure information, summarize and highlight key points and display images and other graphics that add to or support, what is being said.

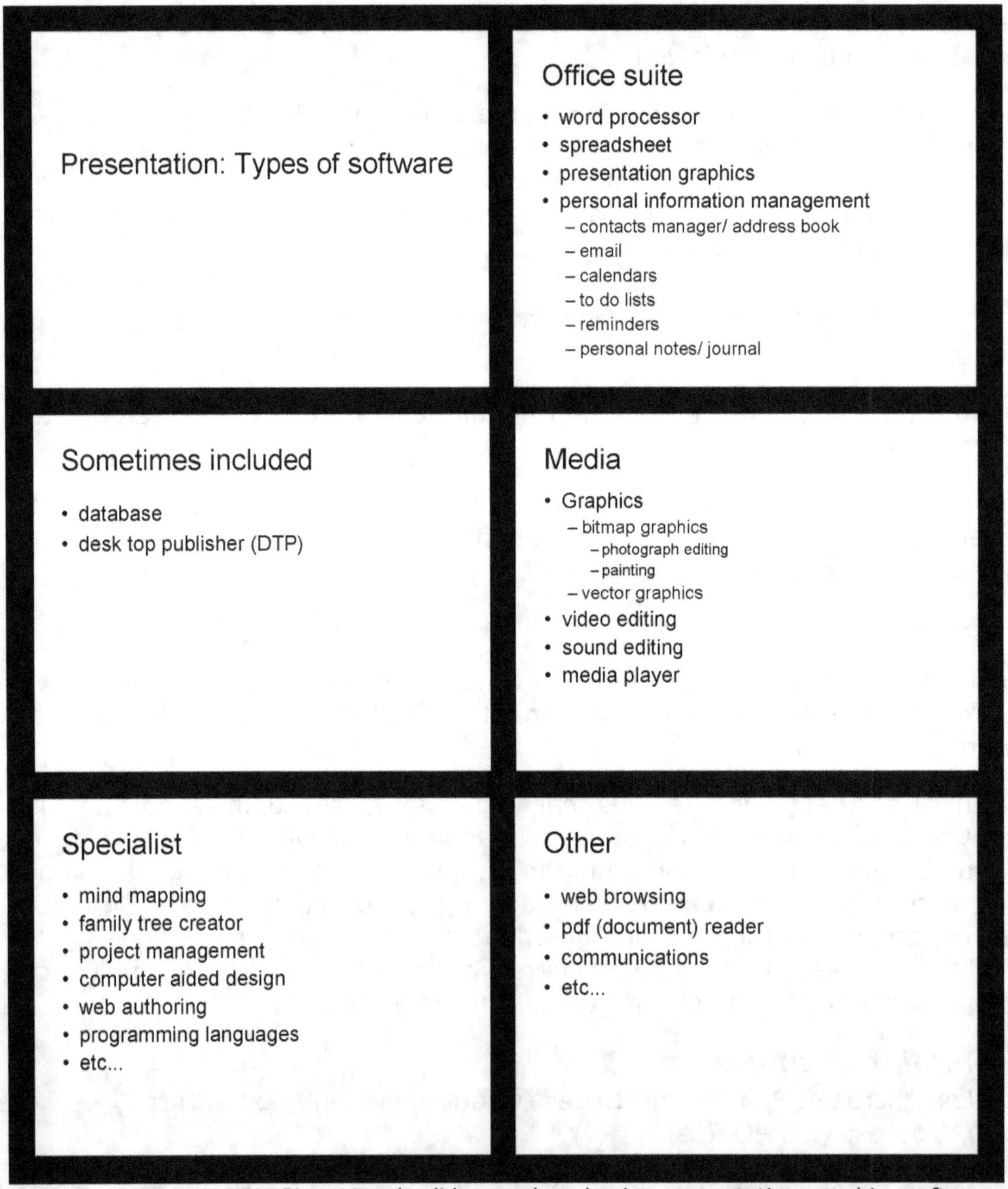

Presentation: Types of software

Office suite
- word processor
- spreadsheet
- presentation graphics
- personal information management
  – contacts manager/ address book
  – email
  – calendars
  – to do lists
  – reminders
  – personal notes/ journal

Sometimes included
- database
- desk top publisher (DTP)

Media
- Graphics
  – bitmap graphics
    – photograph editing
    – painting
  – vector graphics
- video editing
- sound editing
- media player

Specialist
- mind mapping
- family tree creator
- project management
- computer aided design
- web authoring
- programming languages
- etc...

Other
- web browsing
- pdf (document) reader
- communications
- etc...

Six text-only slides produced using presentation graphics software.

Above you can see six text-only slides that show another way of displaying the list of headings first seen in the *Types of software* mind map. Collecting and structuring ideas is another possible use of presentation graphics software.

It is easy to add hyperlinks to slides, that link either to the internet or to other slides in the presentation. This means that the software can also be used to create a quick website or CD ROM prototype, to try out proposed navigation schemes. For example, each slide could represent a different page of a website.

Slide shows can be set to run continuously and are sometimes used to provide rolling information displays.

Desktop publisher

Examples: Adobe InDesign, QuarkXPress, Microsoft Publisher, Scribus (open source)

Desktop publishing (DTP) deals with production of poster, newsletter, magazine and newspaper formats, where the primary focus is on layout. Word processors use pages as the primary unit on which documents are built, whereas DTP documents are based on frames. All page elements, whether text, diagrams, tables, photographs or other graphics, are placed within frames. These can then be moved around the pages of a document until a pleasing arrangement is achieved.

Text frames can be linked so that when the first frame is full, additional text automatically flows into the second frame and then any subsequent frames. The content of all the linked frames is automatically updated whenever text is added, deleted, changed or re-formatted or when frame sizes are altered.

This book is being written using DTP software and three frames have been set up below (grey frames). These have all been linked and some text entered, starting on the left.

These frames were then copied and pasted underneath (black frames). They were arranged in a step pattern, the width of the middle frame was reduced and some of the text had its formatting changed. Some words were also added to the middle frame and now text fills all three - the software worked out where to put everything automatically, as the changes were made.

Each chapter of this book has been written as a separate document, usually with one large frame on each page, linked to the pages on either side. The next page is an exception, having seven text frames in all. Additional frames were then added for diagrams, graphics, photographs and tables.

The DTP software that is being used includes a management utility that allows the whole book to be assembled. Each of the chapters, which have been written as separate documents, can be added to a single publication. They can be reordered and deleted, if necessary. Components like a table of contents, index and preface, can be added and put in the correct place.

A table of contents can be created automatically. The different formatting styles (Heading 1, Heading 2, Heading 3, etc.) are used to indicate the section hierarchy.

> This is frame 1 and when it is full the text will automatically flow into frames 2 and 3 which lie to the right. This is just about to happen,

> here we go, into the second frame! Keeping on with the flow, the text should just reach into the final frame, then it can be copied and

> pasted to show how the auto-flow works.

> This is **frame 1** and when it is full the text will automatically flow into **frames 2** and **3** which lie to the right. This is just about to

> happen, here we go, into the second frame! Keeping on and on and on and on and on with the flow,

> the text should just reach into the final frame, then it can be copied and pasted to show how the auto-flow works.

An index can be created semi-automatically. The user has to indicate which words are required to be in the index. They might also need to indicate which occurrences of each word should be in the index or the software can be asked to find **all** occurrences. The software then does the hard work of finding all the appropriate page numbers, according to the latest versions of all the different components.

The book can then be "published" and a single document is produced, correctly page numbered and with all the sections in the right order. Options can be chosen such as different ways of numbering pages and always starting a new chapter on an odd or even numbered page, by inserting blank pages when necessary.

Desktop publishing software is a specialist tool designed to handle large documents, potentially containing a lot of text and graphics and with a focus on layout. It tends to be more robust and reliable when dealing with longer, more demanding documents.

Although word processors have evolved to include many of the same features, they are more prone to crashing/freezing/misbehaving when working with large documents, lots of graphics and photographs and complex layouts. Word processors are simpler to use with shorter, less demanding documents. No one has yet produced a piece of software that can handle both types of document equally well.

Database

Examples: Microsoft Access, Corel Paradox, Base (LibreOffice), Oracle Database

Databases are probably the type of software that we are the most dependent on, since they form the backbone of most large scale computer systems. Banks, all online and most physical shopping outlets, social media websites, airlines, holiday companies and most other commercial companies, charities and governmental organisations all depend on databases.

Yet, for most people, databases are the type of software that they are least likely to have to set up from scratch. In my professional life I can only recall two occasions when I needed to create a database. However, both were very important pieces of work. One was when I began operating as an independent consultant and this database allows my business to function.

It records the details of all the schools and other organisations that I have worked with, keeping track of key contacts as well as key communications, including phone conversations and emails. It allows me to list all of the training events that I have organised, including all the venue details and all bookings. I can use it to automate physical mail shots and bulk email communications as well as other routine functions, such as producing a list (register) of those attending a training course and printing job sheets that include directions and contact details. It allows me to keep the amount of time spent on administration to a minimum.

A database is a structured set of data, organised for convenient access, that is held on a computer. It can be thought of as an electronic filing system.

A flat file database is the simplest type of database. It can be represented by a *single table*, where each row contains all the information being stored about a single item (i.e. a single **record**). Each column contains data about a single aspect and is called a **field**.

A DVD collection could be stored as a flat file database (see table), where each record would be a different DVD. The fields might include the DVD title, genre, British Board of Film Classification rating (U, PG, 12A/12, 15, 18 and R18), Director, year of release, etc.

In this fictitious example, the field names are **number**, **title**, **genre**, **rating**, **director** and **year**. A few example records are shown. Each record in the database refers to one DVD, for example, record 474 is all about the *Bird on a Spire* DVD.

number	title	genre	rating	director	year
...					
471	Good Morning, Aldershot!	Comedy	15	Anton Trouser	1975
472	Smoked Haddock in the Morning	Romance	18	Rita Largeapron	1997
473	The Merchant of Macclesfield	Drama	PG	Fred Proudstaff	2014
474	Bird on a Spire	Action	15	Anton Trouser	2003
475	Angela's Lashes	Comedy	15	Bunty Bouquet	2011
...					

Each record is given a number to allow it to be uniquely identified. The *title* field could not be used for this, since you might get given a second copy of *Smoked Haddock in the Morning* as a gift, which would require two records with the same title. This would also be the case if you bought the classic 1965 version of *Bird on a Spire* directed by Wilfred Spatchcock or intend buying the 2010 remake of *Good Morning, Aldershot!*.

In the majority of cases, records are allocated a unique record number to act as the **key field**, i.e. the field that is used to uniquely identify each record. Libraries, which may have many copies of the same title, allocate an accession number to each individual book. This would be used as their key field.

Flat file databases allow information to be structured and stored simply and are quite adequate for keeping track of a film or music collection. The data can be automatically searched to find all the comedies in the collection or all the films made by a favourite director. A list of all the PG and U films could be produced in advance of a visit by the grandchildren. All films containing the word *haddock* could be found, for what it's worth! These search results or indeed, the entire database, could be sorted according to one or more fields and the results could be printed out.

However, flat file databases are relatively inflexible and limited in their use. To release the full potential of databases and create something that can be scaled and adapted to meet a variety of evolving needs, requires a **relational database**.

A relational database is constructed from a series of related tables, rather than just a single table. Each one takes on the table structure already seen. A database management system (DBMS), is used to create, modify, and extract information from the database.

Example: Furniture manufacturer

Suppose that a small furniture making business, with a single workshop, develops a relational database. Some of the tables needed would include the following.

Suppliers A table of all the companies from whom materials and components are purchased. Fields would include supplier name, address details and contact phone numbers.

Contacts A table of all the key people, who are external to the business, e.g. the supplier sales people and delivery company contacts. Fields would include title, name, job role and mobile phone number or direct extension.

Communications Details about all key communications - phone calls, letters and emails. Fields would include the type of communication, date it took place, whom it was with and notes summarising the key points.

Invoices (received) A table containing details of all the invoices received from suppliers.

Invoices (issued) A table with details of all the invoices issued by the company to customers.

If a database is not carefully designed, it is possible to end up storing the same piece of information several times. This is to be avoided at all costs. Keeping multiple copies of the same information clearly wastes storage space. Much more importantly, it makes it very difficult to maintain the accuracy of the data on which the company is depending.

For example, suppose that the company owner has an important phone call with the new Head of Sales at a key supplier about an invoice. The name, job role and phone number of this person could be recorded as fields within the **Communications** table. However this information is also relevant to the invoice that was being discussed and could be recorded in the **Invoices** table. Also, a new record should be added to the **Contacts** table.

The same information is now being stored in three places. Suppose that this contact's phone number changes shortly afterwards, when a company mobile phone is issued to them. Anyone trying to update the database has to know to change what has been recorded in all three tables. Trying the find the correct records to amend in the **Communications** and **Invoices** tables is a relatively time-consuming task if the person's name and their employer's name is all that is known.

Over time it is likely that changes may only be made to one or two of the tables and now there is out of date information in the database - with no way of knowing which entries are the correct ones!

A great deal of effort goes into the design of data tables to try and ensure that any piece of information is only stored **once**, in the most efficient way possible. This process is called data normalisation.

In the above example, the name, job role and phone number of the new Sales Manager would be stored in the **Contacts** table. That table would have a ***Contact_Number*** field, a unique number allocated to each record (key field), so that each contact would have their own number. This number would be used in the **Invoices** and **Communications** table to show whom the contact was regarding the phone call about the invoice. When required, the DBMS could look up their details in the Contacts table. The information about the contact is now only stored once, but it can be linked to in any relevant table by storing their ***Contact_Number***.

Databases are incredibly powerful tools that we currently depend on for running most key aspects of government, education, business and commerce. Many specialist pieces of software are effectively databases with a custom interface and perhaps with additional specialised tools.

Restaurant software will need a database to store bookings, as well as having tools to allow menu choices from different tables to be entered, bills to be calculated and payments taken. The menu choices may be communicated directly to the kitchen and reports may be generated, for example to show the relative popularity of different items over a given period. The database functions might be extended to include stock control to monitor food stock levels and assist with reordering, potentially using the internet to connect directly to suppliers.

Accountancy software will use a database to record various aspects of business performance, including the payment of supplier invoices and the raising of invoices for customers. Staff payroll might be included along with the payment of taxes.

Data integrity

A database is only useful if the information it contains is up to date and accurate. As well as data normalisation, much effort usually goes into avoiding data entry and other errors. Data integrity refers to the accuracy and consistency of data.

Data **validation** checks are used to ensure that data is sensible and reasonable, although this alone cannot guarantee that the data is correct. A UK postcode can be as short as **B4 8HW** and as long as **RG17 3FJ**. The following validation checks could be used.

The length of a postcode string will be between 6 and 8 characters, including the space.

The first character is always a letter.

The last two characters are always letters.

The third last character is always a number.

When entering a postcode, the above rules could be used to create an automatic validation check, that only accepts entries that obey all of them. If an attempt is made to enter a postcode that starts with a number, consists of only 5 characters or ends with a number, the database will not accept the entry and will display an error message, prompting the user to try again.

Range checks are often used with numeric entries. Most British secondary schools that have sixth forms will cover years 7 to 13. When recording the year group that a new entrant is placed in on arrival, this could be validated using the range check

6< YearGroupOnArrival <14 or

7<= YearGroupOnArrival <=13

Numbers, such as bank account numbers, national identity numbers and certain product/item numbers, may have check digits appended, according to set algorithms. The data is validated by recalculating the check digit and comparing this with the check digit that was read/entered. If the check digits differ then there has been a data entry error.

EAN-13 item number barcode - check digit

If entering a day of the week, a user may have to select the appropriate day from a drop-down list. This means that they are only allowed to enter one of seven alternatives, all of which are valid days. The wrong day could still be chosen from the list, but it would at least be a valid day. If a user was asked to type the day of the week, they might mistype (e.g. Tuesdya) or misspell (e.g. Thirsdaye). They might even mix up where they should be typing the entries and put something completely unrelated to days of the week.

The more thorough and precise that validation checking is, the more that users are being supported and the smaller the risk of inaccurate data finding its way into a database.

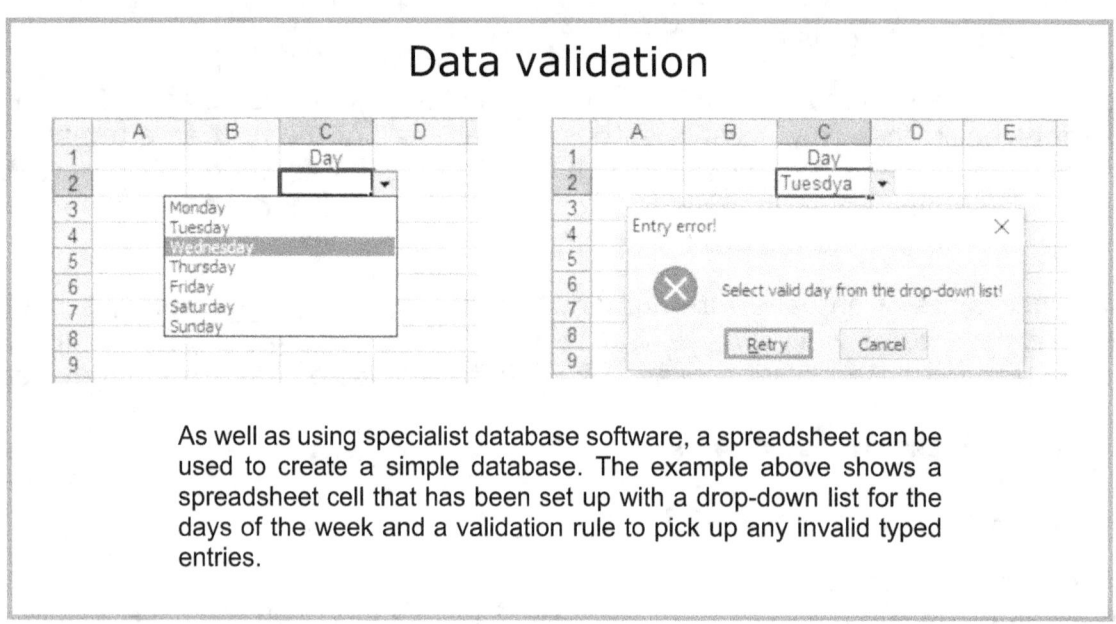

As well as using specialist database software, a spreadsheet can be used to create a simple database. The example above shows a spreadsheet cell that has been set up with a drop-down list for the days of the week and a validation rule to pick up any invalid typed entries.

In some data entry situations, data **verification** may be used. This may simply be a form of proof-reading where a copy of the data that has been entered is compared with the original. Another method is to enter the data twice and get the computer to compare the two versions. The two versions should be identical, so any discrepancies can be highlighted for further checking. For large data sets this is time-consuming and therefore costly, when done manually.

Most readers will have come across dual entry verification when setting up online accounts. User email addresses are frequently the key to identifying and communicating with users and they must therefore be entered twice. If the two versions differ by as little as a single character, the website will display an error message and require that this part of the data entry process is repeated. The same approach is normally taken when a password is being chosen.

Graphics software

Examples (bitmap or raster graphics): Adobe Photoshop, Corel Paint Shop Pro, GIMP (open source), Microsoft Paint

Examples (vector graphics): Adobe Illustrator, Adobe FreeHand, CorelDRAW, Inkscape (open source)

Bitmap images, sometimes referred to as raster images, are made up of a grid of pixels (picture elements). Information is stored about the colour of each pixel. Photographs are examples of bitmap images.

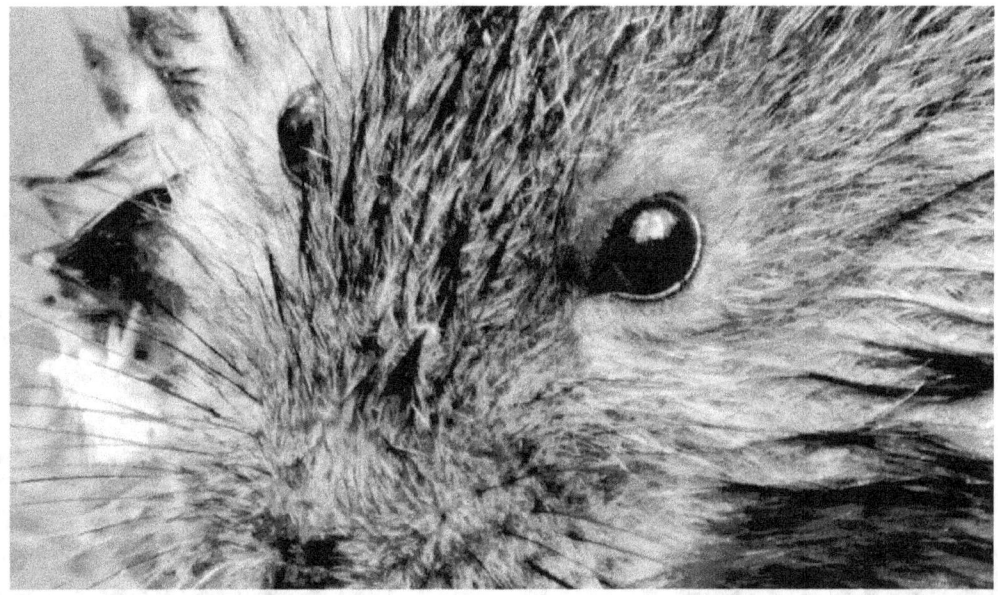

The photograph above shows some of the face detail of the water vole already seen in Chapter 2. At this level of zoom you cannot see the individual pixels that make up the image. The images below show what happens as the level of zoom (right-hand eye) increases, with individual pixels now becoming visible.

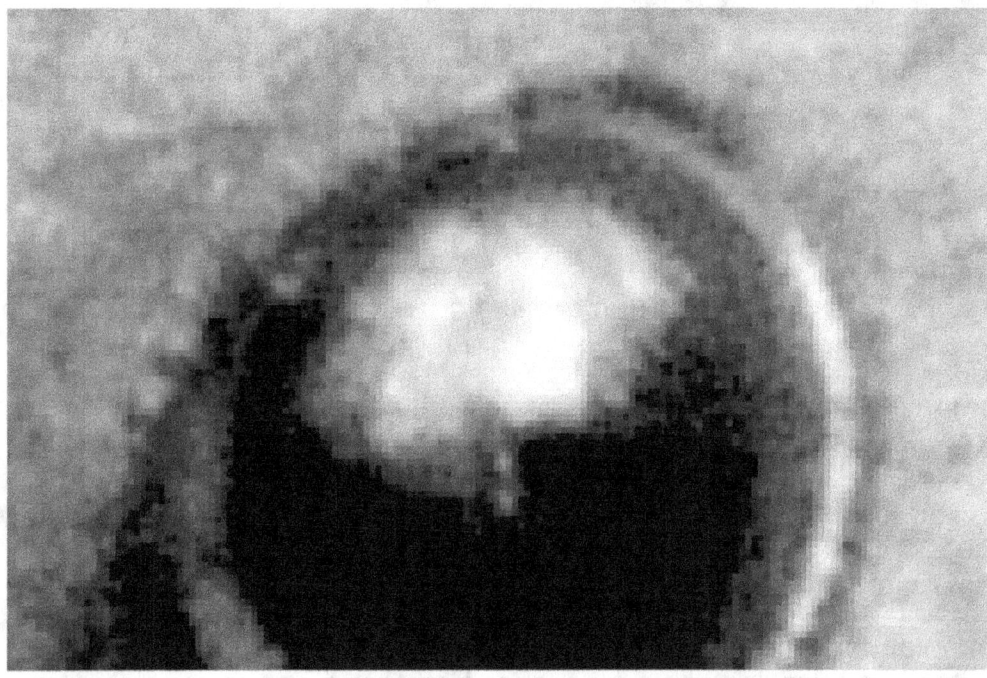

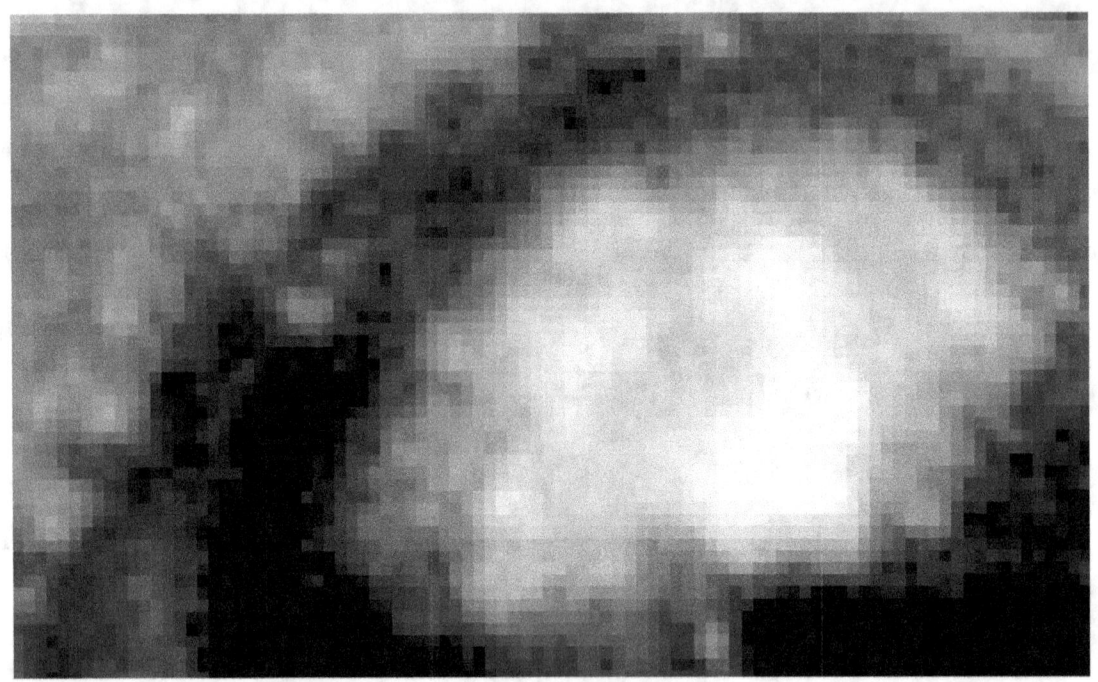

The process of creating a design using bitmap graphics is similar to working with paper and a brush or pen and they are often known as painting programs.

As the chosen colour is applied to the "canvas", individual pixels are changed according to whichever painting tool has been chosen.

Designers will often use a graphics tablet and stylus to do this, since the experience is much more like drawing or painting, offering greater control than when using a mouse or trackpad.

Vector graphics are built up from a series of individual **objects** - circles, squares, lines, arrows and so on. Each object has a range of **properties** defined. The properties of a circle will include the coordinates of its centre relative to the page, its radius, the colour, thickness and style of any outline, the fill colour, and so on. The process of building a vector graphic is therefore completely different from producing a bitmap image.

Both bitmap and vector graphics software will have some tools in common. For instance, tools for drawing common shapes like circles and rectangles. However, the way the image is being constructed is completely different. Below is a vector diagram of a spoon, stirring the contents of a glass, seen as part of the Example Algorithms diagram earlier.

Deconstructing a vector graphic

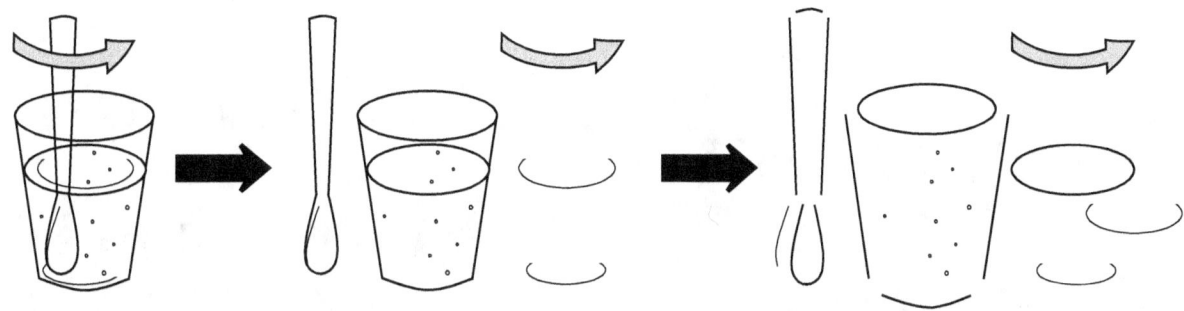

The individual drawing components can be seen on the right. There are straight and curved lines, two ellipses, two partial ellipses and an arrow. The bubbles are tiny circles of different sizes.

Creating diagrams from individual elements can be laborious. However, vector graphics have three big advantages over bitmap graphics. They are usually much easier to edit and they can be resized with ease, whilst maintaining quality. In addition elements used in a vector graphic can be readily copied for reuse, either as-is or subject to further editing. This allows designers to build up libraries of time-saving reusable components. In the example above, the spoon and the glass of water might be useful items to save.

Here is a simple bitmap image, showing three overlapping shapes. Suppose the artist decided that the black hexagon was not needed. An eraser tool would be used to remove it. This will work quite well where the hexagon is above the white background, although it can be time consuming, but it becomes more difficult where the shapes overlap.

An attempt to remove the hexagon resulted in the following (see over).

Editing a bitmap (1)

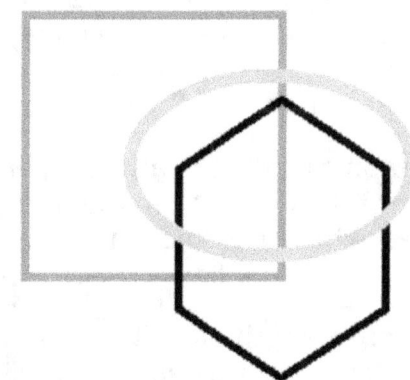

Editing a bitmap (2)

Where the hexagon overlapped the square, removing it was bound to leave white spaces. Where the ellipse sat on top of the hexagon, it would have been possible to leave the ellipse intact, if the eraser had been wielded with great precision. This is unlikely to happen in practice, leading to further damage to the image.

Repairing the image would require zooming in and changing the colours of individual pixels until everything was neatly restored. This would be an onerous task even with this simple graphic, imagine what it would be like with something more complicated!

With a similar vector graphic, the artist would simply need to select the hexagon and either press DELETE or select CUT.

The construction and editing of both bitmap and vector graphics has been made easier by the introduction of **layers** to many graphics programs. Users can create new layers and these can be edited in isolation or combination, depending on which other layers have been **locked**. When the image is finished, the layers are combined to form the final picture.

Most graphics software also supports multiple levels of **UNDO**. This aids editing when mistakes have been made, by restoring an image to its state before the last **n** changes, where **n** is chosen by the user, up to the maximum allowed by the particular software being used. With simple software, $n_{max} = 1$.

The other strength of vector graphics is resizing. Below you can see different versions of the glass and spoon, all scaled differently.

The main quality issue arises if there is preservation of line thickness. This means that as objects are enlarged or reduced, line thickness remains constant.

Enlarging a vector graphic

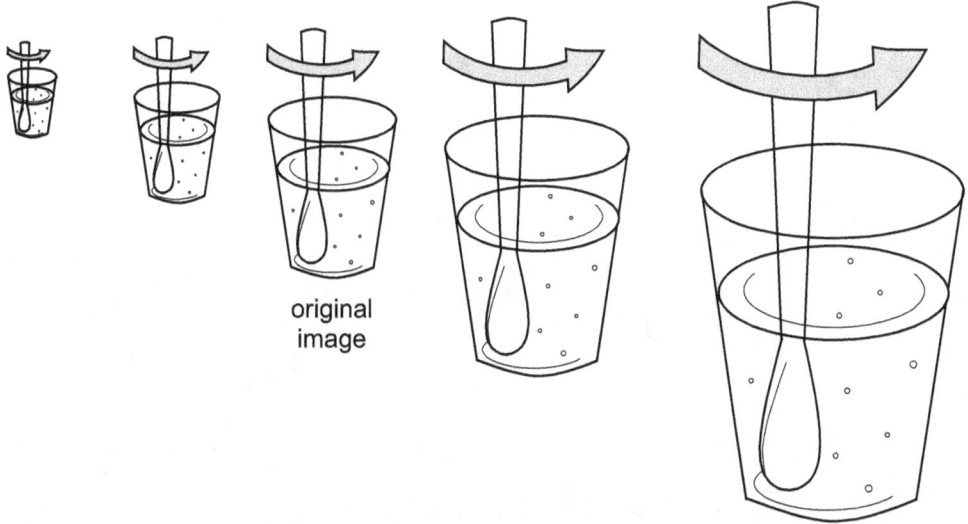

original image

If very significantly reducing the image size, the lines eventually look too thick. If significantly enlarging, they can end up looking too thin. However, within those extremes there is no loss of image quality. In this example, the problem is most apparent with the smallest version of the glass and spoon.

Correcting this issue depends on the complexity of the image. If all lines started out with the same thickness, it could be as simple as quickly selecting all the objects by dragging around them or typing CTRL-A (a common keyboard shortcut for "*select all*") and choosing a new line thickness.

There is much less scope for enlarging or reducing a bitmap image. Curved lines quickly lose their smoothness, as can be seen from the zoomed-in portion of the light grey ellipse on the previous page. What should be smooth curves now appear stepped or jagged, a condition often referred to as "jaggies".

For comparison, the vector graphic of the glass and spoon was copied and pasted into bitmap graphics software, to convert it into a bitmap (below, centre). The resulting image was then enlarged and reduced. The decrease in quality can be clearly seen.

Enlarging a bitmap graphic

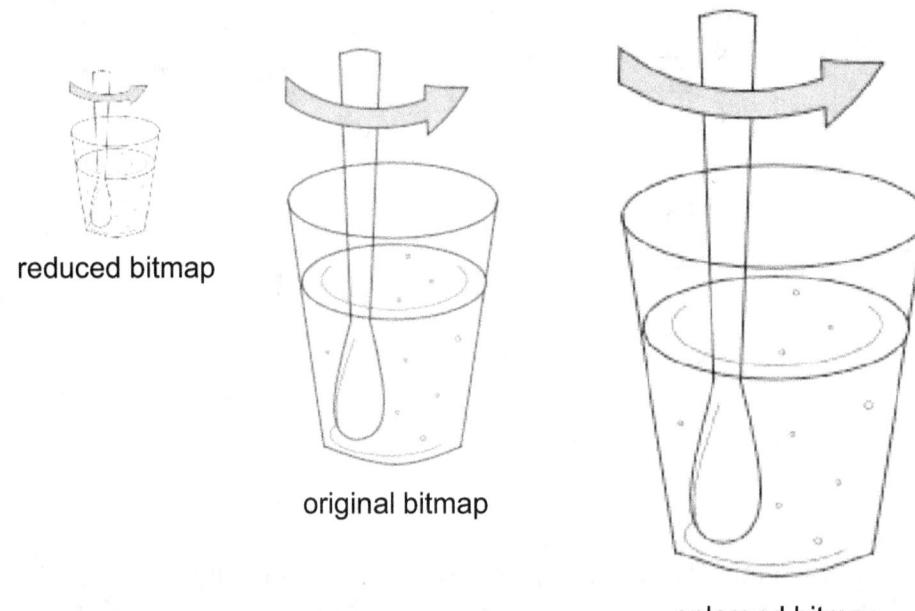

reduced bitmap

original bitmap

enlarged bitmap

Vector graphics are well suited to technical diagrams, as it is easy to select individual objects or groups of objects and align, arrange or transform them in some way.

All of the flowcharts in this book have been produced using vector graphics. However, many from a pure art background would feel more at home using bitmap graphics and the two are complementary. It is very difficult to produce something that looks remotely hand-drawn using vector graphics.

Vector graphics software all use proprietary file formats by default. The Scalable Vector Graphics (SVG) format is the main **open format** for vector graphics, first released in 2001. It is supported by most web browsers and was developed by the World Wide Web Consortium (W3C). By contrast there are several bitmap formats in common use, such as JPG, PNG, TIFF, BMP and GIF.

As with other types of software, there has been something of a convergence over time, with bitmap software offering some vector-type tools and vector software offering some bitmap handling tools. However, as it has proved difficult with word processing and desktop publishing to produce a single piece of software well suited to all document types, so it has proved difficult to produce a single piece of image producing software.

As well as general purpose graphics software, there are also some specialist products available. Photo editing software is a specialist type of bitmap graphics software, with tools to adjust exposure, contrast and colour saturation, along with red-eye reduction, blemish/defect removal and other tools.

Specialist vector graphics tools exist in areas such as computer aided design and the production of specialist diagrams - flowcharts and organisation structure charts, for instance.

Graphics capability is often available within other types of software, such as word processors, desktop publishers and presentation graphics software. Usually a small selection of vector graphics tools are offered.

Web browser

Examples: Google Chrome, Mozilla Firefox, Internet Explorer, Safari, Microsoft Edge, Opera

One of the newer types of software, web browsers are now ubiquitous and for many people will be the software application that they spend most time using. Primarily for viewing pages on the World Wide Web (WWW), they allow users to view pages consisting of text and graphics/photographs and follow any of the embedded hypertext links that are chosen, connecting to other pages and resources. Some browsers support the downloading of add-ons and plug-ins which boost their capability further, to allow, for example, the viewing of video material or the streaming of online radio stations.

Many people equate the internet with the World Wide Web and it is true that when most people use the internet, it is in order to access the WWW. However, the two are not the same. The internet is a global network of computers and one of the services that is offered is the WWW.

Currently, most online browsing is done via mobile devices; smartphones and tablets. This requires leaner page design as these are typically less powerful than most desktop and laptop computers and use much smaller screens.

The growth in the availability of good quality broadband connections, allowing ever faster internet connections has, in turn, led to increasingly ambitious online offerings. Software can now be readily accessed via the internet, using a web browser, without requiring users to install software on their own device. Even demanding applications such as photo-editing are now available online. Many of these applications have been written using the **Java** programming language, which was designed for producing programs that could run on any device that can run a Java Virtual Machine. Most other programming languages have to produce different versions, by using different compilers, in order to run on different families of devices.

Mobile device apps

The term "app" is simply a contraction of "application", which in computing terminology refers to a software application; in other words a computer program firmly aimed at end-users, to help them complete particular tasks. Therefore software like word processors, spreadsheets and web browsers are all apps. However, in my mind, I always associate the abbreviation "app" with software designed for mobile devices, such as tablets and smartphones.

Some mobile apps simply offer users simplified access to one or more websites, whilst others offer programmed tools and services.

Mobile apps have definite characteristics that separate them from applications designed to run on a desktop or laptop computer. Since mobile devices generally have much less working memory and long-term storage, as well as lower powered processors, the software that runs on them must be leaner, requiring much less in the way of computing resources. As a result, mobile apps are generally smaller, being more focused on a limited range of functions. Ease of use, rather than having a large number of features and tools, is the prime consideration. They are designed to work well using a touch screen, the size of which will be many times smaller than conventional computer monitors. Because these apps are used on mobile devices, they are also designed for use "on-the-go".

What is useful to people will vary, but here is a selection of different types.

Mapping apps can integrate with the GPS capability of many devices to pinpoint your current location and show your position on a scalable map. The app may allow you to type in a destination so that it can provide you with walking, driving or cycling route directions. It may integrate with local public transport information to show you any appropriate alternatives, perhaps going as far as telling you precisely which stop or station you should go to and the time of the next departure.

Communications apps are popular, despite the fact that many mobile devices are phones! However, there are messaging apps, that allow users to send photographs and video using their data connections, without incurring separate charges. Mobile access to email adds great convenience to what is already a very popular messaging medium. There are apps and services, some available via web browsers, that effectively turn your device into a video phone, for face-to-face communications and video conferencing.

There are note taking apps for supporting note taking, idea collection and creative thinking. These often support a range of media - sound recordings, video and photographs, along with text.

Social networking apps allow you to take your favourite sites with you wherever you go. Convenience and ease of use mean that many users access these websites via a mobile device out of preference. At the time of writing, the largest was Facebook with over 2 billion active users as of the end of June 2017. It is interesting to note that the largest country in the world at that time was China, with an estimated population of 1.4 billion. Not bad considering the service only launched in 2004.

Next in line after Facebook came YouTube (1 billion users, video sharing, acquired by Google) and Instagram (700 million users, photo-sharing, acquired by Facebook). Other players worthy of note were Twitter (posts/messages, maximum 140 characters), Reddit (USA, social news aggregation and discussion), Vine Camera (video clips up to 6.5 seconds long - arguably the video equivalent of Twitter), Snapchat (photo and video sharing), Ask.fm (Latvia, questions-based), Pinterest (social network using a pinboard metaphor), Tumblr (microblogging and social networking), Flickr (photo sharing), Google+ (social networking) and LinkedIn (professional networking).

There is some convergence between social networking websites that also have linked apps and messaging apps, such as WhatsApp, that could also be considered as social networking tools.

The ideas behind many of these sites/apps are deceptively simple, but that does not mean that the social media entrepreneurs have always had it easy. Alphabet, the new group name for Google, has either launched or bought several social media services, including Orkut, Dodgeball, Latitude, Google Buzz, YouTube, Google+ and Google Friend Connect. Heard of them? YouTube currently dominates video sharing, but Google+ is a relative bit-player and the remainder were closed down; presumably they were not commercially viable. As with many segments of the software industry, the market is dominated by a few big players, with some niche players, whilst the remainder often struggle to survive.

Some services have found it a challenge to deal effectively with online bullying and issues around keeping users safe, especially children and young people. There have also been tensions between user demands for privacy and the desire of some governments to maintain a measure of control over communications, for national security, anti-crime, censorship and other reasons.

Finding a formula that captures the imagination of the large numbers of people needed to make a commercial success of social networking services has proved an elusive dream for many. Others have fallen foul of a fickle public, that can switch their allegiances from one platform to another with a few clicks, according to the whims of fashion. Bebo and MySpace were once the biggest names in social networking. Both fell into obscurity, only to be relaunched - perhaps to return to their former glories or perhaps only to disappear forever. Fierce competition between the providers of social networking services has led to a degree of convergence as each ruthlessly incorporates some of the best features of their key rivals. Sometimes the best shortcut to someone else's functionality is to buy the company and all of their expertise and experience. There has been no shortage of merger and acquisition activity, where the companies with the larger and healthier balance sheets have a clear advantage.

"New kids on the block" turn up regularly or older services suddenly see a surge of interest, or simply reach a tipping point in their growth. Snapchat, Tinder (dating-oriented social networking) and Grindr (social networking "for gay, bi, curious and queer men"[1]) are examples. At one point Facebook was hugely popular with many teens and young people, until their parents, adult relatives and, in some cases, younger siblings, all started joining in. This encouraged moves onto newer, less well-known platforms, in the search for greater privacy.

Here are a few names that have been tipped as up and coming social networking tools, indicating just how vibrant this area is currently. Periscope (video sharing including live broadcast), Blab (topic driven social video platform) Slideshare (PowerPoint presentation sharing), Quora (Q&A), Goodreads (about books and reading), Hyper (photo sharing) and Yik Yak (location-based social networking). Some will fail to reach a mass audience and simply fade away, others that show promise will get bought by competitors, one or two may just be the next big names in social networking...

Beware the 'ware words!

By now readers should know that **soft**ware is another word for computer programs, whilst **hard**ware is computing equipment or something related to computing that has a physical form. However, over the years, many other 'ware words have been adopted into the technical vernacular. I have listed a few below.

abandonware/orphanware	Software that is no longer marketed and whose copyright is no longer defended.
adware	Software that includes advertisements that are displayed whilst the software is running.
bloatware	Software that is slow or unwieldy because it has become packed with too many features.
firmware	Usually software that is stored on a chip that can be overwritten/updated and hence is between hardware and software. Firmware updates are periodically issued for common devices, some install automatically, others require user intervention.
freeware	Free software, fully functional with no advertising.

---
[1] From www.grindr.com/about

malware	An umbrella term for hostile or malicious software that is designed to disrupt, damage or gain authorized access to a computer system.
ransomware	Malware that attempts to extort money from a computer user by hiding, or claiming to have hidden, their data, threatening to publish their data or some other hostile act.
scareware	Security or another type of utility software that is either very poor quality or is itself malware.
shareware	Software that is distributed without payment but is limited in some way to encourage those who want to use it to pay for it.
shelfware	Software or hardware that is not used, underused or remains unsold.
spyware	Software that monitors and reports on the actions of a computer user, for example to harvest bank login details.
vapourware	Software or hardware that is announced publicly and actively promoted, even though it does not exist yet (as a marketing strategy).
wetware	Humorous term for the human brain. Also called liveware or meatware.

Self test

1. What makes a binary search more efficient than a linear search?
2. On a flowchart, what do diamond shaped boxes and rectangular boxes represent?
3. What types of software typically make up a basic office software suite?
4. What three things can be stored in one cell of a spreadsheet?
Number, text or formula
5. What type of generic activity could you use a spreadsheet budget model to help with?
6. What is the difference between word processors and desktop publishers?
7. What is the difference between a flat file database and a relational database?
8. What type of graphics is made up of a series of defined objects?
9. A photograph is what type of graphic (two names)?
10. Give two advantages of vector graphics over bitmap graphics.

Answers:

1. What makes a binary search more efficient than a linear search?
With each comparison/check, the search space is halved.
2. On a flowchart, what do diamond shaped boxes and rectangular boxes represent?
Decisions (questions), processes (actions)
3. What types of software typically make up a basic office software suite?
Word processor, spreadsheet and presentation graphics. Personal information management software is often included, too.
4. What three things can be stored in one cell of a spreadsheet?
Number, text or formula
5. What type of generic activity could you use a spreadsheet budget model to help with?
Review, monitor, predict (answering "what-if" questions)
6. What is the difference between word processors and desktop publishers?
DTP software puts all content into frames, rather than directly on the page and is very much focused on layout. It is particularly good with more complex documents such as newspaper and magazine-type formats, where there are lots of photographs, illustrations and other graphics. Word processors are particularly good for documents that are wholly or mostly comprised of text.
7. What is the difference between a flat file database and a relational database?
A flat file database consists of a single data table, whereas a relational database consists of more than one (usually several) related tables.
8. What type of graphics is made up of a series of defined objects?
Vector graphics
9. A photograph is what type of graphic (two names)?
Bitmap, raster graphics
10. Give two advantages of vector graphics over bitmap graphics.
Any two valid answers, e.g. Vector graphics can retain full quality despite significant resizing and they are easier to edit.

Chapter 3: Key learning points

- An algorithm is a structured set of instructions for carrying out a task or solving a problem. Examples include a knitting pattern, pseudocode sorting algorithm, recipe, method for a science experiment and computer program.
- The three structures that make up algorithms are sequence, selection, repetition.
- Algorithms can be described in many different ways, including pseudocode, flowchart, a series of diagrams and structured text.
- The three basic types of software are UEFI/BIOS (allowing a device to boot-up), operating system (provides basic services to allow other software to be run, as well as the user interface) and applications software (software aimed at end users).
- Utility software is a type of applications software that helps devices to run better by helping to analyse, configure, optimise or maintain them.
- Computers run machine code programs (sometimes called object code). These programs are in binary.
- High level programming languages are much easier for humans to use than programming directly in machine code.
- Programs written using a high level language must be converted into machine code (object code) before they can be run, using special software. There are two types of conversion software, compilers and interpreters.
- A variable can be thought of as a named memory location or box that can contain a single item.
- An array can be thought of as a 'super-variable', containing more than one item. A simple one dimensional array is like a list and is an example of a data structure.
- Pseudocode is a very precise and concise way of representing an algorithm. It looks similar to a computer program.
- Atomic data types cannot be broken down any further and include integer (whole number), real number (any number that can be represented on a number line), boolean (true or false) and character (any text character).
- Data structures consist of more than one item and include array, string (an array of characters) and record (some user-defined set of data types).
- A data table is made up of a set of records. In a student data table one record would contain all the information being stored about one student.
- Each record is divided up into fields, each one holding a single data item, such as date of birth, name, first line of address and post code.

- Each record is identified by a key field, usually a unique record number.
- There is a wide range of different types of applications software including word processors, spreadsheets, databases, presentation graphics, desktop publishers, web browsers, messaging, video chat and graphics software.
- There is a wide range of applications software available for use on smartphones. These programs (apps) are normally smaller in size and more focused in their range of functions when compared with software written for desktop and laptop computers.

4: Computer networks and the internet

What is a computer network?

A computer is a wonderful tool. By installing appropriate software it can be used to support a huge range of tasks. This can range from composing songs, making videos, creating a wide range of graphics, designing just about anything, playing immersive games and authoring articles, papers and books, to running a business, analysing vast quantities of data, writing your own software or creating complex mathematical models. In fact just about any important area of human activity can be supported by the use of a computer.

However, a single computer is an isolated tool. Join computers together so that they can communicate with each other and people can work collaboratively, sharing information, files and software. Users can communicate with each other. Expensive printers or specialist hardware like scanners, can be shared, as can high speed internet connections. Services, such as keeping anti-virus software up to date and backing up data[1], can be controlled centrally for everyone's benefit. Very large amounts of storage space can be added centrally much more cheaply than upgrading lots of individual machines. Now the huge potential of computers is magnified many times over! This joining together of individual computers, so that they can communicate with each other, is fundamentally what computer networks are all about.

As might be expected, there are some disadvantages to computer networks. There is additional hardware to buy and installation to pay for. Large networks can be technically challenging, requiring specialist design, along with on-going management costs. Where computers are connected, it is much easier for malware, such as computer viruses, to spread. It also becomes easier for unauthorised people to gain access to the computers (hacking). However, the advantages of connecting computers together are such, that the vast majority of devices around the world are either permanently connected to one or more networks, or spend much of their time connected in some way.

Computer networks can be classified as either **peer to peer** or **client/server** networks. Peer to peer networks use a decentralised communications model where all the devices have the same network capabilities and any of the network can initiate communication. There is no single computer that is in charge, running the network. This type of network is relatively cheap and easy to set up, but it is not

---

[1] Soon after buying a computer, it is likely that the work and data that is stored on it is worth much more than the device itself. Copies of data should be made regularly in case a hardware fault, computer virus, fire or theft results in its loss. This is known as **backing up** or **making a backup**.

very scalable and therefore only suitable for small networks, for example in a small office.

In a client/server network, servers provide services to the network, whilst clients consume them. A file server will provide storage space, usually on one or more hard disc drives. Larger networks often use arrays of hard discs, configured to keep multiple copies of data simultaneously, in case any one disc fails. A print server will control access to one or more printers, maintaining print queues and sending data to the relevant printer when it becomes available. Client computers can save data centrally on a chosen file server (there could be more than one) and can use any of the printers that have been allocated to a user.

Networks can be wired in different ways, the three main topologies being bus, ring and star configurations.

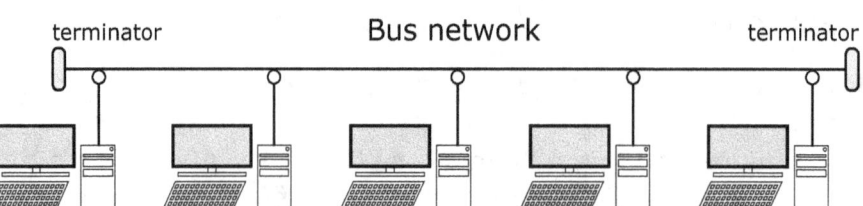

Bus and ring networks require much less cabling than star networks and were very popular in the early days of networking. However they suffered from a serious vulnerability, since if a network link was broken at any point, the whole network would fail. Many early school networks were of the bus type and the cabling was often, at best, informal. Wires would be slung between adjacent computers and left to hang down behind desks. Many lessons were brought to a grinding halt when a child accidentally, or indeed, deliberately, kicked out a leg and pulled out one of the connecting cables. As the only permanent storage available was via the network and all the computers would need to be rebooted to reconnect to the network, any unsaved work would be lost.

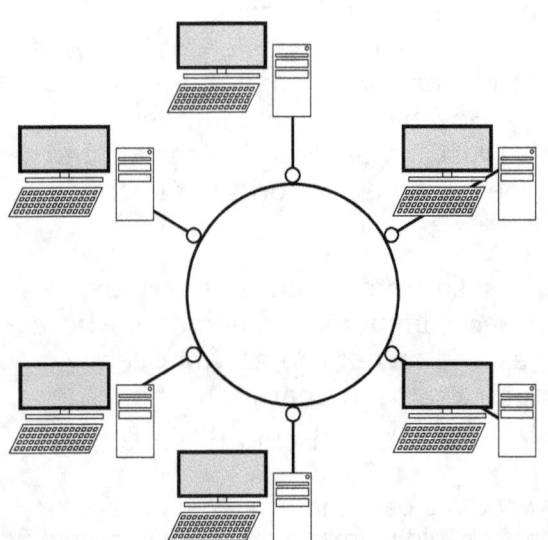

Star configurations, with individual cables going to each computer, are much more resilient. A single connection break will only affect one user, the rest will be able to continue working. As a result, despite the added cost of cabling, this arrangement has become very popular.

Users have to log on/login/sign on to a network, with a username and password that uniquely identifies them. All users will have a profile that will include settings listing which printers and other resources they can use and allocating a maximum amount of space they can take up on the file server. Logging on helps maintain network security, by controlling who can gain access and supports network management through services like resource monitoring and allocation.

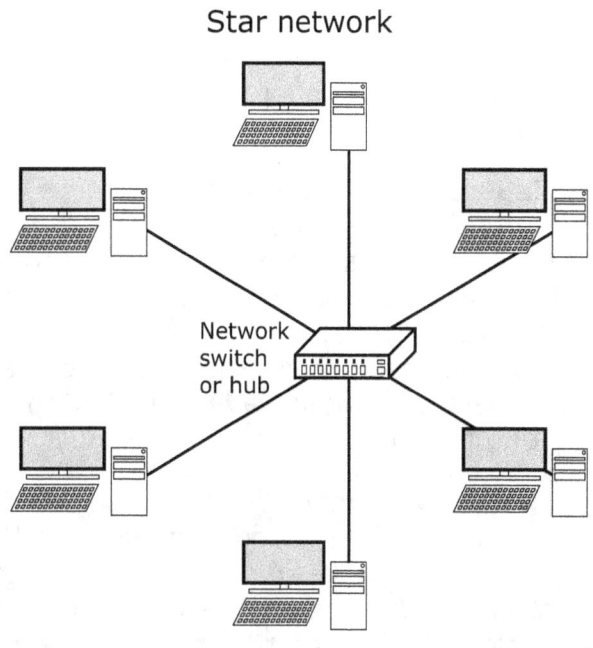

Star network

Networks are also classified according to their scope, although the definitions are slightly vague. A local area network (**LAN**) will connect a group of computers that are in close proximity; a single office, single building or group of adjacent buildings. A wide area network (**WAN**) spans a larger geographic area such as between cities or countries and connects a number of LANs. The intermediate term metropolitan area network (**MAN**) is used for those networks that are bigger than a LAN, smaller than a WAN and may, for example, cover a single metropolitan area. Some university campus networks are referred to as MANs.

Network hardware

Traditionally networks were "hard wired", i.e. local connections were made using copper cable, with the possibility that the telephone network was used for long

Representative LAN configuration

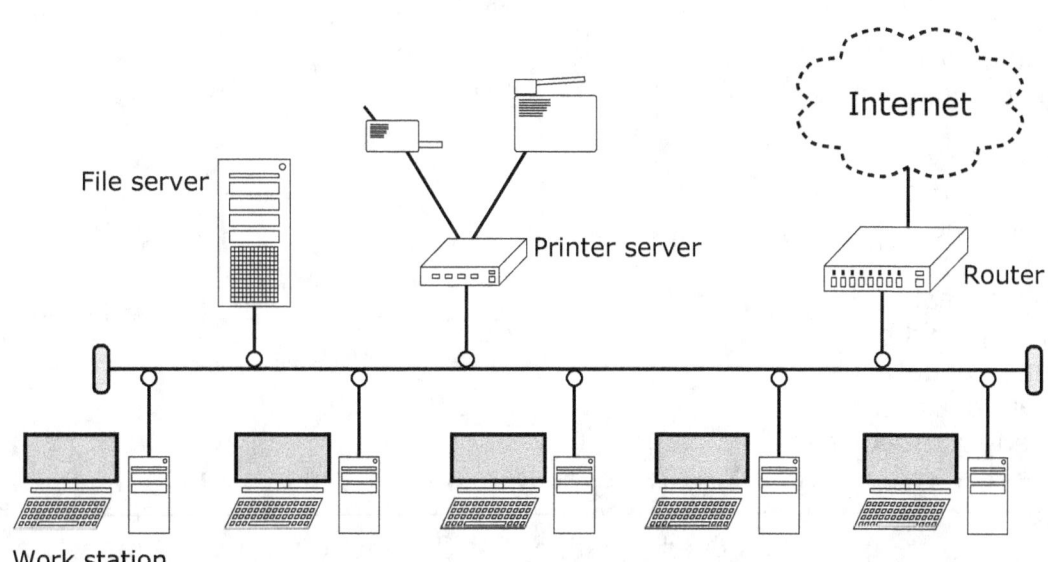

distance connections. Today various wireless technologies, including the use of satellites, are also employed. High speed, long distance communications are often provided by optical fibres, rather than copper wires. However copper still dominates the last mile or so, connecting directly into many homes and other premises.

An industry group that was to become the **Wi-Fi Alliance**, first came together in 1999 to develop standards to drive forward wireless networking technology. The term Wi-Fi™ was coined in 2000 and this technology has seen rapid worldwide adoption. It has either replaced or augmented network connections to many networks, is the default connection medium in many homes and has helped boost the popularity of mobile devices. The availability of Wi-Fi connectivity has become an expectation when travelling, staying in hotels, eating in cafés and restaurants, visiting museums, in fact, pretty much everywhere.

A **hub** allows computers to be connected together, for example, as required for the star topology. They used to be favoured on cost and simplicity grounds. However, when a hub receives data it broadcasts this to all connected computers, which means that they end up having to share the available bandwidth (network capacity). The alternative is to use a **switch**, which is able to determine which computer data is intended for and only send it there. This makes the network much more efficient. Now that switches have become much more affordable, they are usually preferred over hubs.

Routers are devices for joining computer networks together, using wired or wireless connections. They contain a processor, memory and input-output interfaces.

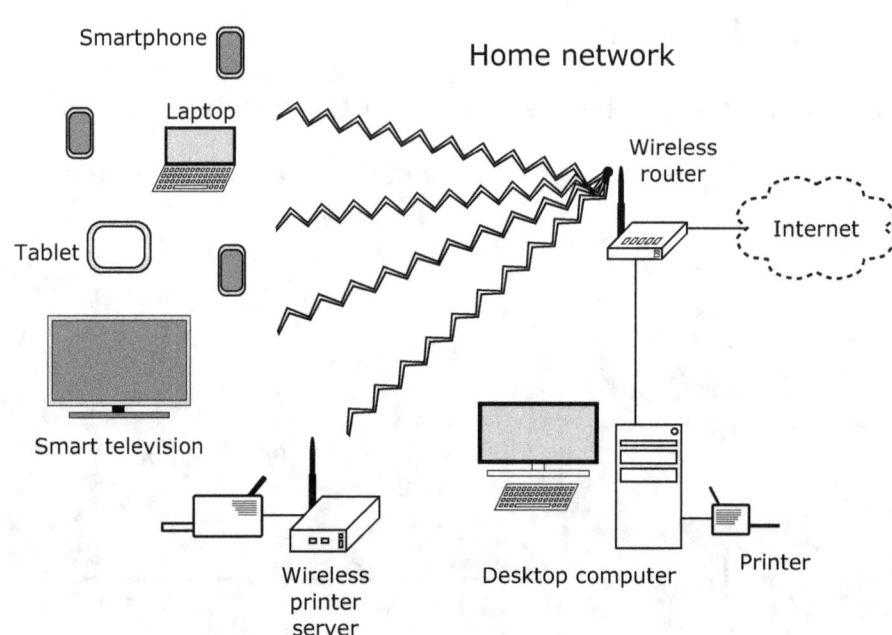

Routers receive, analyse and move data from one network, onto another. If required, they can alter the way that the data has been 'packaged' to make it compatible with the destination network. Wireless routers are commonly used in the home in order to connect the home network to the internet. The inconvenience and technical difficulty of setting them up used to mean that the vast majority of homes did not use any form of network. Devices worked as isolated computers, alleviated only when they were plugged into a phone line to access the internet. Now commercial internet providers offer wireless routers, requiring minimal setting up and making it easy to connect the gamut of domestic internet-enabled devices; laptops, tablets, smartphones and other so-called "smart" devices, such as televisions, fridges and home heating controls.

A **firewall** is a network security device that monitors incoming and outgoing network data ("network traffic") and decides whether to allow or block specific traffic based on a defined set of security rules.

Networks usually employ a firewall to assist with security. It can be included as part of a router, it may be a separate hardware device or it may simply be software that runs on a general purpose computer. The security rules can be configured or amended by the network administrator. Home users are often able to use firewall software that comes with their computer's operating system or has been downloaded separately.

Ethernet

Ethernet networking technology was developed by Xerox PARC (Palo Alto Research Center, California) in the early 1970s. Commercially introduced in 1980, it appeared as a published standard (IEEE 802.3™) in 1983. It has become a dominant technology, used in LANs, MANs and WANs. Originally based on a bus topology using coaxial cable, the more recent variants use twisted pair cable (the same as telephone cabling; much easier to work with and cheaper) and optical fibres, in conjunction with hubs or switches. The original data transfer rate was just under 3 megabits per second (Mbit/s), maximum speeds have since reached 100 Gbit/s and will continue to increase.

Ethernet has shown itself well able to grow and adapt to changing times. The now ubiquitous 802.11™ standard for wireless networking is based on Ethernet and promoted by the Wi-Fi Alliance. Most computers and many other devices are supplied with built-in Ethernet capability.

The Internet

The internet is a global interconnection of a huge number of networks. A metanetwork (network of networks) perhaps, or a meganetwork (a single, giant, network). It is an amazing phenomenon, owned by nobody, controlled by nobody, constantly evolving, amorphous. Ethereal, its precise structure cannot be seen clearly, as though obscured by a cloud and often referred to as, "The Cloud".

Global brain?

Is the internet a global brain? Certainly if it does not already contain the vast majority of recorded human knowledge, that day cannot be too far away. But the

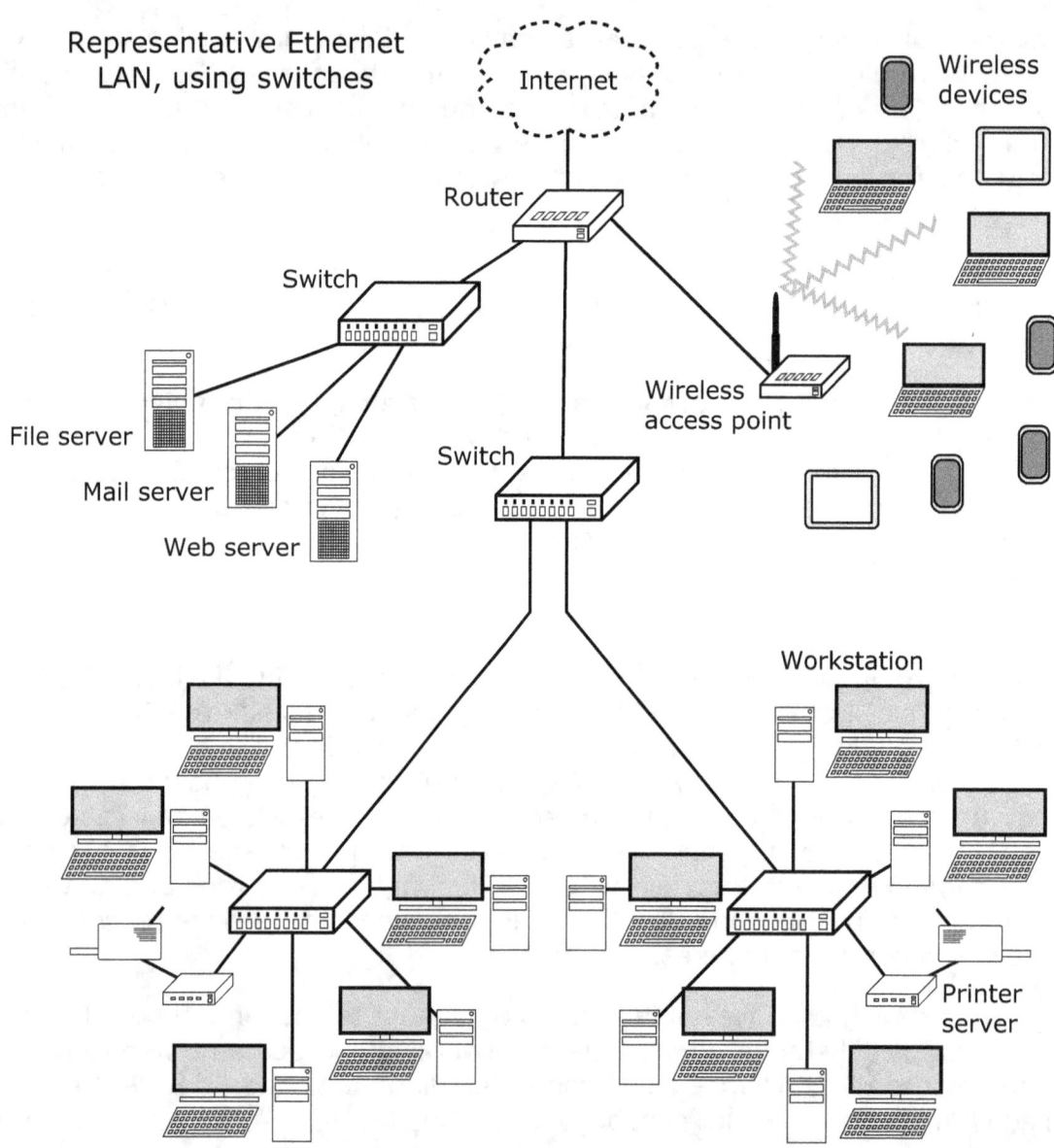

similarity with an organic brain goes further. Each person connected to the internet can connect with others, not dissimilar from neurons (brain cells), each of which can connect with up to 10,000 other neurons. Those internet connections that are used the most will strengthen over time, whilst those that fall into disuse will whither and fade. The connection between two neurons also changes over time, the more that one is used, the stronger it becomes, which is why skills improve with practice.

Groups of people who work together or collaborate regularly using the internet will form their own informal communities, similar to the way in which functionally related neurons connect together to form neural networks. The internet is constantly developing and evolving and the brain exhibits plasticity, being able to adapt its physical structure. This happens the most early in life, as the immature brain organises itself. However it also happens throughout adulthood as something new is learned or memorised and as part of the compensation process should brain injury occur. The structure of the internet can grow and shrink as investments are made and withdrawn by those operating internet-connected equipment. If there is a hardware failure anywhere, the internet can carry on largely as before, as the hardware is repaired, replaced or decommissioned. Using a distributed control model, as opposed to centralised control, gives the internet great resilience. Individual users and commercial providers will come and go over time.

A brain can suffer from conditions and illnesses that impair its performance. The internet can suffer from malicious activities such as spam, denial of service attacks and computer viruses that can seriously affect performance and have the potential to spread via network links.

Internet services

As noted earlier, the terms "internet" and "World Wide Web" are sometimes used synonymously, but this is incorrect. The World Wide Web is perhaps the best known internet service, but it is only one of several. The internet is the single, global computer network, which can be used to access various services. The services that are used the most are **email** and the **World Wide Web** (WWW).

The ways in which the different services operate are laid down in a series of rules or protocols known as the **internet protocol suite**. FTP (File Transfer Protocol) allows the transmission of binary and ASCII text files, for example when downloading a document from an internet source. The Session Initiation Protocol (SIP) governs aspects of instant messaging and internet telephony (voice and video). It often works in conjunction with the Real-time Transport Protocol (RTP) which deals with media streams (audio and video). Telnet is an older protocol that allows users to log in remotely to computers over the internet, whilst IRC (Internet Relay Chat) allows real-time discussions. Interest-based discussion groups can be facilitated by USENET, another older protocol, the predecessor of discussion forums.

Users access some of these via their web browser and most will be unaware that they are using different services.

The World Wide Web is made up of text documents that can include hypertext links that lead to other resources (including video, images, files and other web pages). These resources are identified by their URL (Uniform Resource Locator or web address) and can be accessed by clicking on the appropriate hypertext link. Graphics and photographs can be displayed along with text.

Self test

1. List ten things a computer can help you with.
2. What is a computer network?
3. Give two disadvantages of computer networks.
4. How can you characterise a client/server network?
5. Why is backing up data important?
6. How might data be lost?
7. What are the three main types of network topology?
8. What item of hardware is needed at the centre of a star network?
9. What is the difference between a LAN and a WAN?
10. What is the difference between a switch and a router?
11. What is a firewall?
12. What are the most widely used internet services?

Living in a digital world - Chapter 4: Computer networks and the internet

Answers:

1. List ten things a computer can help you with.
   Any ten reasonable answers. Hopefully having to come up with ten applications provided a bit of a challenge!

2. What is a computer network?
   The linking of individual computers so they can communicate with each other.

3. Give two disadvantages of computer networks
   Some examples: Additional hardware to buy. Cost of design, installation and management. Easier to hack into from outside. Easier for malware like viruses to spread.

4. How can you characterise a client/server network?
   Servers provide resources and clients consume them. For example, file servers provide centralised storage for users and print servers provide access to printers.

5. Why is backing up data important?
   Backing up data is important because its value is likely to far exceed the cost of the hardware. This is due to the time and effort that has gone into its creation and perhaps the difficulty of recreating it if the original is lost. For many businesses and organisations certain data can be essential for smooth, effective, day to day operations.

6. How might data be lost?
   Hardware problems such as a faulty hard disc drive, computer virus, fire, flood, or theft.

7. What are the three main types of network topology?
   Bus, ring and star.

8. What item of hardware is needed at the centre of a star network?
   Switch or hub.

9. What is the difference between a LAN and a WAN?
   A LAN connects computers in close proximity, whereas a WAN can span large geographic areas, e.g. between cities or countries.

10. What is the difference between a switch and a router?
    A switch connects groups of computers in a network, whereas a router connects networks together, for example, a router is used to connect a home network to the internet.

11. What is a firewall?
    A firewall controls in- and out-bound network traffic, enforcing a set of security rules.

12. What are the most widely used internet services?
    Email and World Wide Web.

Internet governance

It has already been said that nobody owns or runs the internet. However, the internet only works because all the linked computers that form the network are following the same set of rules and protocols. It is the same with the different image formats that exist. They only work because the details of the formats have been published and can be followed by software developers all around the world.

There are different groups operating cooperatively to create the policies and standards that maintain the interoperability of the internet, for the general good of all that use it. ICANN (Internet Corporation for Assigned Names and Numbers), based in California, looks after some key aspects, including domain names and internet addresses. It ensures that addresses are not duplicated, just as GS1 maintains the value of EAN numbers, by ensuring that these are unique identifiers for retail and logistics purposes.

The Internet Engineering Task Force takes care of the internet's core protocols, IPv4 and IPv6 (IP = Internet Protocol). According to their website, "The Internet Engineering Task Force (IETF) is a large open international community of network designers, operators, vendors, and researchers concerned with the evolution of the Internet architecture and the smooth operation of the Internet. It is open to any interested individual."

In 2005 a United Nations sponsored summit established the Internet Governance Forum (IGF) that meets annually to facilitate stakeholder discussion of public policy issues related to the internet. The IGF's mandate includes fostering the sustainability, robustness, security, stability and development of the internet.

History of the internet

Interest in networking computers took off around the 1950s and by the early 1960s it was possible to login to time sharing services, accessing a mainframe computer remotely, connecting via a telephone line. The first commercial networks started appearing around this time, although it was not possible for different networks to communicate with each other, initially.

The Advanced Research Projects Agency (ARPA, later renamed Defense Advanced Research Projects Agency or DARPA) was formed by US President Dwight Eisenhower in 1958, in response to the early lead in space exploration taken by the Soviet Union. Eisenhower did not want to be taken by surprise again in matters of technology. Part of ARPA's work was in computing and projects were supported at different universities across the USA. There was a growing community of researchers who wanted to develop computers beyond being giant, glorified calculators. However, it became clear that a lot of money was being spent duplicating expensive computing resources and that the existing infrastructure did not support effective academic collaboration.

Living in a digital world - Chapter 4: Computer networks and the internet

---------- Packet switching illustration ----------

MESSAGE: Dear Father Christmas, please bring me a diamond tie pin as I have been very good this year. Thank you. Love Mark

This message contains 113 characters. Suppose that the standard data packet contains 30 characters. The message will be broken down as follows.

```
Dear Father Christmas, please

bring me a diamond tie pin as

I have been very good this yea

r. Thank you. Love Mark&&&&&&&
```

The final packet has 7 padding characters added to make it up to the 30 character standard size. Each packet has a header added, as well as a hash value for error detection.

Header
From: A
To: G
Packet: 1 / 4

Data: Dear Father Christmas, please

Header
From: A
To: G
Packet: 2 / 4

Data: bring me a diamond tie pin as

Header
From: A
To: G
Packet: 3 / 4

Data: I have been very good this yea

Header
From: A
To: G
Packet: 4 / 4

Data: r. Thank you. Love Mark&&&&&&&

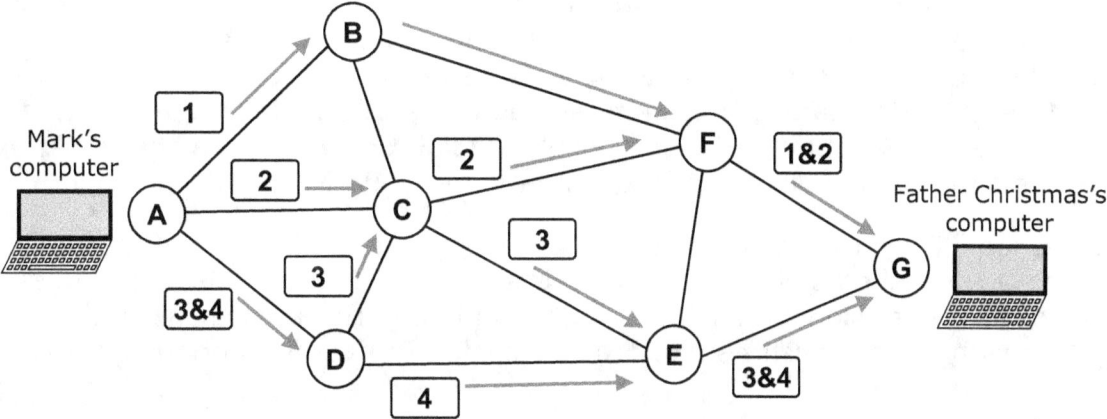

The data packets go onto the network at computer A. Each packet can then follow its own route to the destination, depending on how busy each node (computer) on the network is. Packets can also be routed to avoid any nodes experiencing technical difficulties. The packets can be reassembled correctly at computer G, regardless of the order they arrive, since each packet is numbered. If any packets go missing or contain errors, a message can be sent back to computer A asking for them to be retransmitted.

ARPA's first head of the computer research programme was JCR Licklider. He came from MIT[1] where he had published his ideas for a "Galactic Network" (1962), a globally interconnected set of computers that allowed data and programs to be accessed from any site.

Leonard Kleinrock, also of MIT, published a paper on a key underlying technology, **packet switching**[2] in 1961. Instead of requiring a constant connection when downloading data, in the manner of early telephone calls (known as circuit switching), the data is divided up into a series of equal sized packets. These can be sent independently and reassembled at the receiving computer.

UCLA was chosen to host the first node of the network that was to be known as ARPANET. The hardware was installed in 1969 and the second node at Stanford Research Institute was added shortly afterwards. By the end of the year, two more network nodes had been added at UC Santa Barbara and the University of Utah.

Fifteen sites had been added by the end of 1971, with a large demonstration of ARPANET's potential taking place in 1972. This was the year that the first big network application, **email**, was introduced. One of the critical design principles was that there would not be one computer in overall control of the network. In terms of scope it is interesting to note that the 32-bit IP (internet protocol) addresses only allocated 8 bits to identify the particular network on ARPANET. It was clearly assumed that there would not be more than 256 networks on ARPANET, which would remain a relatively small-scale national network.

The term "internet" started being used as a shortened version of "inter-networking", the joining of different networks. The internet protocol suite was standardised in 1982 and over time organisations other than ARPA, together with various governments, became important contributors of research funding. Public commercial use of the internet began in 1989, it was no longer solely for academic use and rapid growth followed. ARPANET, as a specific project within the US Department of Defense, was decommissioned in 1990. The first web page was served towards the end of 1990 and people outside CERN[3] (where The World Wide Web was born) were invited to join this new community in 1991.

It is perhaps fitting that it is very difficult to identify a precise moment, or event, that can be described as the invention of the internet. Instead there have been a series of policy decisions, technical developments and research collaborations, together with the establishment of broad-based, international working groups, that

---
[1] Massachusetts Institute of Technology (USA)
[2] Some sources credit Welsh computer scientist Donald W. Davies with developing this data transmission concept.
[3] CERN acronym comes from Conseil Européen pour la Recherche Nucléaire, it is now known as the European Organisation for Nuclear Research/Organisation européenne pour la recherche nucléaire.

have contributed to getting the world to where we are today and ARPANET played an important part.

The World Wide Web (WWW)

It is easier to tie down the start of the World Wide Web. Englishman Sir Tim Berners-Lee set out his vision for what would become "the web" in his 1989 document titled "Information Management: A Proposal". By October 1990 he had written the three fundamental technologies that underpin the web. These are:

HTML: **HyperText Markup Language**. The formatting language for the web.

URI/URL: **Uniform Resource Identifier/Locator**. The unique address that is used to identify to each resource on the web.

HTTP: **HyperText Transfer Protocol**. Allows linked resources from across the web to be accessed.

At the time of writing, Sir Tim Berners-Lee is Director of the World Wide Web Consortium (W3C), which has developed standards for the web from its launch in 1994. He is also Director of the World Wide Web Foundation, which began in 2009 to "advance the open web as a public good and a basic right."

The deep, dark web

The terms "deep web" and "dark web" refer to two different aspects of the WWW. The **deep web** is those parts of the web that are not indexed by standard search engines, such as Google, Bing, Yahoo, Baidu, DuckDuckGo and Yippy. The deep web encompasses many standard uses of the internet, such as email and online banking, as well as services that are protected by a "paywall", i.e. they require a subscription or some form of payment. This includes some online newspapers and magazines and other private sites that require the use of a login.

The areas of the internet that are indexed by standard search engines are referred to as the "surface web". An iceberg analogy is commonly employed to explain that the surface web covers but a small part of the whole web, like the portion of an iceberg that sits above the water. More massive by far is the deep web, like the portion of an iceberg that lies below the surface.

By contrast, the **dark web** hosts material that has been intentionally hidden and cannot be accessed using a standard web browser. It forms a small part of the deep web and is designed to allow users and websites to maintain their anonymity, if used properly. This appeals to those concerned with their privacy and the extent to which some companies and organisations are harvesting data from our use of the web - the subjects we are searching for, the websites we are visiting and so on. It also appeals to those who wish to stay hidden for nefarious purposes. There are occasional lurid stories in the press that talk of a dark, murky, frontier type of environment.

Living in a digital world - Chapter 4: Computer networks and the internet

World Wide Web as an Iceberg analogy

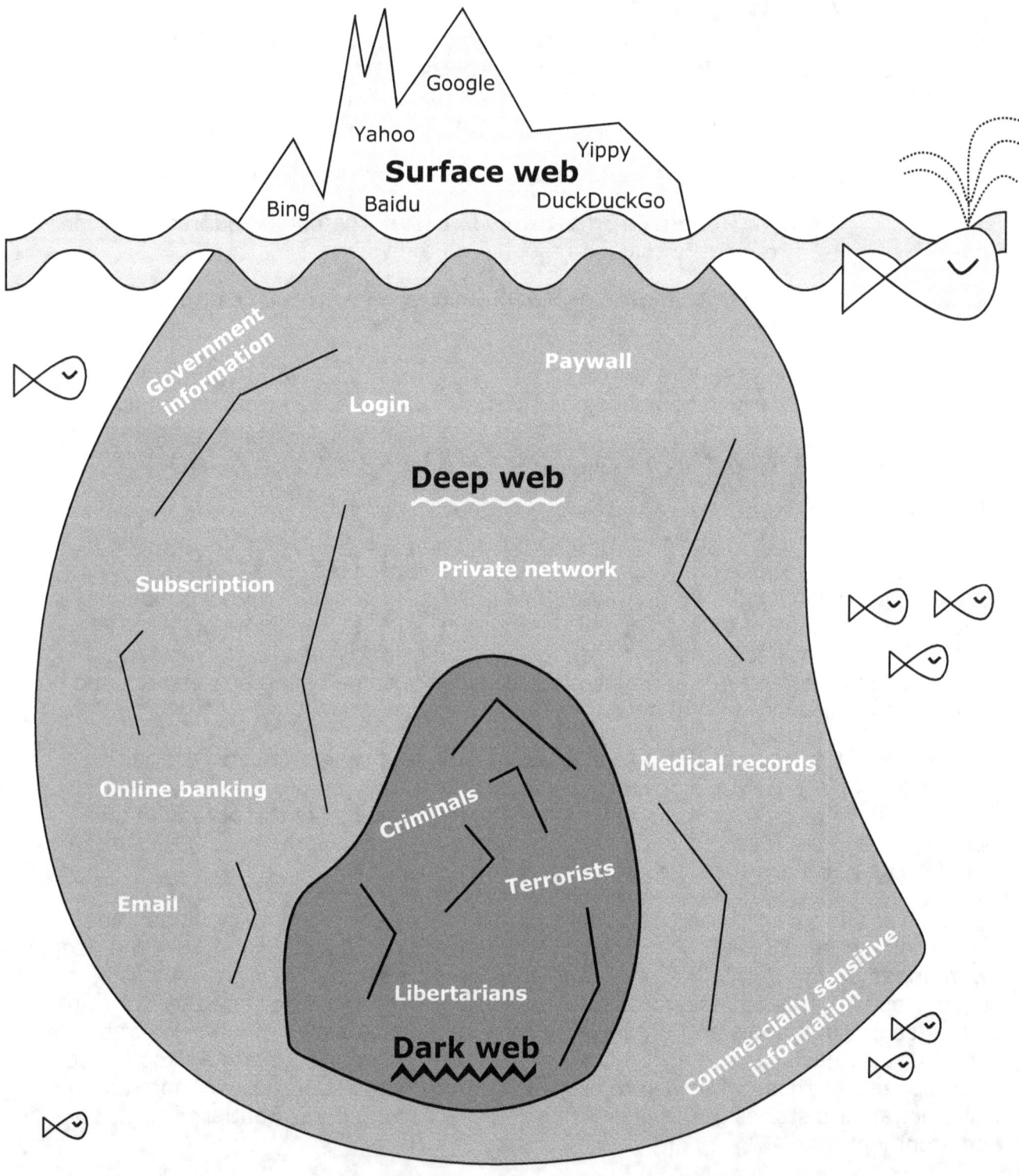

A place frequented by organised criminals and terrorists, where you can purchase drugs, buy weapons, order an assassination and access images of abuse.

No doubt some of this activity goes on (as it does in the surface web) and in 2015 a judge in the USA gave a life sentence without the possibility of parole to Ross Ulbricht. He was convicted of being the mastermind behind the Silk Road dark web marketplace, dubbed the criminal version of eBay. However, it is presumably just as easy for police and security agencies to use the anonymity of the dark web, to set up sting operations and target criminal activity, as it is for criminals to trade their wares. The Silk Road marketplace was set up in 2011 and closed down by 2013, suggesting significant vulnerability.

The Guardian newspaper (UK) posed the following question. "Who is Ross Ulbricht? A libertarian who championed internet privacy out of deep personal conviction, or a ruthless felon who appreciated that secrecy was integral to the successful operation of his multimillion-dollar criminal enterprise?" The US court clearly felt it was the latter.

The internet and in particular the web, has helped to democratise information by making it much harder to control centrally. Governments, as well as big commercial and other organisations tend to want to control and direct. Some want to censor and suppress. This means there is a natural tension between them and the idea of an open internet. At the same time, there will be those who will use opportunities to operate anonymously to impose themselves on others, whether by criminal or terrorist activity or by spreading hate and intolerance. Debates about freedom and privacy versus security and the common good are likely to be ongoing so far as the internet, and especially the web, is concerned. It will be important that as many people as possible get involved, since the decisions taken may have far reaching ramifications for all of us.

Web versions

Like the internet, the web is continually evolving and developing and, in truth, there is no such thing as Web version 1 and Web version 2. However, when the term Web 2.0 was coined it did mark a fundamental milestone or tipping point.

In the early days of the web ("Web 1.0") information was posted on websites by relatively few people and most users would simply visit websites and read or download this information. These pages were often pretty static in nature and the information on them would remain untouched, unless they were manually edited.

Over time improvements in technology brought about websites with greater user interactivity and collaboration, along with greater network connectivity and enhanced communications. Tools like news feeds, RSS and links to social media posts make is easier for websites to be much more dynamic and for users to receive information that is automatically updated in response to external events.

Today users have much richer opportunities for adding their own input through forums, blogs, microblogging, social networking, social bookmarking and curation and other forms of content generation. Users have been transformed from being mostly passive consumers of content to co-contributors. This step-change was labelled "Web 2.0".

It also prompts a follow-up question. What will Web 3.0 look like? It has been suggested that this might be the "Internet of Things" where a myriad of internet enabled digital devices unobtrusively share data throughout each person's environment creating a ubiquitous computing nirvana.

In 2009, Sir Tim Berners-Lee gave a TED Talk arguing for getting more data onto the web in a linked, accessible form - interesting given that one of the issues facing ARPA back in the 1950s and 1960s was academic collaboration. He highlighted how social networking sites generate a great deal of data, but then tend to act as silos, making it difficult for others to access and use this data. Other organisations, including governments, tend to exhibit this silo mentality, although sometimes this is because of a genuine concern regarding the right to privacy of individuals. Collaboration and sharing has been a significant benefit of the internet to date, can we take that on to the next level?

Google Flu Trends was an interesting project that demonstrated the potential value of connected data. It was based on the "digital refuse" of individual internet searches. An analysis of the topics people were using the Google search engine to look for, was employed to help predict large-scale flu outbreaks. For example, a sudden spike in the number of people looking up flu symptoms, details of nearby pharmacies and other related medical searches, could indicate the arrival of an epidemic. In isolation this data might prove volatile, but linked with medical data being collected through regular channels, the approach could produce an enhanced prediction tool.

There was a report suggesting that Google Flu Trends was able to detect outbreaks of flu in the USA up to 14 days faster than the existing reporting mechanism. The methodology certainly showed promise and a similar tool was developed for dengue. However, following some erratic performance, the programme was ended, but it did illustrate how search engine data might be used to better understand current issues and large scale behaviours. Perhaps with further research, more reliable tools will emerge.

> **Practical task:** Reflect on what you would like the internet and in particular the World Wide Web, to become. What services would you like to be able to access? What do you think are the main opportunities in front of us and what are the key threats? Can you find any online videos to help with your reflections?

Markup Languages

Markup languages are for the processing, definition and presentation of text. The term comes from the practice of marking up documents, for example those being sent to printers, often using a blue pencil. This colour was chosen as it would not reproduce when the document was printed using certain lithographic or photographic techniques. Markup languages use codes instead, these are embedded with the text in the same way as blue pencil annotated comments and also do not show on the final document. These codes are called **tags**.

HTML - The language of the web

HTML stands for Hypertext Markup Language, where hypertext is text that includes hyperlinks to other pages and resources. It is the language that is used to produce web pages.

It is based on humble text files. These can simply contain ASCII/Unicode text characters. This makes it possible to produce web pages by "hand coding" using a plain text editor, such as Notepad. There are lots of software tools around that make it easy to produce highly formatted web pages, but a little hand coding can be fun and it demonstrates just how simple the ideas behind web pages are.

Formatting and other instructions needed to produce an engaging web page are coded using HTML tags. All tags appear within the symbols < and >.

The majority of tags always occur in pairs - a start tag and an end tag. To make text appear bold, it must be surrounded by **** and ****. For example:

Author: Mark C. Baker, 2018 *appears as* Author: **Mark C. Baker**, 2018

, makes text italic whilst <sub> and <sup> tag pairs produce subscript and superscript text. There are a few tags that do not appear in pairs, they have no end tags. A horizontal line across the page can be produced using <hr> (for *horizontal rule*), whilst <br> produces a line *break*.

The paragraph tag <p> is something of a special case. In the first version of HTML this was used *on its own* to mark the end of each paragraph (note that browsers ignore the ENTER end of line character, as well as multiple space characters). In later versions of HTML what you could do with the <p> tag was extended and it made sense to surround the paragraph to which it applied, with a <p>, </p> pair.

As a result of trying to maintain compatibility with earlier versions, many browsers will be able to deal with lone <p> tags, particularly on desktop or laptop computers. However, you cannot be sure that this will always work, especially with the browsers on smartphones, which have to be smaller (and therefore simpler), since phones have fewer computing resources available to them. Therefore, these tags should always be used in <p>, </p> pairs.

Hello World!

There is a programming convention, known as the Hello World! program. When learning a new programming language, the starting point is often to produce a program that will output the text "Hello World!" on screen. This is taken as being the simplest type of program that can be written and therefore introduces all the bits that have to be included BEFORE you can start to produce something functional. It introduces basic program structure.

The same thing can be done with HTML and it can be seen on the right. The DOCTYPE declaration at the top is not an HTML tag as such, it is an instruction to browsers to tell them what type of document will follow.

The start and end of the page is marked with **<html>**, **</html>** and within that there is a header section (**<head>**, **</head>**) and a body section (**<body>**, **</body>**).

Hello World web page

```
<!DOCTYPE html>
<html>

<head>
<title>Hello World Page (Title)</title>
</head>

<body>

<p>Hello World!</p>

</body>
</html>
```

The appearance of the Hello World! page is shown above.

The header can contain a range of information, that does not appear directly on the web page. In this example there is simply a title, which appears either on the browser tab, or frame of the browser window. The web page content appears in the body section and in this case is just the words "Hello World!"

To view the file, it should be saved with a **.htm** or **.html** extension, not .txt, which is the usual default for simple text editors. With the correct extension, double clicking on the file should load it into the default browser.

To edit this page, changes are first made using the text editor. These changes must be saved and then the refresh button must be clicked on the browser, to load in the new version of the page.

Typical refresh button

This basic page needs to be extended in order to produce useful web pages.

A representative web page

The next step is to extend the Hello World! page to include all the key elements expected on a basic web page - text with a range of **formatting**, together with one or more **images** and one or more **hypertext links**.

Photographs and other graphics can be included on a web page by using the <img> tag.

<img src="newbury.jpg" alt="Newbury, West Mills" style="width:304px;height:228px;">

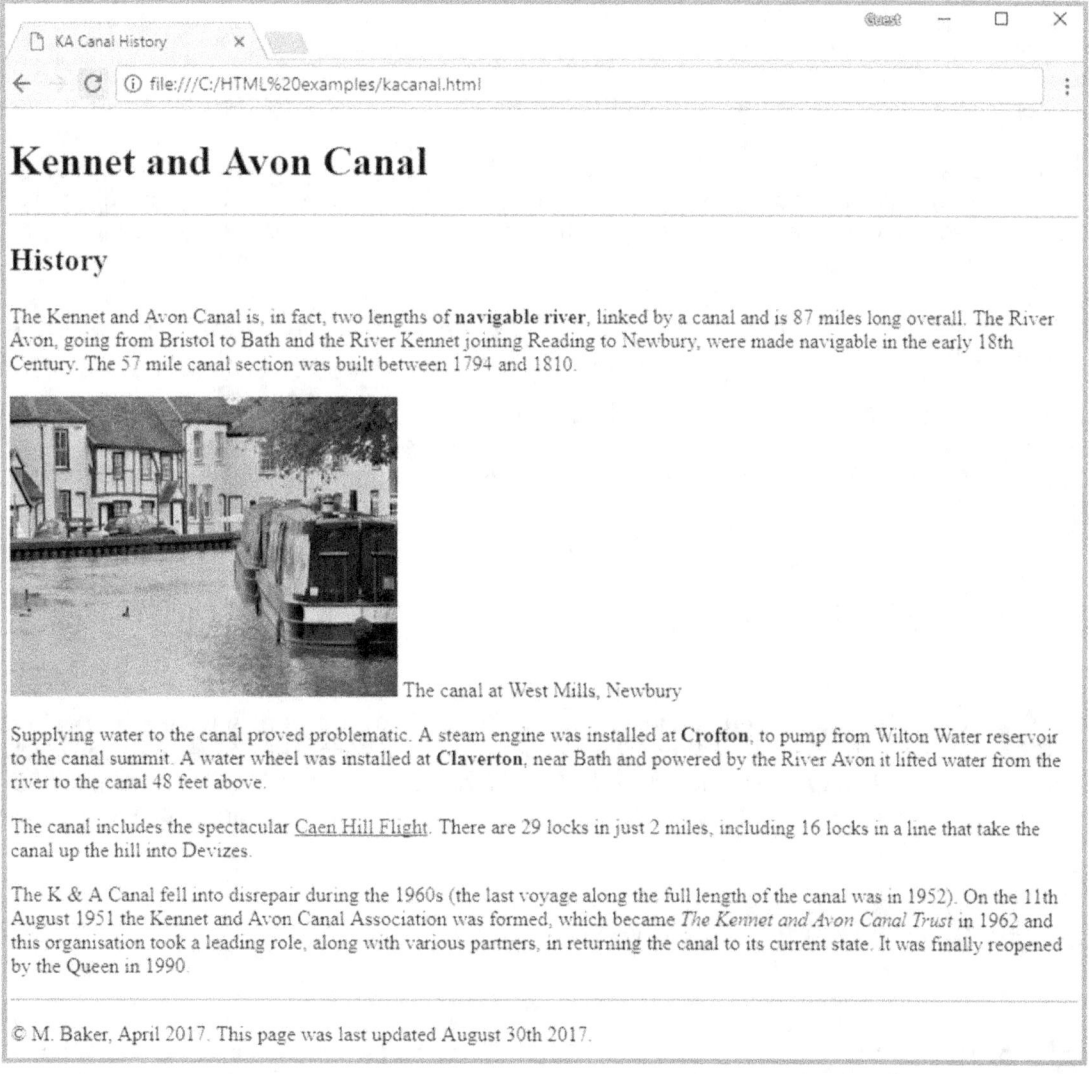

The src value gives the filename and path so that the browser can find the image file. In this case just the filename is given, so this will only work if the image file is stored in the same folder as the web page HTML file. The src value could be a full URL if an image from the internet was being used.

Kennet and Avon Canal web page - html

```html
<!DOCTYPE html>
<html>

<head>
<title>KA Canal History</title>
</head>

<body>

<h1>Kennet and Avon Canal</h1>
<hr>
<h2>History</h2>

<p>The Kennet and Avon Canal is, in fact, two lengths of <b>navigable river</b>, linked by a canal and is 87 miles long overall. The River Avon, going from Bristol to Bath and the River Kennet joining Reading to Newbury, were made navigable in the early 18th Century. The 57 mile canal section was built between 1794 and 1810.</p>

<img src="newbury.jpg" alt="Newbury, West Mills" style="width:304px;height:228px;"> The canal at West Mills, Newbury

<p>Supplying water to the canal proved problematic. A steam engine was installed at <b>Crofton</b>, to pump from Wilton Water reservoir to the canal summit. A water wheel was installed at <b>Claverton</b>, near Bath and powered by the River Avon it lifted water from the river to the canal 48 feet above.</p>

<p>The canal includes the spectacular
<a href="https://canalrivertrust.org.uk/places-to-visit/52-caen-hill-locks">Caen Hill Flight</a>.
There are 29 locks in just 2 miles, including 16 locks in a line that take the canal up the hill into Devizes.</p>

<p>The K & A Canal fell into disrepair during the 1960s (the last voyage along the full length of the canal was in 1952). On the 11th August 1951 the Kennet and Avon Canal Association was formed, which became <i>The Kennet and Avon Canal Trust</i> in 1962 and this organisation took a leading role, along with various partners, in returning the canal to its current state. It was finally reopened by the Queen in 1990.</p>

<hr>
<p>&copy; M. Baker, April 2017. This page was last updated August 30th 2017.</p>

</body>
</html>
```

Kennet and Avon Canal web page - labelled

```
<!DOCTYPE html>
<html>

<head>
<title>KA Canal History</title>              top level heading
</head>

<body>

<h1>Kennet and Avon Canal</h1>
<hr>  ←······································· horizontal rule (line)
<h2>History</h2> ←······································································ 2nd level heading

<p>The Kennet and Avon Canal is, in fact, two lengths of <b>navigable river</b>, linked by a canal and
is 87 miles long overall. The River Avon, going from Bristol to Bath and the River Kennet joining Reading
to Newbury, were made navigable in the early 18th Century. The 57 mile canal section was built between
1794 and 1810.</p>
                    image (photograph)                                           image size in pixels
<img src="newbury.jpg" alt="Newbury, West Mills" style="width:304px;height:228px;"> The canal at
West Mills, Newbury
                                                      text to display if image cannot be found

<p>Supplying water to the canal proved problematic. A steam engine was installed at <b>Crofton</b>,
to pump from Wilton Water reservoir to the canal summit. A water wheel was installed at
<b>Claverton</b>, near Bath and powered by the River Avon it lifted water from the river to the canal
48 feet above.</p>
                                          URL of hypertext link      page text that will form
                                                                     the hypertext link
<p>The canal includes the spectacular
<a href="https://canalrivertrust.org.uk/places-to-visit/52-caen-hill-locks">Caen Hill Flight</a>.
There are 29 locks in just 2 miles, including 16 locks in a line that take the canal up the hill into
Devizes.</p>

<p>The K & A Canal fell into disrepair during the 1960s (the last voyage along the full length of the canal
was in 1952). On the 11th August 1951 the Kennet and Avon Canal Association was formed, which
became <i>The Kennet and Avon Canal Trust</i> in 1962 and this organisation took a leading role, along
with various partners, in returning the canal to its current state. It was finally reopened by the Queen in
1990.</p>

<hr>
<p>&copy; M. Baker, April 2017. This page was last updated August 30th 2017.</p>

</body>         copyright symbol
</html>
```

However, that would mean the image was under somebody else's control and could be moved or renamed in the future. The **alt** value is the text that will be displayed should the browser be unable to locate the specified image file. Finally, the **style** values give the display size of the image, in pixels.

Hypertext links are added by using the **<a>** anchor tags.

<a href="https://canalrivertrust.org.uk/places-to-visit/52-caen-hill-locks">Caen Hill Flight**</a>**

This link points to a page about the Caen Hill lock flight on the Canal and River Trust (CRT) website. The href value gives the URL of the page and the <a>, </a> pair surrounds the 'hot' text that will form the hyperlink. In this case, the words **Caen Hill Flight** will be coloured blue and underlined (the default format for a hyperlink) on the web page. Clicking anywhere on these words will cause the CRT page to be loaded by the browser.

> **Practical task:** Create a new folder and use a plain text editor to make the Hello World! example. Save the file in your new folder and open it with your chosen browser. Add some additional text - can you get the new version to appear on screen?
>
> Add four spaces between **H** and **e** and press ENTER three times after the word **H   ello**. Save the file and refresh the browser. What do you see?
>
> Use the **
** tag to display **Hello** and **World!** on different lines.

Metadata

Metadata can be added by using the **<meta>** tag within the <head> section. It does not appear on the page, but can be used by search engines to understand what the page is about and by browsers to understand how the page should be displayed. Some examples are given below.

<meta name="keywords" content="Kennet, Avon, Canal, Trust, history, river, water">

<meta name="description" content="Brief history of the Kennet and Avon Canal">

<meta name="author" content="Mark C Baker">

<meta http-equiv="refresh" content="120">

The first example allows the page author to list key words that can be used when search engines are indexing the page. When other users make searches, the degree to which their search terms match with the keywords will affect whether this page will be included in the search results and how far up the list it appears. Each search engine uses its own algorithm to produce search results and a whole range of factors may be taken into account, not just any keywords that are listed.

The second meta tag allows the page author to define a short description of the page, whilst the third tag gives the name of the author(s).

The final meta tag ensures the page will be refreshed every 120 seconds. This is not necessary for the example page, where the content is likely to remain static for long periods of time. Indeed, it may never be changed. However, if the page was displaying breaking news items or sports scores then this would be important, to ensure that the information shown was up to date.

Specifying colours on web pages

There is a predefined list of 140 colours that can be used by name. These include some obvious names, such as blue, cyan and DarkGrey. There are also some names that would do credit to the marketing department of a paint company, such as AliceBlue, AntiqueWhite, BlanchedAlmond, LavenderBlush, PeachPuff, SteelBlue, Thistle and WhiteSmoke.

However, page designers can specify precise colours using the 24-bit RGB colour model seen previously. A number system called hexadecimal is used, with two digits each to represent the amount of red, the amount of green and the amount of blue. LightSteelBlue is represented by #B0C4DE, where red=B0, green=C4 and blue=DE.

Hexadecimal is base 16. It requires 16 digits, representing 0 to 15, but we only have the digits 0 to 9. Letters A to F are pressed into service for the digits 10 to 15. The hexadecimal column headings are 1, 16, 16 x 16... or 1, 16, 256... Fortunately it is often just the first two columns that are needed.

Counting to twenty in hexadecimal goes like this:
1, 2, 3, 4, 5, 6, 7, 8, 9, A, B, C, D, E, F, 10, 11, 12, 13, 14

$14_{hex} = 1 \times 16 + 4 = 20_{10}$

$B0_{hex} = 11 \times 16 + 0 = 176_{10}$

$C4_{hex} = 12 \times 16 + 4 = 196_{10}$

$DE_{hex} = 13 \times 16 + 14 = 222_{10}$

$FF_{hex} = 15 \times 16 + 15 = 255_{10}$

Encountering hexadecimal for the first time, it might seem like a bizarre choice of number system. Its beauty is that it is a wonderful accompaniment for binary and the two systems can

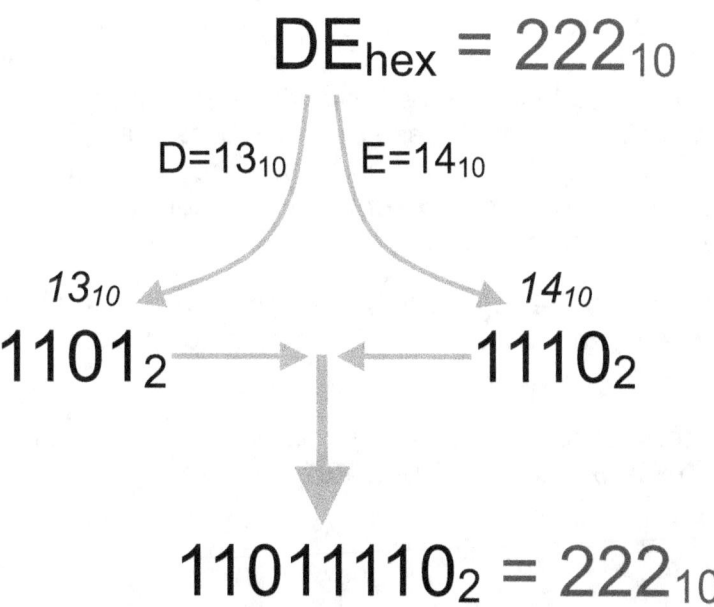

be converted from one to the other really easily. It is used where binary would be the most appropriate choice, but something that is easier for humans to use would be helpful.

To convert from hexadecimal to binary, you take each hex digit and, ignoring place value, convert it into binary. Stick the individual binary chunks together and this is the binary equivalent.

14_{hex} = 0001 0100
= 00010100_2
(= 20_{10})

$B0_{hex}$ = 1011 0000
= 10110000_2

Converting from binary to hexadecimal is equally straightforward.

10100011_2 = 1010 0011
= A   3
= A3

01101101_2 = 0110 1101
= 6   D
= 6D

The 24-bit RGB colour model allows for 256 shades of each of the three primary colours (0-255) which requires exactly two hexadecimal digits per colour, or six for the full definition. So the colour represented by #B0C4DE means 176 red, 196 green and 222 blue, if using decimal numbers.

Page background colours and font colours used to be part of each web page. However, over time cascading style sheets have been developed (CSS), which allow formatting instructions for a whole website to be kept centrally. This makes maintenance much easier and reduces the effort required in producing each page. As a result, the following has been removed from later HTML versions to discourage its use, however browsers should be able to deal with it and it is an easy way to play around with colours, when hand coding.

Changing the top **<body>** tag to **<body bgcolor ="#B0C4DE">** and the page background colour should be changed to LightSteelBlue. *Note the US spelling of colour.*

Alternatively colour names can be used, for example, **<body bgcolor="PeachPuff">**.

As you might expect, #000000 is black and #FFFFFF is white, since in hexadecimal, these represent *no red, no green, no blue* and *full red, full green, full blue* respectively.

Remember, using *bgcolor* is considered bad HTML and has been removed from later versions of the language. It is suggested here only as a quick way of experimenting with colours defined using hexadecimal and colour names.

Hand coding HTML allows a minimalist approach to be taken in terms of the amount of code used. The Hello World! page can be opened in a word processor and saved as a web page, using a new file name. If this is opened with a plain text editor there is likely to be a significant amount of additional HTML that has been added by the software - none of it strictly necessary. This extra code may be referred to, somewhat uncharitably, as bloat.

> **Practical task:** Either in a new folder or in the one created for the Hello World! page, create a new HTML file. Choose your own topic, but try and include a range of formatting, one or more images and at least one hyperlink. Use the Kennet and Avon Canal page as a guide.
>
> *Extension 1:* Look up some additional HTML tags to enhance your page. At the time of writing, the website **https://www.w3schools.com/** has a comprehensive guide and includes an environment in which you can practice.
>
> *Extension 2:* Open a word processor and start a new document. Type in the words, "Hello World!". Save the file as a Rich Text File (.rtf). Open this with a plain text editor, such as Notepad.
>
> Can you find things that you can recognise? The formatting instructions are given inside curly brackets or braces {}, rather than the inequality signs <> used by HTML. There should be some mention of one or more fonts and some RGB colour definitions. Can you find your *Hello World!* text? If you cannot, try using "Edit-Find".
>
> *Extension 3:* To view some raw HTML, view a web page using a browser and choose the *View-Source*, *Page Source* or similar option from the menu. You may need to look under *Developer* or *Developer Tools*. This works better with some websites than others, but you should be presented with the underlying HTML that the browser is using to produce the finished page.

Putting pages on the World Wide Web

For pages to be available to others to view on the World Wide Web at any time, they need to form part of a website and be hosted (stored) on a web server that is permanently connected to the internet.

A website is a series of HTML pages linked together using hyperlinks. There is normally one home page, which is the page that visitors first arrive at. The function of the home page is to help visitors to find their way to the page or pages that are of interest to them, so it acts rather like the table of contents in a document. The diagram below shows the structure of a canal website made up of seven pages.

Structure of a simple website

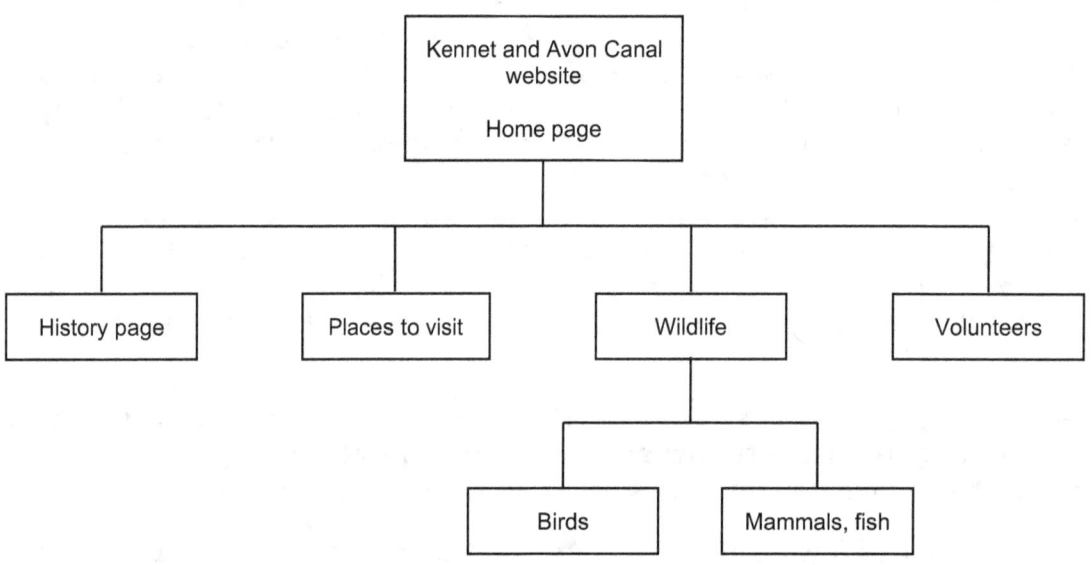

If a domain name is entered into a browser, such as educationvision.co.uk, a browser will normally load up the website's home page. Historically, these had one of two filenames, either index.html or default.html. In the case of this example, the home page URL (or colloquially, the "web address") is
http://www.educationvision.co.uk/index.html.

Most browsers can happily deal with URLs where the **http://** and the **www.** parts are missing, so users often just type in the required domain names, which are relatively easy to remember. A browser must then use the internet's **DNS** (**Domain Name System**) to look up the requested domain name and find out its **IP address** (Internet Protocol address). This is made up of numbers, which would be difficult to remember. The IP address can then be used to fetch the relevant home page. Thus the DNS is acting rather like a phone directory, converting domain names to IP addresses.

For most home users, making a website available involves finding a commercial provider, who will host the pages on their web server. This may come at no additional charge, as part of an internet connection package. Alternatively there are organisations providing website hosting services, either free of charge or as a paid service. Large or specialist organisations may choose to own and operate their own web server(s), rather than use a commercial service. Some website hosting services include online templates or software allowing the production of web pages without users needing to install specialist software themselves.

XML and the SVG graphics format

The SVG or Scalable Vector Graphics format is written in **XML**, which stands for e**X**tensible **M**arkup **L**anguage. XML looks like HTML, but there are some very important differences.

HTML is designed to display data, focusing on how that data looks and is presented. XML is designed to carry data, focusing on what data is. HTML uses a whole raft of predefined tags, the meaning of which can be looked up in an appropriate reference guide. These include <p>, <br>, <hr> and <h1>. XML has **no** predefined tags, document authors must define both the tags and the document structure.

As XML uses plain text files, it provides a method for storing, transporting and sharing data that is completely independent of the hardware being used, since all hardware can handle plain text files. XML is designed to be both human and machine readable, as HTML is.

The **SVG** format was developed to define vector graphics for use on the World Wide Web. It includes support for animation and interactivity. Since SVG images are described using text, they can be searched, indexed, scripted, and compressed. The authors of the SVG format have defined a whole range of tags to describe different types of graphic elements.

The simplest way of seeing how the SVG format works is to embed a graphic in a web page. The following code would produce a web page with a heading and a single circle. The SVG code is shown in bold.

<html>
<body>

<h1>Drawing a circle with text...</h1>

<svg width="400" height="400">

  <circle cx="150" cy="150" r="100" stroke="DarkOrchid"
  stroke-width="8"
fill="yellow" />

</svg>

</body>
</html>

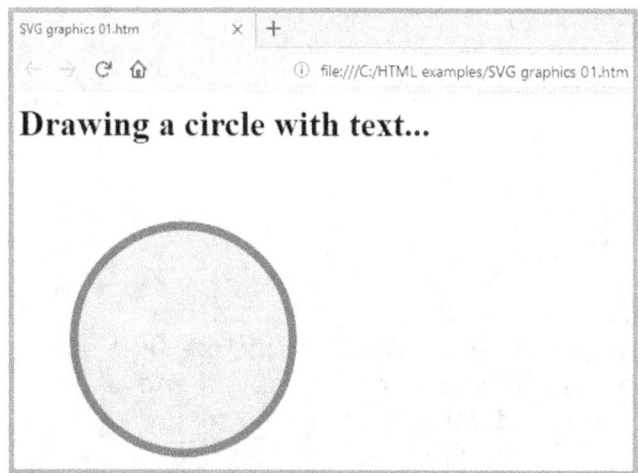

The **width** and **height** values give the size of the graphic in pixels, whilst **cx** and **cy** are the 'coordinates' of the centre of the circle. This is measured from the top left hand corner of the graphic, the cx value going from left to right and the cy value from top to bottom. The circle radius is given by **r**, **stroke** is the line colour and **stroke-width** is the line width in pixels. The fill colour is given by **fill**.

Different graphic elements can be added and a whole range of properties described. The next example includes rectangles and lines, with both colour names and decimal RGB values being used. One of the rectangles is partially transparent.

```
<html>
<body>

<h1>Adding elements...</h1>

<svg width="400" height="400">

  <circle cx="150" cy="150" r="100" stroke="DarkOrchid" stroke-width="8" fill="yellow" />

  <rect x="190" y="190" width="80" height="40" style="fill:rgb(255,255,0);stroke-width:4;stroke:rgb(0,0,0)" />

  <rect x="40" y="80" width="60" height="20" style="fill:rgb(0,255,0); fill-opacity:0.4;stroke-width:2;stroke:rgb(0,0,0)" />

   <line x1="67" y1="20" x2="175" y2="200" style="stroke:rgb(100,100,100);stroke-width:3" />

  <line x1="67" y1="20" x2="155" y2="80" style="stroke:rgb(100,100,100);
stroke-width:3" />

   <line x1="67" y1="20" x2="135" y2="30" style="stroke:rgb(100,100,100);
stroke-width:3" />

</svg>

</body>
</html>
```

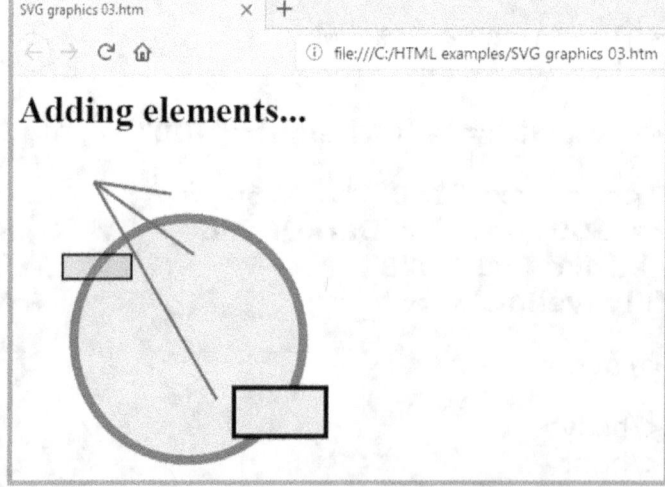

To convert this web page to a Scalable Vector Graphics picture file, all the HTML must be removed and some additional code added to say what the file is and the version of SVG that is used. If you have a vector graphics program on your computer, you can see this by creating a simple graphic, saving it as an SVG file and then opening this file in a plain text editor.

> **Practical task:** Use a plain text editor to make a simple web page with an SVG circle on it.
>
> *Extension:* Add other elements and experiment with their properties. Go online to find out about some of the different drawing elements not covered here and some of the properties that you can control.

Streaming

Typically when a file is downloaded over the internet, the entire file is copied from the source computer to the destination. This does not cause any difficulties when the file is an HTML web page as these simply contain text and tend to be relatively small. The same is true of many documents. However, if the file contains a sound recording or video then it could be very large indeed. It could take many seconds, minutes or even longer before it can be copied to a user's computer and played. Video conferencing, video chat or live broadcasting add the problem that often it is not known when the session will end, or the session will be very long. Those taking part in the conference, or watching or listening to the broadcast, will want to be using the data in real time, as it is happening and not wait to the end when a complete data file could be created and made available.

These problems are overcome by sending out a steady stream of data, that a user's computer can use immediately to form small pieces of the overall video, music or broadcast. If these pieces can be sent out quickly and reliably enough then the user will experience a continuous event. This approach is known as **streaming**.

Suppose that a user wants to view a short video clip of a cat riding a skateboard. Having clicked on the appropriate hyperlink, a request would be sent to the relevant video server via the internet. The diagram below represents the situation part way through viewing the video. Suppose that the video clip will be divided into 12 data packets. The video server has sent 8 packets so far, 6 of which have been received by the user, 2 are still being sent over the internet. Of the 6 that have been received, 2 have been viewed and could be discarded. However, these are likely to be retained temporarily in case the user wants to rewind or replay the video. Packet 3 is currently being viewed, with 4, 5 and 6 waiting in the buffer. Packet 9 is being prepared for transmission, with the data for packets 10-12 waiting for attention.

Clearly streaming can only be contemplated when the data stream can be processed and transmitted quickly enough. If some of the packets are delayed, the receiving computer could run out of data. This would lead to the music or video stopping and starting periodically and potentially becoming unusable. This

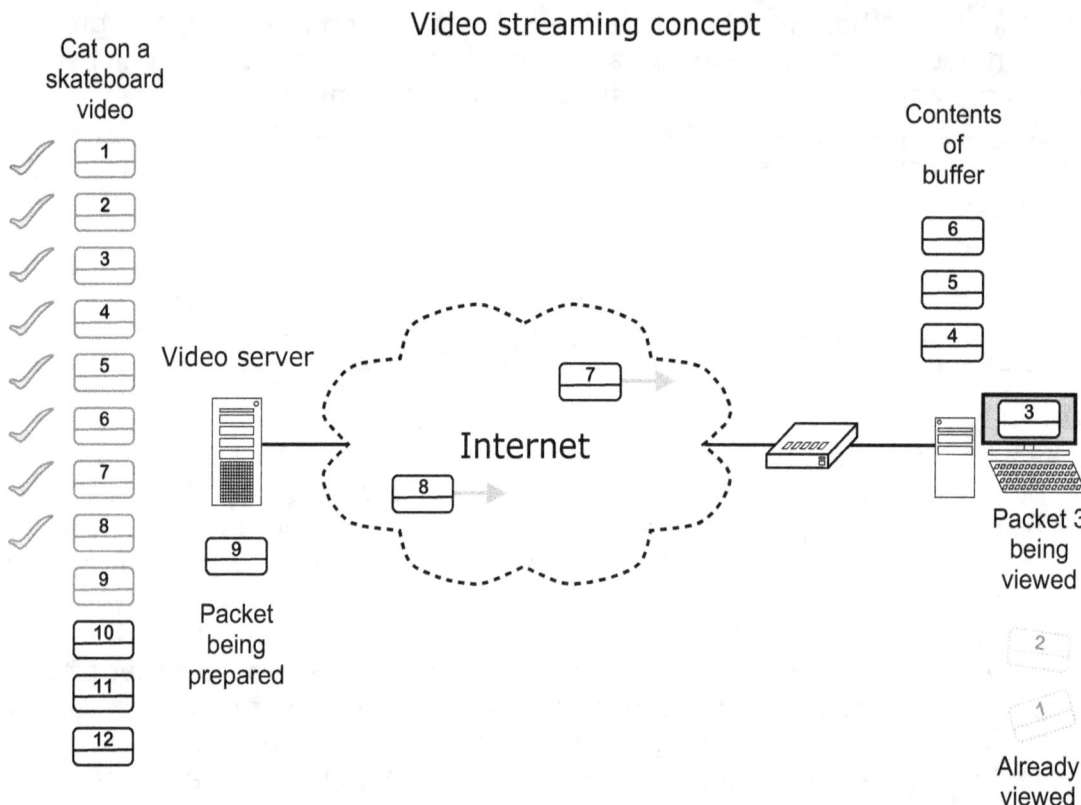

Video streaming concept

technique has only become popular relatively recently as internet connection speeds have increased.

To try and ensure that a user can receive data without any stopping and starting, the aim is to send it out more quickly than it can be used. The excess data is then stored temporarily in memory. This is known as a **buffer** and it can fill and empty depending on how quickly data is getting through; hopefully fast enough to smooth things out and give the user a continuous piece of audio or video.

If the buffer empties and the receiving computer needs to wait for more data to arrive, the message "*Buffering...*" often appears.

To have the best possible experience when streaming requires data to be transmitted with the best possible efficiency. As well as using the fastest possible internet connection speed, the amount of data that is needed should be reduced wherever possible. File compression can be used, however since the data has to be made available in real time, there is a balance to be struck between the degree of compression that can be achieved and the processing time required at both ends to firstly compress and then decompress the data. When viewing video users may be offered different resolutions. Low resolutions are more likely to be viewed smoothly and continuously since much less data has to be transmitted, however the visual quality will be poorer. The same is true of the quality of any transmitted sound.

One issue with streaming is that it is, usually, "unicasting", since each person following a live event, viewing a video or listening to a music track, receives *their own stream* and this uses up a lot of valuable internet bandwidth. Multicasting allows many users to share the same stream and is particularly valuable to popular broadcasting services such as the BBC, ITV and Sky (UK). However whilst this has been a research area for some time, the technical complexities mean that it is not currently widely available.

Web caching

The term cache is used to describe an additional memory store that is designed to speed up future requests for the same data. Caches can be either hardware or software components and can occur in different places. They work on the proven principle that when a particular data location has been accessed it is often the case that the same or related locations will be accessed again in the near future.

The relevant data can be stored in a cache. Hard disc drives are often fitted with a small amount of semiconductor memory for this purpose. This is relatively expensive, but it can be accessed much more quickly. The next time the same data is requested it can be delivered from the cache. If the data sits in the cache for a while and is not requested again, it can be over-written with newer data.

Caches have been found to significantly improve performance in a wide range of situations. Many CPUs have a cache that sits between the processor and the main memory (RAM). Most personal computers use a software web cache when browsing the internet. Users often return to the same pages and having a cache means that page content can be displayed, without having to download it via the internet more than once, saving time and reducing the internet bandwidth that is used. The content is normally stored on the computer's hard disc. Some schools have invested in hardware caches (stand-alone computer controlled 'boxes') recognising that pupils will often be accessing the same pages, images, videos and other resources, often under teacher direction, leading to significantly improved performance.

One disadvantage of a web cache is that some pages are dynamic and change over time. The version of a page that is in a user's web cache might be out of date. Packet headers can include a date/time when a page becomes 'stale' and 'expires', automatically signalling that the cache version should be deleted and a new copy downloaded. As seen earlier, web pages can include metadata to tell browsers how often they should be updated. Browsers also have a refresh button, so that users can manually ensure they have the latest version of important pages.

Internet search engines

One of the strengths of the internet is that it is a mind-bogglingly vast repository of information. This could also be a serious weakness, since at any time the information that is wanted could prove inaccessible, because it is buried amongst all the rest and cannot be found. Even a list of all the pages on a particular topic could prove useless if there are lots of poor quality pages, hiding a few top quality offerings.

Internet search engines have had a crucial role to play in making the internet usable from relatively early on and this continues to be the case. They allow users to enter one or more words as search terms. The search engine then returns a list of, hopefully, relevant web pages.

At the time of writing, the most widely used search engine is Google, to the extent that its name is often used as a verb in everyday speech. It is common to hear people say that they have or are about to google a particular topic. The name Google appears to have come about from a misspelling of the word Googol, which is the number 10^{100} or 1 followed by one hundred zeros. This huge number represented the vast amount of data that had to be searched.

A Googlewhack is two dictionary words that when entered into Google yield a single result. Finding one is quite a challenge as many obscure two word combinations can still yield tens of thousands or hundreds of thousands of results!

Google's global dominance is growing, with a staggering 80% market share worldwide in 2017. Also-rans with shares of between 5% and 7% were Bing, Yahoo! and Baidu. These are all general purpose search engines.

> **Internet snapshot**
>
> Statistics from:
> http://www.internetlivestats.com
>
> 8th September 2017,
> approximate time - 15:30 BST
>
> **Per second:**
> 62,400 Google searches
> (equates to 5.4 billion per day)
> 2,620,000 emails sent
> 71,000 YouTube videos viewed
> 48,212 GB of internet traffic
> 2750 Skype calls
> 1300 Tumblr posts
> 800 Instagram photos uploaded
> 7750 tweets sent
>
> **There were:**
> 3.7 billion internet users
> 1.25 billion websites
>
> **So far this day:**
> 3.3 billion blog posts written
> 56,000 websites hacked
> 2.3 million MWh of electricity
> consumed through internet use

However, Google is not the most popular search engine in every country. Baidu has the largest market share in China, with Yandex dominating in Russia. Naver leads in South Korea, whilst Yahoo! Japan and Yahoo! Taiwan come top in those countries.

There are various niche search engines, as well as the general purpose ones. Specialist engines cover areas such as maps, images, jobs, property/real estate and question & answer. Metasearch engines use the results from more than one search engine. For example, Dogpile brings together search results from Google, Yahoo!, Bing, Ask.com, and others. Kayak is a metasearch engine that specialises in travel.

Yippy is another metasearch engine, that presents its results in clusters, rather than just a straight list. The search term "cell" brings back clusters under headings including cell phone, stem cell, biology, jail, cancer, fuel cell, terror and cell culture.

Some search engines have responded to concerns about competitors tracking user searches, for example to help target advertisements, by promising not to do this. DuckDuckGo is an example.

WolframAlpha is a computational search engine, using its collection of data, algorithms and methods and responding to searches by carrying out dynamic computations.

Conventional search engines, by comparison, index the web using automated software known as web crawlers. These start at a few 'seed' websites and then proceed by following every web link they find, crawling their way around the web, indexing as they go. When a user enters search terms, each search engine uses an algorithm to try and ensure that the most relevant web pages in their index, for that user, come at the top of their list.

Google famously made its name by incorporating a PageRank score in its algorithm. This uses the premise that better quality pages will be linked to more from other pages. Web pages are therefore ranked based on the number of other pages that link to them and the PageRanks of these pages. This innovation achieved excellent results and quickly established Google as the dominant search engine.

The details of search engine algorithms are commercially sensitive and are kept secret, but will include the degree to which the search terms appear within the text on a web page and how well they match with any metadata for that page. The main search engine companies are constantly trying to refine and improve their algorithms, in response to the relentless growth of web content.

Self test

1. What is packet switching?
2. What are the three technologies that underpin the World Wide Web?
3. What is the difference between the deep web and the dark web?
4. What does HTML stand for and what is it used for?
5. Describe the basic structure of an HTML web page.
6. Convert $A7_{hex}$ to binary.
7. Convert 11111001_2 to hexadecimal.
8. What does SVG stand for?
9. What is streaming?
10. What is a buffer?
11. What is a web cache?
12. What is a metasearch engine?

Living in a digital world - Chapter 4: Computer networks and the internet

Answers:

1. What is packet switching?
   Data that is to be transmitted over a network is divided into a series of standard packets. Each packet can follow its own route to the destination, where the original data can be reconstructed.

2. What are the three technologies that underpin the World Wide Web?
   HTML, URI/URL and HTTP.

3. What is the difference between the deep web and the dark web?
   The deep web are those parts of the internet that are not indexed by standard search engines. It includes subscription services and private networks. The dark web hosts web material that has been intentionally hidden and cannot be accessed using a standard web browser. It is designed to allow users and websites to maintain their anonymity.

4. What does HTML stand for and what is it used for?
   Hypertext Markup Language is used to produce web pages.

5. Describe the basic structure of an HTML web page.
   The start and end of a web page is marked with <html>, </html> tags. Within that there is a header section (<head>, </head>) and a body section (<body>, </body>). Page content must be in the body section. Metadata and other information that does not appear directly on the page is placed in the header section.

6. Convert A7$_{hex}$ to binary.
   10100111

7. Convert 11111001$_2$ to hexadecimal.
   F9

8. What does SVG stand for?
   Scalable Vector Graphics.

9. What is streaming?
   Streaming is a technique for sending out music, video or live broadcast material as a steady data stream.

10. What is a buffer?
    A buffer is a temporary store, e.g. when watching a streamed video, data that has not yet been viewed is kept in a buffer until it is needed.

11. What is a web cache?
    A web cache is a store of web page content, so that if recently visited pages are returned to, the page data is immediately available, without having to download it again via the internet.

12. What is a metasearch engine?
    Metasearch engines, such as Dogpile and Yippy, combine the search results from more than one search engine, to smooth out the bias inherent in each individual search algorithm.

Chapter 4: Key learning points

- A computer network is formed when individual computers are linked so that they can communicate with each other.
- Computers are much more powerful when they are networked. This allows information and file sharing, communication and the sharing of expensive hardware resources and high speed internet connections.
- Data backups should be made regularly.
- A local area network (LAN) connects computers that are in close proximity. A wide area network (WAN) spans a much larger geographic area, normally connecting multiple LANs.
- The internet is a global network joining a great many networks together - a massive network of networks.
- The internet is not owned or governed by anyone. There are various international groups that take care of different aspects, ensuring that there are standard rules and protocols for everyone to follow, ensuring interoperability as the internet grows and develops.
- A key internet technology is packet switching. Instead of sending data altogether, at once, it is broken down into a series of equal sized packets. These are reassembled at the receiving computer.
- The World Wide Web is just one service that can be accessed using the internet. Other services include email and FTP (for transferring files).
- The term "Web 2.0" refers to developments in the WWW that allowed ordinary users to move from being passive consumers of content to being content generators.
- Web pages are produced using HTML. These are text files with embedded text tags, (codes) within < and > symbols. These tags tell web browsers how to present the page and can include page metadata.
- HTML colours can be specified using predefined colour names or six digit hexadecimal RGB values.
- Streaming is often used when sending music, video and live broadcast data. A steady stream of data packets are sent out. As soon as one packet is received, the user can start to listen/watch and providing data arrives at least as quickly as it is being listened to/watched the user experiences a continuous piece of audio or video. Data that has arrived, but not been played yet, is stored in a buffer until it is needed.

- A cache is an additional memory store that speeds up further requests for data that has already been requested or data that is stored near to previously requested data.
- Conventional search engines use web crawler software to automatically index the web. The index is then used to respond to each user search and present a list of relevant pages, selected and ranked according to a search algorithm.

5: How some stuff works

You may have correctly surmised from the title of this chapter that I had some difficulty coming up with a suitable heading. After the chapter on *Algorithms and software* it seemed logical to follow that with a chapter about hardware. As detailed planning commenced however, it soon became clear that it would not be primarily about hardware, rather it would examine a selection of technologies, looking in detail at certain aspects. It also became clear that *Computer networks and the internet* deserved a chapter to itself.

I opted to stay with my working title *How some stuff works* since this actually sums up the chapter very well. Technologies have been chosen, in part, because of their relative importance, although this was not the only consideration. They must also have aspects that are readily accessible to a non-specialist audience and should ideally reinforce or build on ideas encountered in previous chapters.

The choice of topics may, at first sight, appear somewhat eclectic, but they hopefully support the key objective of helping to demystify digital technology.

Handshaking

Handshaking is the term given to the automated "conversation" that takes place between two devices that are trying to connect. Handshaking is also applied to the periodic, on-going chatter between two devices, that supports smooth communication, once data transfer has begun. It could be a computer connecting to a printer or to a server, it could be two smartphones setting up a Bluetooth connection or, in the olden days, two modems connecting via a telephone line.

Modems would sit between each computer and the telephone sockets that they were plugged into, much as a home broadband router does today. They allowed two computers to communicate over a telephone line, by changing binary data into sound when transmitting. When receiving, the sounds were converted back into binary. When the connection was first made, users would hear the phone number being sent, followed by some fairly harsh warbling and squealing noises as the modems at either end of the phone line started handshaking. Usually, once the handshaking had been successfully completed, the modem speaker would be turned off automatically.

A key part of the handshaking process was deciding what speed to communicate at. This would alter depending on the quality of the phone line, which could be variable. The modems would start by trying to communicate at the fastest speed they could both handle. If there were too many errors, the speed would be stepped back until reliable communication was possible.

Hello, I am computer A! I would like to transfer some data to you.

Hello, I am computer B! I am able to receive your data.

I am authorised to connect to you.

That is good, because I am authorised to connect to you!

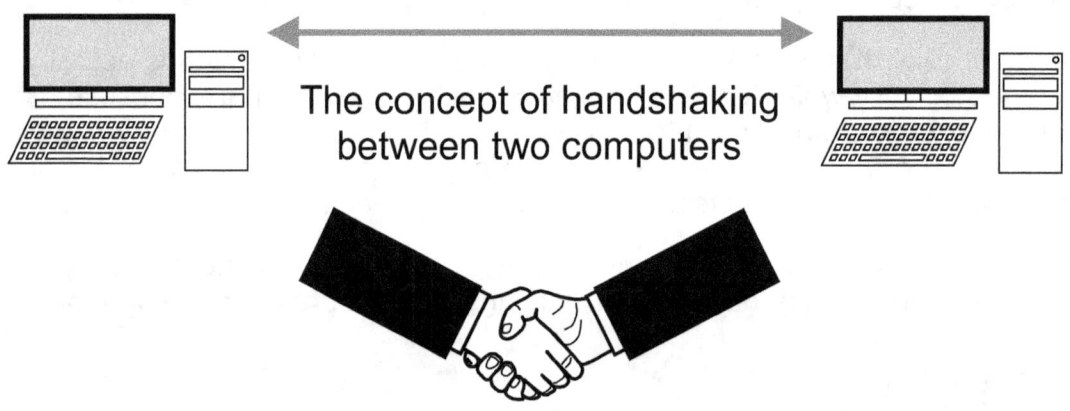

The concept of handshaking between two computers

Which protocol (set of rules) would you like to use while we communicate?

Let's try a quick test and see how quickly we can communicate using this connection today.

Okay, lets start transferring data…

If transmitting text, the handshaking must establish which character code set is to be used. There are also checks to ensure that the two computers are authorised to communicate with each other and to establish the precise communication protocol (set of rules) that will be used. If the data is to be encrypted before transmission then the appropriate details must be exchanged to allow the data to be decrypted when it arrives. The details of any error detection to be used must also be agreed, e.g. if using parity, whether it will be odd or even parity. If sending the data in packets then establishing the composition and size of the packets will form part of the "conversation". Some of these details will be covered by the rules of whichever protocol is to be used and will not need to be negotiated individually.

Universal Serial Bus (USB)

The USB Implementers Forum, Inc. (USB-IF) is a non-profit, industry backed, organisation. It was established in 1995 to support and accelerate the adoption of USB compliant peripherals and is based in the USA. It has very successfully standardised the connection of computer peripherals to personal computers and has become the default means of connection for all sorts of hardware including keyboards, mice, flash

USB type A connector

memory drives, digital cameras and external hard disc drives. As well as allowing data transfer, USB cables can also provide power to peripherals. However, there are limits to this and some higher powered devices are supplied with their own power adaptors, to ensure reliable operation. More recently, USB cables have become the standard means of charging mobile phones, ending the very wasteful practice of manufacturers producing a wide range of proprietary chargers.

USB mini B connector

USB type B connector

A standard USB cable has a type A connector that normally plugs into a computer and may have a type B connector that plugs into the device.

USB micro B connector

However, peripherals like mice and keyboards are usually "hard wired", with a cable exiting the device directly and not via a socket. As well as standard connectors, there are smaller mini and micro connectors to allow greater miniaturisation. These have the same width, but the micro connector is much thinner. It was introduced in 2007 with the aim of replacing the mini connector.

A key use of the micro plug was expected to be with mobile phones, where significant use of charging cables, with potentially rough handling, was expected. The specification therefore called for a more rugged rating of at least 10,000 connect-disconnect cycles, more than the mini B (5,000) and the standard A (1500) connectors.

USB device: Flash memory drive, USB type A connector

USB 1.0 was introduced in 1996 with data rates of either 1.5 Mbit/s (*low speed*) or 12 Mbit/s (*full speed*). USB 2.0 followed in 2000, capable of speeds up to 480 Mbit/s (*high speed*). USB 3.0 debuted in 2010 offering speeds up to 5 Gbit/s (*SuperSpeed*), with lower power consumption and increased power output, whilst remaining **backward compatible** with USB 2.0, i.e. all USB 2.0 devices should be able to work with the new USB 3.0 sockets. USB 3.0 type A and B plugs and sockets incorporate blue inserts for easy identification.

Before the introduction of USB compliant devices, personal computers used a range of parallel and serial interfaces. Setting up a new peripheral could be time consuming and fraught with issues. The USB standard has produced a means of

USB topology

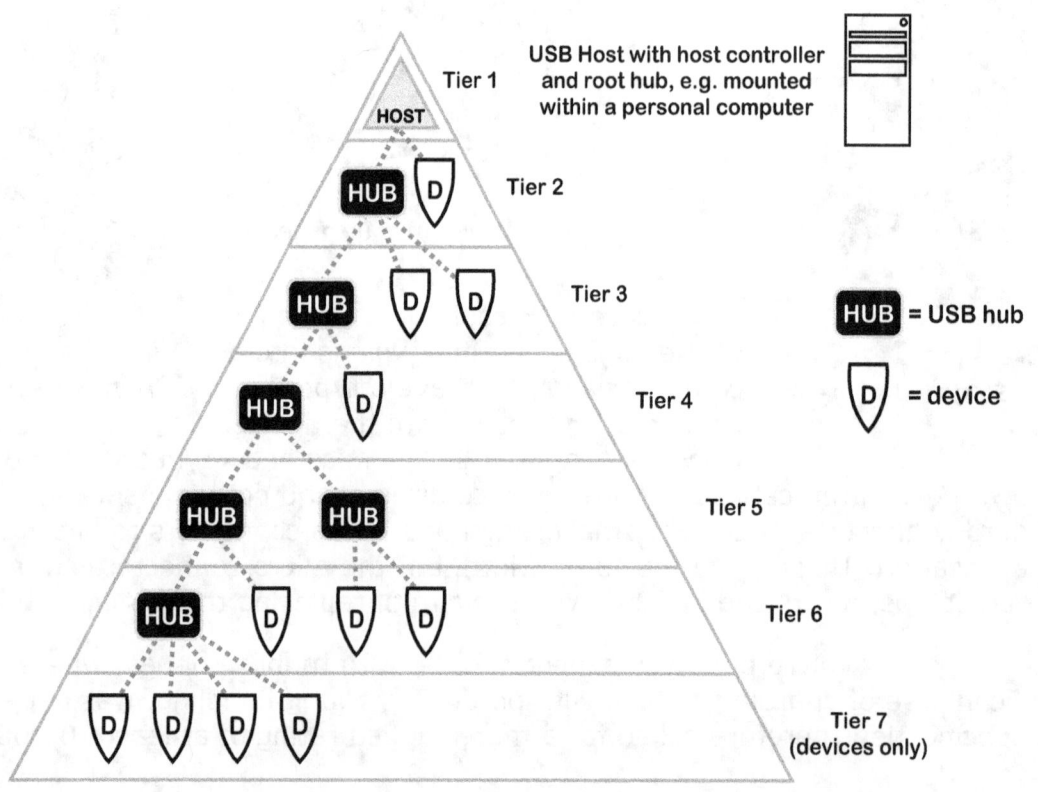

connection that is largely plug-and-play, with the installation of software drivers and the setting up of connections taking place automatically in the majority of situations. The impact of this technology in improving the usability of personal computing devices should not be underestimated.

The USB standard defines the communications protocols, connectors and cables for connection, communication and power supply between computers and other devices.

USB devices connect in what is known as a tiered star topology. A personal computer with USB sockets will contain a USB controller and root hub. That can be either directly connected to USB devices or to one or more USB hubs, which will have multiple sockets into which other devices and hubs can be connected. The chain of hubs and devices can be up to 7 tiers long, but the last tier can only contain USB devices.

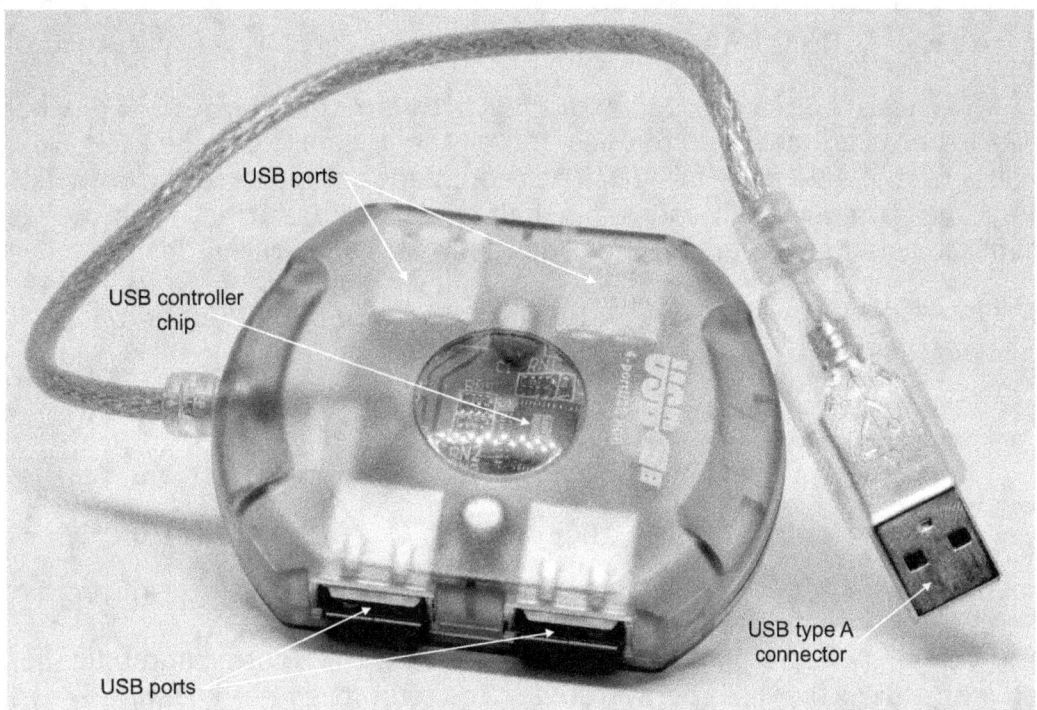

Inexpensive 4-port USB hub

In theory, up to 127 hubs and devices can be connected to a USB host, however you are unlikely to reach that number before running out of power and/or bandwidth, with the service to each device becoming unacceptably slow. Power issues can be alleviated by including hubs and devices in the chain that have their own power supply and do not rely on what the host can deliver.

USB data is transmitted in packets. There are start of packet and end of packet signals, with data in between. The first byte is a packet identifier (PID), a code number that corresponds to a particular meaning and type of packet. There are five types of USB packet, each with their own format. The first packet to be sent in any transaction is a **Token** packet which gives the address of the device or hub that the data is being sent to and the purpose of the transaction. **Data** packets carry the necessary data, whilst **Handshaking** packets are used as required. Finally, **Start Of Frame** and **Split** packets are used as part of the transaction control process.

There are four handshake codes within the PID code set.

Name	Code	Description
ACK	0100	Data packet accepted
NAK	0101	Data packet not accepted; please retransmit
NYET	0110	Data not ready yet (USB 2.0)
STALL	1110	Transfer impossible; do error recovery

All 4-bit PID codes are transmitted with their **bitwise complement** (i.e. what you get if all the zeros are changed to ones and all the ones are changed to zeros; flip each digit), to make up an 8-bit PID. The redundant data is used for error detection. The resulting 8-bit codes are then transmitted, starting with the least significant bit (lsb first, reversing the order as it appears written down).

Name	Bitwise complement	Code	Combined	Transmitted byte (lsb first)
ACK	1101	0010	1101 0010	0 1 0 0 1 0 1 1
NAK	0101	1010	0101 1010	0 1 0 1 1 0 1 0
NYET	1001	0110	1001 0110	0 1 1 0 1 0 0 1
STALL	0001	1110	0001 1110	0 1 1 1 1 0 0 0

The early versions of USB only allowed the USB host to initiate communication. This changed with USB 3.0, which permitted devices to start communication with the host.

Solid state memory

Memory or storage is a critical component of any computing device, being required to store the software that is to be used, any input data and the final output data. Long term, permanent storage, has commonly been provided by various magnetic media, such as magnetic tape, floppy discs and hard disc drives. It is also possible to use punched media, such as paper tape and punched cards and optical media, such as compact discs and DVDs.

All of these media rely on hardware that has moving parts, which makes them less resilient because of the risk of mechanical failure. Another type of memory is solid state memory, where data is stored on semiconductor chips and there are no moving parts. Drop a USB flash memory drive or an SD card and you are very unlikely to lose any data. Drop a hard disc drive and there is a good chance that it will be damaged beyond repair.

Solid state memory is formed from large arrays of certain types of transistor, a basic building block in micro-electronics. Ordinary transistors are simple components, made up of three electrical terminals. Electrons can flow from the **source** terminal to the **drain** terminal (sometimes called the *emitter* and the *collector*). However, that current can only flow if there is a (small) minimum voltage on the third terminal, the **control gate** (or *base*). The transistor therefore can act as a simple switch. Apply a voltage to the control gate to turn it on, remove that voltage to turn it off.

Types of solid state memory

RAM Random Access Memory is unfortunately named, as the access is anything but random, being very precise indeed. "Random" was probably chosen because, unlike sequential media, such as paper or magnetic tape, where data had to be gone through in order, starting from the beginning, a computer could *directly* access any memory location in RAM, at any time. Anyway, the name has stuck.

RAM is described as *volatile memory*, since any software and data contained within it is lost when the power to it is turned off. RAM is relatively high speed, but expensive. It is used on computers, in relatively small amounts, as working memory. If a computer appears to freeze or behaves inappropriately this is often because there is a minor error or bug. Either the working memory has become full or part of the memory has become corrupted (contains errors). The first thing to try is to reboot the computer (turning it off, then on again), which turns the power off briefly, resetting the memory to its blank state, before starting the computer again.

ROM Read-Only Memory is a chip that has software and data permanently formed into it when it is manufactured. It cannot be subsequently altered in any way. If a fault is discovered after a batch of ROM chips have been made, the only solution is to scrap the entire batch, including removing any that have been assembled into products. Each different ROM requires a custom design, which lengthens the production process and increases costs. ROMs are normally only used for large production runs and where any software to be encoded is well proven. This is *non-volatile* memory, since any software and data on the chip is retained when power is turned off.

PROM Programmable Read-Only Memory takes the form of a blank memory chip. High voltages are used to permanently break or make links on the chip (*fuses* and *anti-fuses*), meaning that the chip can be programmed once. Chip costs are kept down since the blank chips can be produced in very large production runs. These are ideal for producing prototypes. First generation software can be "burnt" onto a few PROM chips, which can be assembled into final products and tested. Upgraded software can be burnt onto new chips, until satisfactory performance is achieved. PROM chips may still be used for relatively small production runs, since it is not worth paying for a custom built ROM. The cost of having to program each PROM chip individually for very large production runs, might make a custom ROM more attractive economically.

A major weakness with PROM memory is that to benefit from any improvements to the software made after manufacture, would require the physical replacement of the chip.

EPROM Erasable Programmable Read-Only Memory has a similar physical structure to EEPROM, but is manufactured with a small quartz window over the silicon memory chip. The chip can be reset to its blank state by shining a strong ultraviolet light through this window. Once programmed, the window is often covered with a sticker to prevent accidental erasure. Repeated UV exposure will eventually damage the chip, typically they are capable of around 1,000 rewrite cycles.

EEPROM Electrically Erasable Programmable Read-only Memory can be rewritten electrically. This makes it possible for it to be reprogrammed in situ, without being removed from a product, such as a digital camera or Blu-ray player.

One type of EEPROM is **flash memory**. The most popular version at the time of writing is NAND flash memory, launched by Toshiba in 1987. Modern flash products offer relatively fast rewrite times, high storage capacities and high endurance.

Flash memory transistor, storing binary 1

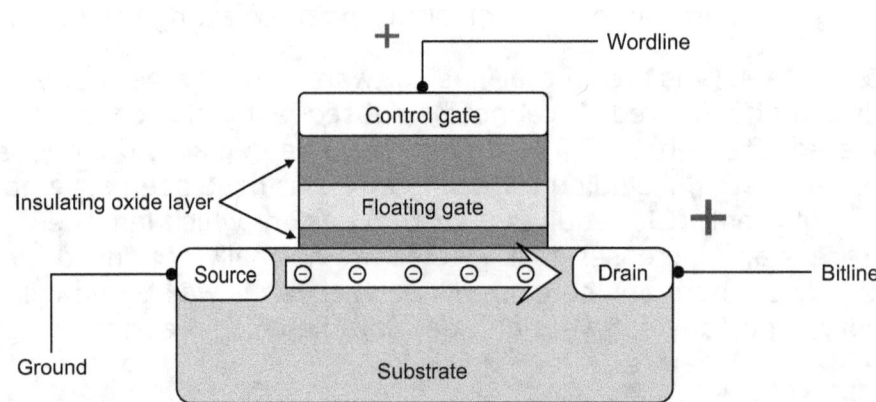

It is not entirely clear why flash memory was so named. One suggestion is that the erasure process was reminiscent of a camera flash going off, another is that things happen "as quick as a flash". Either way, this is another name that has stuck!

How flash memory works

Flash memory transistors are similar to basic transistors, but they have an additional gate, known as the floating gate. This sits within a thin layer of insulating oxide. In its default state, which is represented above, these transistors store binary 1.

As with a normal transistor, applying a small voltage to the control gate will effectively switch the transistor on, so that when a voltage is applied between the source and the drain, electrons can flow. The state of the transistor can be checked by applying this voltage and if there is a current flow then the transistor is storing binary 1.

Flash memory transistor, higher voltage applied

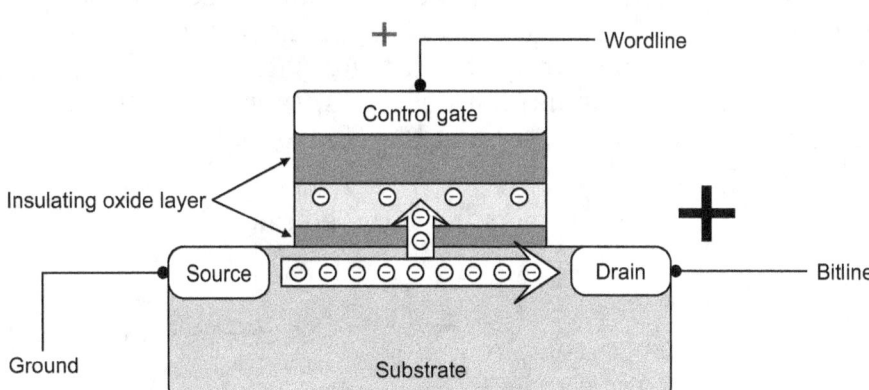

To change the transistor so that it is storing binary 0 a larger voltage is applied between the source and the drain. As before, there is a flow of electrons between the source and the drain. However, the flow is greater and the electrons have more energy. Some of these electrons are able to pass through the thin insulating oxide layer, by a process known as *tunnelling*. However these electrons do not have enough energy to pass all the way to the control gate and when the voltage is removed, they become trapped indefinitely within the floating gate. This gives the floating gate a negative charge.

This negative charge effectively cancels out the effect of the small voltage being applied to the control gate, turning the transistor off. When a normal voltage is applied between the source and the drain to check the state of the transistor, there is no current flow, representing binary 0.

Flash memory transistor, storing binary 0

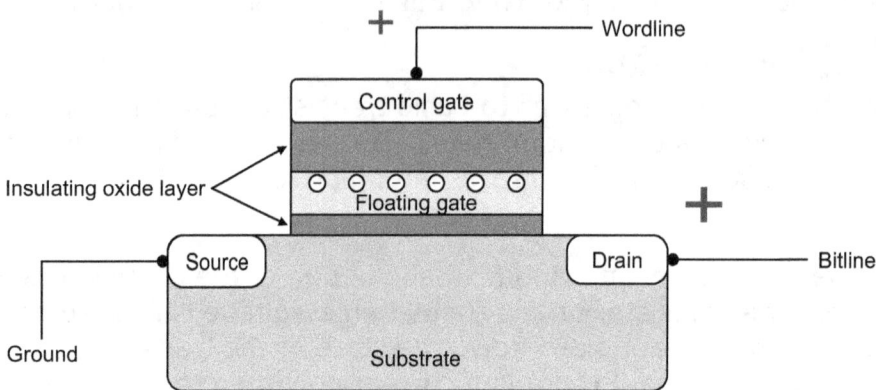

To "erase" the contents of this transistor, i.e. to reset it so that it is storing binary 1, the electrons in the floating gate must be cleared out. To do this, the voltage at the control gate is removed and a larger than normal voltage applied between the drain and the floating gate. The previously trapped electrons now have enough energy to tunnel their way back out of the floating gate and out of the transistor, via the drain (below). As the floating gate empties, there is no current flow from source to drain since there is no voltage at the control gate.

Flash memory transistor, erasing 0

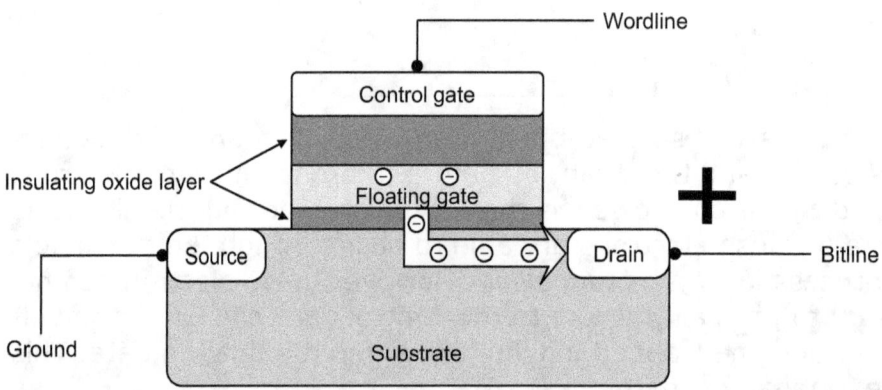

Eventually, after a very large number of rewrite cycles, the insulation surrounding the floating gate will become permanently damaged and the memory location will fail. This could take as many as 1,000,000 write cycles or it could happen sooner, especially if there have been any manufacturing variances. In any case, no memory media should be regarded as being permanent; all can, and probably will, eventually, fail. Important software and data should always be backed up, so there is at least one further copy available should the original be lost. **Wear levelling** algorithms have been developed to try and ensure that all memory locations are used evenly, in order to prolong the overall life of flash memory devices.

Flash memory devices have evolved so that they offer compelling performance in terms of memory capacities, portability, reliability, speed of operation and price. They are a popular form of **backing storage**, that is long term storage of data and software.

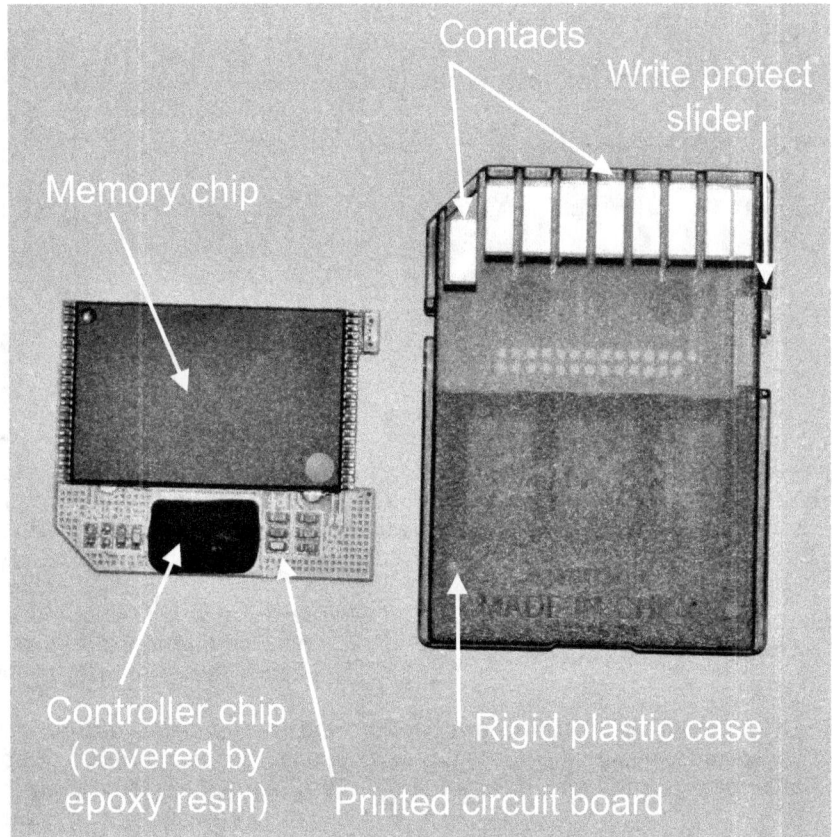

Flash memory SD card, innards on the left

Solid state drives or SSD

For very large capacities, of the order of terabytes or more, for example as the primary backing storage for personal computers, hard disc drives still reign supreme. However, solid state drives (SSD) are making inroads into this market segment, their much faster performance reducing boot-up times and boosting operating speeds in general. Most use NAND flash memory and are increasingly being used as primary storage on personal computers. As well as boosting performance, SSDs have no moving parts, making them quiet and highly resilient if dropped or physically shocked.

Self test

1. What is handshaking?

2. What do blue inserts in a USB plug or socket indicate?

3. What is the maximum number of tiers supported by the USB topology?

4. How is USB data transmitted?

5. How does a simple transistor work?

6. What does EEPROM stand for and what is it?

7. How does flash memory work?

Answers:

1. What is handshaking?
   An automated conversation between two devices, such as that which takes place when they try to connect. It can also refer to on-going "chatter" that supports smooth communication.

2. What do blue inserts in a USB plug or socket indicate?
   USB version 3.

3. What is the maximum number of tiers supported by the USB topology?
   Seven tiers including the host. The seventh tier can only contain devices. This is a maximum, you are likely to run out of power and/or bandwidth before reaching this.

4. How is USB data transmitted?
   It is transmitted in packets.

5. How does a simple transistor work?
   There are three terminals, the source, the drain and the control gate. If a voltage is applied between the source and the drain, a current will only flow if there is a small voltage applied to the control gate. The control gate therefore acts as a switch, turning the transistor on and off.

6. What does EEPROM stand for and what is it?
   Electrically erasable programmable read only memory. Flash memory drives and memory cards such as Compact Flash and SD cards are examples of EEPROM.

7. How does flash memory work?
   Flash memory transistors have an additional floating gate that sits between the control gate and the rest of the transistor. When larger than normal voltages are applied, the floating gate can fill with electrons or have them emptied out, affecting how the transistor behaves and therefore the value that is being stored.

Magnetic backing storage

There is a relatively long tradition in computing of using magnetic media for backing storage. Magnetic material can be magnetised either N-S (north-south) or S-N. The magnetic polarity can then be sensed when the data needs to be read.

Magnetic media with longitudinal recording used to store 0s and 1s

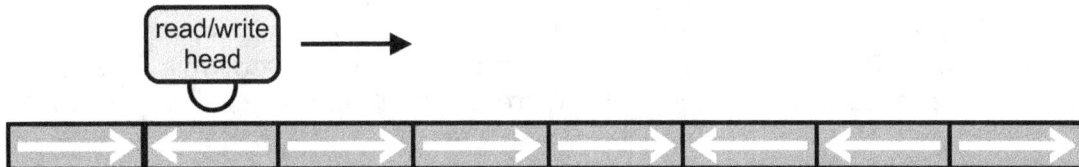

Perpendicular recording was developed to allow higher data densities on hard disc drives

Magnetic tape

Magnetic tape was widely used as it was cost effective and extended to the use of audio cassette tapes on early inexpensive personal computers. However, tape was slow and it might be necessary to search all the way through a particular reel in order to find the required data. In addition, audio tape readers could be unreliable, requiring multiple attempts, before a piece of software could be successfully loaded.

Floppy discs

Floppy discs were developed which used discs of flexible plastic film with a magnetic coating, inside a plastic case. Over the years these developed to be cheap and reliable media and since they offered direct, rather than sequential access, were much faster. Storage densities improved over time, resulting in the different generations of discs getting smaller, whilst offering greater capacities.

The first floppy disc (1971) had a diameter of 8 inches. Next came the 5.25 inch floppy disc (1976). This had a write protect notch and the disc could be made read-only by putting a sticker over it. A small hole was punched into the magnetic disc which would pass by the index hole once each revolution. The start of each magnetic track was indicated by using a light and light sensor in combination, to sense when the two holes were aligned. The 3.5 inch disc (1982, high density HD version introduced in 1986) used a slot on the metal hub to align each disc with the disc drive spindle. It avoided the use of stickers by having a reusable plastic slider built into the case, to cover/uncover the write-protect hole.

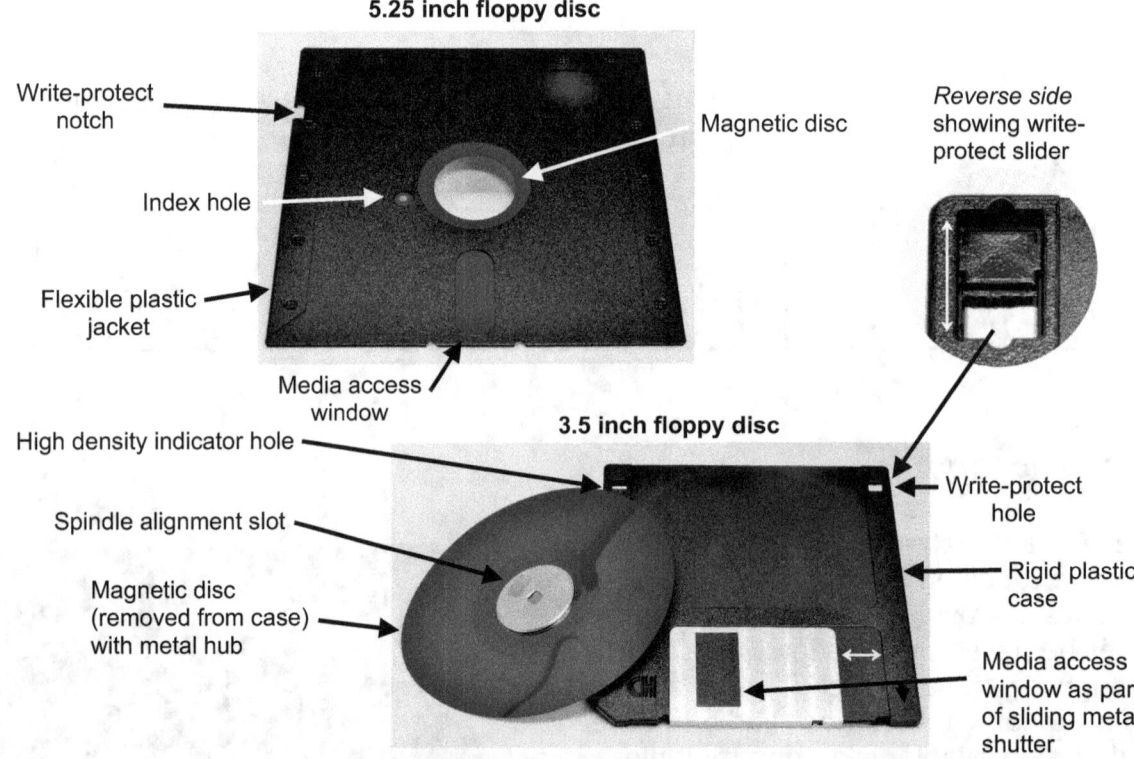

Floppy discs

Both types of disc used a fabric liner to sit between the magnetic disc and the cover. This both reduced friction between the spinning disc and the cover and collected any loose debris and dust. The 3.5 inch floppy disc being both small enough to put into a pocket and having a rigid outer case, was a big improvement in terms of portability. The HD (high density) version had a capacity of 1.44 MB.

Other magnetic media

Travan magnetic tape cartridge

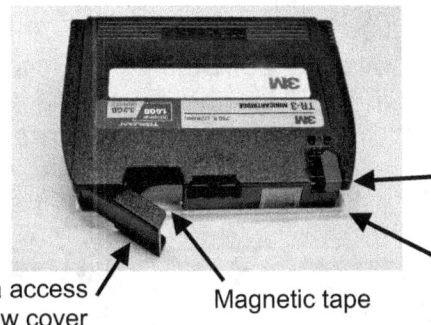

This 8mm tape cartridge from 3M has a capacity of 1.6 GB (uncompressed) and was used in tape backup drives. Tape drives are still sometimes used for backing up.

Write-protect slider

Metal base for added rigidity and to help with heat dissipation

Media access window cover

Magnetic tape

Sony introduced the MiniDisc (MD) in 1992. The discs have a layer of ferromagnetic material sealed beneath a plastic coating. It is a type of magneto-optical media, using a magnetic head together with a laser when recording. The laser heats a tiny portion of the disc to allow its magnetic polarisation to be changed. This change is made permanent when the temperature drops. The MD format proved popular with audiophiles and was used in professional recording equipment. It was superceded for personal audio by MP3 players (using flash memory) and Sony shipped its last MD devices in 2013.

MiniDisc (MD)

Sliding metal shutter

Disc

Write-protect slider

Sliding metal shutter

Reverse side

Disc with case

Iomega Zip was a relatively high capacity proprietary floppy disc format, with a 100 MB capacity at launch. Higher capacity discs followed. Introduced in 1994 they initially sold well, but sales started to decline in 1999 and the format was effectively killed off by other technologies, such as large capacity HDDs, recordable CD/DVDs and flash memory drives.

Zip disc

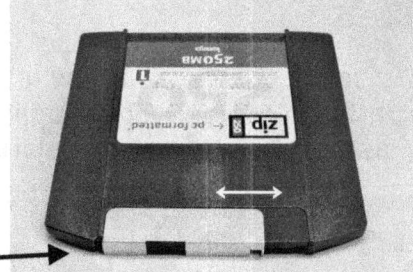

Sliding metal shutter

Hard disc drives

Partitioning a hard disc creates regions so that operating systems can manage each region separately. Partitions are allocated their own drive letter and appear to users as though they are separate drives. If a disc is to be partitioned, this must happen before it is formatted. Using partitions allows files to be isolated/protected by being stored in different regions. It also allows more than one operating system to be installed on a single computer, with each one residing in a separate partition.

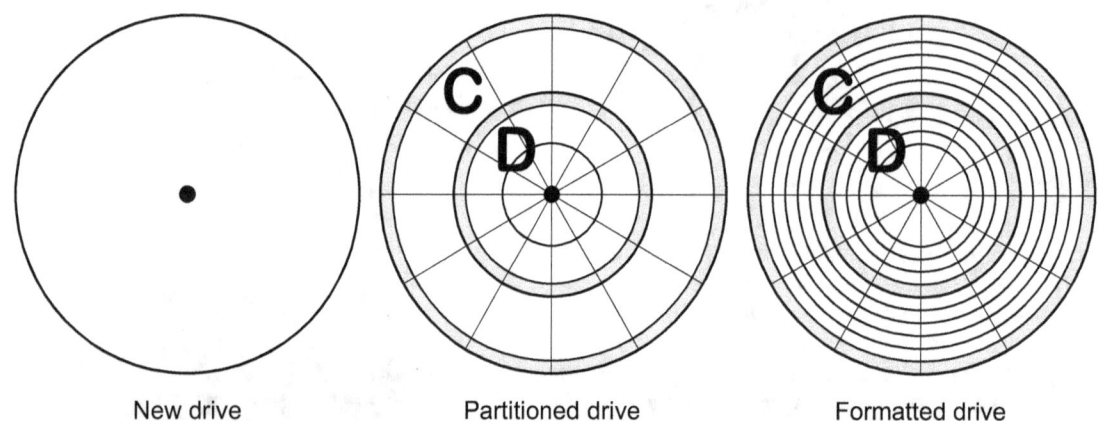

New drive   Partitioned drive   Formatted drive

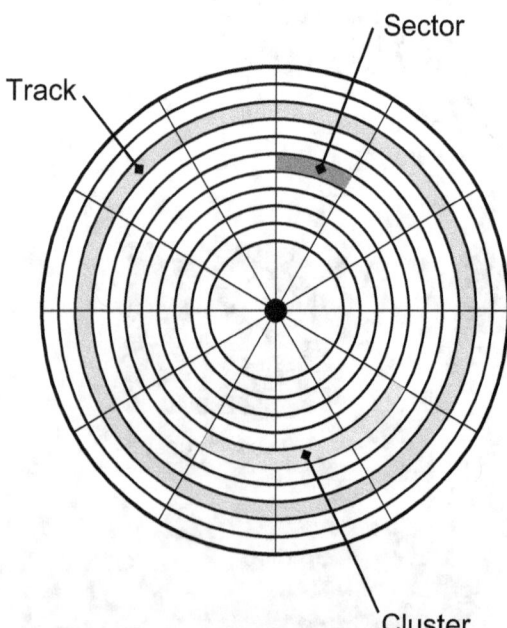

Computer manufacturers often set up a hidden partition, also known as the recovery or restore partition. This allows computers to be returned to factory settings without needing the operating system CD or DVD.

A volume is a single accessible storage area, also known as a logical drive. The diagram shows two volumes, labelled C and D. Low level formatting is usually carried out by the manufacturer and it divides a disc into cylinders, tracks and sectors. Each sector has to be organised, for example with an identification section and a data area. It is usually only done by a user to change the way the drive is partitioned or as a last resort, e.g. if the drive has become badly corrupted or there is a very serious virus problem.

Floppy discs needed similar low level formatting, although they only ever used a single partition. Some were supplied ready-formatted. Users might reformat a floppy disc as a quick way of deleting all the content.

A **cluster** is the smallest unit that a disc drive can access at one time and is made up of one or more sectors. A file will take up a minimum of one cluster. Having a small cluster size reduces the waste associated with very small files, but using larger clusters tends to speed up the operation of the disc drive.

High level, **logical** or **quick** formatting organises the storage of file management information, such as the file allocation table (FAT). Any bad sectors that can no longer be used may also be marked, but this process can be time consuming. Any data that was previously stored on the drive will be lost, however data recovery might be possible.

Hard disc drives (HDD) often contain multiple discs, each one is called a **platter**. The corresponding track on each platter form what is known as a **cylinder**. The platters are spun at high speed, typically over 7,000 rpm, although faster and slower speed drives are available. Read/write heads (one for each side of each platter) float or fly, just above the surface, to read and write data.

File Allocation Tables are a type of file system introduced in 1977 by Microsoft, that has proved sufficiently robust to still find use today. The most recent version is known as **FAT-32**, it is often used with USB flash drives and memory cards. It lists all the files, together with all the clusters where they are stored. FAT-32 is unable to use volumes larger than 2 TB, so a 4 TB HDD would have to be broken down into 2 x 2TB partitions. It can only support files up to 4 GB in size and high definition uncompressed movie files can be around 30 GB. **NTFS** (New Technology File System) is another Microsoft file system, introduced in 1993 with Windows NT 3.1, that has been widely adopted. It has largely replaced FAT on personal computers, with a massive volume limit of 16 EB (exabytes).

2.5 inch internal HDD, 160 GB, taken from a laptop computer

Deleting and recovering files

Files are often moved into a special folder/directory when they are deleted, which is in fact a pre-delete stage. This allows files to be found and undeleted (restored) if a user wants to 'undo' the original delete command. When this recycle or trash folder is emptied, the files are then deleted. However, this does not mean that each file is destroyed. To save time, a file is simply marked as being deleted (for example, the first character of the file name in the file system record might be replaced with a reserved character, such as **?**), so that the operating system knows that the disc space can be used for another file, if needed. Specialist data recovery software can scan a disc to list all the deleted files that it can find. Any that are still intact can be recovered. Sometimes partially complete files can have what is left recovered, too.

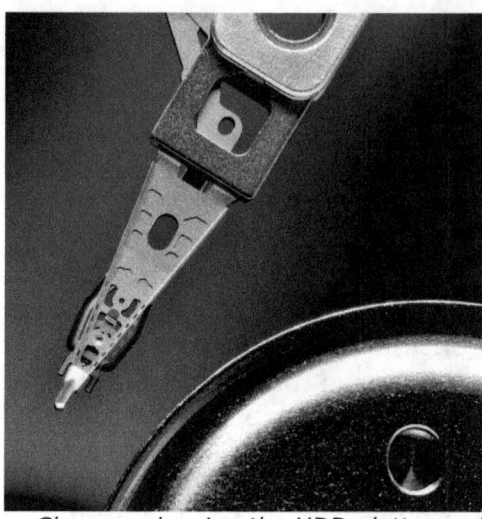

Close up showing the HDD platter and the actuator arm with one of the read-write heads

Occasionally a user will want to 'destroy' a file for security reasons, perhaps it contains bank information or other sensitive data. Such a file should be wiped using specialist utility software, which involves over-writing the file data, either with all 1s, all 0s or with randomly generated data. There have been frequent reports of classified or sensitive government and other data being found on equipment sent to

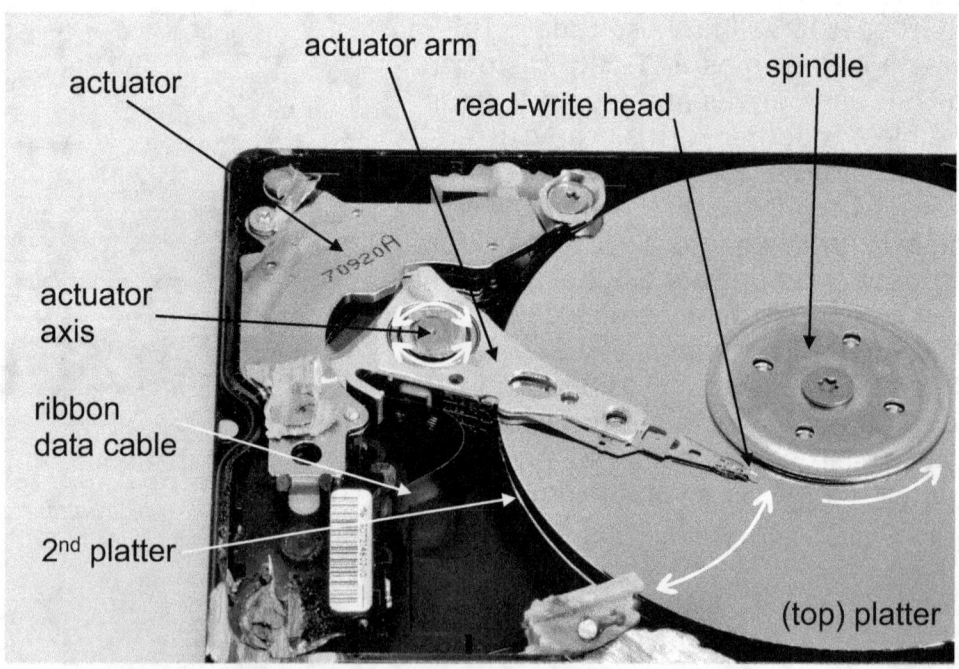

landfill at the end of its life. It is now well established good practice to ensure that computers have their hard drives either securely wiped or physically destroyed before they are scrapped and sent for recycling.

How a hard disc drive works

The 2.5 inch internal hard disc drive shown in the photographs was used in a laptop until it failed. Its data capacity was 160 GB and it was made up of two double sided platters. These spin together at high speed around the spindle. The left end of the actuator arm (not visible) has a coil of wire, sitting inside a magnetic field and when a current passes through the coil, this causes the arm to rotate about the actuator axis, moving the read-write heads backwards and forwards across the surface of the platters. It is known as a voice coil actuator and is similar to those found in loudspeakers, that move the speaker cones backwards and forwards.

The actuator arm in the photograph has four read-write heads in a stack, on the right hand end of the arm. Only the top one is visible, but all four move together. This allows both sides of the two platters to be used. If a large file can be saved to sectors in the same cylinder, this speeds up the writing and any subsequent reading. In this case, once the start of the file has been found, the actuator arm does not need to move again.

The platters are polished to an exceptionally high degree of smoothness and the read-write heads are aerodynamically designed so that they literally fly, nanometers above the surface. The drives are assembled and sealed in clean-room conditions, to ensure that everyday dust does not contaminate them. Getting the read-write heads closer to the platter surface allows more data to be stored, however should the head touch the surface (for example if a laptop is dropped whilst the disc drive is operating), permanent and probably irretrievable damage will occur.

Drive letters

Drive letters are often assigned to volumes to act as identifiers. Windows operating systems (and the predecessor DOS operating systems) assign **A** to a computer's primary floppy disc drive, with **B** being reserved for a second floppy disc drive, should one be present. The primary hard disc drive is allocated **C**, which is the first drive letter used by most modern personal computers. A user's personal or home directory on a network is often allocated **H** by convention, with other network volumes being further down the alphabet, to differentiate between them and local drives. External hard drives, flash memory drives, memory cards and any other local drives, have drive letters allocated dynamically, when they are first plugged in (or *mounted*), depending on what letters are available.

Where is my data stored?

To be absolutely sure, you need to know what storage volumes are available to the particular device being used, but the following is a good rule of thumb for personal computers.

Drive C will be the primary hard disc drive of the computer and the letters that immediately follow are likely to be any other local hard drives/partitions or USB devices that have been connected to your computer, such as flash memory drives, memory cards and external hard disc drives.

Important data saved to your own computer or to local devices should be treated as being vulnerable and should be manually backed up as appropriate.

Network volumes (likely to apply to work/corporate computers only) will probably use letters further down the alphabet, but remember, H has often been used for each user's home network directory. Files saved to a network should be more secure as they will be protected by any centrally enforced backup system.

Cloud (i.e. internet) storage services, such as Dropbox, Google Backup and Sync and Microsoft OneDrive allow files to be shared across many devices. Each device normally has a copy of the storage folders and files can be opened and updated. The next time the device is connected to the internet, the folders on your device are synchronised with those being stored on a remote server by the service provider. If you then move to another device and connect it to the internet, it has its copy of the folders updated. All your devices should therefore be working from the latest copies of each file, unless a file was changed on a device that has not been connected to the internet since.

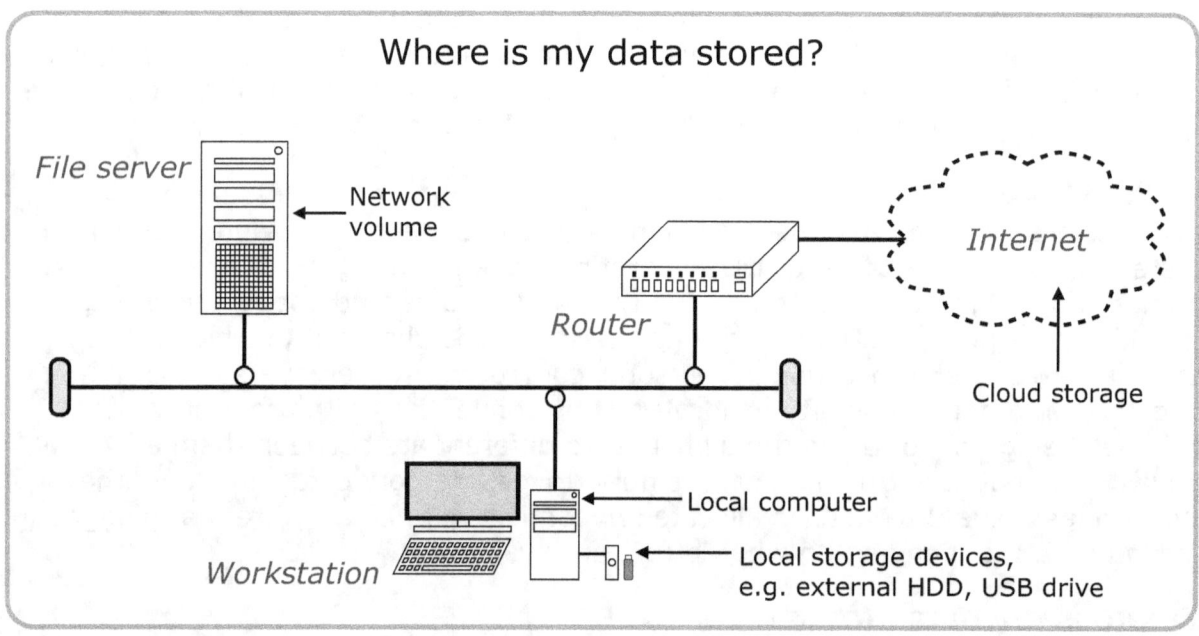

One advantage of these services is that one copy of your folders is being kept remotely, in a professionally run facility, so that even if you lose all your devices there should still be one set of intact folders that you can access. In effect, these files are being backed up automatically and should be much more secure, provided the service provider maintains a high level of security to defend against hacking attacks. A major service provider is more likely to attract the attention of hackers, than an individual internet user, so local storage has its attractions. Not least of which is that the storage devices are under the control of the user.

It should be noted that some cloud storage services simply keep your files at a remote location, with no local copy. When the files are needed the user has to be connected to the internet in order to be able to download them, i.e. copy them to the user's computer. They can then be worked on and the edited versions saved back to the cloud.

When storing data using internet services and also when uploading material to social networking sites, attention should be paid to the sometimes lengthy and often daunting terms and conditions. Legal aspects, such as copyright and whether the service provider has any rights to use your content, will be governed by the laws of the country in which the file servers reside, as well as the service Ts & Cs (terms and conditions). This may not be the same as your country of residence, in which case local laws may not apply.

Depending where you choose to save it, your data could be saved in any of the following.

- **Local computer**, usually an internal HDD or SSD
- A **local storage device**, e.g. flash drive, external HDD, memory card
- **Network** volume (if part of a LAN or WAN)
- **Cloud** storage, i.e. somewhere in the world via the internet, perhaps with a copy held locally on your computer and any other devices you use, where the service has been installed

Living in a digital world - Chapter 5: How some stuff works

Self test

1. Why is a floppy disc so-called?

2. What is an HDD partition?

3. Why does a disc need low level formatting?

4. What does high level or quick formatting do?

5. Why might it be possible to recover a file after it has been deleted?

6. Why is the primary hard disc drive allocated the drive letter C by some operating systems?

7. When saving data, where might it be physically stored?

Answers:

1. Why is a floppy disc so-called?
   Data is stored on a flexible plastic disc covered with a magnetic coating. The larger floppy discs were protected by flexible jackets, however the 3.5 inch floppy was mounted inside a rigid plastic case.

2. What is an HDD partition?
   Each partition is a separate storage area or logical drive. It allows files to be protected by being isolated from each other and more than one operating system can be installed on a single computer by installing each one on a separate partition.

3. Why does a disc need low level formatting?
   This prepares a disc for storing data by dividing it into tracks and sectors. With a multi-platter hard drive it also creates cylinders.

4. What does high level or quick formatting do?
   This organises the storage of file management information, such as the File Allocation Table (FAT) or New Technology File System (NTFS).

5. Why may it be possible to recover a file after it has been deleted?
   Modern operating systems usually place a "deleted" file into a pre-delete trash or recycle bin, from which files can easily be selected and restored to their original folder. When these bins are emptied the files are simply marked as having been deleted and the disc space is made available should it be needed. However, the file will only disappear once that disc space has been used for something else. Prior to that, special utility software can be used to scan for files that can still be recovered.

6. Why is the primary hard disc drive allocated the drive letter C by some operating systems?
   This is an historical hangover from the days when A and B were reserved for floppy disc drives.

7. When saving data, where might it be physically stored?
   Your local computer, a local storage device, a network volume or in the Cloud (the internet, i.e. anywhere in the world).

Optical media

Optical media use a spinning disc, marked with patterns of lands and pits, that are read by precisely focused laser light. The main types currently in use are all based on 120 mm diameter plastic discs, with some form of reflective coating.

Compact disc (CD)

Pits and lands on a CD do not represent 0s and 1s. Instead, the player reads the changes. Changing from a land to a pit, or a pit to a land represents binary 1. No change represents binary 0. A similar change/no change method is used for the electrical signals in USB cables and for HDD magnetic storage.

Compact disc, typical composition

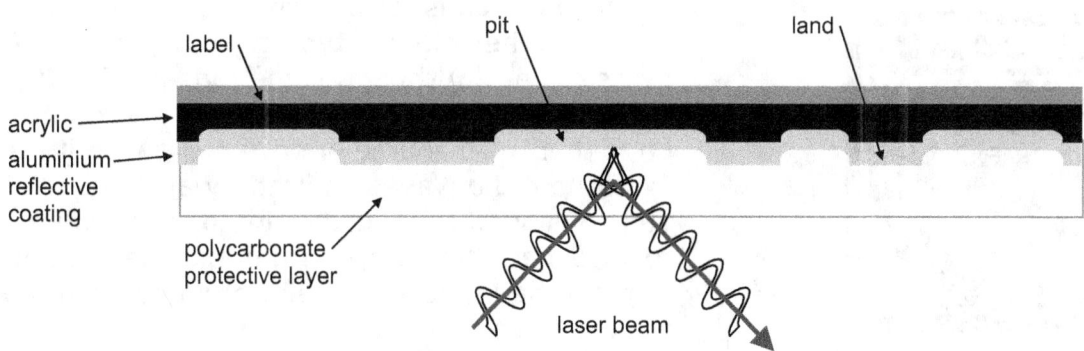

A CD is a mere 1.2 mm thick and the label side is much closer to the lands and pits than the clear, polycarbonate side. Therefore scratches on the label side are much more likely to ruin the disc. On the polycarbonate side, defects may well be out of focus and not interfere with the reading of the disc. Otherwise problems may be solved by polishing the surface or filling scratches with a material with similar optical properties to the polycarbonate.

Compact discs are usually read-only media, injection moulded using metal formers created from a glass master disc. However, there are also recordable compact discs (CD-R, record once only) and rewriteable compact discs (CD-RW).

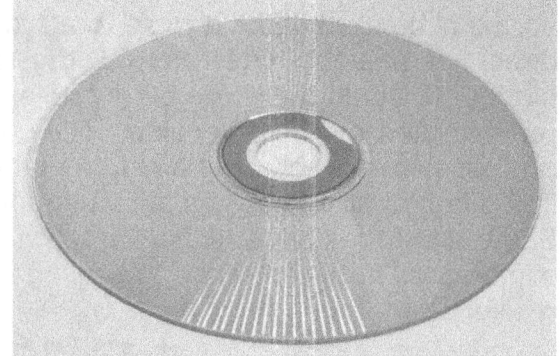

Compact disc, polycarbonate side upwards

Different types of optical media

Type	Variant	Storage capacity
Compact disc	Single layer	700 MB
DVD	Single layer	4.7 GB
DVD	Dual layer	8.5 GB
DVD	Single layer, double sided	9.4 GB
DVD	Dual layer, double sided	17 GB
Blu-ray	Single layer	25 GB
Blu-ray	Dual layer	50 GB

Radio-frequency identification (RFID)

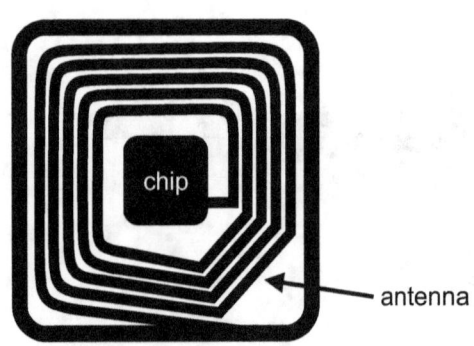

An RFID tag consists of a small chip and an antenna. The chip can typically carry up to 2,000 bytes of data. Although some tags are fitted with batteries, the majority are *passive* and do not have their own source of power, drawing it instead from the radio waves emitted by an RFID reader. Tags designed to be used with lower power readers need to be large, to maximise the power that can be induced in their antennas from reader radio signals.

A typical RFID reader will work within a few feet of a tag, accessing whatever data is stored in the chip. However there are specialist high frequency readers that can operate at up to 20 feet or even further. RFID tags can be used for inventory control in a similar way to barcodes, however standard 1-D barcodes, such as those used to encode EANs, can only store a single number. In addition, barcodes normally have to be held close to a scanner in order to be read and certainly in direct line of sight, whereas RFID tags can be further away from the reader and hidden. It would therefore be possible to rapidly scan someone's shopping without removing it from the shopping trolley, reducing handling and speeding up the process considerably. Initially RFID tagging was mostly used in retail for high value items only, but its use has become more widespread as costs have decreased. Some retail tags have relatively delicate antennae, so the tags are usually sandwiched between other packaging materials or under stickers, to improve resilience.

RFID tags come in a range of sizes, typically from a few centimetres square down to around the size of a grain of rice or smaller. RFID tags have been used to "chip" animals such as dogs (in case of loss), cattle and horses (tracking and anti-theft). They have even been glued to ants and bees for animal behaviour studies. They can be used for access control for electronic locks and automated barrier access (personnel barriers in buildings, car park barriers, toll road/bridge use) as well as for making fast, contactless payments using credit or debit cards. Public transport cards, such as London's Oyster cards, that can be topped up by making periodic payments, often use RFID technology. Many countries' passports now incorporate these tags. Sports events that use transponder timing are also using RFID tags and they can be used in a retailing environment to set off alarms as an anti-shoplifting measure, as well as for inventory tracking.

RFID technology has been around for a long time, but its adoption has been relatively slow and both the costs and lack of common standards have been blamed for this. However costs have been coming down and work on standards is ongoing, leading to an increasing range of applications and wider adoption of this technology.

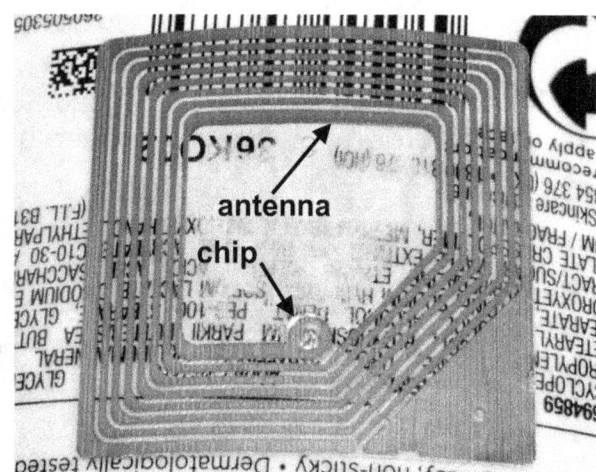

Work has been done on linking sensors with tags, so a possible future application would be to tag, e.g. joints of meat and record the temperatures over, say, the last week. This would make it possible to monitor storage conditions more accurately and therefore the likely condition of the meat. It would also facilitate the detailed investigation of different storage methods, to establish which is the most effective.

RFID inventory tag on a plastic bottle, originally mounted under a paper barcode label

One concern has been that these tags can remain readable long after they are no longer needed, which raises privacy issues, such as when they are used in retailing. They can be embedded in products or attached with ferocious adhesives making their removal impractical (this may also cause contamination issues when items are recycled). When leaving a store, having bought a high value item, it is possible that anyone with an appropriate reader could detect what has been purchased, even once it is inside a vehicle. Clearly this is a security issue, as well as a privacy concern. Some tags can be switched at the point of sale, so that they can only be read at very short distances or are effectively disabled. In either case, full functionality could be restored in the event of the item being returned to the store. However this approach relies on store equipment functioning properly and being used consistently by staff. Contactless payment cards are designed to function only at very close distances, as part of the overall approach to security, which has been stepped up following early concerns about vulnerabilities. Nevertheless, some people will be uncomfortable about the contribution these tags could make to a "surveillance society".

Barcodes

Barcodes epitomise simplicity. The "traditional" 1-D barcode, such as an EAN-13 barcode, usually encodes a single number or string of characters, normally a code that identifies an item, or one of its properties. Made up of light (space, S) and dark (bar, B) modules or areas, they can be accurately printed on the most basic printer, making it possible to print out auto-read boarding cards at home or present them to a scanner on the screen of a mobile phone. They can be easily incorporated onto all manner of packaging and documentation and have become ubiquitous.

The anatomy of an EAN barcode

Each EAN-13 symbol character is made up of **seven modules**, put together to make **four elements**, two dark (often black) and two light (usually white).

Example EAN-13 symbol character

space/bar modules character	S	B	S	B
9 (set A)	3	1	1	2

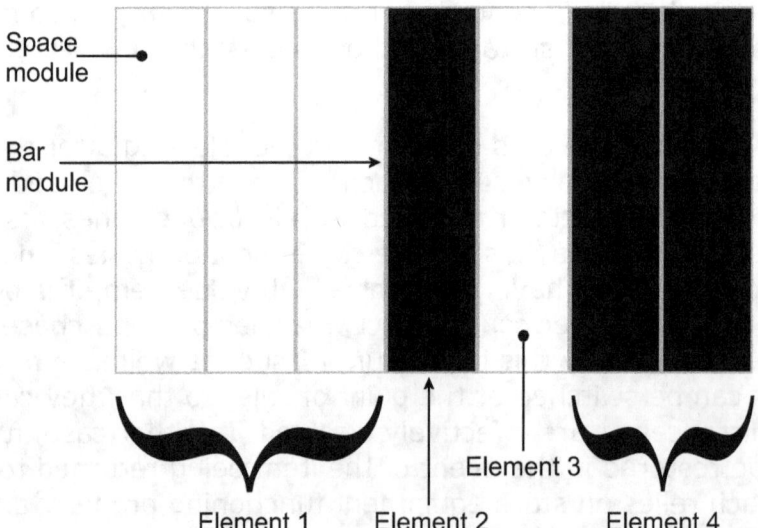

The normal guard bar is made up of 3 modules; **B,S,B** whereas the centre guard bar comprises 5 modules; **S, B, S, B, S** with the result that at first glance they appear identical.

EAN symbology

Character	Set A (odd)	Set B (even)	Set C (even)
0			
1			
2			
3			
4			
5			
6			
7			
8			
9			

Note: Take the Set A symbol characters and invert all the modules (i.e. change all the dark modules to light and all the light modules to dark) to get the corresponding Set C symbols. Take the Set C symbol characters and put them in reverse order (horizontal reflection) to get the corresponding Set B symbols.
Set A symbol characters all have an odd number of dark modules. Sets B and C all have an even number of dark modules.
Sets A and B always start with a light module and Set C always ends with a light module so that symbol characters in positions 1 and 12 do not merge with the start/end guard bars.

Living in a digital world - Chapter 5: How some stuff works

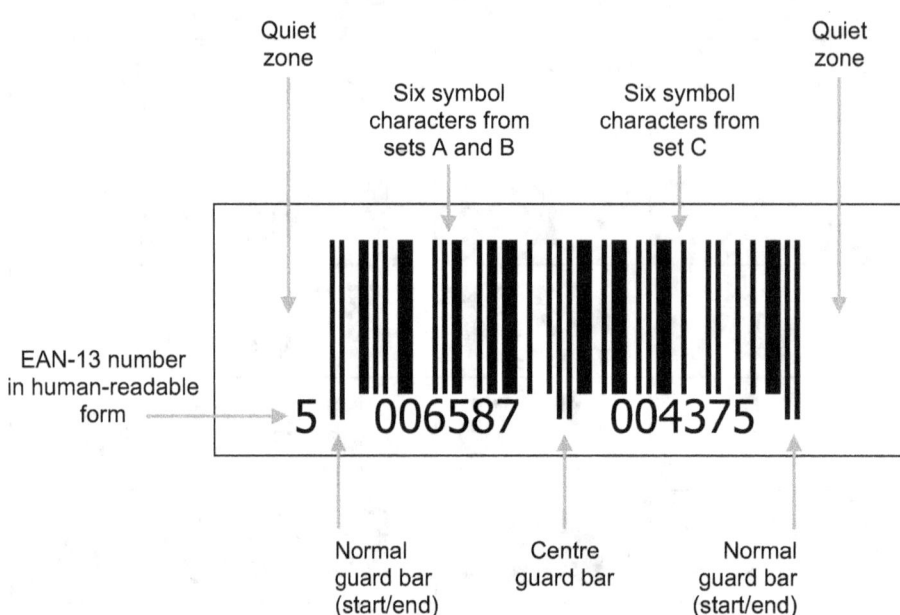

An EAN-13 barcode is made up of 12 symbol characters, but in fact encodes 13 digits. The number on the extreme left (the leading digit, 5 in the diagram above) is not directly represented. It is encoded by the mix of sets A and B used for the left-hand six symbol characters. This clever sleight of hand allowed EAN-13 barcodes to remain compatible with the American predecessor 12-digit UPC-A barcodes on which the EAN-13 system is based. This was important as it meant the existing US barcodes could fit within the system that was designed for use throughout Europe and which has since become fully international.

Leading digit, implicitly encoded	Sets used for the left half of an EAN-13 barcode					
	Symbol character position					
	1	2	3	4	5	6
0	A	A	A	A	A	A
1	A	A	B	A	B	B
2	A	A	B	B	A	B
3	A	A	B	B	B	A
4	A	B	A	A	B	B
5	A	B	B	A	A	B
6	A	B	B	B	A	A
7	A	B	A	B	A	B
8	A	B	A	B	B	A
9	A	B	B	A	B	A

Set C uses odd parity, which means that when a scanner sees six symbol characters all with odd parity, it must be scanning the right half of the code. If it sees three with even parity and three with odd parity, this must be the left half of the code. The scanner can therefore determine the orientation of the code, i.e. is it right-side up or upside down. If the scanner sees six symbol characters with odd parity and six with even parity, it knows it is dealing with a UPC-A code, since the leading digit is zero. If the even parity ones are read first then the code is upside down. UPC-A codes use the same guard patterns and also comprise a total of 95 modules.

Structure of an EAN-13 barcode				
Left guard pattern	Characters 12 through 7 (left half)	Centre guard pattern	Characters 6 through 1 (right half)	Right guard pattern
3 modules	6 x 7 = 42 modules	5 modules	6 x 7 = 42 modules	3 modules
95 modules, excluding quiet zones				

The quiet zones are a minimum of 9 modules each, making the minimum width of an EAN/UPC-A barcode 113 modules.

Examples of other 1-D barcodes

PostNet

Standard 2 of 5

Interleaved 2 of 5

Pharmacode

Codabar

Code 128

MSI Plessey

> **Practical task:** If you have a smartphone with a barcode reading app, try and scan the codes above. Are you able to read any of them?

2-D barcodes

One dimensional barcodes, such as EAN-13 have one big drawback. They may only be able to represent a very limited set of characters (e.g. numbers only) and they become very large (and impractical) if attempting to encode a significant amount of data. Two dimensional barcodes, such as QR (Quick Response) codes, offer the opportunity to store up to around 3,000 bytes of data or over 4,000 alphanumeric characters, or in some cases, even more.

Examples of 2-D barcodes

QR Code   Datamatrix   PDF417   Aztec

The above barcodes all encode the text, "Hello, I hope you are enjoying reading "Living in a Digital World - Demystifying Technology". Kind regards, Mark Baker"

QR Codes have high fault tolerance and fast readability. QR Codes that are commonly seen can store of the order of 35-395 characters. Standardised QR Codes are free to use.

Datamatrix barcodes can have a tiny footprint and therefore they are often used to label small items. The specification was placed in the public domain by its developers (Acuity CiMatrix/Siemens), however there have been attempts by third parties to assert patent rights in respect of its use.

PDF417 barcodes can hold over 1 KB of machine readable data in a very compact form. They are free to use.

Aztec codes are commonly used for transport tickets and airline boarding passes. They have high readability even when reproduced with poor resolution and can be used reliably when presented on a smartphone, or poorly printed. Invented by Honeywell, the ISO specification is in the public domain and it is free to use.

QR Codes

History

The limitations of 1-D barcodes were particularly felt in Japan, where there was a demand to be able to store more data to enable the coding of Kanji and Kana characters, as well as the standard alphanumeric ones. Mashahiro Hara and a colleague at Japanese company Denso Wave set about developing a solution. Denso Wave was a subsidiary of Denso Corporation, once wholly owned by Toyota. As a global automotive components group, they worked closely with a range of car makers, including their old parent company.

A key design objective was to be able to read the new code as quickly as possible and this led to its name, QR or Quick Response Code. A big step forward was taken when it was decided that adding positional information to the code might speed up the process of the reader knowing when there was a code present, waiting to be read. A key characteristic of QR Codes are the large square marks that allow a code to be spotted and its orientation known. Problems can occur with orientation patterns if there are any similar marks nearby when the code is read. The square marks were chosen after examining large quantities of printed matter and they represent the least used ratio of dark and light areas. Readers hunt for this ratio to identify a QR Code. Similar to EAN barcodes, QR Codes require a white border, or quiet zone.

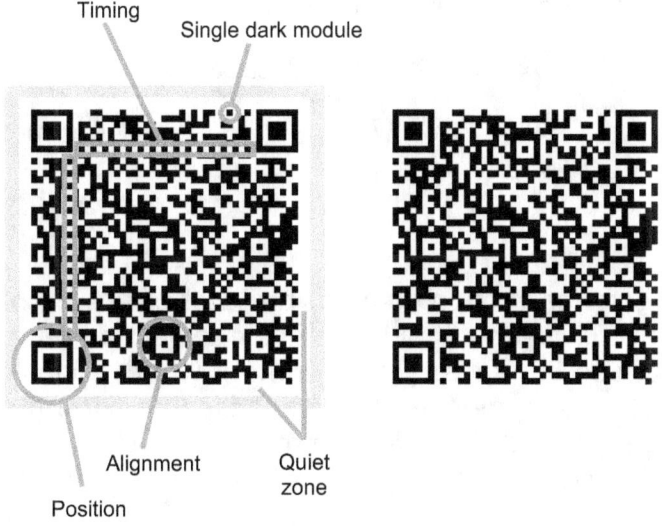

Labelled and unlabelled copies of the same QR Code, showing some of the functional elements

QR Codes were announced in 1994, after about 18 months of development work. Crucially, although Denso Wave retained the patent rights, they announced that they would not exercise them and would publish the specifications. Therefore the new code could be used without any legal complications or payment of licence fees. QR Codes were widely adopted by the auto industry and were also used for product tracking purposes in the contact lens, pharmaceutical and food industries. In the latter case, the use of the codes was boosted by food scares, such as bovine spongiform encephalopathy ("mad cow disease"). Global expansion of QR Code use has also been boosted by its inclusion in various national and international standards, being recognised by ISO in 2000.

In 2002, the marketing of mobile phones in Japan that could read QR Codes, brought these eye-catching patterns to the attention of the general public for the first time. Now it was possible to use a phone to capture a web address, obtain a special offer coupon or add business card details to your contacts list, in seconds.

Some detail

QR Codes come in different sizes, referred to by their version number. Version 1 is the smallest code, made up of 21 x 21 = 441 (square) modules and capable of storing between 10 and 25 alphanumeric characters. Version 40 can store over 4,200 alphanumeric characters or almost 3,000 bytes of binary data, however this depends on the level of error correction chosen. Version 40 QR Codes are densely packed (177 x 177 modules = 31,329 modules), requiring the use of very small modules, which some readers/cameras will struggle to read reliably. Each version adds another four modules in each dimension, so Version 2 is 25 x 25 modules and Version 3 is 29 x 29 modules.

Four levels of error correction are offered.

Error correction level	Approx. data correction capability	Recommended use
L (Low)	7%	Clean environment
M (Medium)	15%	Somewhat unclean...
Q (Quartile)	25%	Factory
H (High)	30%	Factory

The higher levels of error correction come at the cost of having reduced data capacity as more space is taken up with the error correction data. Levels Q and H are recommended for use in a factory environment where codes could become dirty or marked, with Level L recommended for use in clean environments. The compromise Level M appears to be used the most. The Reed-Solomon error correction algorithm is used.

Illustration of the effect of error correction on QR Codes

Error Correction Level = LError Correction Level = MError Correction Level = QError Correction Level = H

The above barcodes could all be read. The black circles represent splodges of oily mess and their radiuses were decreased until the barcode could just be read. The reader was a smartphone with a moderate/poor camera and the codes were displayed on a computer monitor.

The original QR Code is referred to as Model 1 (available in versions 1-14), with the improved Model 2 being developed subsequently. Model 2 performs better when the code has been distorted, perhaps because it is displayed on a curved surface.

Illustration of the effect of error correction on QR Codes

Error Correction Level = LError Correction Level = MError Correction Level = QError Correction Level = H

The above barcodes could all be read. The black circles represent oily mess splatter and the number on each code was decreased until the barcode could just be read. The reader was a smartphone with a moderate/poor camera and the codes were displayed on a computer monitor.

Other types of QR Code have been developed, including the Micro QR Code, which has only one positional marker. This comes in four flavours, referred to as M1, M2, M3 and M4. M1 codes are 11 x 11 modules and can encode a maximum of 5 digits only. The others can encode between 5 and 21 alphanumeric characters. M4 codes are 17 x 17 modules.

Micro QR Code (M4)

An iQR code, compared with a regular QR code of the same size, can hold 80% more data. Alternatively, when storing the same amount of data, iQR codes are 30% smaller than QR codes. They can be produced as squares or as rectangles. In the latter case they can be used to overprint standard 1-D barcodes and can be used, e.g. to label thin cylindrical objects, where a square barcode might wrap around too far to be read. Version 61 can store over 40,000 characters. Error correction of up to 50% is available.

Uses of QR Codes

It is very easy to create your own QR Codes using one of the numerous code generating websites or a specialist piece of software. Having selected the type of code required, the data is entered via an on-screen form. The code can then be generated and there is often a number of image formats to choose from. Where SVG is available, it is to be recommended. It scales easily, without the image degradation that can occur with bitmap formats. Once generated and saved, the code can be added to documents, emails, posters, business cards and presentations, in the same way that any other image or graphic would be.

> **Practical task:** Search online using terms such as *QR Code generator* and try producing your own QR Codes. How could you use them?

Some alternative uses of QR Codes for automatic data capture

Website URL

Contact details meCard format (fictitious business card)

WiFi details (fictitious conference)

Email (fictitious promotion)

Bookmark the above website

Google Maps: Canals of central Birmingham

vCalendar event (fictitious conference)

Call phone number (fictitious)

The diagram above shows some of the specific applications offered and at first sight it might seem amazing that all these things can be represented by a simple pattern of dark and light blocks. It is another example of elegant simplicity. All the uses rely on the ability of QR Codes to store text. Website URLs are stored as-is and scanning software should be capable of recognising them and browsing directly to the sites. Maps use the URL of the mapping website with the location details added to the end.

For some other applications, standard metadata is added so that the scanning software knows how to handle the code, once it has been read. Semicolons are used as field separators, with colons after field names. Here are some examples.

QR Code type	Data encoded
Call phone number:	**TEL:**01632 927338
Bookmark website:	**MEBKM:TITLE:**Education Vision Consultancy - home;**URL:**http://www.educationvision.co.uk
Email:	**MATMSG:TO:**sales@megastoreengland.co.uk; **SUB:**Special seasonal offer;**BODY:**Please send me your special offer coupon, a copy of your brochure and add me to your emailing list. Thanks!;;

TEL, MEBKM and MATMSG tell the scanning software what sort of information will follow. TITLE, URL, TO, SUB and BODY are all field names. SUB is the email subject, BODY is the message text and so on. The metadata must be defined in a standard for this to work, but once that is done, all these applications become possible. All that remains is for the barcode app on your mobile phone to be correctly programmed and it will be able to handle all these examples and more.

Custom QR Code linking to Education Vision Consultancy website

The ease of scanning QR codes with smartphones means that they have been widely used in consumer advertising, especially for promoting websites. They have appeared on notes and coins. They can be scanned from the sides of buses and vans. Train companies have used them to link to electronic copies of timetables. They have been embedded on gravestones to link to virtual grave sites that include photographs

Decorative custom QR Code linking to Education Vision Consultancy website via an advertisement

and other details of the deceased. Graphic elements can be added, such as company logos, or to produce aesthetically pleasing custom QR Codes with added impact, taking advantage of the in-built error correction capability. However, there is a greater chance that decorative codes will be unreadable, especially to lower quality scanners and mobile phone cameras, or if printed very small or using lower quality processes or paper. The standard codes, printed black on white, have the best readability.

Another custom QR Code

Types of barcode reader

Pen- or wand-type readers have a light source and a photo diode to read the intensity of the light reflected back from the barcode, mounted in a cylindrical pen-like container. The wand has to be moved over the barcode at a fairly steady speed, so reading is not always reliable. Barcodes that are not flat or are located on vertical surfaces can be difficult to scan. Once a lower cost option, these are not commonly used any more.

CCD or LED readers use an array of light sensors and LEDs arranged in the head of a hand-held reader, to illuminate the barcode and measure the light that is reflected back. Only 1-D barcodes that are less than the width of the reader can be read. The reader does not have to be in contact with the code, but it does need to be within a few centimetres.

Hand-held laser scanners work in a similar way, but they use laser light and either a rotating prism or reciprocating mirror to dynamically scan across barcodes. Barcodes that are bigger than the scanning head can be read and some laser readers can read at a distance of several metres. Most supermarkets use more sophisticated versions that are permanently mounted as part of Point of Sale terminals and use a scanning pattern designed to read the barcodes regardless of their orientation.

Some supermarkets offer customers the option of self-scanning as they shop, using hand-held barcode scanners powered by rechargeable batteries.

Camera readers use image processing techniques to read both 1-D and 2-D barcodes. Apps are available that allow everyday mobile devices such as smartphones to read different barcodes.

Most readers give an audible beep or similar signal to indicate a successful read.

An example barcode reader

The pictured hand-held CCD reader can scan 33 barcode types and their variants, including EAN/UPC, Codabar, Code 128 and GS1 DataBar, although only some of these are enabled by default. It cannot read 2-D barcodes. It has a 1500 pixel sensor and uses red LED light. It has a 4KB transmit buffer, so that it can store up to 256 EAN-13 scans, until the computer to which it is connected is ready to receive data.

The scanner is configured (set up) using a series of command barcodes which are printed in the user manual. A user simply has to read the correct sequence of barcodes in order to change a setting. For example there is a reading redundancy setting. With "No Redundancy" the scanner will only require a single successful reading to make the reading valid. If Three Times (the maximum) is selected, a total of four successful readings will be required to achieve a valid reading, the first, plus three redundant readings. All four readings would have to be identical. The Three Times setting increases reading security, at the expense of reading speed and would be adjusted in the light of experience with the particular barcodes being used.

CCD hand-held barcode reader, with USB connection

Using a keyboard wedge interface with older computers, or the equivalent software wedge for USB connections, means that the scanner behaves as though it is a keyboard. This means that input from the scanner can be accepted by all software that can also accept keyboard input. The scanner can even be configured to add an ENTER character at the end of the barcode digits, just as if they had been typed in!

Communications

In the 1960s mass public communication was catered for by telephone, postal and telegraph services. Telephone networks were built on cables that ran to telephone points in individual homes and offices. Cables ran from those telephone points to telephones. To make a voice call, the telephone network had to make a cable connection between the two participants and keep this in place for the duration of the call, so-called **circuit switching**. Large numbers of public telephones were maintained to allow people to stay in contact when away from home or office. These were easier to find in densely populated urban areas and much less common in rural regions. Radio systems did

Radio equipment mounted on a water tower, United Kingdom

exist, but size, weight and power requirements meant that these were mostly limited to specialist vehicle installations. The concept of personal communicators that could be carried in a pocket or handbag, with calls being made "on the go" existed, but only within the realms of fanciful science fiction.

One of the big changes over the last three decades or so has been the explosive growth of mobile telecommunications. Using radio connections between users and a series of base stations has allowed rapid expansion. Base stations serving a significant area can be installed much more quickly than laying cables and installing all of the associated infrastructure required by a wired system.

Mobile telephony

Mobile telephony allows users to communicate via their nearest base stations. The area covered by the base station is called a cell. Hence the US term **cell phone**, which has nothing whatever to do with prisons, despite the popularity of the technology in those environments. Each base station connects initially with the provider's network, via a regional Mobile Telephone Switching Office (MTSO) and through that, if necessary, to the wider national or international telecommunications network (PSTN or Public Switched Telephone Network).

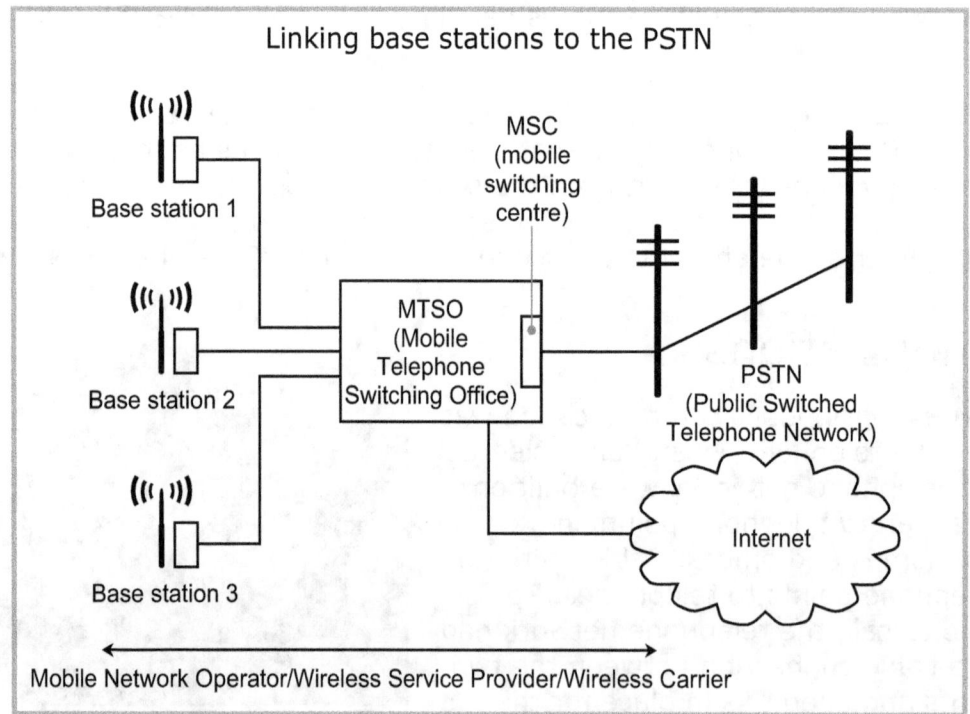

To make or receive a call, a mobile phone will require access to a communication channel. A channel is made up of two frequencies, one for transmitting to the base station and one to receive data from the base station. The same channels cannot be used in adjacent cells, because of radio interference effects, however they can be reused in cells that are a minimum distance apart. This distance will depend on the power of the transmitter serving each base station. A group of cells that are located adjacent to each other and within which no channels are reused, is called a **cluster**. The diagram (right) shows a cluster of 7 cells. These can be designed so that adjacent clusters (below) can reuse the same frequencies, since the corresponding cells are far enough apart to avoid radio interference.

Cluster of 7 cells

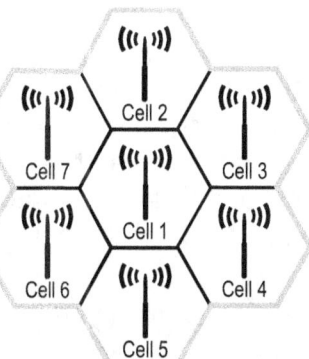

If a user is moving towards the edge of a cell, the base station will notice that their signal strength is reducing. At the same time, the base station of the cell they are moving towards will see their signal strength increasing. The two base stations coordinate via the MTSO and at the appropriate moment a hand over (*US: hand off*) is executed, passing control from one base station to the next. At the same time, the mobile phone switches frequencies to ones used by the new cell. Handovers happen so quickly that users are not aware of them taking place. Handing over proved difficult to implement in the early days of mobile networks, especially if a user was moving quickly in a vehicle or train, leading to connections being dropped and calls ending prematurely. However, this aspect of performance has been refined and improved over time.

Frequency reuse

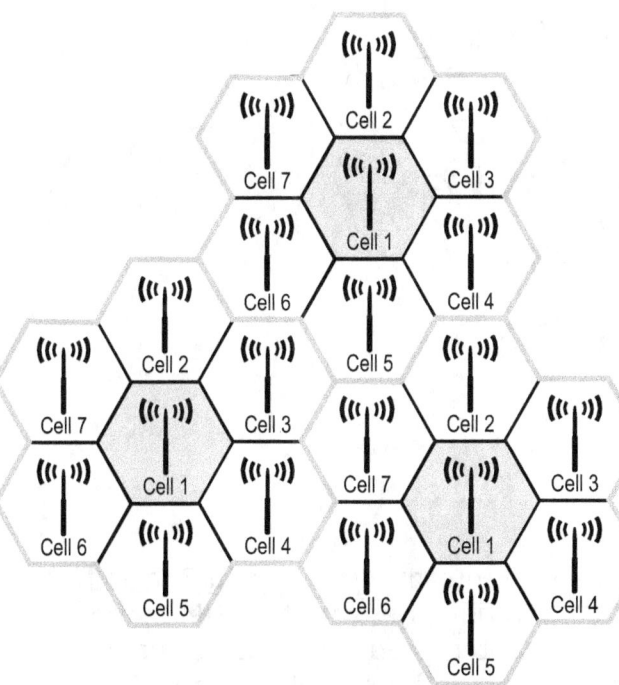

Mobile phone cells will not have nice clean edges as the diagrams suggest. Cells can be thought of more realistically as being roughly circular, with areas of overlap and, in some cases, areas of zero coverage. Local geography, together with the type and siting of the base station and the location of any large buildings or structures, will all affect the actual shape of each cell. Depending on its design, a single cell may only be able to serve a few hundred subscribers at a time.

Densely populated urban areas will have to serve a greater user density than sparsely populated rural areas. One way of dealing with higher user densities is to use a larger number of smaller cells. Large sports stadiums, with their very high user densities, are particularly challenging for the mobile phone network operators.

There are two principal mobile telephony standards worldwide. The most popular is GSM (Global System for Mobile). In the USA, most providers follow CDMA (Code Division Multiple Access), although GSM is also used. Under CDMA each company keeps a list of all the phones that are authorised to use their network, linking this to each phone's electronic serial number. GSM phones are authorised by inserting a valid SIM (Subscriber Identification Module, also *SIM card*).

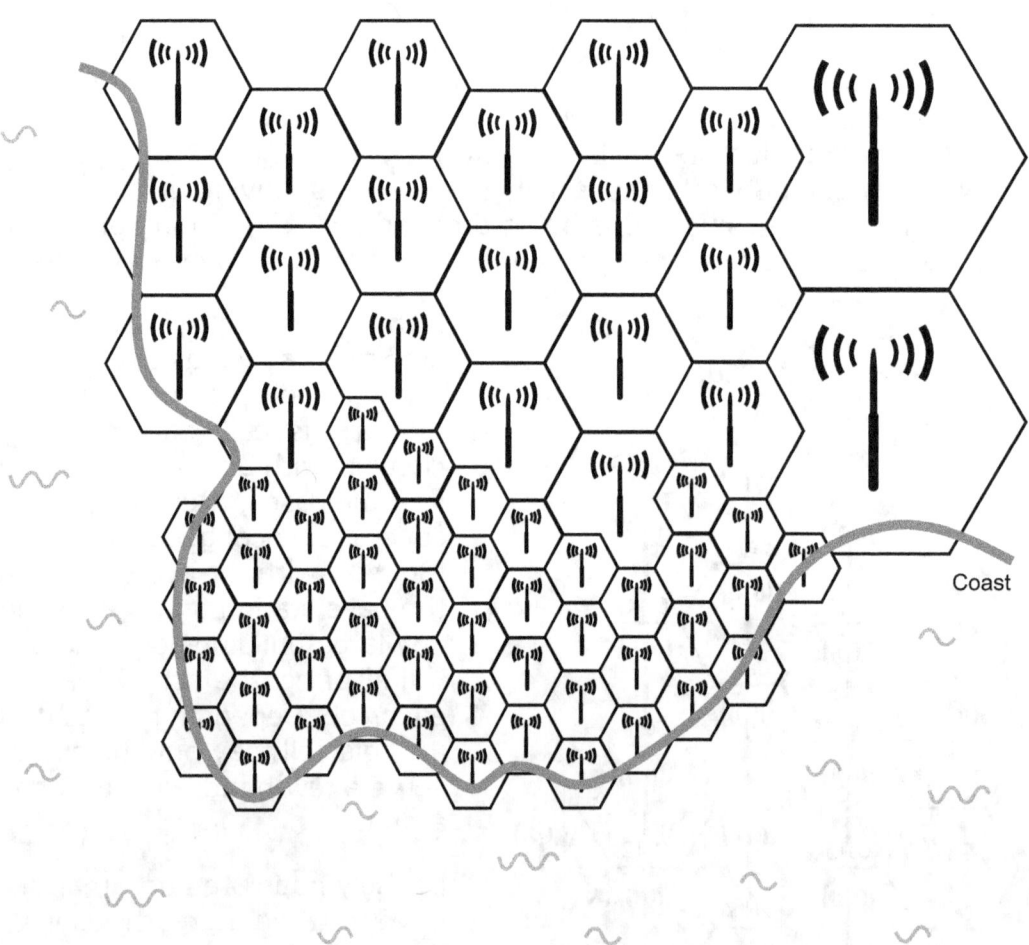

Coastal town - more urban cells, fewer rural cells

A SIM contains a microchip that holds an IMSI (International Mobile Subscriber Identity) number and details of the particular mobile network the SIM user is authorised to use. It also contains the ICCID (Integrated Circuit Card Identifier), a unique identifier which is both stored on the card and physically engraved upon it.

The ICCID is made up of three numbers, the user's account number, one which identifies the SIM issuer and a check digit (Luhn algorithm).

SIMs can store kilobytes of data and used to be important for holding SMS messages and details of contacts, but their capacity is now tiny in comparison with phone internal memory and any added memory card storage.

SIMs make it easy to switch between GSM compliant phones, as all the user needs to do is to swap it from their old phone,to the new one. It also makes it possible to have multiple SIM phones, so that a user can have a single phone and use different accounts/service providers, e.g. for work and personal use.

Mobile phone mast (base station) disguised as a palm tree, Morocco

A GSM service provider can implement software on the phones they provide, so that they only accept SIM cards from their network. If a SIM from another network is used, the phone will not work. However, phones can be unlocked for a small fee or for free. UK government intervention in 2016 led to the major networks abolishing unlocking fees, for pay monthly customers who had served their minimum contract term.

Network generations, approximate timeline
- 1G 1979 Analogue
- 2G 1991 Digital, limited data services including SMS text messages
- 3G 2002 Mobile broadband
- 4G 2009 Faster speeds, reduced network congestion
- 5G 2018-2020? Faster still... higher user densities, improved latency

Audio latency, sometimes referred to as mouth to ear delay, is the time delay that occurs as a result of the processing and transmission of sound. High quality voice calls require maximum latency of the order of tens of milliseconds. Once it is around 150 - 200 milliseconds, then it becomes very difficult to converse, with both parties inadvertently interrupting and speaking over each other. Audio latency ("*delay on the line*") is sometimes apparent during television interviews, when the interviewer and interviewee are in different studios, perhaps in different countries. It can make it difficult to maintain a conversation and can be rather annoying to listen to.

Smartphones
Smartphones are a miracle of miniaturisation with a huge amount of technology crammed into a very small container, sometimes referred to as *technology convergence*. There could be as many as five different radio systems. Apart from

the phone itself, you will usually find NFC (near-field communication, used for example, for contactless payments), Wi-Fi, Bluetooth and GPS. Despite being packed tightly together, none of these must be allowed to interfere with the others.

Typical smartphone components

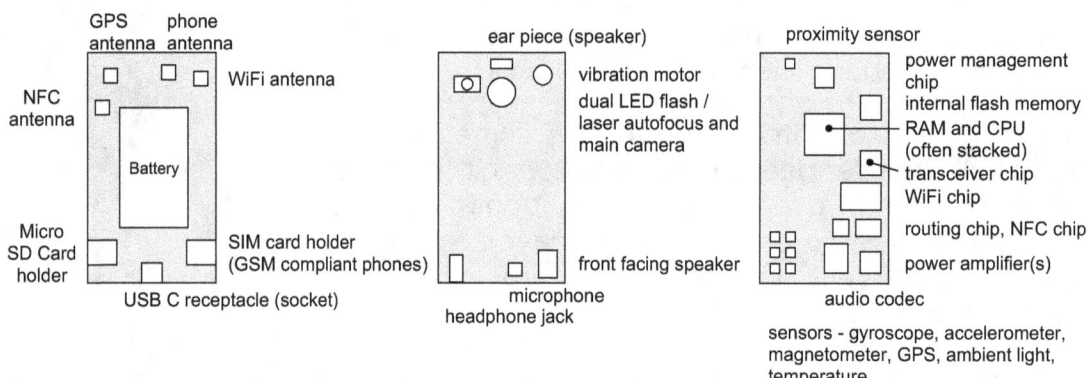

Interfaces are likely to include a USB receptacle for plugging in a charger and possibly for data exchange and perhaps a headphone socket.

The precise components used in smartphones will obviously vary, but there are common functions to be taken care of and much similarity. The transceiver chip handles the transmission and reception of phone signals, whilst the routing chip deals with internet data in much the same way as a home broadband router. The audio codec looks after the analogue to digital and digital to analogue conversion of voice data as well as its compression/decompression. Some chips may be mounted under thin metal plates, that act as rudimentary heat sinks.

Modern smartphones include an array of different sensors, again, exactly what each phone includes will vary, but the most common ones are as follows.

- Camera(s), usually two, one front facing and one rear facing
- Accelerometer for sensing movement along 3 axes
- Gyroscope for more accurate positioning information
- Proximity sensor incorporating an infrared LED and a light sensor so that the phone knows when it is being held up to a user's ear and can therefore turn the display off and disable touch-sensitive controls
- Magnetometer (for measuring magnetic fields, e.g. to provide an electronic compass)
- Ambient light sensor for adjusting the screen brightness according to current conditions

Living in a digital world - Chapter 5: How some stuff works

Diagram illustrating a mobile-mobile phone call

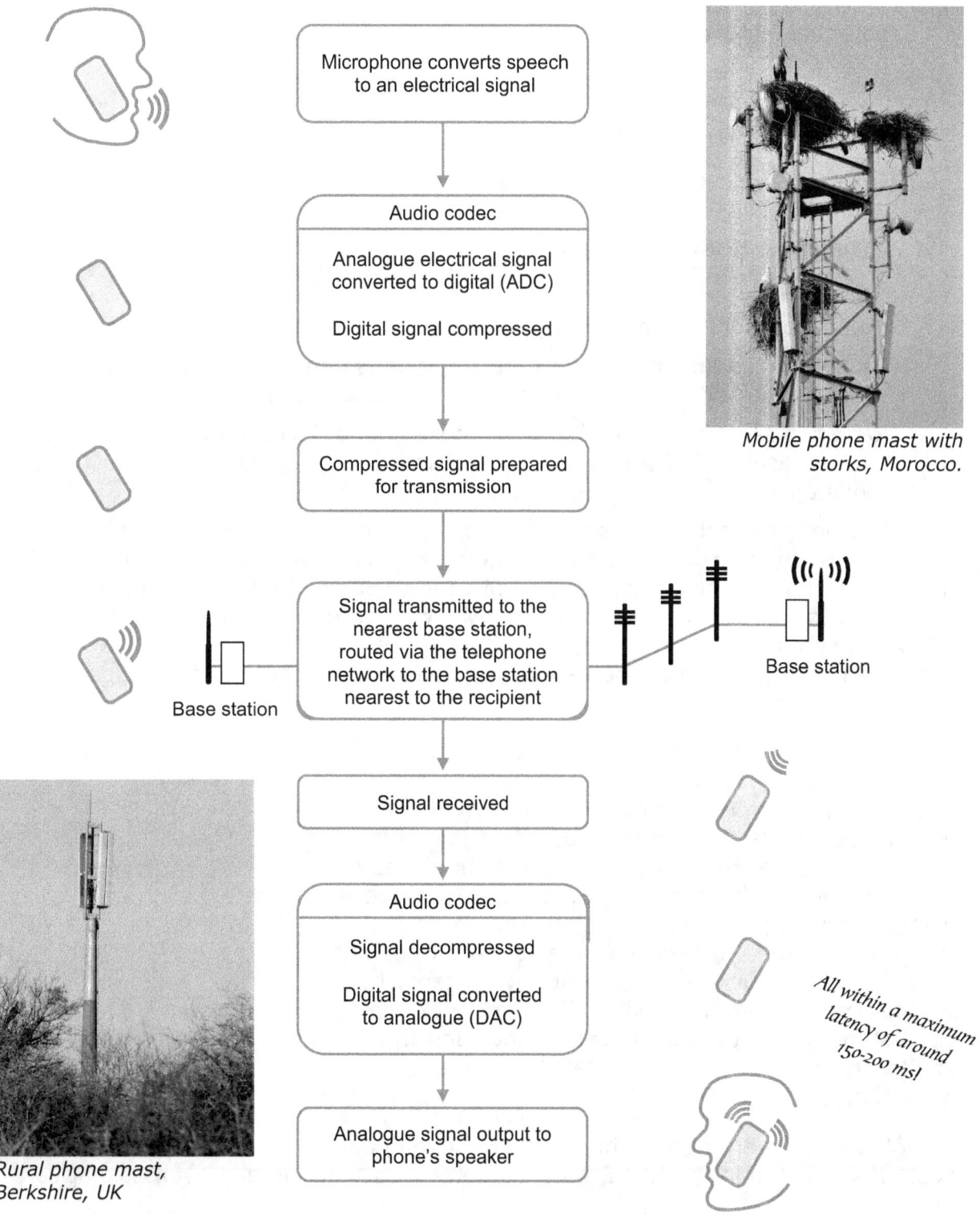

Mobile phone mast with storks, Morocco.

Rural phone mast, Berkshire, UK

All within a maximum latency of around 150-200 ms!

> Temperature sensor - whilst a phone may have an ambient temperature sensor, it will certainly have at least one for monitoring conditions within the phone, in particular the temperature of the CPU and the battery. This allows potential faults to be diagnosed and, if necessary, to shut down the phone to avoid damage.

Other more esoteric sensors that have found their way into some models have included the following.

> Fingerprint sensors, so that only the owner of a phone can unlock it (user authentication)

> Iris scanner (for user authentication)

> Air humidity

> Heart rate monitor - measuring the pulsations of tiny veins in the finger

> Pedometer - although steps can be counted using an accelerometer, a specialist sensor is both more accurate and uses less power

> Radiation sensor - featured in a Japanese phone, following the Fukushima nuclear disaster in March 2011 and subsequent concerns about exposure to radiation.

Microelectromechanical systems (MEMS) are microscopic devices, especially those that have moving parts. Manufacturing methods have developed from those used to make semiconductor products, such as microprocessors. The key techniques are building up thin layers of material by deposition, patterning using photolithography, followed by etching to produce the necessary forms. MEMS techniques allow the production of tiny mobile phone sensors, such as accelerometers, gyroscopes and magnetic compasses.

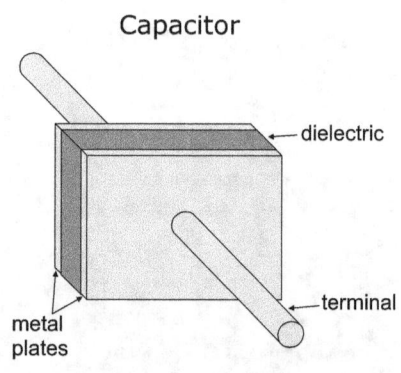

One MEMS accelerometer design is based on the electrical property of capacitance. A capacitor is a fundamental electronic component that is made up of two conducting plates, separated by a thin layer of insulating material known as a dielectric. The dielectric can be air. When a voltage is applied across the plates electrons are stripped from one plate and are attracted to the other plate, but because of the dielectric there is a break in the circuit and no current flow. A capacitor therefore stores electrical charge. The amount of charge it can store is measured by its capacitance and the smaller the gap between the plates, the higher the capacitance.

A single axis accelerometer is only able to move in one direction, along a single axis. This is shown in the MEMS accelerometer diagram. There is a mass, that can move backwards and forwards against the springs, for example, if the phone it is part of, is shaken. Suppose the mass is moving to the right. The gap C1 will be increasing and the capacitance between the fixed plate and the moving plate to its right will be decreasing. The gap C2 will be getting smaller and the electrical capacitance between the fixed plate and the moving plate to its left will be increasing. Sensing changes in the capacitance allows the accelerometer to determine what sort of acceleration is being experienced. The forces causing this

MEMS accelerometer

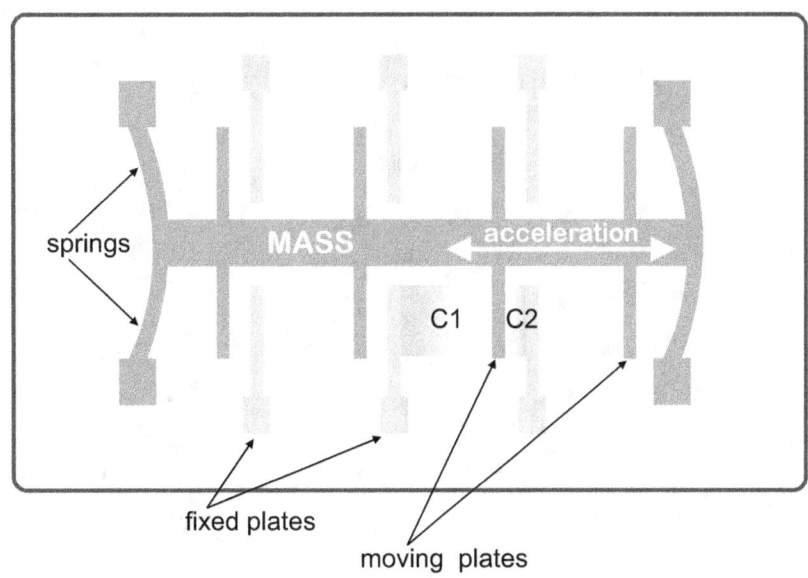

acceleration could be static, for example, gravity or they could be dynamic, caused by moving or vibrating the accelerometer. MEMS accelerometers are of the order of 2.0 mm x 2.0 mm x 1.5 mm in size, although some are smaller than this, with a total volume of less than 1 mm³.

To give a full, three dimensional picture, the accelerometer must measure the acceleration along three, orthogonal axes, i.e. three axes all at right angles to each other. These are sometimes referred to as the x, y and z axes. In other words, the component shown in the MEMS accelerometer diagram would need to be repeated three times, with one lying along each of the three different axes. More usually, two of the above design are used to detect horizontal motion along the x and y axes, with a slightly different design used to detect vertical movement along the z axis.

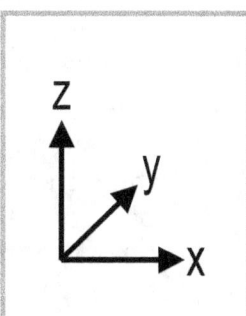

Satellite communications

The concept of geostationary communications satellites was proposed by science fiction author Arthur C Clarke in a 1945 paper. The first artificial Earth satellite was the Soviet Union's 1957 Sputnik 1, but the first dedicated communications satellite was NASA's Echo 1, a balloon that floated 1,000 miles above the planet. Launched in 1960, it was a **passive reflector**, as were all of the early communications satellites. This meant they simply reflected signals beamed to them, back down towards a receiver. The signals that are received from passive satellites are obviously going to be very weak and most modern satellites are active, amplifying the received signal before re-transmitting it.

Satellite - passive reflector

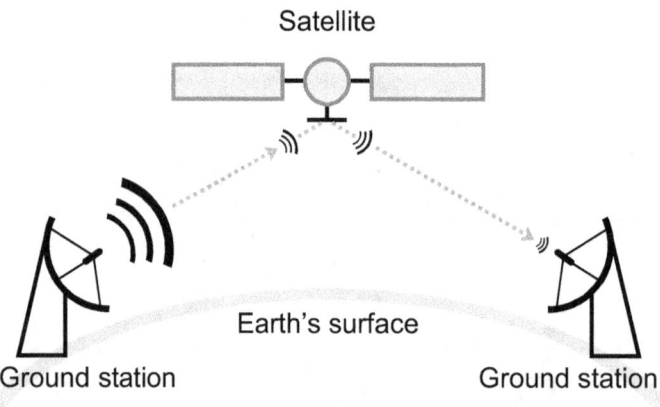

Communications satellites generally have one of three types of orbit.

> Geostationary satellites orbit at an altitude of over 22,000 miles, chosen so that the satellite moves in time with the rotation of the earth. Therefore, from the perspective of someone on the Earth's surface, the satellite does not appear to move and the terrestrial transmitting/receiving equipment will always point in the same direction.

> Low Earth orbits range from around 100 to 1200 miles, which makes the satellites that use them cheaper to launch. As they are closer to the ground, they do not need as high signal strength. However, they do change their position relative to the ground quite quickly and will eventually disappear below the horizon, so several will be needed to maintain continuous service.

> Medium Earth orbits sit in between these two.

A set of satellites working together is known as a satellite **constellation**. The Iridium system uses a constellation of 66 low Earth orbit satellites (plus six in-orbit spares) to provide a global satellite phone service.

Communications satellites are used to provide services to telephone and internet companies, as well as to broadcasters. They are also used for military communications.

The inverse square law

Suppose that the strength of a radio signal is measured at one 1 km and 2 km from the transmitter. The signal covering 1 m² at 1 km will be covering four times the area at 2 km, because both the width and height being covered will have doubled. The signal is spreading out in two dimensions. It will be four times more spread out and the signal strength at 2 km will be one quarter what it is at 1 km. Treble the distance and the signal strength goes down by nine times. Quadruple the distance and the signal is 16 times weaker.

Signal strength - inverse square law

one ninth of the signal strength

one quarter of the signal strength

x 1   x 2   x 3

The signal strength goes down by the *square* of the distance. This is known as the **inverse square law**.

A geostationary satellite, with an altitude of just over 22,000 miles, is roughly 22 times further away than a satellite in low Earth orbit, with an altitude of 1,000 miles. Therefore the signal reaching the geostationary satellite will be approximately $22^2 = 484$ times weaker.

Satellite navigation systems

The Global Navigation Satellite System (GNSS) has as its core two medium earth orbit satellite constellations, the American Global Positioning System (GPS, 32 satellites) and the Russian Global Navigation Satellite System (GLONASS, 24 satellites). Both countries offered free use of their systems to the international community. The Chinese BeiDou Navigation Satellite System (BDS, will comprise 35 satellites) and the European Union Galileo system (will comprise 24 satellites plus spares) are under construction at the time of writing.

The basic GPS service has an accuracy of about 8m, 95% of the time, anywhere on or near to the earth's surface. Restricted military users have access to increased accuracy down to a few centimetres. It is based on working out the difference between the time that a satellite signal is sent and the time that it is received. That is why the satellites have to carry atomic clocks, since they need access to extremely accurate time measurements. Once the time difference is known and adjustments made for various atmospheric effects, the distance between the satellite and the receiver can be computed.

Given information about the ranges to three satellites, together with their locations when the signals were sent, the receiver can work out its three dimensional position. If a signal can be received from a fourth satellite then there is no need for the atomic clocks and the receiver can calculate latitude, longitude, altitude and time.

Artificial intelligence

Whilst taking an artificial intelligence course at The University of Birmingham in 1992, I was interested to find that the computer science students were joined by a group of cognitive scientists. The computer scientists were clearly there to learn how machines could be given what might pass for a measure of human-like intelligence. The cognitive scientists were presumably there to see what insights could be gained into real cognition, from the study of attempts to make hardware "think".

It is a measure of how complex it is to make devices that are "truly intelligent", that what passes for artificial intelligence (AI) currently, refers to a narrow or weak form of intelligence, focused on a tightly defined task or range of tasks. It is also why the field has fragmented into a number of specialised areas, such as the following.

Gaming - for example, strategy games such as Go, chess, poker, draughts and noughts and crosses.

Natural language processing - understanding spoken language.

Expert systems - these attempt to capture the knowledge of specialists and make it available to others providing advice and explanation. Expert systems have been built to support activity in many different areas, including automated customer service using chatbots, process automation, e.g. loan approvals and insurance claims management, analysis and prediction of customer behaviour, crime prevention support, purchasing recommendation engines, contextual advertising, simplifying access to scientific knowledge, knowledge sharing and medical diagnosis. An early medical expert system was called Mycin and it helped doctors to identify bacteria and then recommend appropriate antibiotics and dosages. Typical expert systems have two key components, a **knowledge base** containing all the expert knowledge that is to be applied and an **inference engine** which draws conclusions, using the knowledge base and data about the particular situation being dealt with.

Vision systems - for example, identification tasks (e.g. facial recognition, number plate recognition), automatic inspection, control (e.g. robotic machinery, self-driving vehicles) and organising information (e.g. automatic indexing of images)

One classification of vision systems uses four Rs.

- Recognition - recognising objects
- Reconstruction - for example, using a series to 2D images to create a 3D environment
- Registration - tracking or alignment. A self-driving car might track pedestrians (for avoidance) as well as lane markings and road boundaries
- Reorganisation - unsupervised learning, mirroring how children learn about the world around them, without being told anything

Neural networks - these attempt to process information in a similar way to the human brain and "learn" from experience. They can derive meaning from complicated or imprecise data and can be used to extract patterns and detect trends. A neural network would be needed for a computer vision system based on reorganisation.

Robotics - there are many applications, including material handling and machine loading, welding, cutting and drilling, material removal, product assembly, product polishing and painting and order picking and palletising in warehouses.

Fuzzy logic systems - these attempt to model real thinking, by allowing for degrees of truth. Instead of being "short" or "tall" (a binary choice), a person may have "0.72 of tallness". Fuzzy logic ideas are used in areas such as expert systems and neural networks. Fuzzy logic systems produce acceptable output in response to incomplete, ambiguous, distorted, or inaccurate (i.e. fuzzy) input, something that the human brain is good at doing.

A more recent term is **artificial general intelligence** (**AGI**) which refers to devices that have a rounded, complete type of artificial intelligence - perhaps the intelligent android, much beloved of science fiction.

How the growth in computing power over time has changed the technologies that are in common use

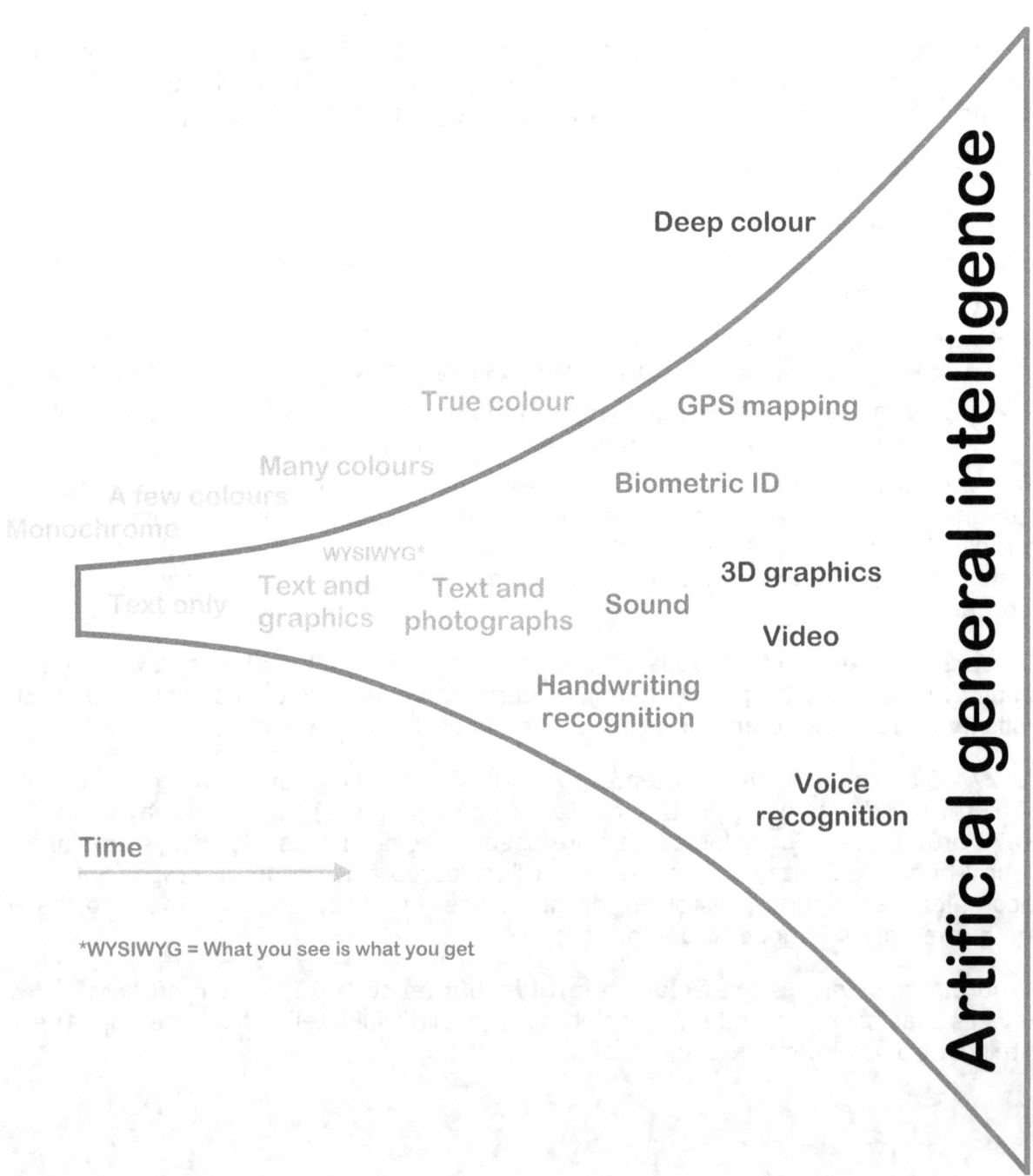

*WYSIWYG = What you see is what you get

There is some dispute around the scope of AI as devices become increasingly capable. Handwriting recognition is now very well developed and voice recognition has reached the stage where it is appearing as part of consumer products, either for giving simple commands to devices, as part of automated dictation software or for automated customer service helplines. This can result in some tasks being removed from the definition of AI, leading some to comment that, "*AI is whatever hasn't been done yet.*"

It has been predicted that within 30 years there will be readily affordable computers with greater processing power than the average human brain. Others foresee the technological singularity, a point in time where the invention of devices with intelligence far in excess of the brightest human minds, trigger runaway technological growth, with entirely unforeseeable consequences. Others, such as Paul Allen, co-founder of Microsoft, suggest that progress is likely to be much slower. We are reminded of how complex human cognition is and how brittle many AI applications are, trapped within rigid constraints and set algorithms, unable to generalise.

This seems to be born out by our experience to date. Hardware capabilities have marched on relentlessly, as typified by Moore's Law. In 1965, co-founder of Intel, Gordon Moore, noted that the number of transistors per square inch on integrated circuits (silicon "chips") had roughly doubled every two years since their invention. In fact, in the following decades, this doubling has typically only taken about 18 months, staggering exponential growth. However, this pace is showing signs of slowing and could be reaching the limits of current technology. Whilst the processors have become more and more powerful and the amount of working memory and long term storage that is affordable, has exploded, the capability of humans to exploit this technology has grown more sedately. Our understanding of human cognition is at a relatively low level, with much left to be discovered. Whilst sudden step changes in understanding and/or technology cannot be ruled out, it seems likely that any singularity is a long way ahead.

Artificial intelligence has been around about as long as electronic computers. In 1950 Alan Turing introduced what has become known as the Turing Test[1] for evaluating intelligence. The term artificial intelligence was coined in 1956 by US computer scientist John McCarthy, often referred to as the father of AI.

For a while it was comforting to know that although computers existed that could calculate far more rapidly and accurately than the best humans, when it came to the complex strategies required for games such as chess, the best humans could always beat the best machines. The human brain was clearly doing something, or

---

[1] The Turing Test involves an interrogator questioning a human being and a computer, using text, without knowing which is which. Turing's view was that if the interrogator could not tell which was the machine and which was the human following this "imitation game", then the machine could be described as being intelligent.

perhaps many things, that made it superior when it came to complex tasks. A seminal moment was reached in 1997 when the then world chess champion, Garry Kasparov, was beaten by the Deep Blue chess computer, created by IBM. In 2016 the AlphaGo program defeated Go[1] grandmaster and many times world champion, Lee Sedol (Korea). A successor program, AlphaGo Zero (AGZ), trained itself from scratch in three days and crushed its "colleague", AlphaGo, winning all of the 100 games played. Both programs were produced by DeepMind Technologies, a UK company founded in 2010 and acquired by Google in 2014.

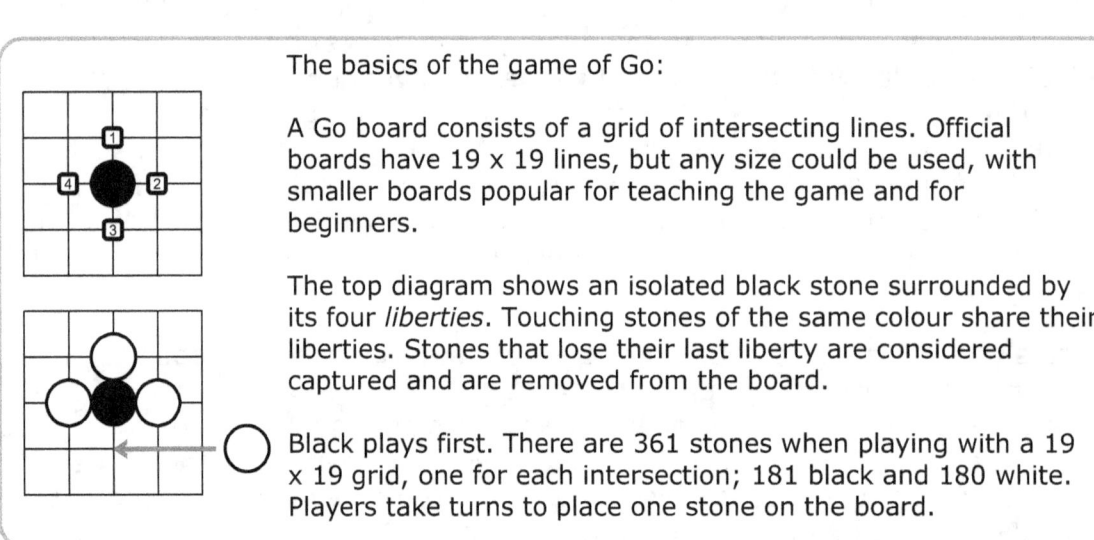

The basics of the game of Go:

A Go board consists of a grid of intersecting lines. Official boards have 19 x 19 lines, but any size could be used, with smaller boards popular for teaching the game and for beginners.

The top diagram shows an isolated black stone surrounded by its four *liberties*. Touching stones of the same colour share their liberties. Stones that lose their last liberty are considered captured and are removed from the board.

Black plays first. There are 361 stones when playing with a 19 x 19 grid, one for each intersection; 181 black and 180 white. Players take turns to place one stone on the board.

There was an interesting difference in the approaches taken by the two programs. AlphaGo had the results of thousands of previously played Go games as part of its programming. AGZ was simply provided with the rules of the game and played itself, starting with random play and without any human supervision. The software used a neural network to continually learn from its experiences. Although training only took three days, thanks to modern processing power, it played 4.9 million games with itself, effectively being its own teacher. It developed from playing like a naïve beginner to become an expert, eventually creating some new strategies of its own. This is a significant shift from older approaches, which have often been based on collecting large amounts of data relating to human attempts at tasks and trying to build models that imitate human activity. These older approaches could be described as "brute force AI", based on sheer computational power and/or large amounts of collected data. It is claimed that the AlphaGo Zero algorithms can be applied generally. If true, this could be a big leap forwards.

It is reminiscent of the world's first iron bridge, built, would you believe it, in the village of Ironbridge, Shropshire. Constructed in 1779, this cast iron bridge uses a number of woodworking joints. Cast iron was a new material and what was

---

[1] Go is an ancient board game. In its conception it is simpler than chess, however in terms of the number of moves, it has many times more possible combinations.

understood at that time was how to work with wooden structures. More efficient ways of designing with this novel material had yet to be developed. Perhaps our early attempts at AI are similar to using woodworking methods when working with iron. Will the use of neural networks provide a major boost on the road towards artificial general intelligence? Or will it prove to be a false dawn?

Why is AI so difficult?

Consider one example of AI, computer vision. With a human, vision comes via the eye and a 2-dimensional image that is formed on the retina. This image is then processed by the brain. A quick glance at the left hand image below and it is easy to see that it is some sort of room, containing some chairs, a table and some stools.

But how could you program a computer so that it could recognise the items in the image and work out that it is a room? Which objects are close to the camera and which are further away? There are two identical chairs, but they are at different angles to the camera and therefore do not make identical shapes in the image. The chairs do not have four legs, as might be expected, so how would you define "chair" for the computer? One of the chairs has no legs at all and is hanging from the ceiling! Detecting edges is one approach to separating objects and the image on the right has been processed to show these. But the strong lighting has produced shadows and the edges, e.g. of the stools, are not showing clearly. How can a computer work out what is shadow and what is an object? Humans can do these things incredibly quickly and without any thought. However, it is hugely challenging to try and devise a method to allow a digital device to carry out the same, "simple" task of interpreting what it is seeing.

There is a great deal of research currently into autonomous, self-driving vehicles. These will need to be able to identify a range of objects, including other vehicles, people, animals and road furniture if they are to be able to respond appropriately and operate safely. How could "car" be defined for a computer? A starting point might be something that has a wheel at each corner, but already there are problems. The Morgan Motor Company (still in production) and the Reliant Motor

Williams FW08B Formula 1 test car. Picture courtesy of Williams F1.

Company are both well known for their three-wheeled vehicles. In 1982 the Williams Formula 1 race team unveiled the six-wheeled FW08B, that proved to be around 3 seconds a lap faster than the opposition during an open testing day. A rule change quickly followed, limiting the number of wheels to four and this prototype never raced in a Grand Prix. Again, the human brain has no difficulty in identifying the FW08B as a racing car. It handles "fuzzy data" in its stride. Sure, the car has an unheard of[1] number of wheels, but it clearly shares enough in common with other racing cars to be identified for what it is. Having a strict definition of an object clearly causes problems, because there are likely to be exceptions, with the prospect of potentially radical new designs in the future. How do you give a digital device common sense? What are the clues that tell us that the FW08B must be a racing car?

The task becomes more daunting if you want a computer to be able to interpret a full range of images - indoors and outdoors, taken in different countries, at different times of the day, at different seasons of the year and in different weather conditions, including a full range of everyday objects. This is why early AI applications could only operate under very restricted conditions, to limit the huge possible range of variation, that human brains usually take happily in their stride. Humans can cope pretty well with objects that they have never seen before - perhaps using some sort of pattern matching to make assumptions about what unknown objects might be, until more can be learned.

Williams FW08B Formula 1 car being tested. Picture courtesy of Williams F1.

Consider reading, an altogether more simple task, you might think. How do humans read? Thinking back to early school days, it would seem obvious that each word and its spelling is

---

[1] To be fair, they were not entirely unheard of - other teams experimented with 6-wheeled cars around the same time.

looked at, in order to identify it and then add all the words together to make a sentence.

Here is a quick test of that idea. Each word in the following paragraph has had its letters jumbled up. It should not be possible to read it.

tBu ti epsarpa hatt sgtihn aer otn ttha pselmi! ouY nca umeblj pu lal teh lettesr ni heac ordw nda os gnlo sa eht tsfri dan stal leestrt aer ni eht otcrerc paecl, eht ettx nca isllt eb daer. imnAagz!

Some readers may have managed to read bits, but it will have been hard work. A similar test is to keep the first and last letter of each word in their correct places and only to jumble up the rest. Clearly all 3, 2 and 1 letter words will be correctly spelt, but none of the remainder.

But it aeppars taht tgihns are not taht smplie! You can jmuble up all the lteters in ecah wrod and so lnog as the frist and lsat lretets are in the crorcet palce, the txet can sitll be raed. Azimnag!

Or to put it another way...

But it appears that things are not that simple! You can jumble up all the letters in each word and so long as the first and last letters are in the correct place, the text can still be read. Amazing!

Here are some similarly jumbled headlines taken from the BBC website, 26th October 2017. How many can you decipher?

1. Travel story: Wmoan is olny pngeesasr on hlidoay jet

2. Heartwarming headline: Colpue kpet arpat by scrtit fthaer mrary 40 yares ltear

3. African political story: Kyena eoetlcin: Vintog bgenis in re-run aimd teitnehgd sieurtcy

4. Ecological disaster: Tsehe flaotolerbs' McpyaSe & Bbeo aucnctos are paek neiohgtus

Okay, so I lied about number 4, but I did it for a good reason! The headline had nothing to do with ecology, disastrous or otherwise. In fact, it was about footballers. The sentence is quite tough anyway and being misled about the context probably makes it unreadable. With the first three headlines, having the correct context should have made decoding the headlines easier. The correct headlines are printed below.

There is clearly more to reading than just knowing the spelling of individual words, since it is possible to make sense of sentences where most of the words are incorrectly spelt. The jumbled sentences[1] demonstration suggests that part of the reading process may be scanning whole words. Perhaps we only look in detail at the spelling of any words that we don't immediately recognise. It is also likely that context plays an important role.

This is the challenge faced by those working in AI. Tasks that humans may find straightforward and carry out seemingly without thought, such as reading and understanding text and seeing and understanding what is in front of us, turn out to be very complex tasks, that prove to be incredibly challenging to fully understand and then to try and implement in digital devices. However, progress is being made and greater "intelligence" is being built into a growing number of gadgets and gizmos, including many serious, commercial applications.

Headlines in their original state.

1. Woman is only passenger on holiday jet

2. Couple kept apart by strict father marry 40 years later

3. Kenya election: Voting begins in re-run amid tightened security

4. These footballers' MySpace & Bebo accounts are peak noughties

The study of artificial intelligence does throw up some interesting philosophical questions, such as what is intelligence? Is human and machine intelligence effectively the same thing? If it is not, what are the differences? One that has been explored by various films and television dramas is, can machine intelligence reach the point where robots should have rights? Another is the post-singularity conundrum, will artificial intelligence eventually seek to displace mankind and take over the world...? Before becoming too fearful, it should be remembered that Deep Blue could play chess and beat a world champion. But that was all it could do, unless it was reprogrammed for another task. AlphaGo Zero is potentially a different story with its ability to self-learn, but nevertheless, I expect that humans will continue to rule the roost for some time to come.

Bitcoin and other cryptocurrencies

There are now hundreds of cryptocurrencies in circulation, the ten largest by market capitalisation in October 2017 were Bitcoin, Ethereum, Bitcoin Cash, Ripple, Litecoin, Dash, NEM, BitConnect, NEO, and Monero. To understand how it is possible for these to exist at all, it is necessary to consider the nature of money.

---

[1] Readers interested in finding out more about reading jumbled sentences might enjoy this web page: https://www.mrc-cbu.cam.ac.uk/people/matt.davis/cmabridge/

What is money?

Turning back the clock to a time before money was invented, people relied on the barter system. They would swap whatever they had, in order to get what they wanted. Suppose that Farmer Ugg grew lots of different types of fruit and that strawberries were currently in season. If he wants a chicken he could take a basket of berries to Farmer Zogg and swap them. That system works fine, so long as the two parties want whatever each of them have to swap. However, Farmer Zogg might not need any berries, instead she wants a cooking pot. Now Ugg cannot get his chicken, unless Zogg is prepared to take the risk of accepting the strawberries and finding a potter who will accept them in return for a cooking pot. There is added risk because the strawberries will only stay fresh for a limited time, so if Zogg cannot find a strawberry-wanting potter, she could have given up a chicken for nothing. Farmer Ugg has a problem too. His livelihood is largely seasonal, with lots of produce to exchange in the late summer and autumn and very little the rest of the year. It would help if he could cash in on the good times and store some of the value of his crop, until he needs to use it in winter and spring.

This is where money comes in, as a means of exchange and a store of value. Now Ugg can take his strawberries to market, or sell them to visitors to his farm, in exchange for money. He can then take money to Farmer Zogg to buy a chicken and she can then use it to buy the longed-for cooking pot. Money eases and boosts trade, making life better for everyone. Ugg can make as much money as possible when he has fruit to sell and keep some of it back to use when he has no produce.

In the Hitchhiker's Guide to the Galaxy series of books[1] there is a spaceship, the Golgafrincham Ark Fleet Ship B, which is filled with all that planet's middlemen, such as management consultants, hair dressers, and telephone sanitation engineers. The ship crash-lands on a new home world, covered in forests. Not having any money, they decide to adopt the leaf as their currency. One of the problems with their choice is its abundance in their new home, which drives its value down. In effect, this causes a severe bout of hyperinflation. This is recognised belatedly by one of the management consultants.

"So in order to obviate this problem," he continued, "and effectively revalue the leaf, we are about to embark on a massive defoliation campaign, and...er, burn down all the forests."

In this fictional example, although wilfully ignoring the ecological consequences of the proposed action, the management consultant did at least show some appreciation of the importance of money supply. The amount of money in an economy needs to be constrained or controlled, to prevent runaway inflation. It also shows the desirability that money should be durable. It should not crumble or rot and ideally should be resistant to fire and water, in order to hold its value.

---

[1] *Restaurant at the End of the Universe* by Douglas Adams

In 1923 the Weimar Republic in Germany responded to an economic crisis by printing more and more banknotes, resulting in growing inflation, which was met with yet more banknote printing. The more bank notes that were printed, the less they were worth. Hyperinflation took hold and people were dragging sacks and wheelbarrows full of banknotes around in order to go shopping. It is reported that a woman in Munich left a suitcase full of money outside a shop briefly, whilst she went inside. She returned to find that someone had run off with the suitcase, after dumping all the banknotes in the street! Faith in the German currency collapsed and many of those that had things to exchange reverted to bartering instead. Anyone who had savings or pensions saw their value wiped out.

This shows three further key characteristics of money. It needs to be portable and there should be general agreement about its value, which ideally should not fluctuate wildly.

Prisons are environments where inmates do not have open access to money and other informal currencies are often adopted. These have included tobacco, ramen noodles, spice/flavour enhancers, tinned tuna and phone credit. Cans of mackerel became a popular currency in the US after Federal prisons banned cigarettes. Inmates were limited to buying 14 cans each per week and generally no one wanted to eat the contents, so there was a predictable supply of new currency. *Money macks* (outdated tins) had around 75% of the value of so-called *eating macks*.

When a large quantity of macks were confiscated from one wealthy prisoner, the prison authorities were able to undermine this part of the informal prison economy by leaving the stash in a bin, available to all. This introduced hyperinflation, wiping out the value of a mack overnight.

Cowry shells have an honourable history as currency. They are small, easy to transport, durable, recognisable and resistant to vermin. Their physical form makes them almost impossible to forge. Their similarity in size and shape means that weighing, rather than counting, was often enough to determine the value of a payment. The cowry was accepted in large parts of Asia, Africa and Oceania. The earliest recorded use dates back to the 13th Century BC and they were still being used as currency into the 20th Century.

Coins have been produced for over 2500 years, usually made from metals and metal alloys, with silver and gold being popular for higher value transactions. The value of gold coins is the value of the gold that they contain. It should be remembered that precious metals usually do not have much inherent value. It is true that gold is used in a few industrial processes, giving it some "real value", but most of its value is because everyone regards it as being very desirable. This is no doubt due to some combination of its colour and lustre, durability and relative scarcity. However, the idea of gold having value could be regarded as an artificial construct, rather like assigning value to a cowry shell. Despite this, gold has remained a popular choice of metal for coins throughout much of history.

China has used aluminium for some low value coins. At one time, a spike in international metal prices meant that the coins were worth more as scrap than their face value. Large numbers disappeared from circulation. More recently low value Indian ferritic steel coins were also worth more as scrap. Many were melted down, smuggled to neighbouring Bangladesh and turned into razor blades and jewellery, leading to coin shortages. In the USA it costs more to produce the 1 cent coin than its face value, although this is due to manufacturing and distribution costs, rather than the value of the metals used.

In the 19th and early 20th centuries, many western countries adopted the gold standard for their national currencies. This meant that the value of each currency was fixed relative to each other and to the value of gold. Bank notes were issued on the basis that they could be redeemed for an equivalent amount of the precious metal. This meant that the central banks had to keep large stores of gold to deal with redemptions. Meanwhile, trade could be conducted using paper money, much easier than having to move quantities of heavy gold around.

Countries have abandoned the gold standard over time, usually in response to crises where it looked likely that the quantity of gold in the nation's vaults was going to be insufficient to meet redemption demands. The UK abandoned the gold standard in 1931 and the pound saw a significant fall in its international value as a result. This helped the economy to recover from the ravages of the Great Depression by boosting exports and slowing imports. The USA abandoned the gold standard in 1971.

Now countries issue their own *fiat currencies* that are backed by the national governments, but are not convertible into gold. Fiat currencies offer governments more flexibility in responding to important financial events, such as major stock market slumps and banking crises. We are also in an era where the use of cash is declining in the face of an onslaught from various forms of electronic money. This consists of nothing more than a series of electronic ledger entries, that record the various credits and debits made to our accounts, using credit and debit cards, online bank transfers and similar means.

The first widely used wire transfer service for money, an early form of e-money, was launched by Western Union in 1872. Someone could go into their nearest Western Union office and pay over the amount they wanted to send, plus a transaction fee. A telegraph operator would then send the transaction details to the office nearest to the recipient, using coded instructions. The recipient could then visit this office to collect the money. This process is summarised in the diagram below.

It can be seen that there are two key points about money.

> All forms of money are entirely artificial. More than anything, they depend on the faith that the majority of people have in them.

> A good currency has certain properties, for example it is durable, portable, hard to forge and its supply is controlled so that its value is stable, changing slowly when necessary and generally avoiding wild fluctuations. It must support high and low value transactions and be supported by large numbers of people, who all assign a similar value to it.

The funds (telegraphic/wire) transfer principle

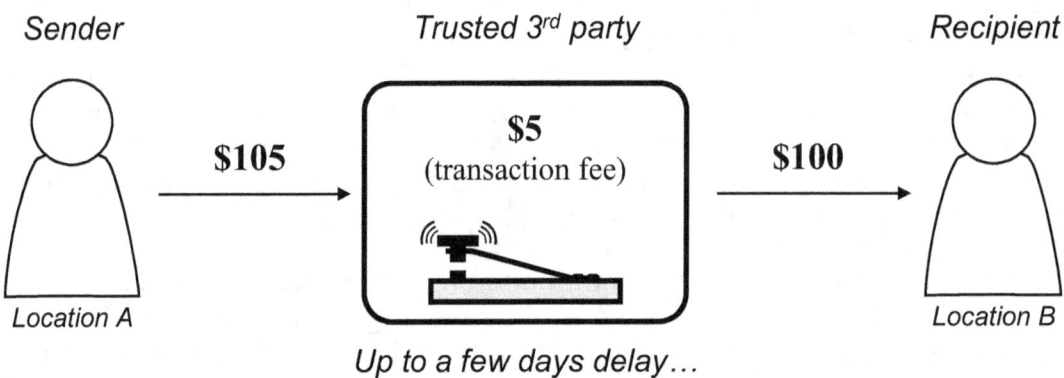

Up to a few days delay...

Public key cryptography

Public key cryptography, also known as **asymmetric cryptography**, plays an important role in cryptocurrencies, giving rise to the **crypto-** prefix.

Symmetric cryptography uses a single, shared key. A physical analogy would be a strongbox that can be opened with a single key. Two people, who both have a copy of the same key, can both access the strongbox and use it to pass items between themselves securely.

Symmetric cryptography uses a single code key. Two people sharing the same code can use it to encrypt and decrypt messages that pass between them. The internet poses a problem however, namely that many people need to exchange information securely who never meet. How can they both end up with the same shared key? Sending the key over the internet is not an option, since it is possible that a third party could intercept it and use it to access any messages secured using that key.

This gave rise to asymmetric cryptography where each user has two keys, a public key that is available to anyone and a private key that must be kept secret for this system to work. Both keys are randomly generated, very large numbers. They are related to each other mathematically, such that a sender can use the public key of a recipient to encrypt a message and the recipient then has to use their private key to decrypt it. The encrypted message could be intercepted by a hostile third party and the recipient's public key is readily available. However, the third party does not have access to the recipient's private key and cannot therefore decrypt the message.

The clever mathematical part is selecting the two keys so that one can be used to encrypt data whilst the other has to be used to decrypt the data.

Asymmetric or public key cryptography

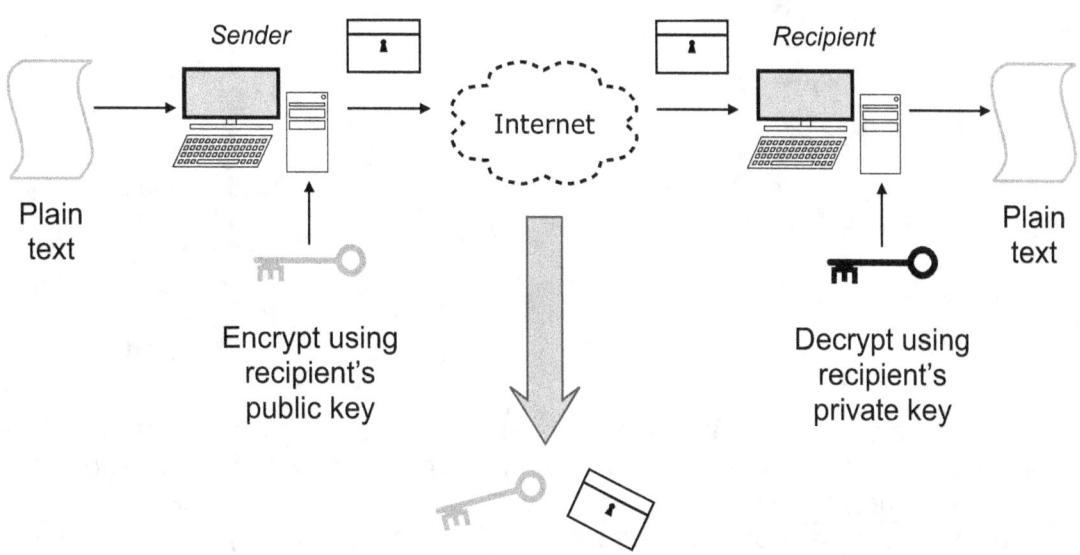

Possible interception by 3rd party

It is virtually impossible to work out the private key if the public key is known. This could only be done by a trial and error process that would require many years of computer processing to carry out a trial and error search. Long code numbers are chosen so that the time required to do this means that for all practical purposes the information can be considered secure.

Public key cryptography can also be used for digital signatures.

A published hash function is calculated for the message content and this is transformed using the sender's private key and added to the message. When the message is received, the recipient recalculates the hash function and transforms it using the sender's public key. If the two results agree the recipient knows that the message must have come from the sender (which cannot be denied later) and that the message content has not been altered in any way during transmission. The text is therefore verified.

These two techniques can be combined to send a message that is both encrypted and signed.

Digital signature using public key cryptography

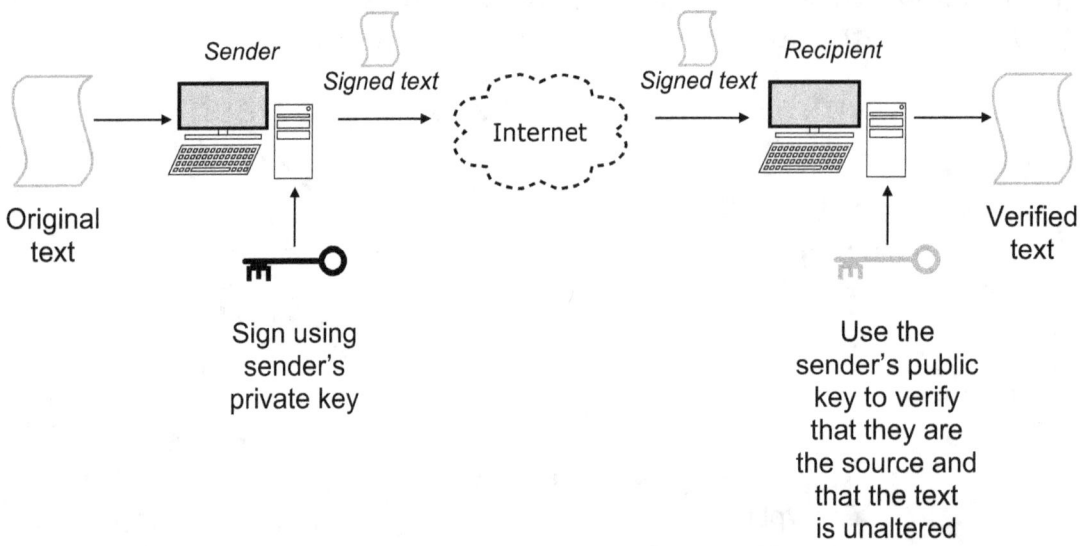

Readers may be aware that some websites are "secure", using encrypted communications, whereas the majority are open/insecure. Banks are examples of institutions that operate secure websites, to allow customers to access their account details and make transactions. Browsers usually display a small, closed padlock icon, or similar, to indicate that a website uses an encrypted connection. Looking at site URLs also tells you about the type of connection. URLs normally begin **http**, whereas those using encrypted communication start **https** (**s** for "secure").

The https protocol actually uses symmetric cryptography, but the common key is shared using asymmetric cryptography. Agreeing the encryption key and all the encrypting and decrypting is handled automatically by the browser software, without users needing to be involved.

How does bitcoin work?

Bitcoin was created by a person, or perhaps a group of people, going by the name of Satoshi Nakamoto, in 2009. The identity of Satoshi has not been established beyond doubt. It followed the publication of a paper titled *Bitcoin: A Peer-to-Peer Electronic Cash System*.

Bitcoin does away with the need for a trusted third party (usually a bank or similar organisation), replacing it with a peer to peer network of users. It also seeks to significantly improve the time it takes to move money and to drastically reduce the cost. It aims to be a more appropriate form of money for our digitally driven world.

A bitcoin is nothing more than an entry in a huge, shared ledger - rather like a bank account record. This ledger records every bitcoin transaction and by late 2017 it contained around 107 GB of data.

Using a paper ledger analogy, each "page" of transactions is called a block. Each new block that is added includes a hash value calculated from the data in the previous block. This helps to forge the blocks into a continuous chain, hence the term "**blockchain**", used when referring to the bitcoin ledger.

There is no central, trusted third party to maintain the crucial blockchain. Instead, anyone can volunteer to assist with this process, the basic idea being that everyone checks everyone else. Instead of relying on a single, trusted organisation, bitcoin users are trusting that distributed control will stop a single rogue user. When any bitcoin transaction takes place it must be announced to the entire bitcoin community so that ledgers can be updated, giving the account the money is coming from, the account it is going to and the number of bitcoins being sent. Fractions of a bitcoin can be exchanged, as small as one hundred millionth (named a Satoshi by the community, after bitcoin's founder).

Some issues that bitcoin attempts to address

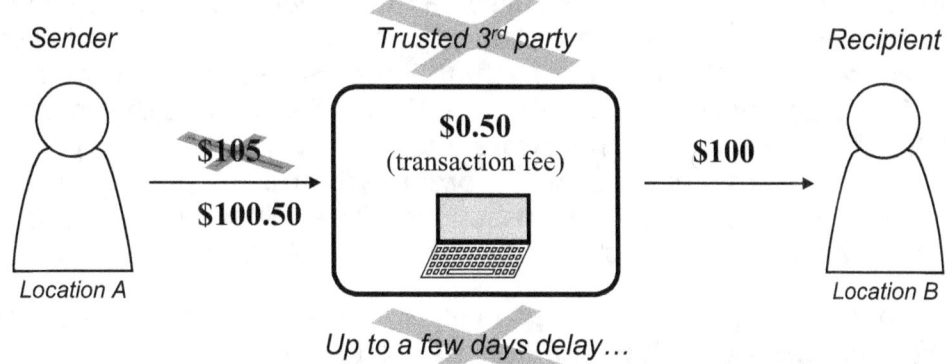

Up to a few minutes delay...

The number of transactions in a block is updated periodically, so that a new block is created approximately every ten minutes. The people maintaining the bitcoin blockchain could be anywhere in the world and it is highly likely that all will be receiving transactions at slightly different times from each other. Only one user is allowed to update the next block to resolve these differences and establish the 'true' version. The updating process, which has become known as *mining*, aims to ensure that the task of updating the blockchain is distributed around many users. This helps maintain security since it is very unlikely that the same person will be able to update two or more consecutive blocks, making it much easier to spot and correct any anomalies/attempts at fraud.

Those volunteers who want to be involved in updating the blockchain, known as miners, have to use their computers to solve a complex hash function, by trial and error searching, that has been chosen because it takes around 10 minutes for a computer to do this. Whoever solves the hash function first (essentially a fairly random selection process) is chosen to update the next block.

The chosen miner is rewarded with bitcoins. This is the only way that new bitcoins are created and the mechanism used regulates/constrains the rate at which this happens. Initially miners received 50 bitcoins for each block that they updated, however the reward halves every 210,000 blocks or approximately every four years. This was chosen as a way of modelling what happens in a typical mine as the target material gets progressively more difficult to obtain, until the mine is exhausted.

Eventually the reward for mining will drop to zero and no more coins will be created. This is expected to occur around 2140, when slightly fewer than 21 million coins will have been created. After launch in 2009, bitcoins were only worth a few pennies, rising to $0.30 the next year. The value has gone up exponentially since; over $13 in 2012, $735 in 2013. 2017 saw it grow from just below $1,000 to a maximum just below $20,000. Mining was initially carried out by enthusiasts, many using their laptop or desktop computers when they were not needed for anything else. It has now become a highly specialised and competitive activity. Miners buy expensive, specialised mining 'boxes', dedicated computers optimised for solving mathematical problems. These run at such an intensive rate that they generate a great deal of heat and need to be cooled effectively. This means that miners need to spend a lot of money, both on hardware and electricity, so it is no longer possible for an individual to make a profit using an ordinary home computer. It is likely that when mining rewards drop to zero, transactions fees will have to be introduced, so that incentives can still be offered to miners to maintain the blockchain.

Small scale operators often join a pool, where a group of miners join their resources and are rewarded every time the pool gets to add the next block, according to how much mining they carry out.

There are two other important areas of infrastructure to allow bitcoin to work. Exchanges are needed to allow bitcoin users to either buy more bitcoins or to swap some of their bitcoins for other, 'normal' currencies, or indeed, other cryptocurrencies. Recently there have been times when the rates on different exchanges have varied by a few thousand dollars, suggesting that the bitcoin market is far from efficient at establishing "true value". Bitcoin users also need wallets. These do not hold their bitcoins, since these will be on the blockchain. Instead they are software that hold a user's credentials as a bitcoin user, essentially the private and public keys. When a purchase is made, a wallet will check with the bitcoin network to make sure that the user has enough bitcoins to cover the cost.

Transactions have to be signed with a user's private key to authenticate their identity. One user claimed to have lost their wallet in 2013 and access to 7,500 bitcoins, when the hard drive it was stored on was accidentally thrown out. There was no backup and at USD $20,000 per bitcoin they would be worth $150 million. Those coins are now lost to the bitcoin community, unless the hard drive is ever rediscovered in working order and the private key can be obtained.

Is bitcoin a real currency?

At the time of writing, bitcoin users can probably best be characterised as belonging to one of the following groups.

- Miners. Making money from helping to maintain the bitcoin infrastructure.
- Speculators. Hoping to make money by purchasing bitcoins at a lower value, relative to other currencies and selling them at a higher value.
- Libertarians. Those who do not trust the normal banking system and/or dislike the manipulations of governments and central banks.
- Criminals. Ironic, given that all transactions are published to a shared ledger! However, users are only identified by their public keys, so bitcoin offers pseudoanonymity and less official oversight and risk of discovery than using traditional banks.
- Normal commercial use. This has been growing, with millions of bitcoin users and tens of thousands of organisations now accepting bitcoin payment, including some large multinational companies. Bill Gates, co-founder of Microsoft, has pointed out how useful cryptocurrencies could be for the world's poorest people. They often do not have access to normal banking facilities. Many of their purchases are for small amounts. This makes other forms of payment, which often have a *fixed price plus a percentage* charging structure, disproportionately expensive. Increasing numbers *do* own a smartphone however, giving them access to cryptocurrency wallets. Bitcoins may also appeal to citizens of countries whose own currencies are in crisis or where the national economy is failing, in much the same way as gold and currencies like the dollar, euro and pound are often viewed as relatively safe havens in times of crisis.

In terms of the characteristics of money described earlier, bitcoin meets many of them. It is certainly artificial. A growing number of people and organisations are showing faith in bitcoins as currency, although this is still a small minority. It is portable, being available via a smartphone and there is a controlled supply. It can support both high and low value transactions.

Perhaps the biggest failing of bitcoin to date has been its volatility, due in part to significant variation in its perceived value, as well as the disproportionate role played by speculators in determining its price. It is still establishing itself as a currency and as more people actively trade using bitcoins and more organisations accept bitcoins as payment, it might be expected that its volatility will fall. One big attraction is the ability to trade internationally without incurring large currency exchange costs. However, as with all currencies, much depends on market confidence and any significant bad news, such as a large, successful fraud, could cause that confidence to evaporate quickly. The same can happen to individual banks and the currencies of countries that are less well developed economically, however because of the experimental nature of cryptocurrencies, they could be expected to behave in a more brittle, less resilient way.

At the time of writing (January 2018) each bitcoin was worth around $14,000 having started 2017 at around $1,000 and peaked at nearly $20,000. Its lowest value during this period was $739, the biggest daily rise in value was 27% and the largest daily fall was 16%. The rapid increase in the value of each bitcoin meant that it largely stopped being used as a means of exchange, since bitcoin holders wanted to keep all their coins so that they could benefit from the ballooning exchange rate. The situation suggested a massive bubble that could burst at any time. Chinese authorities decided to close the country's bitcoin exchanges, whereas Japan and Australia passed laws to bring cryptocurrencies within their regulatory frameworks. One estimate has suggested that the process of bitcoin mining and recording transactions now uses more electricity every year than Ireland, which also throws up questions about its long term sustainability. Where next for bitcoin...?

Cryptocurrencies are a fascinating experiment, but it is too early to say with any conviction whether they are a flash in the pan or the future of money. If devastating crashes can be avoided and sensible valuation levels achieved, they could have a rosy future. There is growing interest in what cryptocurrencies offer and provided effective solutions are found to problems as they occur (for example, some wallets have proved vulnerable to hackers, who have been able to take control of accounts and empty them), they should remain with us for some time to come.

Other applications of blockchain technology
Regardless of whether cryptocurrencies are able to grow to self-sustainability in the world economy, the blockchain technology that sits behind them might well end up supporting a range of activities and industries. The use of large, distributed, shared ledgers is currently being investigated for a range of other applications.

One problem with the digital world as it stands, is that it is often hard to know anything about the people that we come across and want to interact or trade with. A global blockchain could be used to store an individual's qualifications, certifications and other information about them to create a portable identity. Some of that information exists online already, but it is spread around in numerous locations and its accuracy is often unknown. Digital identity blockchains could be developed for use in refugee crises, to support those who do not have any official documents.

Physical tracking is another promising application. Food, other products, shipping containers and livestock can all be tracked as they move around supply chains or between farms, studs and abattoirs, to authenticate their provenance. Where did items originate and where have they been to since? This is very useful information, especially where food safety is concerned or where bloodlines are key to an animal's value. Diamonds can have their identifying features recorded to counter the trade in blood diamonds and stolen stones. Other high value items could be recorded on blockchains as an anti-counterfeiting measure.

Banks are investigating using blockchains to improve the SWIFT system for making international payments. The US stock exchange NASDAQ is using a blockchain to carry out share trades, looking to reduce the risk of fraud.

It is early days for all of these applications, as it is for cryptocurrencies. However, blockchain technologies offer a number of potential benefits.

- Reduced costs
- Speeding up transactions
- Easing international transfers
- Reducing regulatory burdens (regulators could be given access to a blockchain rather than having to go through a distinct regulatory process)
- Helping mediate disputes (by providing an authenticated audit trail)
- Improved transparency

Self test

1. How are the binary digits stored on a CD?

2. Where does a passive RFID tag get its power from?

3. Give three uses of an RFID tag.

4. Barcodes normally require a light border area. What is this called?

5. EAN barcodes display 12 symbol characters, but actually encode 13 numbers. How is the 13th digit encoded?

6. What links the base stations of mobile network operators to the public switched telephone network?

7. What is special about the adjacent cells in a mobile phone cluster?

8. With regard to making a phone call, what is audio latency?

9. Name three radio systems commonly found in a smartphone.

10. Name five sensors found in smartphones.

11. What is the difference between satellites in geostationary orbit and those in low earth orbit?

12. Name three specialist areas of study within artificial intelligence.

13. Why is bitcoin referred to as a cryptocurrency?

14. What is a bitcoin?

Living in a digital world - Chapter 5: How some stuff works

Answers:

1. How are the binary digits stored on a CD?
   Changing from a land to a pit or a pit to a land represents binary 1, whereas no change represents binary 0.

2. Where does a passive RFID tag get its power from?
   The current induced in the antenna by the radio waves from the tag reader.

3. Give three uses of an RFID tag.
   Any relevant applications, including chipping pets/other animals, access control, inventory control, race timing, contactless payment cards and passports.

4. Barcodes normally require a light border area. What is this called?
   Quiet zone.

5. EAN barcodes display 12 symbol characters, but actually encode 13 numbers. How is the 13th digit encoded?
   The most significant digit of an EAN barcode is encoded by the pattern of code sets used for the first six symbol characters. For example, if all six come from code set A the leading digit is zero.

6. What links the base stations of mobile network operators to the public switched telephone network?
   The MTSO or mobile telephone switching office.

7. What is special about the adjacent cells in a mobile phone cluster?
   None of them use the same radio channels in order to prevent interference.

8. With regard to making a phone call, what is audio latency?
   Ear to mouth delay, i.e. the time delay between a person speaking into one phone and it being heard by the person they are calling.

9. Name three radio systems commonly found in a smartphone.
   Three from mobile phone, WiFi, Bluetooth, NFC and GPS.

10. Name five sensors found in smartphones.
    Any five valid answers, may include cameras, accelerometer, gyroscope, magnetometer, ambient light, proximity, fingerprint and temperature sensors.

11. What is the difference between satellites in geostationary orbit and those in low earth orbit?
    It is much more expensive to put a satellite into geostationary orbit since it is much further above the Earth's surface which requires a much more powerful launch vehicle. However, once in orbit, these satellites move with the rotation of the earth and therefore sending and receiving hardware does not need to track their position. Satellites in low earth orbit must be constantly tracked and will eventually move below the horizon. Multiple satellites will be needed to provide constant coverage. Since the radio signals will be travelling less far and therefore spreading out less, communicating with a satellite in low earth orbit requires much less power from both the ground station and the satellites.

12. Name three specialist areas of study within artificial intelligence.
    Any three valid areas, which may include gaming, natural language processing, expert systems, vision systems and neural networks.

13. Why is bitcoin referred to as a cryptocurrency?
    Because cryptography plays a crucial role in the way that bitcoin operates.

14. What is a bitcoin?
    A bitcoin is an entry in a widely distributed ledger. It is a cryptocurrency, one of many.

Chapter 5: Key learning points

- The USB (Universal Serial Bus) standards have made a significant contribution to making it easier to connect peripherals to a digital device, making the process largely "plug and play".
- There are different types of solid state memory. RAM (Random Access Memory) is used as working memory. The contents of ROM (Read-Only Memory) are permanently stored when the chip is manufactured and cannot be changed later.
- Electrically erasable programmable read only memory or EEPROM can be modified electrically, without removing the memory chip(s) from the host device, allowing operating software to be updated flexibly. EEPROM is also the basis for popular backing storage options, such as SD cards, flash memory drives and SSD drives.
- Eventually flash memory transistors will fail, usually only after many rewrite cycles. However it is important not to rely on a single backing storage device.
- There is a long tradition of using magnetic storage media, including hard disc drives.
- Deleted files are not "removed" from a storage device until the space they occupied is given to another file or special utility software is used to securely "wipe" the file by overwriting its location on the disc with other data.
- It is important to know where your data is being stored, because that will indicate to you whether you need to take responsibility for backing up anything important, or whether that is being done for you.
- RFID tags can be attached to or embedded within products/items. Passive tags use an antenna to draw power from radio signals emitted by reader devices. This allows the data stored on a chip to be broadcast and picked up by readers. Data can be read from several feet away, or further if using higher powered readers. Line of sight between reader and tag is not required.
- 1-D barcodes may only be able to display a limited number of characters, e.g. numbers only. They are not suitable for encoding large amounts of data. 2-D barcodes can hold a great deal more data and are much more flexible in how they can be used. There are websites that will generate many of the common 1-D and 2-D barcodes as a downloadable picture file. Many of these are free to use, or offer both free and premium accounts.
- One important advantage of barcodes is that they can be easily printed onto a variety of media.
- QR Codes include error correction data, so that it may still be possible to read them, even if they are dirty or damaged. This makes them suitable for more challenging environments, such as factories and postal services.

- Smartphones contain a great deal of miniaturised technology, including up to five different radio systems and many different sensors.
- The exponential growth in computing power witnessed since the introduction of the first electronic computers, has determined the technologies that can be used routinely; progressing from a monochrome, text-only world to one of deep colour, incorporating high definition graphics, video and growing degrees of artificial intelligence.
- Artificial intelligence has progressed relatively slowly, as it has proven extremely challenging to understand in detail how human cognition works and then find ways of implementing similar systems in electronic devices. However, increasing amounts of AI are being incorporated in a range of products and software.
- Public key cryptography makes it possible for two people/parties who may never meet to exchange data securely. Each party's public and private keys can be used to encrypt/decrypt transmissions (be they text or other data). They can also be used to sign transmissions, validating both the source and that the content has not been tampered with during transmission.
- Cryptocurrencies do have some of the key characteristics of money, and offer some advantages over other forms of money, although it remains to be seen if they will become firmly established and have a sustainable future. The blockchain, or distributed community ledger, that forms the core of a cryptocurrency, has wider potential. Blockchains can support other applications to reduce costs, speed up transactions, ease international transfers and improve transparency.

6: Some technology issues

Technology has a fundamental impact on all aspects of our lives, so it is unsurprising that a wide range of social, ethical, economic and political issues are heavily influenced by it. Some of them are explored in this chapter.

The pace of technological change

The text for this section is based on a paper titled "Shift happening – taking charge" and first published on my educationvision.co.uk website.

Around the time of The Millennium there was a news article reporting the death of an elderly lady, perhaps Britain's oldest citizen at the time, aged about 110 years. It prompted me to reflect on the incredible changes that had taken place during her lifetime. Transport developed from being predominantly wind, steam and animal powered, to the point at which astronauts were successfully landed on the Moon and returned to Earth, an international space station was under construction and countless satellites orbited the planet. Countries merged, fractured, were created and disappeared. Empires grew and disintegrated and the balance of world power ebbed and flowed, a process punctuated by many different conflicts, both global and local. Medical science took massive leaps forward, as did technology, especially in the field of electronics. There were huge social and cultural changes, often following other developments.

I imagined her lifetime represented by a graph with a ski-slope profile, with change increasing exponentially and reflected on this with a sense of awe. It was not until later that I started to consider my own place on the latter half of that graph, where the slope was increasing rapidly. I tried to extrapolate mentally where the graph would get to, should I live to a similar age – what changes would I end up living through? Will the rate of change eventually start to slow?

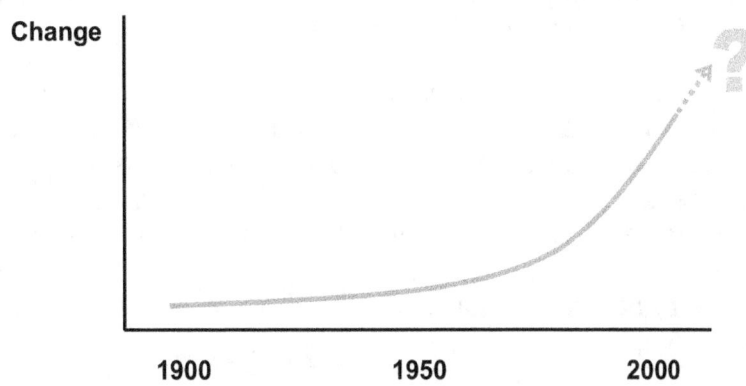

It is easy to think back on some of the changes seen already – mobile phones, the birth of the internet, the fall of the Berlin Wall, the introduction and subsequent over-use of antibiotics, the emergence of AIDs, a growing awareness of global warming and the need for sustainable living and so on. It is less easy to identify the changes that I am living through now, let alone predict those yet to come, but one thing seems certain. I am likely to live to see far greater change than the Millennium Lady.

Whilst technology can change very rapidly indeed, our ability to fully exploit new developments and ideas can lag behind significantly. This will continue to provide fuel for future change as new applications of older technologies emerge.

Gondolier on his mobile, Venice.

In the face of rapid change, it is easy to drift towards one of two possible extremes. One involves sticking your head in the sand and refusing to accept new ideas, whilst clinging desperately to increasingly outmoded ideas and customs. The other extreme is enthusiastically rushing to adopt every new idea and trend with little thought about the consequences. Perhaps one of the greatest challenges is trying to decide what we should grab hold of with determination and what we should just let go.

Taking just one example, I tend to guard my privacy zealously, whilst others seem content to share all sorts of intimate details and photographs with the world, via numerous social networking and other outlets. Is one way better than the other? Is this trend an unstoppable cultural change and my approach that of an increasingly obsolete older generation? Or does being older give me the benefit of wisdom and should we in education do our best to encourage younger learners to treat their personal privacy with greater respect? I won't pretend to have the answer to this. I am confident of one thing however, we cannot hang on to all the "old ways." Trying to maintain a focus on an evolving vision of what we want the future to be like, will give us greater control over the eventual outcomes.

Developing technology and increasing rates of change point towards growing international competition for jobs and the likelihood that today's learners will be changing roles, jobs and careers, far more than previous generations. This highlights the importance of developing relevant and readily transferable skills, as well as associated attitudes and characteristics, such as greater flexibility and resilience. The importance of developing life-long learning capability seems clear. These ideas have been circulating for some time.

The changes will bring further challenges. For example we have access to ever-growing oceans of data and information, to the extent that it becomes increasingly difficult to find what we need the most, in order to achieve the greatest impact. The crucial is lost, all too often, within the mundane. New tools and services will help with this, but we will need to work smarter too.

Not all aspects of life are improving with increasing rapidity, following the ski-slope profile. Cultural change tends to be slower. What would the graphs of health or happiness look like? The graph of world peacefulness or fairness?

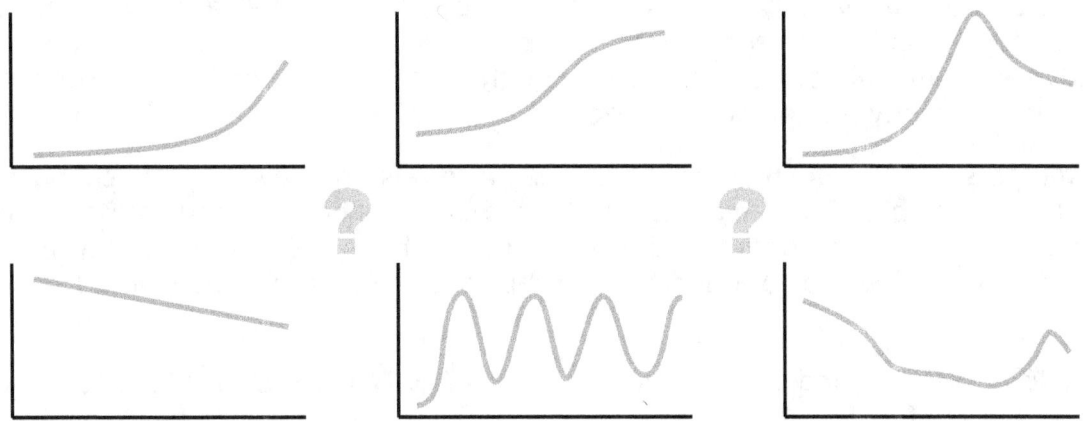

Whilst guessing the future is fraught with difficulty and error, we do appear to have a clear choice. We can sit back and allow technological changes to drive what we do. Alternatively we can develop a vision of what we want the future to look like and take charge of technology to try and make sure it delivers what we want from it. This whilst educating young people so that they have the skills and the confidence to do the same in their turn.

The pace of change creates a range of issues, beyond the ability of individuals to keep up with all the developments. Hazards and areas of risk associated with technology keep changing as new technologies are introduced. The implications for our digital footprints are also changing and legal systems, which tend to work in arrears anyway, can struggle to deal with new and emerging problems.

Online safety

As use of the internet has grown, so too have concerns about the ways in which young people in particular may be putting themselves at risk. In truth all ages can put themselves at risk from their online activities, but the young are particularly vulnerable. From time to time, particular issues may hit the headlines such as online grooming and sexting (taking and/or passing on sexually explicit photographs, usually using a mobile phone). Lurid headlines and heartbreaking stories can support the idea that online safety is all about combating these one or two problem areas, often with simple "Don't do x..." messages. However the situation is much more complex.

In 2007, four American researchers gave brief presentations to a Congressional internet interest group and then answered questions from the floor.[1] Danah Boyd introduced the idea of the internet's ability (and indeed that of technology in general) to **mirror and magnify**, a particularly powerful and appropriate description. Life online reflects offline life. You see the same things in both; the good, the bad and the ugly. In real life there are bullies, thieves and swindlers, as well as many people of integrity, who would only want to help others. You find exactly the same online. However, the big difference with the online experience is its ability to greatly magnify any impact.

A single person can launch an online campaign to raise money for a life-changing operation for a child. They might easily reach hundreds or thousands of people or perhaps even more, via social media and other methods. Offline they might be lucky to reach a few tens of people or perhaps a few hundred if they work really hard.

If a child is being bullied at school it is no longer confined to the playground or classroom, but it can continue within what should be the safety of their own home, around the clock, with unkind texts, emails and social media posts. The impact is greatly magnified.

Reports of internet trolls have shown how some individuals can become emboldened by their relative anonymity to launch prolonged and bitter attacks on people they have taken a dislike to. Harassing, threatening and stalking, sometimes with very negative consequences.

A sexual predator might attempt to groom a limited number of young people by hanging out at the same places where they choose to go.

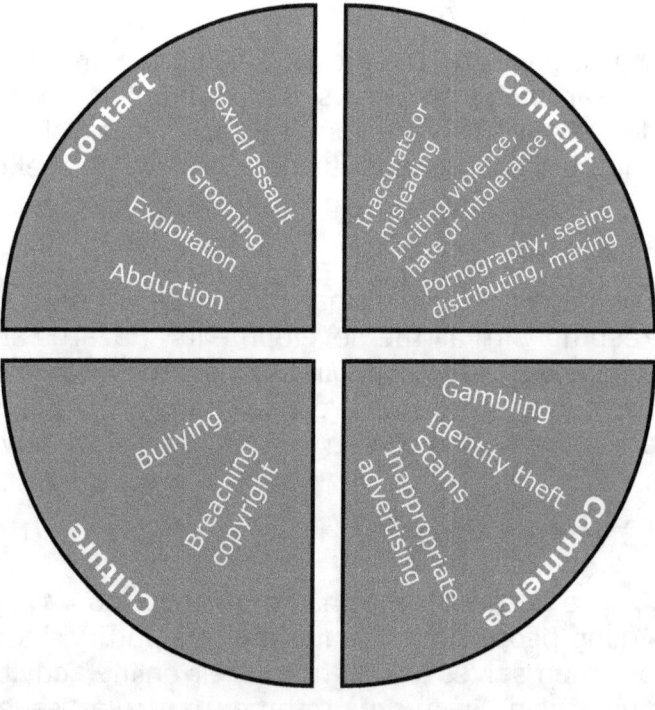

The four Cs, reduced

[1] Just The Facts About Online Youth Victimization (video), Committee to the Congressional Internet Caucus. https://www.youtube.com/watch?v=x-qybCYuYPY

Online they can come into contact with hundreds of young people via gaming and social media sites and keep a log of all their contacts in a database to help manage their interactions. Mirroring real life <u>and</u> magnifying it. Interestingly, often leaving more of an evidence trail of their activity, through emails, text messages and similar.

It is important to recognise that the hazards are many and varied. They are not just limited to people being mean and criminals trying to perpetrate fraud. With new internet services and new technologies come positive new opportunities, but at the same time these opportunities can often be exploited by those that would like to do harm to others, or exploit them in some way. Whilst a few simple safety messages may have their place, the approach has to be focused on educating people around a general hazard awareness and making appropriate responses to problems when they occur. The need is to equip people for the broad array of hazards that surround them already and to prepare them for all those unknown hazards that are yet to come.

A better understanding of technology must be part of this. Understanding what happens when a photograph is posted to the internet, for instance, will help people realise why it can be a very bad idea to upload an overly revealing image. It may seem like fun at the time, but once posted control is lost and it is unlikely that the picture can be effectively removed, should there be a later change of heart. It may have been copied and forwarded a huge number of times before any attempt is made to retrieve it. Questionable uploads of both text and images have come back to haunt individuals later in life. As well as well publicised errors of judgement by the rich, famous and powerful, many others have lost education and job opportunities when their internet footprints have been examined by recruiters.

At the same time it is essential not to lose sight of the huge benefits that being online can bring. This, after all, is why it is well worth exposing everyone to the hazards, whilst trying to educate them in how to manage the risks. There is a strong parallel with driving around in cars. That is probably the most high risk activity that most people regularly take part in willingly. The benefits of easy access to personal transport are also huge and most people only give passing consideration to the risks involved, once everyone has put on their seat belts.

To put this into some kind of context, in 2005 there were 39 murders of children in England and Wales. The crime statistics did not record whether technology played a role in any of these, but it would only have been a tiny minority of cases, if at all. In the same year, 141 children died on the roads in Great Britain (i.e. England, Wales and Scotland) and 3331 were seriously injured.

However, since then stories have emerged of deaths where technology was definitely involved. The most common seems to be where two people have met online and then agreed to meet up physically and one has murdered the other. It is difficult to know how many of these are primarily to do with technology, since meeting online is such a common occurrence now. Intuitively it would seem to be relatively high risk behaviour to meet following an online encounter, since you may know little about the other person and deception is so much easier.

There have been cases of predators lying about their age and gender when getting to know someone online. But then the bars and night clubs of the world must be littered with folk who have lied about their age, gender, job, house, car and/or economic status. However, some lies are harder to get away with when you are sitting opposite someone, as opposed to communicating on screen using text-only messages. Online, a 50-year-old man can hope to get away with pretending to be a

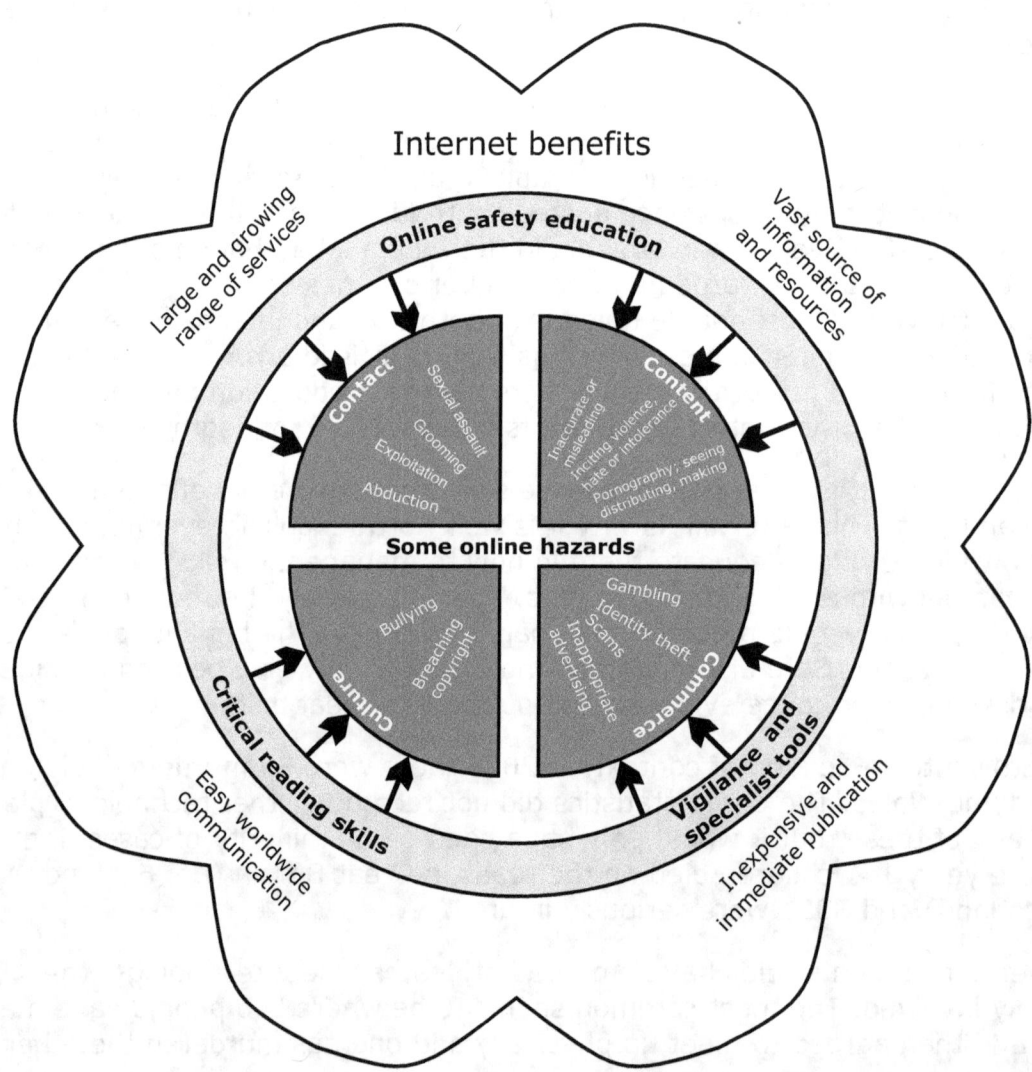

15-year-old girl, which must be tough to achieve in real life. Of course it is equally possible for a 13-year-old girl, desperately seeking friends, excitement or freedom from an abusive home environment, to potentially put herself at risk by pretending to be a glamourous 18-year-old and looking for 18 to 21-year-old boys to hang out with. As has already been said, mirror and magnify.

Deaths have come about for other reasons, too. There are websites that promote suicide or self-harm that may have contributed to some deaths and cases where individuals have received a torrent of horrendous online bullying and abuse, perhaps whilst in a fragile state of mind, that seems likely to have been instrumental in eventual suicide attempts. There have been cases where a criminal from one country has "befriended" a young person in another country, often pretending to be of a similar age and opposite gender. The young person is flattered and carefully groomed until they are coaxed into sharing pictures or video of themselves in ever more revealing states of undress. The criminal then either demands more sexual content, that can be sold on for profit, or seeks to extort money, threatening that otherwise the materials already collected will be shown to friends and family, or posted online. This can lead to tragic consequences.

There have also been a few reports of people dying from dehydration after marathon online game playing sessions. Online games can prove very addictive and in some cases it seems likely that completing a first 24-hour session is seen as a right of passage, leading to a culture where those who play the longest sessions have the highest status.

However there are also reports of games where the more experienced players act as very positive role models, guiding, supporting and if necessary, reining in, the younger, more inexperienced players. Some people are able to escape from abusive, isolated or difficult environments and find a positive support network online. Those who are old, disabled, suffering from disfiguring conditions or any sort of prejudice are judged by what they contribute, not what they look like or sound like. They can also look for communities of like-minded people who normally they could not expect to come into contact with.

One teenage British boy was a big fan of a football (soccer) game and enjoyed going online to find others to compete with. He got to know a Russian lad of a similar age and they played regularly. In time they started to teach each other their respective languages. They started, as you might expect, with all the swear words, but progressed onto general conversation. This anecdotal story must have been repeated many times and what a fabulously rich experience for those two boys to share, something that is only possible because of technology.

Technology is a neutral tool. It has the potential to be used for great benefit or great harm. Just like driving a car.

Online hazards and areas of risk matrix

	Commercial	Aggressive	Sexual	Values	Health and wellbeing
Content (child as recipient)	Adverts Spam Sponsorship Use of personal information	Violent/hateful content, including in games	Pornographic or unwelcome sexual or sexualised content including in games, music videos	Bias Racist Harmful e.g. promoting self harm, suicide or extreme dieting Misleading or extreme information or advice	Body image Addictive behaviour Physiological issues (RSI, muscle and joint issues, eye strain, etc) Reduced ability to interact socially Lower self esteem or self confidence Less physical play especially during childhood More sedentary lifestyle Negative digital footprint Criminalising themselves
Contact (child as participant)	Tracking Harvesting personal information	Being bullied, harassed or stalked	Being groomed (for sex) Sexting (forwarding images received) Use of webcams Meeting strangers	Promotion of self-harm, suicide Unwelcome persuasions Being groomed (extremism)	
Conduct (child as actor)	Illegal downloading Hacking Gambling Financial scams Funding terrorism	Bullying or harassing another Mimicking violent behaviour seen	Creating and uploading/sharing inappropriate material, including sexting and revenge porn Encouraging others to watch inappropriate content	Providing misleading info/advice Encouraging others to take risks, act in a harmful way Encouraging others to become extremists or engaging in creating extremist content	

Once we have learned how to drive safely, passed our test, fitted air bags and put on seatbelts, we should celebrate the freedom and all the benefits that this technology offers us. The same applies to the use of digital technology. There are risks and hazards that need to managed, but beyond that there are massive benefits that should be enjoyed and celebrated.

Becta[1] produced a hazard matrix that is useful in illustrating the broad scope of online hazards, originally built around four Cs, contact, content, culture and commerce. This was later restructured around three Cs, content, contact and conduct[2]. It was aimed at children and young people, but is applicable to all ages, perhaps with some adaptation.

Adults are more likely to fall prey to fraudsters, who use deception to extract money or financial information through which they can gain access to bank and investment accounts. Posting holiday photos can tell burglars that your home is empty and lead to break-ins. Dating and other scams have been used to target vulnerable people in order to get money from them. As in the offline world, fraudsters and swindlers look to take advantage of any weaknesses they can find. Technology makes it easier for them to target large numbers of people. Only a small percentage of attempts need to yield any money to make this a financially worthwhile operation.

It would be a mistake to take the Becta matrix, or any other, as including all hazards, it is probably impossible to be comprehensive. In addition, technology and society is changing all the time, throwing up new risks and opportunities. However, it is hugely valuable in illustrating the broad range of hazards. It also helps to show why safety education cannot simply address a few known areas of risk. It must encourage resilience and the developing of broad skills and knowledge that can tackle a wide range of hazards, including those that have not yet surfaced. The matrix can also be useful as stimulus material, challenging audiences to find areas of risk that are not covered and to come up with their own categories.

A few years ago I updated[3] the original hazard matrix, primarily adding a column covering health and wellbeing. The content/contact/conduct categories were retained since they point towards different levels of engagement. However, as various communications technologies become more embedded, e.g. within web pages, the distinction between content and contact in particular, is becoming less well defined. The new version can be seen on the preceding page. The next page has an attempt at an online benefits matrix.

---

[1] UK government agency charged with leading the national drive to ensure the effective and innovative use of technology throughout learning. Becta was closed down in 2011, as a cost cutting measure.

[2] Contains public sector information licensed under the Open Government Licence v3.0. http://www.nationalarchives.gov.uk/doc/open-government-licence/version/3/

[3] Acknowledgement: Various colleagues made valuable suggestions, particular thanks to *Katie John* (who also had the idea for a benefits matrix) and *Jon Tarrant*.

Online benefits matrix

	Education	Employment	Entertainment	Everyday life	Social
Access to information	Subject research Finding material in different languages Search for images Search for videos, including "How to" videos	Searching for vacancies Research potential employers, clients Keeping up to date or preparing for a new area of work	Venue and event information Personal research	Finding reviews, best deals, price comparisons, etc Researching holidays, trips, visits Access to health and medical information and advice	Information on events, sports and social clubs, etc Finding like-minded people or people with similar interests, problems, etc
Access to data, software and services	Advanced search tools Access to large and specialist data sets	Acquiring skills for employment and self-employment	Computer games Audio, video and photo editing	Access to interactive maps and GPS navigation Managing accounts, paying bills Online shopping Booking travel and holidays, peer-to-peer ridesharing	Purchasing event tickets or making reservations or bookings
Communication and collaboration tools	Learning from others Sharing and combining research Take part in specialist forums, email groups, etc Video conferencing	Virtual meetings, remote working or working from home Professional networking Interact with employment agencies, respond to posted vacancies Keeping up to date with new developments	Competitive or collaborative gaming with others from around the world Fan clubs	Messaging - text, audio or video Take part in or launch local, national or international campaigns Buy/sell/exchange/give away items, products Finding support from other people	Staying in touch with family and friends, social networking Online dating Sharing photographs and videos Sharing hobbies and interests
Personal publishing	Peer review Establish your name/reputation	Post CV or personal profile Self publishing Sell from your own website	Produce your own books, websites, etc		Promoting community projects or campaigns

When working with children and young people, the key tool that adults and in particular parents, have at their disposal, is their ears. From the earliest time that children are accessing the internet, it is crucial to talk with them about what they are doing online, the sites that they are visiting and the people they are interacting with. By *talking with*, I really mean *listening to*, more than anything. There will be opportunities to build up their ability to navigate the online world, as well as to find out what they are up to. If children are not used to having these sorts of conversations with parents and other key adults, there is evidence that when things go seriously wrong, their first instinct is to keep quiet. Their big concern is often that they may have their device(s) taken away. But with some problems, such as inappropriate contacts, they can get drawn in deeper and deeper and be less and less likely to turn to an appropriate adult, until an issue has ballooned into a very serious problem. The sooner these types of issues are confronted, discussed and dealt with, the better.

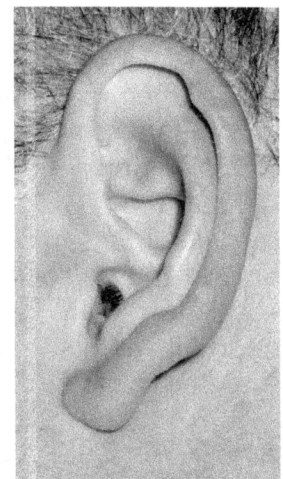

Using technology can be quite addictive and sleep can often be the first casualty, going to bed later and later as the next level of a game is finished, or just one more text message is sent. This in itself can result in too much time being spent sat down in front of a screen and not enough time spent moving around outside, leading to an excessively sedentary lifestyle. When activities have additional addictive qualities the problems can be multiplied. Some individuals have suffered from technology fuelled addictions to things as diverse as shopping, gaming, pornography and gambling. These can have very detrimental long-term impacts for some.

> **Practical task:** Look at the *Online hazards and areas of risk matrix*. Can you think of any hazards that should be added? Can you think of a better way of grouping and presenting the hazards? Consider these questions in relation to the *Online benefits matrix* also.
>
> How can people best protect themselves and manage the associated risks and still enjoy the benefits that can be derived from being online? What are the key messages for children and young people?

Digital footprint

Digital footprint is the term given to all the traces (data) that each person leaves behind them through their use of the internet. It may be relatively large items such as blog posts, websites and photographs. It may be intermediate items such as tweets, messages and responses to the posts of others. It may be tiny fragments of automatically generated data, such as cookies (see below). It will include material that others have written or posted about you and may also include website features like purchasing wish-lists and contact lists, which may default to being publicly readable. Privacy issues are usually governed by service/website terms and conditions, which are often indigestible and can change frequently, making it difficult for users to stay up to date. Unless you know otherwise, it is worth assuming that any comments you make or files you upload to any social media or similar website, are there for eternity, for the whole world to read. Be sure that what you are happy to publish today, you will be happy with tomorrow...and the day after...and the day after that...

All devices leave some sort of digital footprint. Smartphones tend to leave larger marks in the mud. They have been designed as consumer devices with a lot of emphasis on ease of use and convenience. This means that much more is hidden from users and there is a heavy emphasis on directing appropriate information based on physical location. This also means that users have much less control.

Turn on any mobile phone and your approximate location is immediately known by your mobile phone carrier. They can link this to your phone number and personal details. Your phone will hold data relating to your use of the internet and the various apps that you have installed and used.

Data on a smartphone might be seen by the mobile phone carrier, the device vendor, app developer, operating system developer, other service providers (e.g. retailers, social media sites) and the internet service provider. The sharing of data may be governed by local laws and the terms of use of the various service providers, but the terms and their implications may not be clear to users, who have little or no control. When installing a new app a user will be asked whether they agree to give the app access to certain data, but it is an *all or nothing* choice. Users cannot pick and choose which data to allow access to. Decline access and the app cannot be installed. This is part of the economic bargain - in return for access to useful software, users agree to share information with the app developer (and potentially, others), that they will want to exploit commercially.

The footprint left by laptop and desktop computers is usually limited to that left by the browser software that is in use. Location information is usually less specific and can be inaccurate and cookies (small data files) can be periodically cleared by

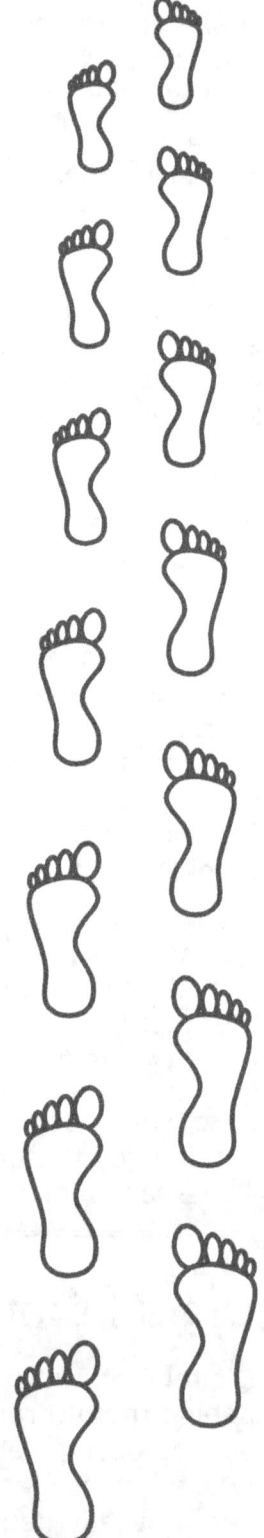

users. However, this may well change over time in the face of commercial pressures.

Consumers are getting used to the idea of "free" software and services. However, app developers and those running social media sites, for example, have to pay programmers and a whole range of other staff, they must invest in servers and other computer equipment. Content must be paid for, along with marketing and promotion. There are big bills to meet and profits to be made. Advertising pays for much of this and those offering "free" software and services need to extract as much value as they can from their customers. This means finding increasingly creative ways of generating revenue from their investment - exploiting user data is a key part of this for many companies. Offering additional premium services that have to be paid for is another approach, whilst some only charge corporate customers, offering them a professional level service, whilst using a lower level, free consumer offering, to get established in the marketplace.

Cookies

Cookies are small files that are commonly left on each user's computer when they browse the internet. They may help to make the internet more usable, for example recording website login details or your personal details, so that you do not have to remember and keep entering them, every time you visit a particular website. They can track your choices and preferences and offer users a more individualised experience. But in tracking activity, they can also be used for targeted marketing (some users may welcome this over random marketing) and to build profiles of site visitors, as potential future customers, as well as building up more knowledge about existing customers.

The key functions of the cookies that are left on a computer by a website can be summarised as to track user activity, customise their experience and support marketing activities.

Cookies are stored by web browsers either as individual files in a single system folder or grouped together in a single file. They comprise a single string of characters that is largely meaningless; fiendishly coded strings that can only be fully interpreted by those that deposited them on the computer in the first place. When a website is next visited, any cookies that have been previously stored on the device by the website, are sent back, returning information about the user's last/previous visits.

A quick investigation of one computer revealed cookies that varied in length from 70 to 1077 characters. However, given that an HDD cluster is likely to be a minimum of 1K (1024 characters), each cookie will take up a minimum of 1K of disc space. This is relatively wasteful, since large numbers of these tiny files are likely to be stored and is presumably why the designers of the Firefox browser opted to collect all the cookies together and store them in a single, custom file.

Here are two examples of individual cookies left by two UK online safety websites.

FDLKI4V5.cookie
CMSPreferredCultureen-gb360safe.org.uk/256001269902720
30647930361456387030574504*CMSCurrentTheme360safev3
360safe.org.uk/25600173846438430599421108500478530 59220*

JOUM83O7.txt
__cfduidddde90fb853aba0205e4cc78bdb8e13361444662366
childnet.com/921642526645763054894422476120173 0475519*

Care should be taken when using any public or widely available computers/devices, not to store sensitive login details, if given the option. These could then be available to anyone else who later uses the same computer. This is not an issue when using a personal device, unless it is later lost or stolen.

Cookies can be cleared periodically, either using the appropriate browser(s) or by using specialist *cleaner* or *privacy* utility software. This may mean that login details for some sites will be cleared (some browsers store these details separately, perhaps as form entries or as complete logins), but it can help to protect privacy.

To link or not to link? That is the question.

Supermarket loyalty card schemes have become very popular in the UK. Shoppers are attracted by the quarter or half percent discount (usually in the form of store credit) deducted from their grocery bills, with the promise of further periodic offers, exclusively for card holders. The economic bargain is that the supermarkets get to build up a large amount of data on individual, identified consumers. This means they can get to know their clientele better and market at them more effectively. Customers can be classified from their purchases - young families, those whose children have recently gone to college/university, retired couples, the recently separated and so on. Loyalty card schemes are large scale data mining operations, supported by big, powerful databases and analytical tools.

Some may welcome targeted marketing, since the offers and advertising they see are much more appropriate to their needs and wants. Some may be proud of the fact that they get through eight packs of XL condoms every month, or six bottles of whiskey, or three tubes of pile cream and be happy for others to know that. Some may regard this as an unwarranted intrusion into their personal privacy.

The information collected about an individual from different sources becomes much, much more powerful if it can all be linked together. If banking, shopping, medical, employment and other records could be linked for individuals, there would be a very rich, deep source of valuable information. Apart from better marketing, people could be tracked over many years to examine lifestyle risk factors for a whole range of medical conditions. This could support better research and allow warnings to be issued to those who might be risking ill health, by working too long hours, eating particular foods, or not exercising enough. Analysing varied, massive data sets for useful information is commonly referred to as *big data*.

There is a clear tension, though. Better quality information comes at a price, beyond a simple violation of privacy. Link information sources about people and you start to concentrate power in the hands of those who have access to this information. It could be used to steal identities, work out when people are most likely to be away from home and therefore the best time to attempt to burgle their properties (and indeed, the sorts of items likely to be found there), or how best to extort money from or swindle them.

An early principle of data protection, particularly information held by governments, was that data held by different agencies should NOT be linked. This would help to protect individuals by limiting the possible abuses of that data. Therefore, records kept by the police, social services, education and health were deliberately kept under the control of separate bodies and linking was not allowed. Then there were some tragic deaths, especially of abused children. The serious case reviews that followed often established that "the system" held enough information to ring warning bells, in time for preventative action to have been taken, had it all been put together in one place and shared between professionals. Here again is this tension between maintaining privacy and preventing abuses of information on the one hand and making the best use of all the information that has been collected, on the other. This is likely to be an ongoing challenge, with no easy solutions.

The Internet Archive and the Wayback Machine

For centuries there have been extensive physical records of human activity. Most of these have been on paper, but there have also been records kept on parchment (animal skin), papyrus, clay tablets, as well as stone inscriptions, as part of monuments and friezes. Historians have based much of their work on these records. With the emergence of the internet and in particular, the world wide web, it was realised that increasingly there would only be electronic records being kept, with the danger that in the future historians would have nothing to work with.

In 1996 The Internet Archive was launched, with the bold mission to, well, archive the internet. The archive comprises over 300 billion web pages. In 1996 I started to build a website to share some teaching material and related ideas. It was primarily a learning exercise, to teach myself about this emerging technology. The site was later expanded to also act as a sales platform for programs that I had written, as the shareware industry that I had previously used, withered and died. The site was last updated in 2007 and was left on a free hosting site. This company eventually either went out of business or stopped offering free hosting and markchrissoft.co.uk 'left' the internet, waiting for me to give it a major redesign and find another site to host it, should I ever find the time.

However, the site has been stored by The Internet Archive and previous versions can be accessed using their Wayback Machine[1]. The most recent copy dates from May 14th 2013. This illustrates how persistent a digital footprint can be, with old web material living on in places like The Internet Archive.

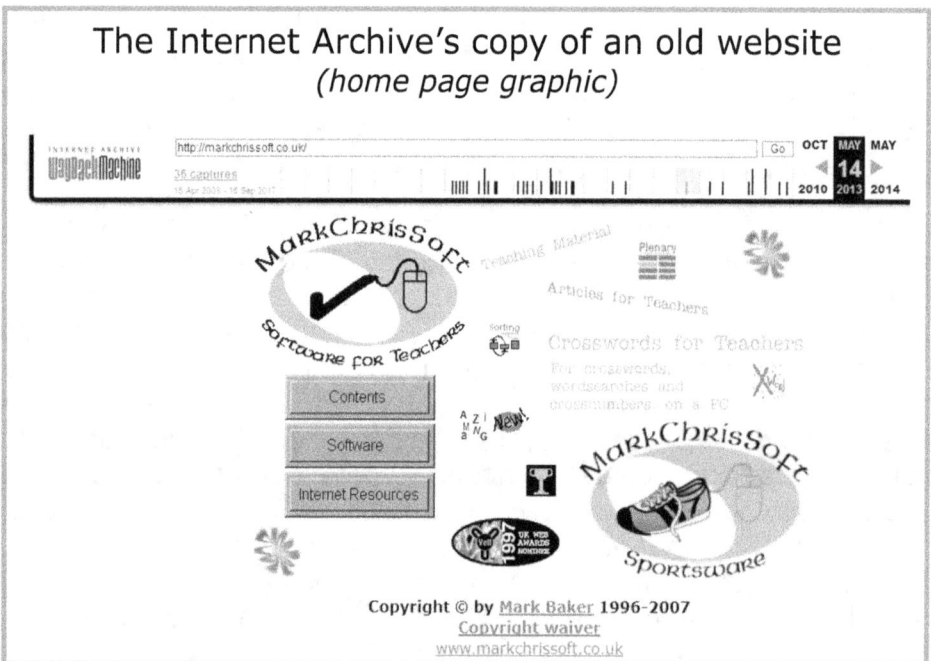

Digital footprint - what is at stake?

For individuals, this can be be summarised as follows.

- Protecting reputation
- Maintaining the ability to decide where and how personal information is shared
- Preventing financial loss, for example as a result of identity theft
- Preserving your freedom; government tracking of internet activity poses a real threat for dissidents and legitimate opposition, in some countries

The damage caused by throw-away comments or over-exuberant behaviour can be further magnified if they are not seen within the context in which they occurred, which is often the case with digital footprint material. *Mirror and magnify!*

The snooper's charter

The Investigatory Powers Act 2016 became law in the UK in November 2016. It has become known as "the snooper's charter". It requires web and phone companies to store everyone's web browsing histories for 12 months, giving access to the police, security services and other official agencies. It has been described as one of the

---
[1] https://archive.org/web/

most extreme surveillance laws ever passed by a democracy and illustrates the tension between state security and individual freedoms.

The right to be forgotten and the GDPR

By contrast, the EU General Data Protection Regulation (GDPR) took effect in 2018 and attempted to update this aspect of European legislation in the face of rapid change. It introduced the **right of erasure**, more commonly known as the *right to be forgotten*. This enables an individual to request the deletion or removal of personal data where there is no compelling reason for its continued processing. It is a tricky concept that has to balance freedom of expression and the right of others to know, with the desire of an individual for something to be 'forgotten'.

Suppose that an individual has a conviction that was reported in the local press. When they later apply for jobs, potential employers carry out internet searches, finding related articles and rejecting this applicant. Under what circumstances should this person have the right to require this information to be deleted? Perhaps after a certain time period has elapsed, particularly if local laws include a rehabilitation period, after which convictions no longer have to be disclosed on application forms. Perhaps if the conviction occurred whilst the person was a child. Perhaps if the conviction was for a relatively minor misdemeanour. What about the rights of potential employers to know what is, after all, a matter of public record? With various conflicting interests and many factors that can influence a final decision in each case, this is not an easy area to legislate on. Living in a digital world does mean that people generally leave more evidence of their activities than in the time before the internet and that this evidence is relatively easy to find.

The GDPR gives individuals the right to have data erased and to prevent further processing only under certain circumstances:

- Where the personal data is no longer necessary in relation to the purpose for which it was originally collected/processed
- When the individual withdraws consent
- When the individual objects to the processing and there is no overriding legitimate interest for continuing the processing
- The personal data was unlawfully processed (i.e. otherwise in breach of the GDPR)
- The personal data has to be erased in order to comply with a legal obligation
- The personal data is processed in relation to the offer of information society services to a child

Data processors can refuse to comply with a right to erasure request where personal data is being processed for any of the following reasons.

- to exercise the right of freedom of expression and information

- to comply with a legal obligation for the performance of a public interest task or exercise of official authority
- for public health purposes in the public interest
- archiving purposes in the public interest, scientific research historical research or statistical purposes
- the exercise or defence of legal claims

The bullet points above illustrate the complexity being dealt with, with much hinging on how this legislation is interpreted in practice. The following gives the full list of individual rights covered by the GDPR.

- The right to be informed *(transparency regarding the use of personal data)*
- The right of access *(the right to access your own personal data)*
- The right to rectification *(inaccurate or incomplete data must be rectified)*
- The right to erase *(the right to request the deletion of personal data where there is no compelling reason for its continued processing)*
- The right to restrict processing *(whilst other rights are being asserted)*
- The right to data portability *(obtaining your data to reuse it across different services, without hindrance to usability)*
- The right to object *(including to direct marketing and profiling)*
- Rights in relation to automated decision making including profiling *(the right not to be subject to a decision when it is based on automatic processing AND it produces a legal effect or a similarly significant effect on the individual)*

Legal systems generally only take action after issues and problems have been identified, which means they are usually behind, playing catch-up. Never more so than in the rapidly changing world of technology.

Technical tools that support online safety

There is a wide range of tools available to help users of digital devices to stay safe.

Firewall
A firewall acts as a barrier between an internal trusted network (for example a home network) and an non-trusted external network, such as the internet. It monitors incoming and outgoing traffic and either allows or disallows it based on a set of security rules. Firewalls are the first line of defence and they can be software, hardware or both.

Anti-malware / Anti-virus software

Malware is malicious software. Computer viruses are one type of malware. Others include:

- Adware (forced advertising)
- Spyware (steals sensitive information)
- Ransomware (uses encryption to hide a user's data from them, a ransom is demanded to be paid before the data is released)

The best defence against malware is to be a cautious internet user, avoiding opening attachments, clicking on links or running programs that seem suspect, avoiding websites that seem questionable and making sure that good quality **anti-virus software** is installed and kept up to date.

A computer virus is a program that is written to change how a computer operates, whilst also spreading from one device to another. It is analogous to the flu virus, which will infect a person and change how their body functions, whilst also looking to spread and infect other people. Some computer viruses are simply playful, perhaps displaying a rude message on screen. Others are malicious, potentially causing severe damage, such as erasing data.

Viruses can spread in different ways. Infection can occur by opening email and text message attachments, or by clicking on seemingly legitimate links within websites or emails. They could be hidden within messages claiming that a prize has been won, that there is an invoice outstanding, that a penalty notice has been issued for speeding or parking violations or any number of often plausible looking fake cover stories. Apps for mobile devices from questionable sources may infect smartphones and tablets.

Anti-virus software often looks out for evidence of viruses and other malware whilst a computer is being used, carrying out tasks like scanning incoming emails or checking programs before they are run. It can also be used periodically to carry out detailed scans of your computer, including storage devices (in particular your hard disc drives and SSDs) in case any viruses have managed to sneak their way in. Scans can be initiated manually or scheduled to start regularly at particular times. Scanning can slow down a computer significantly, so it is best done when the computer is not needed for other activities.

Zombies are computers that have come under the control of a remote attacker using malware, who then uses them to transmit items to other computers via the internet, including viruses and spam emails.

New malware is appearing all the time, in much the same way as the flu virus is always mutating and changing. It is therefore important that anti-virus software is updated regularly to ensure that it can deal with the latest threats.

Parental controls and filtering

Internet service providers may offer parental controls and filtering. Filtering is a type of content control, where websites that are on a list are automatically blocked. Often different lists are available, covering different types of website and users can opt in or out as they wish. A standard list in the UK is the IWF (Internet Watch Foundation) child sexual abuse images list. This allows sites displaying images that are illegal in the UK to be blocked. Other lists might include legal pornography, online gambling, social networking, sites promoting terrorism/hate/extremism, sites promoting self harm/suicide/eating disorders and malware websites.

UK schools are expected to use internet filters to protect children, but this is not the case in all countries. Filtering can lead to over-blocking, where sites containing useful information find their way onto filtering lists. Worse still, it might give a false sense of security and allow difficult issues to be avoided - until young people are at college or away from home and unsupervised, perhaps without having been given the skills, knowledge and confidence to navigate their online lives safely. Filtering can also lead to concerns about censorship and freedom of expression. It is hard to see any reason not to use something like the IWF list, but some of the other lists are more open to debate. Organisations often use filtering to try and ensure that corporate resources are used for work purposes rather than personal entertainment, as well as trying to maintain harmony in the workplace, as part of their duty of care for their staff, for example anyone who may have a gambling addiction and to protect their corporate reputation. As new websites are appearing all the time, filtering cannot be expected to be 100% effective, since it will take time to identify and evaluate new candidates for the filter lists.

There is a case to be made for exposing children, at appropriate ages, to questionable material, so that they can recognise and discuss it, understand the potential dangers and develop strategies for dealing with it. Filtering should allow users to create their own *allow* and *disallow* lists, offering a degree of local control. This can help to counter problems with either over-blocking or under-blocking.

Parental controls may go further, for example allowing parents to control the times of day that the internet will be available, ensuring a good night's sleep for all!

Encrypting devices including laptops, smartphones and flash memory drives

Periodically there are news stories about memory sticks or laptop computers being left in taxi cabs or found in the street, containing sensitive material. Perhaps is it a government minister with details of a forthcoming budget or a bank employee with details of individual accounts and their owners. If these devices have not been encrypted, then all the information on them can be read by whoever finds them.

However, software can be used to encrypt storage devices and smartphones with a password. The software to do this may be included as part of the device operating system. Without the correct password the data will appear as random garbage. The user needs to enter the password each time they want to use the device, but has the peace of mind of knowing that should it ever be lost, the data on it will be secure. The main disadvantage is that if the password is forgotten then the user loses their data.

Device tracking and disabling

Software exists that allows users to remotely track, lock and even wipe the data from their devices, usually portable devices like laptops, smartphones and tablets, that are most at risk of being lost or stolen. This software may come as part of the device operating system or be a stand-alone specialist utility.

This type of software does not work in all situations, since the device needs to be switched on and connected to the internet for it to function. This is more likely to be the case with a phone, than a laptop. It is not an alternative to encrypting the device, particularly when sensitive or valuable data is being stored and some software can be defeated by carrying out a device factory reset, using the operating system. However, it does add another layer of security.

This software can also be used on smartphones to track children, the elderly and others considered vulnerable to wandering off and getting lost, perhaps due to the early stages of dementia. However, the phone must be charged, switched on and able to connect to the internet, for this to work.

Some might have concerns about the sinister overtones of using a digital device to track another person, especially if they have not consented to this. It could also result in too much faith being put in the capabilities of this technology, with insufficient effort being put into other, perhaps more effective approaches, to handling the issues being dealt with. However, it is another interesting application for this technology.

Virtual Private Network (VPN)

A VPN is a secure, encrypted connection or tunnel, between two or more devices. It allows a private network (such as a corporate intranet) to be extended across a public network, such as the internet. It protects web traffic from snooping, interference and censorship. It also hides a user's IP address and location and can therefore reduce their digital footprint.

A individual can set up their own VPN or can sign up to an online subscription service and use it in order to browse the internet, to maintain their privacy and anonymity. Free VPN services are available over the internet, although they may slow down internet access, with payment required for faster speeds.

Proxy server

A proxy server acts as an intermediary in a computer network for client requests for resources from other servers. Web proxies are a common type.

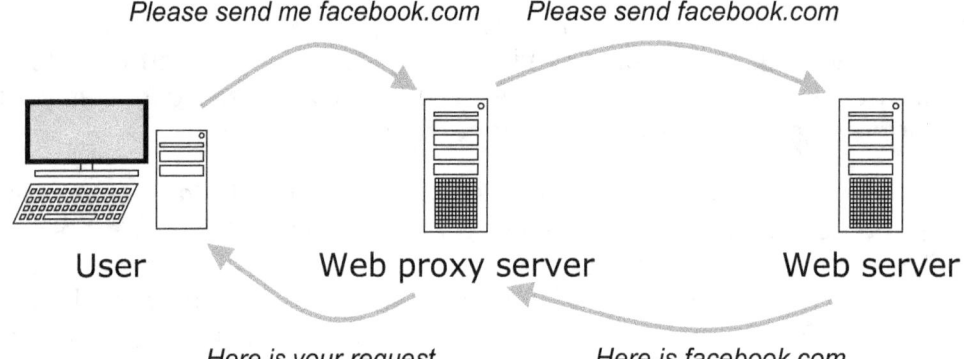

A web proxy server allows a user to surf the web anonymously, since it forwards requests from the user for web pages, so that they appear to come from the proxy. A proxy server can be used to bypass web filtering, provided the web proxy itself is not on a filter list, since the pages received by the user appear to come from the proxy. Pupils have been known to use proxy servers to bypass their schools' web filters. A web proxy can also be used to cache web pages.

War and peace and fake news

It has been said that the next world war will take place on the internet. It is certainly true that the world is becoming increasingly dependent on technology in general and especially the internet. This is nicely illustrated by a news story from March 2011. Armenia lost its connection to the internet for five hours, after a 75-year-old woman in neighbouring Georgia accidentally damaged a fibre optic cable with her spade. She was scavenging for unused copper cables to sell as scrap. Denying organisations and countries access to the internet can bring many activities grinding to a halt. In this case the loss of internet access was limited to a few hours, but it will still have had a significant impact on the economy, as well as confidence in the country and its institutions. More recently, concerns have been expressed about the vulnerability of submarine communications cables, that often carry a lot of internet traffic.

Whilst the Armenia example appears to have been an unfortunate accident, the world has entered into an era where governments and potentially terror organisations and others, are seeking to use the internet as a vehicle for launching aggressive attacks.

In May 2017 a ransomware virus known as WannaCry was released worldwide. The UK's National Health Service (NHS) was badly effected. According to a National Audit Office report, 81 out of 236 NHS trusts and a further 603 primary care and other NHS organisations were infected by the virus, including 595 doctors' practices. No ransom was paid, but the attack had a huge impact. It was estimated that over 19,000 medical appointments had to be cancelled and in 5 areas patients had to travel further than normal to access hospital accident and emergency departments. Significant costs will have been incurred in responding to and countering the attack.

WannaCry could have caused much more disruption if a cyber researcher had not found and activated some code within the virus (referred to as a "kill switch") that stopped it replicating.

It was reported that the Democratic People's Republic of Korea (DPRK, better known as North Korea) was responsible for this attack, having stolen the code in the first place from the US National Security Agency. It targeted vulnerabilities in Microsoft's Windows operating systems. Those writing malware usually target the most popular operating systems and other software, in order to maximise their impact. Software that is no longer actively supported by the vendor is often particularly vulnerable, as fixes may not be released for any new weaknesses that come to light.

North Korea was also thought to be responsible for a hacking attack on Sony Pictures, just prior to the release of *The Interview*, a satirical film mocking leader Kim Jong-un. Internal emails and employee records, along with some unreleased films, were accessed and leaked. Any cinemas showing the film were threatened with attack. Cinema chains withdrew their support for the film in response and it was pulled from general release at the last minute. The studio opted for a lower key, digital-only publication in the USA, via online pay-to-view outlets. However all the publicity surrounding the film may well have given it an added boost, with reportedly high demand within North Korea for bootleg copies.

It is alleged that in 2010 the USA and Israel were responsible for the Stuxnet virus (a type of virus known as a worm, that can spread through a network by itself, without needing unwitting human intervention) that caused around 20% of Iran's highly specialised nuclear centrifuges to spin out of control and be temporarily closed down or destroyed (reports differ). These centrifuges were being used to enrich uranium and were a key part of Iran's nuclear programme. It is reported that this followed an earlier cyber attack that harvested essential information that helped the attackers to understand how computers were being used to control the centrifuges. Estimates of the impact vary from equipment having to run at reduced capacity for a few days, up to delaying Iran's nuclear programme by 18-24 months.

The virus caused the load on the centrifuges to be increased, possibly by varying their speed to introduce excessive vibrations, whilst reporting normal operating conditions back to the control room. Previously the most likely way to damage this sort of equipment would be to blow it up, either by planting explosives or dropping bombs. The virus was probably introduced via an infected USB memory drive. Once a computer was infected, any other memory drives that were inserted into it would also be infected, as would other machines that these drives were subsequently used in.

The Stuxnet virus eventually "escaped" and spread via the internet, which led to its wider identification. This illustrates another serious issue with state-sponsored malware. Countries have the resources to create incredibly complex software, but once this is released others can find it, copy it and then reverse engineer it to discover how it works. The technology then becomes available to potential enemy countries, cyber-criminals and others.

The United States Cyber Command started operating in 2009 as a part of the US Strategic Command. Cyber attacks targeting Iran's nuclear programme allegedly began during the administration of President George W Bush and continued under President Obama. Flame is another cyber weapon that is reported to have collected information from the computers of Iranian officials and it may have been used as a precursor to Stuxnet, although its origin is officially unconfirmed.

Russia has been accused of hacking the Democratic National Committee in the USA and leaking some of their internal files in an attempt to influence the 2016 presidential election. It is also alleged that they hacked at least one voting technology company. They used the information gathered to launch a spear-phishing campaign (a type of email spoofing attack). Posing as the e-voting vendor, they tried to trick local government employees into opening documents that were carrying malware, which appeared to come from a known person, usually someone in authority.

In 2017, UK Prime Minister, Theresa May accused the Russian government of attempting to "weaponise information". As well as hacking the Danish ministry of defence and the German parliament, she claimed that false stories and images were being planted to sow discord in the west and influence the outcome of elections. Control of information has long been sought by governments and is particularly important during times of conflict and tension, as well as during elections.

The Guardian newspaper reported in 2017 that a viral image of a Muslim woman appearing to ignore victims of a terror attack, as she walked across Westminster Bridge in London, was shared by an automated Russian social media account. If this was a planted fake news story then it would clearly come under the heading of sowing discord, with the potential to stir up hatred and incite "reprisals".

Example tweets

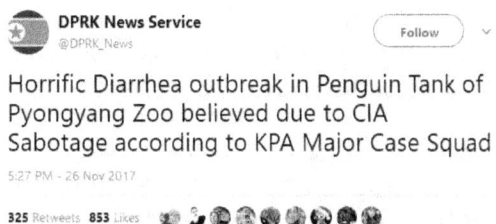

DPRK News Service @DPRK_News
18 hours ago
KPA Major Case Squad reports major decrease of public urination incidents after crackdown on Chinese Tourists.

DPRK News Service @DPRK_News
21 hours ago
Supreme Leader Kim Jong-Un likely to be named Time Magazine "Person of the Year," once again, according to highly placed sources.

DPRK News Service @DPRK_News
Nov 25
Black colored pants expected to be best fashion trend of 2018, sources say.

DPRK News Service @DPRK_News
Nov 25
Supreme Leader Kim Jong-Un saves Italian man choking on Tiger Prawn with swift sure punch of high quality and accuracy.

DPRK News Service @DPRK_News
Nov 24
"Black Friday" is US holiday on which affluent technocratic elites mock the poor, for aspiring to own consumer products.

DPRK News Service @DPRK_News
Nov 24
Director of US media criticism at Ministry of Information is reassigned to Nampo Sewage Inspections Department, for inability to conjugate English verb "to be."

DPRK News Service @DPRK_News
Nov 22
Donald Trump to spend US holidays with his "Twitter," and his childish, impotent rage.

DPRK News Service @DPRK_News
Nov 21
"Thanksgiving" is United States ritual in which the rich devour as much food as possible, to prevent it from falling into hands of the poor

DPRK News Service @DPRK_News
Nov 21
United States goes nearly eighteen hours without sexual abuse scandal.

It is hardly surprising that governments would try to influence events by creating false or heavily manipulated stories and by creating false social media accounts, thereby trying to shape public opinion. It is a case of "Reader beware!" Sources should be treated with suspicion until they have established their credentials and key facts have been checked. It would be naïve to assume that just one country has been involved in this type of misinformation campaign.

It should be noted that as these types of stories affect national security, details are often unconfirmed, and may in some cases be speculation. Often at best, only "unnamed sources" are quoted. It is likely that some of these stories are themselves attempts at disinformation or propaganda or their impact is exaggerated. However, malware that goes on to infect general internet users does provide something for investigators to examine and attempt to draw conclusions about.

In 2017 the UK's National Cyber Security Centre wrote to all government departments warning against using Russian anti-virus software in systems relating to national security. There were concerns that it could be exploited by the Russian government as part of espionage activities. Kaspersky Labs, a Russian security company with around 400 million users worldwide, is thought to be the main target of this advice.

There have been some entertaining attempts to create fake websites to illustrate how easy it can be to generate fake news or misleading information, or in some cases, just as a light-hearted prank. One site offered to sell cans of dehydrated water, whilst another detailed the culturally crucial haggis hunts that take place in Scotland. Natural history sites explained about creatures such as the tomato spider and the tree octopus, whilst another went into the history of Victorian robots. Google has even joined in, explaining how their pigeon ranking algorithm uses live pigeons to help rank the relevance of web pages, in response to searches.

Parody social media accounts can also be found. On first reading, Twitter account @DPRK_News uses the sort of bellicose propaganda style that gives it a ring of authenticity as a mouthpiece of the North Korean government. It has reportedly fooled a number of major news organisations, at least temporarily, including the New York Times, Washington Post, Newsweek, USA Today and Fox News. In fact, this feed is run by two friends, Derrick the data analyst (West Coast, USA) and attorney Patrick (North Carolina).[1]

Social media accounts are easy to set up and there must be many bogus examples. Some will have been set up for comedy purposes and no doubt some governments will have experimented/are experimenting with using them as a propaganda/ misinformation tool, including using accounts run by bots. The foreign policy objectives of one country could easily benefit from small swings in public opinion in

---

[1] Acknowledgement: My thanks to Derrick and/or Patrick for agreeing to me reproducing some of their tweets here.

another country, especially in close national elections or important referendums, for example the 2016 UK Brexit referendum (to decide whether the UK would leave the European Union) and the following 2017 UK general election.

In carrying out research for this book, there have often been important discrepancies between accounts of the same event and it can be difficult to be sure which facts are actually true. Historians have no doubt had to deal with this problem ever since historians were invented. However, with so many people using the internet for their sources, it is much easier for myths to propagate, as the same errors get repeated with growing speed. They can then become the accepted truth, simply because of the number of people repeating them! This is another example of the mirror and magnify principle. Usually there is no malicious intent, but sometimes there will be.

There is a chance that future conflicts will erupt for more traditional reasons, such as control of resources and our growing dependence on technology could be the underlying cause. Lithium-ion batteries, currently the dominant rechargeable battery technology, require lithium, cobalt and manganese. Solar technologies consume indium, tellurium and gallium, whilst rare earth metals are used in high performance magnets and a range of other technologies. Rare earth metals include neodymium, yttrium and erbium. All the elements listed are, to a greater or lesser extent, in relatively short supply and known sources are concentrated in a small number of countries.

The vision thing

During the early part of my career in education I would not have been described as a great strategic thinker. I was much more focused on the management of the day to day detail, getting through the relentless demands of lesson preparation and delivery, marking, assessment and pupil management. However, as I took on more responsibility it became obvious that I could not lead effectively unless I had a clear idea of where I wanted to get to. I wanted to encourage those that I worked with to develop their own personal subject visions and realised that I could not expect others to work at this if I did not have one of my own!

As with the design of a digital system, a good vision starts with a focus on the desired outputs/outcomes. Concentrating on that and taking a lot from the UK's National Curriculum for ICT[1] at the time, I developed my personal vision for ICT education around 2002 and it can be seen on the following page. It was based, as the National Curriculum was, on developing a single, broad outcome, *ICT Capability*.

---

[1] ICT = Information and Communications Technology. This was the National Curriculum subject for many years, having changed from the earlier curriculum areas of Computer Studies, then Information Technology (IT) and before morphing into Computing.

Living in a digital world - Chapter 6: Some technology issues

A personal vision for ICT

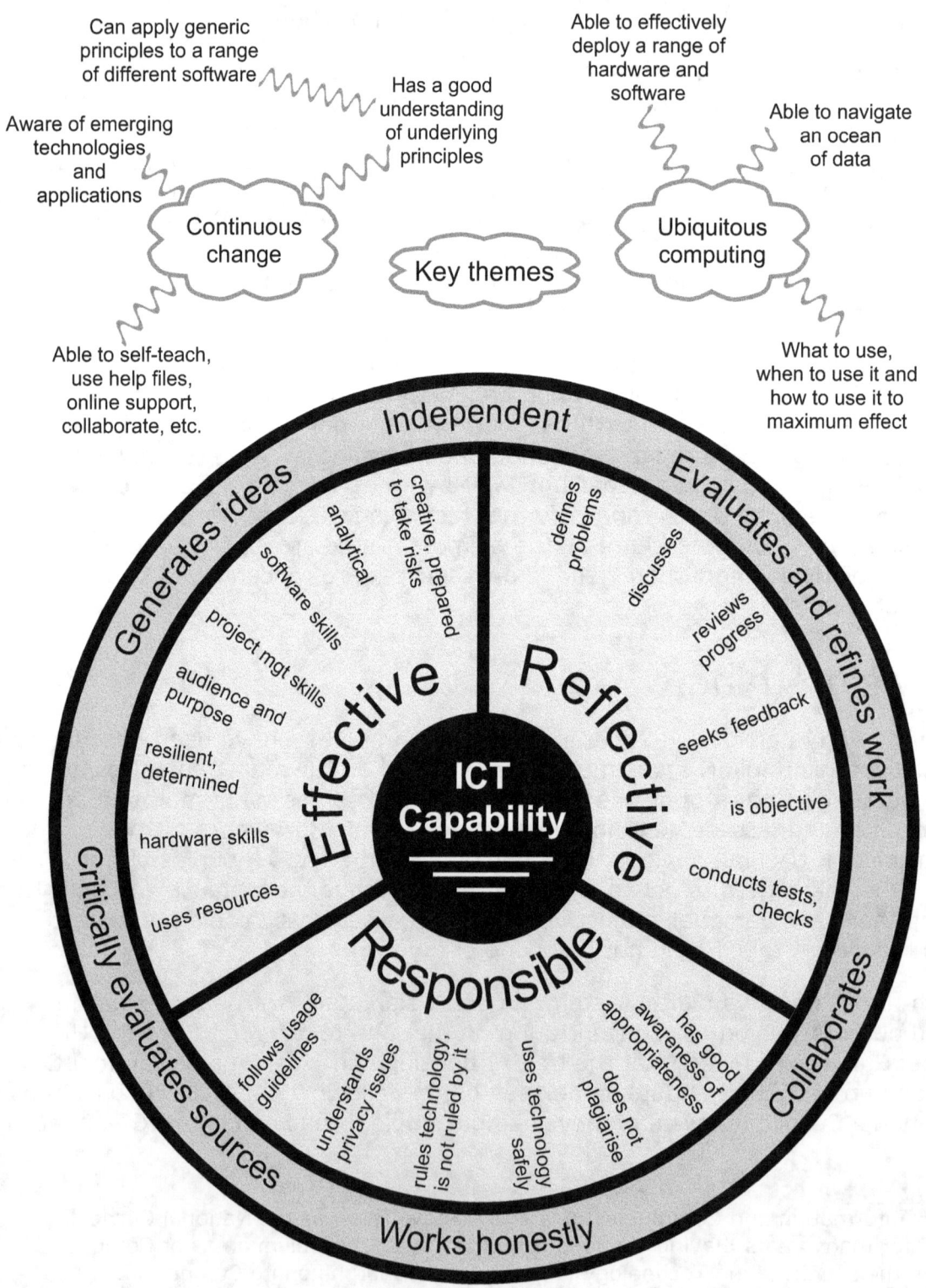

I classified the components of this under three characteristics, namely being **effective**, **reflective** and **responsible**. It has been modified since, but much remains of the original.

I include it here because I have mentioned in the text already how we should aspire to drive technology and not be driven by it. This requires a vision of where we want to get to. Although the vision was written for use in schools, it can be applied much more widely. It is not a description of curriculum content, rather it is a list of skills and characteristics to be developed in order to function well in a digital world. Ranging from being able to design with regard to audience and purpose, to seeking feedback and using technology safely.

I encourage readers to reflect on the diagram and think about which parts you think are really important and relevant. How would you change it? Are there important bits that are missing? What would you leave out? Could it be better expressed another way? What would your personal vision for education in preparation for the digital world be and how would you show it?

Self test

1. Explain the mirror and magnify principle as it applies to life online.
2. Give two significant categories of internet benefits.
3. List five online hazards.
4. List five individual benefits to being online.
5. What is your digital footprint?
6. What is a cookie?
7. What is the Wayback Machine?
8. Give two of the individual rights under the EU General Data Protection Regulation.
9. What is a computer virus?
10. What is website filtering?
11. Suggest two ways in which one country may use the internet as a vehicle for launching an aggressive act on another country.

Living in a digital world - Chapter 6: Some technology issues

Answers:

1. Explain the mirror and magnify principle as it applies to life online.
   What goes on in the real world is mirrored online; the good, the bad and the ugly. However, technology tends to greatly magnify its impact.

2. Give two significant categories of internet benefits.
   Any valid answers, for example access to a large and growing number of services, a vast information resource, easy worldwide communication/publication, etc.

3. List five online hazards.
   Any valid answers, see the online hazards and areas of risk matrix earlier in this chapter. Remember though, that this matrix will not include all hazards.

4. List five individual benefits to being online.
   Any valid answers, see the online benefits matrix for some ideas.

5. What is your digital footprint?
   This refers to all the data on the internet that relates to you as an identifiable individual. It includes online comments, blog posts and uploaded photographs. It also includes information posted by other people about you and automatically generated data about you and your online activities.

6. What is a cookie?
   A small file left on your computer by a website. They are normally used either to customise your experience/record your preferences, to track your activity and to build up a profile about you. This information is often used to target marketing information.

7. What is the Wayback Machine?
   This allows access to archive copies of websites, for historical and other research purposes.

8. Give two of the individual rights under the EU General Data Protection Regulation.
   Any two from the rights to be informed, of access, to rectification, to erase, to restrict processing, to data portability, to object and rights in relation to automated decision making.

9. What is a computer virus?
   A computer virus is a type of malware that changes how computers operate and can spread from one device to another. They can vary in impact from being annoying to being downright destructive.

10. What is website filtering?
    This prevents a device from accessing a list of websites, usually because they are considered to contain undesirable content. Sites may be put into categorised lists, allowing users to opt in and out of specific categories, according to their requirements.

11. Suggest two ways in which one country may use the internet as a vehicle for launching an aggressive act on another country.
    Any two valid answers, may include espionage, sabotage, denying access to the internet or attempting to influence the outcome of elections or referendums.

Chapter 6: Key learning points

- The pace of technological change has been rapid and is still increasing. This impacts on social and cultural development. Legal systems can struggle to keep pace and some people feel increasingly left behind.
- Technology is a neutral tool. It can be of great benefit or it can cause great harm.
- When considering safety issues it is important to balance the risks and the benefits that digital technology brings.
- There is a wide range of hazards and areas of risk with technology, especially when online. These could be grouped under the following headings: Commercial, Aggressive, Sexual, Values, Health and Wellbeing. However, other classifications are possible.
- There is a wide range of benefits to being online and using technology. One possible classification is to use these headings: Education, Employment, Entertainment, Everyday Life and Social.
- Each person has a digital footprint, identifiable online information about them. This will be mostly made up of data posted by the individual. However it can include information about the person posted by others and automatically generated information generated from their online activities.
- A person's digital footprint may affect them when applying for jobs or to colleges and universities. It may affect their reputation and professional standing. It tends to be persistent and items can easily be taken out of context.
- There is a natural tension as to whether databases containing personal information should be able to be linked, in order to make much better use of all the information stored or whether they should be kept separate to protect individuals' privacy and reduce opportunities for the information to be abused/misused.
- There are key tools to support online safety which include firewalls and anti-virus software. These must be kept updated in order to deal with ever-changing threats.
- Personal privacy protection can be enhanced by the use of tools such as VPNs and proxy servers.
- Filtering can be used to try and block access to websites with undesirable content. However it can result in over- and under-blocking and could make it easier to avoid addressing the underlying issues that these sites raise.
- Devices can be encrypted so that any data they hold will appear as garbage unless an assigned password is entered.

- Software exists to allow mobile devices in particular, to be tracked, locked and/or wiped, in case they are ever lost or stolen.
- The internet has been and in all likelihood will continue to be, used by some national governments and other organisations for aggressive acts. These may include espionage, sabotage, misinformation, radicalisation of individuals and inciting them to commit acts of violence and attempting to manipulate public opinion in another country. Some governments monitor internet use by their own citizens, seeking to control or crush internal dissent or opposition.

Appendix A: SI prefixes - kilo, mega, giga

Prefixes are widely used in computing as very, very small numbers may be needed, for example when discussing component sizes on silicon chips. Very, very large numbers are often needed, for example when describing storage (usually measured in bytes) and data transmission speeds (bits per second). Prefixes allow this to be done easily and readers will probably be familiar with, or at least heard of, kilobytes, megabytes, gigabytes, terabytes and possibly even petabytes.

Standard prefixes give us multipliers that allow numbers of widely different sizes to be easily expressed. A kilometre is 1000 metres and a kilogram is 1000 grams, since kilo is the prefix meaning "x 1000".

Factor	Name	Symbol	Multiplier
10^{24}	**yotta**	Y	x 1000 000 000 000 000 000 000 000
10^{21}	**zetta**	Z	x 1000 000 000 000 000 000 000
10^{18}	**exa**	E	x 1000 000 000 000 000 000
10^{15}	**peta**	P	x 1000 000 000 000 000
10^{12}	**tera**	T	x 1000 000 000 000
10^{9}	**giga**	G	x 1000 000 000
10^{6}	**mega**	M	x 1000 000
10^{3}	**kilo**	k	x 1000
10^{2}	**hecto**	h	x 100
10^{1}	**deka**	da	x 10
10^{-1}	**deci**	d	x 0.1
10^{-2}	**centi**	c	x 0.01
10^{-3}	**milli**	m	x 0.001
10^{-6}	**micro**	μ	x 0.000 001
10^{-9}	**nano**	n	x 0.000 000 001
10^{-12}	**pico**	p	x 0.000 000 000 001
10^{-15}	**femto**	f	x 0.000 000 000 000 001
10^{-18}	**atto**	a	x 0.000 000 000 000 000 001
10^{-21}	**zepto**	z	x 0.000 000 000 000 000 000 001
10^{-24}	**yocto**	y	x 0.000 000 000 000 000 000 000 001

Strict interpretation examples:

50 Mbps = 50 x 1,000,000 = 50,000,000 bits per second transmission speed

4 Gbytes = 4 x 1,000,000,000 = 4,000,000,000 bytes of storage

Those working in computing have, by convention, *adopted their own version* of these prefixes, based not on powers of ten, but on powers of two, since this is often much more useful to them. The prefix kilo was the nearest power of two to 1000, which is 2^{10} or 1024. The prefix mega is therefore, informally, 2^{20} or 1 048 576.

In the world of standards, where precision is everything, it is clearly a problem to have one set of prefixes meaning two different things, depending on the context and leaving it up to the individual to decide which meaning to apply. More recently, some suppliers of memory products have applied the correct interpretation of the SI prefixes, producing flash memory where kilo means only 1000 and not 1024, etc. Plug this memory into a device running operating systems that still use the 1024=1 kbyte interpretation and the reported free space available appears much less than that claimed by the supplier. This is particularly true with large capacity memory devices in the gigabyte range or above.

The International Electrotechnical Commission (IEC) published a binary prefix standard in 1998 to deal with this problem, however adoption has been patchy to date. Given the ambiguity problem, it seems likely that these prefixes will become more widely used in the future.

IEC binary (bi) prefixes

Factor	Name	Symbol
2^{80} or 1024^8	yo**bi**	Yi
2^{70} or 1024^7	zebi	Zi
2^{60} or 1024^6	exbi	Ei
2^{50} or 1024^5	pebi	Pi
2^{40} or 1024^4	tebi	Ti
2^{30} or 1024^3	gibi	Gi
2^{20} or 1024^2	mebi	Mi
2^{10} or 1024	kibi	Ki

Appendix B: Computing timeline

Understanding the historical developments that led to the modern world of digital devices helps to give valuable context. Below is a personal selection of items that form part of that timeline.

The Abacus The abacus was invented at some point, somewhere! Its precise origin is uncertain. This device, which is still in use today in certain parts of the world, can be used by an experienced person to calculate more quickly than is possible with an electronic calculator.

3500-3000 B.C. The Wheel The wheel was invented by Sumarians in Mesopotania during this period, which allowed machinery to be developed.

3400 B.C. Egyptian numbers The Egyptians started using a special symbol for the number ten.

200-300 B.C. Arabic numbers Arabic numerals, which developed into the system we use today, were first developed by the Hindus in India. The system was in use during the third century BC, later spreading to the Arab world.

628 Zero defined mathematically (India)

1623 Schickard's Calculating Clock (Germany) A 6-digit adding machine.

1644-5 Blaise Pascal's "Pascaline" (France) Not as good as Schickard's, but it establishes the idea of a computing machine.

1674 von Leibiz's "Stepped Reckoner" (Germany) Able to multiply, answers up to 16 digits long, not always reliable.

1775 Charles, 3rd Earl Stanhope (UK) Makes a successful multiplying calculator.

1770-6 Mathius Hahn (Germany) Also makes a successful multiplying calculator.

1786 J H Mueller (Germany) Comes up with the idea of the "Difference Engine".

1820 Charles de Colmar's "Arithmometer" The first mass-produced calculator.

1822 Charles Babbage (1791-1871, UK) Starts trying to build a difference engine.

1836 Charles Babbage (UK) Designs his "Analytical Engine", working closely with **Ada Lovelace**.

1843-53 Scheutz and Scheutz (Sweden) Complete the first difference engines, both include printers.

1890 Herman Hollerith (US) Produced punch card tabulators to help process the US census results.

1892 William Burroughs (US) Invents a machine that starts the office calculator industry.

1937 Alan Turing (1912-1954, UK) Publishes his paper on "computable numbers".

1938 Konrad Zuse (Germany) Makes a prototype mechanical, programmable calculator.

1942 Atanasoff and Berry (US) Build a calculator with 300 bits of memory and a clock speed of 60Hz.

1943 Mark 1 Colossus The world's first programmable electronic computer, designed, constructed and tested under the direction of Thomas "Tommy" Flowers of the GPO (General Post Office, UK, the telecommunications unit of which became British Telecom, then BT). It was later delivered to and used at the Bletchley Park code breaking centre. Its existence remained a state secret for many years.

1946 ENIAC (US) Eckert and Mauchly build an programmable electronic calculator. Weighs 30 tons, covers 1000 sq ft and consumes around 190kW. Clock speed 100kHz, capable of 6000 additions per second.

1947 Transistor invented

1948 Mark I (UK) Newnam and Williams at Manchester University complete the first computer with stored program capability. It uses CRT (cathode ray tube) memory.

1949 EDSAC (UK) Wilkes and team (Cambridge University) build the first non-prototype stored program computer. It uses paper tape input/output.

1952 EDVAC (US) John von Neuman and team build a stored program computer first described in von Neuman's famous 1945 report.

1958 Integrated circuit developed

1964 DEC PDP-8 mini computer

1965 Commercial timesharing begins in the UK.

1969 ARPANET Started by the US Dept. of Defense for research into networking.

1971 i4004 Intel's microprocessor launched.

1972 Burrough's ATM (Automatic Teller Machine) appears

1972 Pong Arcade game released by Atari.

1973 First international connections to ARPANET

1973 Motorola produce prototype hand-held mobile phone Weighing over 1 kg, a 10 hour charge would give about 30 mins talk time.

1974 i8080 The first general purpose microprocessor.

1978 i8086 A 16-bit microprocessor.

1978 Commodore Pet introduced With 8K RAM, cassette deck and 9" monitor.

1978 Microsoft Bill Gates and Paul Allen found their software company.

1978 Space Invaders Arcade game released by Taito.

1979 VisiCalc The first spreadsheet is launched taking personal computers forwards from being "toys for techies", to serious business tools.

1979 1G, first generation, automatic analogue cell phone system (Tokyo)

1980 Sinclair ZX-80 computer The first computer for under GBP £100. It had 1Kb RAM, which could be expanded to 16kB, a processor that ran at 3.25MHz, used a TV for display and a cassette drive for storage.

1981 The first 32 bit microprocessors

1981 DOS 1 Microsoft's original operating system for personal computers.

1981 IBM PC launched Its success helped to standardise much of the disparate personal computing market, driving this technology forwards.

1982 The first BBC micro produced Hugely popular computers in UK schools.

1983 Commodore 64 launched One of the best-selling home computers.

1984 DOS 3 Operating system from Microsoft.

1984 Apple Macintosh Iconic microcomputer.

1985 Intel's i80386 chip launched

1985 DTP Aldus PageMaker launched for the Apple Mac, marking the birth of DTP (desktop publishing).

1987 NAND flash memory Launched by Toshiba.

1989 Intel's i80486 chip launched

1990 Windows 3.0

1990 First products from SunDisk Based on their 4 MB flash chips. Sun Disk was the original name of SanDisk.

1991 World Wide Web Created by Sir Tim Berners-Lee and released by CERN.

1991 Ban on business use of the internet is lifted

1991 Psion 3 Psion 3 handheld computer launched.

1991 2G digital mobile phone networks Introduced data services for mobile phones, starting with SMS text messages.

1992 Simon Personal Communicator The world's first smartphone launched by IBM.

1993 Intel's Pentium chip launched

1993 DOS 6 Operating system from Microsoft.

1994 Kodak digital camera Kodak demonstrates a digital camera based around a Nikon P90 and costing in excess of GBP£8000.

1994 CompactFlash memory cards (4MB) Launched by SunDisk.

1994 PlayStation game console launched by Sony

1995 Windows 95 launched

1996 Windows CE The first hand-held computers with this cut-down Microsoft operating system are launched.

1996 USB 1.0 launched

1997 First portable MP3 player launched (South Korea)

1997 Garry Kasparov beaten at chess by a computer World chess champion Garry Kasparov beaten 3½ - 2½ by IBM's computer, Deep Blue.

1998 Google founded Group name later changed to Alphabet, Google was retained as the name of their search engine.

1999 SD memory card Launched by SanDisk, Panasonic and Toshiba.

2000 First USB flash memory drives sold (8 MB capacity)

2000 64 MB SD card from SanDisk

2000 US President Clinton orders military to stop scrambling GPS satellite signals. This led to a mass market for vehicle satellite navigation systems, within a few years.

2000 USB 2.0

2001 Windows XP Operating system from Microsoft.

2002 3G mobile phone networks First commercial 3G network launched in South Korea. Applications not previously available to mobile phone users include GPS, location-based services, mobile TV, video on demand and video conferencing.

2003 First BlackBerry smartphones

2004 Facebook launched Social networking service.

2005 1GB SanDisk microSD memory card

2005 Xbox 360 game console Launched by Microsoft.

2006 Twitter founded Microblogging service.

2006 Wii game console Launched by Nintendo.

2007 First Apple iPhone released

2007 Fitbit founded Producing wearable technology relating to physical activity tracking, with the aim of promoting healthier lifestyles.

2008 First Android smartphone released

2009 Bitcoin launched The world's first blockchain-based cryptocurrency.

2009 Windows 7 launched Operating system from Microsoft.

2009 WhatsApp released Messaging service.

2009 Uber founded Ridesharing backed by a social network to validate both drivers and riders.

2009 4G mobile phone networks Commercial deployment begins. Entirely based on packet switching (IP telephony).

2009 64GB SanDisk Extreme Pro CompactFlash Memory Card.

2010 Apple iPad released

2010 USB 3.0

2010 Most computer motherboards no longer support floppy disc drives.

2010 Instagram launched

2011 Researchers set a new record for the rate of data transfer using a single laser of 26 terabits per second. At those speeds, the entire Library of Congress collections (see box) could be sent down an optical fibre in 10 seconds.

2011 Snapchat launches (as Pictaboo)

2011 More calls in the UK made by mobile phones than using wired devices (estimated).

2012 First Raspberry Pi device released. A computer for under $40.

2012 Hard disc drives with a capacity of **1-2 TB** commonplace.

According to the **Library of Congress** website (2017)...

The Library of Congress was founded in 1800 and contains more than 164 million items on 838 miles of shelving. There are over 38 million books and other printed materials, 3.6 million recordings, 14 million photographs, 5.5 million maps, 8.1 million pieces of sheet music and 70 million manuscripts.

The Library receives around 15,000 items each working day, adding roughly 12,000 to the collections. Most are received through the US copyright registration process. About half of the books are in languages other than English.

It employs over 3,000 staff.

2015 Windows 10 launched Operating system from Microsoft.

2015 Navya Arma The first fully autonomous vehicle, able to carry 15 people and drive at speeds up to 45 km/h.

2016 Self-driving taxi service First taxi service using self-driving vehicles launched in Singapore.

2016-2017 5G mobile phone networks Initial field trials begin. 5G offers higher data rates and is capable of supporting much higher user densities, with greater reliability.

2018 First pedestrian killed in collision with a self-driving vehicle (USA)

Appendix C: Failed IT projects

This appendix contains some outline details of a few notable IT project failures from around the world, chosen to illustrate a fairly common phenomenon. The aim is to illustrate the difficulty of successfully concluding large IT projects and the degree of risk often involved, whilst touching on some of the possible causes and contributory factors.

Major failures by governments and other public bodies are often followed by detailed investigations and reports. Much less information is generally published about commercial failures. However, at their worst, large scale IT project failures can cost tax payers millions or billions (name your currency of choice) and have the potential to put companies out of business.

Issues can include poor research and preparation at the beginning, underestimating the complexity of what is being undertaken, lack of management oversight or clear accountabilities, issues between contracting partners, frequently changing requirements and poor implementation. The latter can include failing to communicate adequately with and gain the support of affected employees, weak or flawed training and not having workable fall-back alternatives should problems arise with the new system.

"Big Bang" projects where, on a given date, the old system is turned off and a new system turned on, are particularly high risk. Working practices have evolved in response to repeated failures and cost overruns and so-called agile project methods have developed to allow a lower risk, more evolutionary approach. The term "agile" was popularised following publication of the Manifesto for Agile Software Development[1] in 2001. The main declaration and key principles will be found at the end of this appendix. Many agile software development frameworks have been created and continue to evolve.

Some failed IT projects - UK Government and related bodies

Project: London Ambulance Computer Aided Dispatch System, 1992
Intention: System to cover ambulance dispatch, map display and automatic vehicle location.

Problems: Shortly after it was introduced, on October 26th 1992, the system was unable to cope with the normal load that it was experiencing. The response to emergency calls could be several hours, ambulance communications failed and

---

[1] http://agilemanifesto.org

some ambulances were lost from the system. Lives were undoubtedly lost, although there is disagreement over the precise number. The system finally collapsed on 4th November 1992, 9 days after its launch.

Issues identified: Procurement weighted towards best price tender. There was ambiguity about who in the successful consortium was to be the lead contractor. Software was often delivered late and of suspect quality. Questionable consultations with the ambulance crews in drawing up the original requirements. Possible resistance of crews to the tracking component and problems with training and communications/industrial relations. Technical problems reduced staff confidence in the new system. Issues arose from problems with procurement, design, implementation and introduction of the new system. There was no secondary fall-back system available.

Project: NHS National Program for IT, 2002

Intention: To provide what would have been the world's largest non-military IT system, including a national patient record system.

Problems: Frequent delays with the delivery of some core systems halted due to concerns that they were not fit for purpose. Some patient records were lost, delaying treatment and causing significant additional costs. By March 2012 an estimated £3.7 billion of benefits had been achieved at a cost of £7.3 billion.

Issues identified: Poor negotiating capability, changing specifications, technical challenges and disputes with suppliers. Weak programme management and oversight.

Project: Department for Transport Shared Services Centre, 2005

Intention: Cut costs by £57 million by creating a single site for all payroll, finance and personnel services

Problems: Instead of saving money the project ended up costing £81 million.

Post project report: House of Commons Committee of Public Accounts

Issues identified: Over optimistic deadlines leading to rushed implementation including insufficient testing and poor initial setting up.

Project: Defence Information Infrastructure, 2005

Intention: To create a secure military network to help British troops to operate more effectively around the world. Initial cost estimate was £5.9 billion.

Problems: Delays; by 2008 the project was 18 months behind schedule with only 29,000 of the contracted 63,000 terminals provided, with none of the contracted secret capabilities. Final cost in excess of £7 billion.

Post project report: National Audit Office (NAO)

Issues identified: No suitable pilot carried out, insufficient research on the buildings where the system was to be installed.

Project: Common Agricultural Policy Delivery Programme, 2014

Intention: To allocate farm subsidies, forecast cost £155 million.

Problems: Payments to farmers delayed, penalties incurred from the EU, final cost around £215 million.

Post project report: House of Commons Committee of Public Accounts

Issues identified: The original vision and design of the programme was narrow. Furthermore there were differences in strategic direction and vision between the Cabinet Office, Department for Environment, Food & Rural Affairs, the Rural Payments Agency (RPA) and other delivery bodies. Many fundamental changes were made to the programme, significantly increasing the level of innovation and risk. The collaboration between the various Government bodies was ineffective and undermined their ability to deliver a successful rural payments service. The often poor availability of good quality broadband in rural areas at the time, was not taken into account.

Some failed IT projects - worldwide

Project: State of Washington License Application Mitigation Project, begun 1990, USA

Intention: Automate the state's license renewal and vehicle registration systems.

Problems: Projected costs kept increasing, running costs were likely to be six times that of the system it was replacing.

Outcome: The project was abandoned in 1997 after incurring costs of $40 million.

Project: FoxMeyer Drugs ERP Program 1993 - 1996, USA

Intention: To implement warehouse automation software, integrated with enterprise resource planning (ERP) software. Estimated cost $35 million over 18 months.

Problems: The first warehouse to be automated suffered from sabotage. Inventory was damaged and some orders were not fulfilled. By 1994 the new system was only processing 10,000 orders per night compared with 420,000 under the old system.

Outcome: FoxMeyer was a very large US distributor of pharmaceuticals, worth around $5 billion in 1993. The company became bankrupt in 1996 and was eventually sold for $80 million.

Issues identified: Deadlines were too optimistic. Warehouse employees whose jobs were under threat were unsupportive. It was alleged that the contracting companies had used the automation project as a training opportunity for junior employees, instead of deploying their best personnel. The resulting legal cases were not resolved until 2004.

Project: National Firearm Registration System, 1997, Canada

Intention: Expected net cost of CAD$2 million, taking gun licensing fees into account

Post project report: Canada's auditor general released a report in 2003 saying that estimated project costs had increased to CAD$1 billion by 2005, offset by CAD$140 million of licence fees.

Outcome: The requirement to register non-restricted long guns (a large part of the initial project) was repealed in 2012.

Issues identified: Over 1000 change orders were made in the first 2 years, following pressure from the gun lobby and others. These changes had to interface with the computer systems of more than 50 other agencies. Since integration work was not part of the original contract, costs ballooned to $688 million by 2001, with annual maintenance costs of $75 million per annum. There were high error rates in the applications submitted by gun owners. A lack of precise standards meant that one person was able to register a soldering gun!

Project: Sainsbury's Warehouse Automation, 2003, UK

Intention: Install an automated fulfilment system at a distribution centre covering much of London and southeast England.

Problems: Technical problems, mainly barcode reading errors.

Outcome: Project scrapped with IT assets of £150 million written off. The total cost to the business will have been much larger.

Issues identified: Outsourcing the project to another company, with a lack of oversight by Sainsbury's management was suggested as one possible cause. This was exacerbated by poor communications and insufficient attention to business and IT risk management.

Project: Queensland Health Payroll and Rostering System, 2006, Australia

Intention: To provide payroll and rostering services to 78,000 Queensland Health staff

Problems: Delayed by 2 years, when it went live thousands of employees were underpaid, overpaid or not paid at all. The total cost to taxpayers has been estimated at AUS$1.2 billion.

Outcomes: By October 2008, having been paid $32 million of the $98 million contract, the supplier had not achieved any of the contracted performance criteria.

Issues identified: Issues between the contracting partners resulting in "silo-working". There were also frequent changes to requirements.

Post project report: Commission of Inquiry

Conclusion: "The replacement of the Queensland Health payroll system must take place in the front rank of failures in public administration in this country. It may be the worst." Commission of Inquiry

Manifesto for Agile Software Development

We are uncovering better ways of developing
software by doing it and helping others do it.
Through this work we have come to value:

Individuals and interactions over processes and tools
Working software over comprehensive documentation
Customer collaboration over contract negotiation
Responding to change over following a plan

That is, while there is value in the items on
the right, we value the items on the left more.

Kent Beck, Mike Beedle, Arie van Bennekum, Alistair Cockburn, Ward Cunningham, Martin Fowler, James Grenning, Jim Highsmith, Andrew Hunt, Ron Jeffries, Jon Kern, Brian Marick, Robert C. Martin, Steve Mellor, Ken Schwaber, Jeff Sutherland, Dave Thomas

© 2001, the above authors

This declaration may be freely copied in any form, but only in its entirety through this notice.

Principles behind the Agile Manifesto

We follow these principles:

1. Our highest priority is to satisfy the customer through early and continuous delivery of valuable software.

2. Welcome changing requirements, even late in development. Agile processes harness change for the customer's competitive advantage.

3. Deliver working software frequently, from a couple of weeks to a couple of months, with a preference to the shorter timescale.

4. Business people and developers must work together daily throughout the project.

5. Build projects around motivated individuals. Give them the environment and support they need, and trust them to get the job done.

6. The most efficient and effective method of conveying information to and within a development team is face-to-face conversation.

7. Working software is the primary measure of progress.

8. Agile processes promote sustainable development. The sponsors, developers, and users should be able to maintain a constant pace indefinitely.

9. Continuous attention to technical excellence and good design enhances agility.

10. Simplicity--the art of maximizing the amount of work not done--is essential.

11. The best architectures, requirements, and designs emerge from self-organizing teams.

12. At regular intervals, the team reflects on how to become more effective, then tunes and adjusts its behavior accordingly.

Sources

INTRODUCTION

https://www.census.gov	US census history
"Digital Natives, Digital Immigrants" By Marc Prensky From On the Horizon (MCB University Press, Vol. 9 No. 5, October 2001) from http://www.marcprensky.com	Digital natives, etc.

CHAPTER ONE: Input, process, output

http://www.tutorialspoint.com/microprocessor/	details on 8085 and 8086 microprocessors
https://en.wikipedia.org/wiki/Intel_8085, https://en.wikipedia.org/wiki/Intel_8086	details on 8085 and 8086 microprocessors
http://www.teach-ict.com	von Neumann architecture
https://www.bluetooth.com	Bluetooth
http://www.practical-home-theater-guide.com/SACD.html	Compact disc
https://www.raspberrypi.org	Raspberry Pi

CHAPTER TWO: Digital devices and data

https://en.wikipedia.org/wiki/ASCII	ASCII
http://www.asciitable.com/	ASCII
https://en.wikipedia.org/wiki/UTF-8	UTF-8
https://www.w3schools.com/charsets/ref_html_utf8.asp	UTF-8
http://giflib.sourceforge.net/whatsinagif/bits_and_bytes.html	Graphic file formats
https://techterms.com/definition/gif	Graphic file formats
https://en.wikipedia.org/wiki/JPEG	Graphic file formats
https://jpeg.org/about.html	Graphic file formats
http://www.libpng.org/pub/png/	Graphic file formats
https://www.w3.org/TR/PNG/	Graphic file formats
https://en.wikipedia.org/wiki/Portable_Network_Graphics	Graphic file formats
http://www.fileformat.info/format/bmp/egff.htm	Graphic file formats

https://en.wikipedia.org/wiki/BMP_file_format	Graphic file formats
http://whatis.techtarget.com/definition/TIFF-Tag-Image-File-Format	Graphic file formats
https://en.wikipedia.org/wiki/TIFF	Graphic file formats
http://www.fileformat.info/format/tiff/egff.htm	Graphic file formats
http://www.livescience.com/27853-who-invented-zero.html	Zero
https://www.mathsisfun.com/numbers/bases.html	Number bases
http://ryanstutorials.net/binary-tutorial/binary-floating-point.php	Number bases
https://en.wikipedia.org/wiki/Luhn_algorithm	Luhn algorithm
https://www.rosettacode.org/wiki/Luhn_test_of_credit_card_numbers	Luhn algorithm
https://en.wikipedia.org/wiki/International_Article_Number	GS1, EAN
http://www.gs1.org/	GS1, EAN
https://www.gs1uk.org/	GS1, EAN

CHAPTER THREE: Algorithms and software

https://www.howtogeek.com/56958/htg-explains-how-uefi-will-replace-the-bios/	BIOS, UEFI
https://en.wikipedia.org/wiki/BIOS	BIOS, UEFI
http://searchcloudsecurity.techtarget.com/definition/BIOS-rootkit-attack	BIOS rootkit attack
http://www.bbc.co.uk/education/guides/ztcdtfr/revision	Operating system
http://www.webopedia.com/TERM/O/operating_system.html	Operating system
https://wiki.scratch.mit.edu/wiki/Programming_Language	Scratch
https://en.wikipedia.org/wiki/Scalable_Vector_Graphics	SVG format
https://www.w3.org/Graphics/SVG/About.html	SVG format
https://www.w3schools.com/graphics/svg_intro.asp	SVG format
https://www.dreamgrow.com/top-15-most-popular-social-networking-sites	Social media
https://www.forbes.com/sites/neilpatel/2015/09/28/5-underrated-up-and-coming-social-media-platforms-you-need-to-join-right-now/#67a14a4d422e	Social media

http://bookdoctorgwen.blogspot.co.uk/2009/11/50-types-of-computerware.html	'ware words

CHAPTER FOUR: Computer networks and the internet

http://www.bbc.co.uk/schools/gcsebitesize	Networks
https://occupytheory.org/advantages-and-disadvantages-of-computer-networking	Networks
http://whatis.techtarget.com	Networks
https://www.wi-fi.org	Wi-Fi
https://www.lifewire.com/how-routers-work-816456	Routers, switches and hubs
https://www.computerhope.com/jargon/r/router.htm	Routers, switches and hubs
https://www.cisco.com/c/en_uk/products/security/firewalls/what-is-a-firewall.html	Firewalls
https://en.wikipedia.org/wiki/Ethernet	Ethernet
https://www.wired.com/2011/07/speed-matters	Ethernet
IEEE Standard for Ethernet by LAN/MAN Standards Committee of the IEEE Computer Society	Ethernet
http://www.computerhistory.org/timeline/networking-the-web	Networks
http://www.human-memory.net/brain_neurons.html	Neurons and the brain
https://sharpbrains.com/blog/2008/02/26/brain-plasticity-how-learning-changes-your-brain	Neurons and the brain
Wikipedia (various)	Internet protocols
https://www.intgovforum.org	Internet governance
https://www.icann.org/resources/pages/welcome-2012-02-25-en	ICAAN
https://www.ietf.org/about/	IETF
"*Where Wizards Stay Up Late: The Origins of the Internet*" Paperback – 21 Jan 1998, by Katie Hafner and Matthew Lyon	History of the internet
http://www.internetsociety.org/internet/what-internet/history-internet/brief-history-internet	History of the internet
http://searchnetworking.techtarget.com/definition/ARPANET	History of the internet
https://www.darpa.mil/	History of the internet
https://en.wikipedia.org/wiki/Internet	History of the internet
https://webfoundation.org/about/vision/history-of-the-web/	History of the internet

https://www.w3.org/People/Berners-Lee/	History of the internet
https://webfoundation.org/about/	History of the internet
https://en.wikipedia.org/wiki/Deep_web	Deep web
https://www.theguardian.com/technology/2015/may/31/ross-ulbricht-silk-road-jail	Dark web
https://www.ted.com/talks/tim_berners_lee_on_the_next_web	The next web
https://www.ted.com/talks/tim_berners_lee_a_magna_carta_for_the_web	Magna Carta for the web
https://www.wired.com/2015/10/can-learn-epic-failure-google-flu-trends	Google Flu Trends
https://www.w3schools.com/html	HTML, including practice editor
http://www.bbc.co.uk/webwise/guides/about-streaming	Streaming
https://www.w3schools.com/graphics/svg_intro.asp	SVG format
https://en.wikipedia.org/wiki/Web_search_engine#Market_share	Search engine, market share

CHAPTER FIVE: How some stuff works

http://www.usb.org/home	USB
https://en.wikipedia.org/wiki/USB	USB
http://www.usblyzer.com/usb-topology.htm	USB
http://www.usb.org/developers/docs/devclass_docs/CabConn20.pdf	USB
http://www.flash25.toshiba.com	Semiconductor memory
http://www.usbmadesimple.co.uk/index.html	Semiconductor memory
https://howflashdriveworks.wordpress.com/what-is-a-flash-drive	Semiconductor memory
https://en.wikipedia.org/wiki/Read-only_memory	Semiconductor memory
https://en.wikipedia.org/wiki/Floppy_disk	Floppy discs
https://www.powerdatarecovery.com/hard-drive-recovery/recover-formatted-hard-drive.html	Hard disc drives
https://en.wikipedia.org/wiki/Disk_formatting	Hard disc drives
https://en.wikipedia.org/wiki/Disk_partitioning	Hard disc drives
https://en.wikipedia.org/wiki/Optical_storage	Optical storage
http://www.explainthatstuff.com/cdplayers.html	Optical storage

https://www.thoughtco.com/what-are-cds-made-of-607882	Optical storage
http://www.madehow.com/Volume-1/Compact-Disc.html	Optical storage
https://en.wikipedia.org/wiki/Magneto-optical_drive	MiniDisc
http://www.rfidjournal.com/	RFID
http://www.technovelgy.com/ct/Technology-Article.asp?ArtNum=1	RFID
https://en.wikipedia.org/wiki/Radio-frequency_identification	RFID
https://www.gs1.org/sites/default/files/docs/barcodes/GS1_General_Specifications.pdf	EAN
http://www.qrcode.com/en/history/	2-D barcodes
http://www.qrcode.com/en/about/version.html	2-D barcodes
https://www.scandit.com/types-barcodes-choosing-right-barcode/	2-D barcodes
https://en.wikipedia.org/wiki/QR_code	2-D barcodes
https://keremerkan.net/qr-code-and-2d-code-generator/	Barcode generator
http://online-barcode-generator.net/	Barcode generator
http://www.visualead.com/	Barcode generator
https://www.qrcode-monkey.com/	Barcode generator
http://www.makeuseof.com/tag/why-do-cellphones-need-a-sim-card/	Mobile telephony
http://www.radio-electronics.com/info/cellulartelecomms/cellular_concepts/handover_handoff.php	Mobile telephony
http://fieldguide.gizmodo.com/all-the-sensors-in-your-smartphone-and-how-they-work-1797121002	Mobile telephony
https://www.youtube.com/watch?v=pKl4I7hwgW4 What's Inside an Android Smartphone?	Mobile telephony
http://howtomechatronics.com/how-it-works/electrical-engineering/mems-accelerometer-gyrocope-magnetometer-arduino/	MEMS sensors
https://en.wikipedia.org/wiki/Communications_satellite	Comms satellites
https://www.faa.gov/about/office_org/headquarters_offices/ato/service_units/techops/navservices/gnss/gps/howitworks/	Satellite navigation
http://www.esa.int/Our_Activities/Navigation/Galileo_begins_serving_the_globe	Satellite navigation

http://en.beidou.gov.cn/index.html	Satellite navigation
https://singularityhub.com/2017/03/31/can-futurists-predict-the-year-of-the-singularity/	Artificial intelligence
https://www.tutorialspoint.com/artificial_intelligence/artificial_intelligence_overview.htm	Artificial intelligence
https://gizmodo.com/stunning-ai-breakthrough-takes-us-one-step-closer-to-th-1819650084	Artificial intelligence
https://futurism.com/kurzweil-claims-that-the-singularity-will-happen-by-2045/	Artificial intelligence
http://www.investopedia.com/terms/m/mooreslaw.asp	Artificial intelligence
http://www.turing.org.uk/scrapbook/test.html	Artificial intelligence
https://www.doc.ic.ac.uk/~nd/surprise_96/journal/vol4/cs11/report.html#Introduction%20to%20neural%20networks	Artificial intelligence
https://deepmind.com/blog/alphago-zero-learning-scratch/	Artificial intelligence
http://www.agi-society.org/	Artificial intelligence
https://www.youtube.com/watch?v=eQLcDmfmGB0#_ga=2.34266465.1133212114.1512728280-1864101239.1512728280 How Computer Vision Is Finally Taking Off, After 50 Years	Artificial intelligence
https://www.nbbmuseum.be/en/2007/01/cowry-shells.htm	Money
http://alphahistory.com/weimarrepublic/1923-hyperinflation/	Money
https://www.thebalance.com/what-is-the-history-of-the-gold-standard-3306136	Money
http://www.zerohedge.com/news/2017-03-06/prisoners-explain-why-pack-mackerel-gold-standard-currencies-americas-prisons	Money
https://www.theguardian.com/society/shortcuts/2016/aug/23/what-do-british-prisoners-use-as-currency	Money
https://en.wikipedia.org/wiki/Wire_transfer	Money
http://searchsecurity.techtarget.com/definition/asymmetric-cryptography	Public key cryptography
https://www.globalsign.com/en/ssl-information-center/what-is-public-key-cryptography/	Public key cryptography

https://medium.com/@vrypan/explaining-public-key-cryptography-to-non-geeks-f0994b3c2d5	Public key cryptography
https://www.tutorialspoint.com/cryptography/public_key_encryption.htm	Public key cryptography
https://www.youtube.com/watch?v=kubGCSj5y3k Bitcoin: How Cryptocurrencies Work	Cryptocurrencies
https://www.youtube.com/watch?v=l9jOJk30eQs How Bitcoin Works in 5 Minutes (Technical)	Cryptocurrencies
https://www.youtube.com/watch?v=93E_GzvpMA0&t=188s What is Blockchain	Cryptocurrencies
https://www.youtube.com/watch?v=r6mOUh_NY8M&t=181s The Strongest Believer Of Bitcoin - Bill Gates	Cryptocurrencies
https://www.youtube.com/watch?v=RplnSVTzvnU How the blockchain will radically transform the economy, Bettina Warburg	Cryptocurrencies,
https://en.wikipedia.org/wiki/Bitcoin	Cryptocurrencies
Blockchain Mania, Fortune, 01 September 2017, issue 11	Blockchain
The Rise of Bitcoins, Investors Chronicle, 23-29 June 2017, issue 25	Blockchain

CHAPTER SIX: Some technology issues

http://www.zephoria.org/thoughts/archives/2007/05/11/just_the_facts.html	Online Youth Victimization
https://www.youtube.com/watch?v=x-qybCYuYPY, Just The Facts About Online Youth Victimization: Researchers Present the Facts and Debunk Myths	Online Youth Victimization
https://www.internetsociety.org/tutorials/your-digital-footprint-matters/	Digital footprint
https://www.theguardian.com/world/2016/nov/29/snoopers-charter-bill-becomes-law-extending-uk-state-surveillance	Snooper's charter
https://ico.org.uk/for-organisations/guide-to-the-general-data-protection-regulation-gdpr/	Data protection
https://us.norton.com/internetsecurity-malware.html	Malware
http://searchsecurity.techtarget.com/definition/malware	Malware
https://us.norton.com/internetsecurity-malware-what-is-a-computer-virus.html	Computer viruses

https://www.howtogeek.com/192949/how-to-remotely-track-any-lost-smartphone-tablet-or-pc/	Remote tracking, locking
https://www.expressvpn.com/what-is-vpn	VPN
https://en.wikipedia.org/wiki/Proxy_server	Proxy server
https://www.theguardian.com/world/2011/apr/06/georgian-woman-cuts-web-access	Loss of internet access
http://www.nytimes.com/2012/06/01/world/middleeast/obama-ordered-wave-of-cyberattacks-against-iran.html?pagewanted=1&_r=1&hp	Stuxnet virus, Iran
http://www.businessinsider.com/stuxnet-was-far-more-dangerous-than-previous-thought-2013-11?IR=T	Stuxnet virus, Iran
https://www.nao.org.uk/report/investigation-wannacry-cyber-attack-and-the-nhs/	WannaCry virus, NHS
http://www.independent.co.uk/news/world/asia/north-korea-responsible-wannacry-ransomware-microsoft-brad-smith-cyber-attack-nsa-a8000166.html	WannaCry virus, NHS
https://www.theguardian.com/politics/2017/nov/13/theresa-may-accuses-russia-of-interfering-in-elections-and-fake-news	Russian alleged hacking, fake news
https://www.thedailybeast.com/the-men-behind-the-infamous-fake-north-korean-twitter-account	@DPRK_News
http://www.bbc.co.uk/news/uk-42202191	Warning about Russia

APPENDIX A: SI prefixes - kilo, mega, giga

http://www.npl.co.uk/reference/measurement-units/si-prefixes	SI decimal prefixes
https://physics.nist.gov/cuu/Units/binary.html	IEC binary prefixes

APPENDIX B: Computing timeline

https://www.loc.gov/about/fascinating-facts	Library of Congress
Wide range of internet sources consulted	*Important dates, etc.*

APPENDIX C: Failed IT projects

http://www.softwareadvisoryservice.com/blog/biggest-uk-government-project-failures	Large IT project failures

http://www.computerworld.com/article/2533563/it-project-management/it-s-biggest-project-failures----and-what-we-can-learn-from-them.html?page=2	Large IT project failures
https://1026139pm.files.wordpress.com/2013/05/london20ambulance20case20study.pdf	Large IT project failures
https://ifs.host.cs.st-andrews.ac.uk/Resources/CaseStudies/LondonAmbulance/LASFailure.pdf	Large IT project failures
https://publications.parliament.uk/pa/cm201314/cmselect/cmpubacc/294/294.pdf	Large IT project failures
http://www.parliament.uk/business/committees/committees-a-z/commons-select/public-accounts-committee/news/npfit-report	Large IT project failures
https://www.nao.org.uk/wp-content/uploads/2011/05/1012888es.pdf	Large IT project failures
https://www.nao.org.uk/wp-content/uploads/2008/05/0708481es.pdf	Large IT project failures
https://www.nao.org.uk/report/ministry-of-defence-the-defence-information-infrastructure/	Large IT project failures
https://www.nao.org.uk/wp-content/uploads/2015/11/Early-review-of-the-Common-Agricultural-Policy-Delivery-Programme-Summary.pdf	Large IT project failures
http://community.seattletimes.nwsource.com/archive/?date=19970322&slug=2529983	Large IT project failures
https://prezi.com/tnr_cop39sxx/canadas-gun-registration-failure	Large IT project failures
https://www.forbes.com/sites/danielfisher/2013/01/22/canada-tried-registering-long-guns-and-gave-up/#6bd1ad85a1b9	Large IT project failures
http://www.computerweekly.com/news/2240058411/Sainsburys-writes-off-260m-as-supply-chain-IT-trouble-hits-profit	Large IT project failures
https://writepass.com/journal/2017/02/analysis-of-the-warehouse-automation-failure-at-sainsburys	Large IT project failures
http://www.smh.com.au/it-pro/government-it/worst-failure-of-public-administration-in-this-nation-payroll-system-20130806-hv1cw.html	Large IT project failures
http://statements.qld.gov.au/Statement/2013/8/7/action-over-health-payroll-bungle	Large IT project failures
http://agilemanifesto.org	Agile software development

Glossary

alpha channel	This relates to computer graphics and specifies the degree of transparency or opacity of a pixel. Fully transparent pixels can be used in an image to create an irregularly shaped object cut-out.
analogue	A continuously varying physical quantity, such as temperature.
application, app	Software that directly benefits an end user, e.g. a word processor or web browser.
ASCII	American Standard Code for Information Interchange (character code set)
bandwidth	The rate or speed of data transfer, usually measured in bits per second.
big data	Informal term for huge quantities of varied data that have the potential to be mined for useful information.
bit	**B**inary dig**it**, i.e. a one or a zero.
bitmap	Representing an image as a matrix of dots or pixels.
blog	Truncation of "web log", informal diary-style text.
Bluetooth	A particular type of wireless technology for exchanging data over short distances.
bot, internet bot	Runs automated tasks over the internet, e.g. a web crawler. Also known as a web robot.
bug	An error or fault in a computer program.
byte	A fixed number of bits, typically eight, the number required to represent one character.
cloud (the)	Informal term for the internet.
CD ROM	Once common for the structured storage of information, e.g. an electronic encyclopaedia. Largely superceded by the World Wide Web.
compiler	Software for converting a program written in a high level programming language into machine code. Compilers attempt to convert the entire program before running the resulting object code.
compression	Reducing the size of a computer file.
compression, lossless	Lossless compression reduces file size with no loss of detail, by finding more efficient ways of storing the data.

Living in a digital world - Glossary

compression, lossy	Lossy compression usually achieves greater compression, but there is some loss of information (detail). The greater the loss, the higher the compression that can be achieved.
CPU	Central processing unit. See *microprocessor*.
DAB	Digital Audio Broadcasting. A digital radio standard used in Europe, Middle East and Asia Pacific.
data	Numbers, which may form the input to a digital device, be stored on a digital device or be output from a digital device.
debug, debugging	Recognising, locating and fixing errors in computer code (programs, software).
denial of service attack	A cyber attack that aims to make a digital device or network resource unavailable for its intended purpose, often by generating a flood of superfluous requests in order to overload the available capacity.
digital	Pertaining to numbers. A digital device uses numbers for all its operations.
digitise	Convert analogue data into numbers.
domain name	An identification string that represents an internet resource, e.g. educationvision.co.uk is the domain name of a website.
DOS	Disc Operating System. Most often used to refer to MS-DOS, Microsoft's family of text-based operating systems that predated MS Windows. However there were many other operating systems that included DOS in their names.
EEPROM	Electrically erasable, programmable, read-only memory.
Ethernet	A dominant networking standard.
EXIF data	Exchangeable Image File, a standard format for recording image and sound information by digital cameras, including scanners.
file	A computer resource that holds/records data. Files can be opened, read, changed and closed. There are two basic types of file, text files and binary files.
filename extension	This is a suffix to a filename, that often comes after a full stop (period), e.g. *myfile.txt* has the extension **txt** and the extension indicates that it is a plain text file.
GPS	Global Positioning System. A space-based radio-navigation system owned by the United States government.

hardware	Computing equipment, items that have physical form.
hacking	Gaining unauthorised access to the data held within a computer or a network.
hash function	A hash function takes a variable amount of input data and produces some output (number or string) that has a fixed size. A simple hash function that could be applied to short email messages would be to take the ASCII codes for all the characters used in the message and add up all the binary ones. This would result in a single number.
HDD	Hard disc drive. A data storage device capable of storing very large quantities of data.
Hz, kHz, MHz	Hz measures frequency in terms of the number of times per second. 1,000,000 Hz = 1,000 kHz = 1 Mhz = 1 million times per second.
ICT	Information and communications technology.
information	The meaning given to data.
interface	A boundary, e.g. between two devices, where data may need to be processed or translated to be meaningful to both. It may comprise any or all of hardware, software and cables & connectors.
interpreter	Software for converting a program written in a high level programming language into machine code. Interpreters convert one line of programming at a time, execute it and then convert the next line.
IT	Information technology.
intranet	Private network, usually run by a particular organisation, to facilitate internal communication and collaboration.
keyword	A word or phrase that helps to describe some content, such as a photograph or web page. A photograph showing a group of lions might include the following keywords as metadata. **Lions, mammals, pride, Africa, resting, grassland, wildlife, wild, natural history, outdoors.**
LAN, local area network	Connected computers that are all in close proximity, i.e. in the same room or same/adjacent buildings.
machine code	Binary program code that can be executed directly by a computer.
malware	Malicious software that aims to disrupt, damage or gain access to a computer system.

metadata	Data about data, or data that describes data. Metadata can include keywords that can help describe content, such as a web page or photograph.
microblog	A social media site where users make short, frequent posts, such as Twitter.
microcontroller	A small, embedded computer. These are found in all sorts of modern equipment, such as microwave ovens, digital cameras, washing machines, mobile phones, etc.
microprocessor	The "heart" of a computer, also known as the CPU, or processor. A single integrated circuit that includes an arithmetic and logic unit and a control unit. Most of the key data processing is done by it.
monitor	Screen or visual display unit (VDU). Crucial part of the interface between a computer and its user.
multi-tasking	Being able to run more than one program simultaneously.
network	Where two or more computers are connected so that they can share resources, including data and communicate with each other. Connections can be wired, wireless or a mix of the two.
object code	Machine code that is the output of a compiler.
open format	A file format for storing digital data that is defined by a published specification that can be used by anyone.
open source software	Software where the source code is made available with a licence allowing anyone to change and distribute it. It is often used for projects where software is developed in a public, collaborative way.
operating system	Software that allows a digital device to work. Provides common services for the different programs to use, as well as a user interface, where required.
pixel	From *picture element*. The smallest dot or square that makes up an image.
program	Computer program or software (i.e. a series of instructions) that can be executed (run) by a computer or digital device.
protocol	A standard used to define a method for exchanging data, e.g. the internet protocol (IP).
PVR	Personal video recorder
RSS	Really simple syndication or rich site summary. A means for delivering regularly changing web content. Many news-related sites will offer one or more RSS

Living in a digital world - Glossary

	feeds. Users subscribe to any that interest them and any new content is automatically notified to them via feed reader software.
software	Computer program(s).
spam	Email spam is unsolicited, undesired or illegal email messages. It is sent indiscriminately in bulk, often for commercial purposes (mostly advertising), seeking to distribute malware or as a part of financial scams.
SSD	Solid state drive. Used like an HDD, but uses solid state memory (EEPROM) and has no moving parts.
tag	A keyword assigned to a resource. Some social networking sites may encourage users to tag uploaded photographs with the names of the people appearing in the picture. However, for reasons of privacy this should only be done if they have given their permission.
touchpad, trackpad	A pointing device that uses a touch-sensitive surface, often built into laptop computers and normally located in front of the keyboard.
URL	Universal resource locator. The address of a web resource, e.g. http://www.educationvision.co.uk
utility	Software that aims to help analyse, optimise, configure or maintain a computer.
user interface	User and computer exchange information (including the user giving instructions) via the user interface. Screens, keyboards and mice are often crucial components of user interfaces.
virus	Malicious software that changes how a computer works and attempts to replicate itself, so that it can spread from one computer to another.
WAN, wide area network	Computer network that spans a large geographical area, e.g. between cities or between countries. Usually connects multiple LANs.
Windows	Widely used family of operating systems from Microsoft.
WYSIWYG	Pronounced "whizzy-wig", this stands for What You See Is What You Get, the ability of a piece of software to show on screen exactly what will be produced, e.g. by a printer.
ZIP	Lossless data compression file format in common use.

Index

'ware words 144

A

abandonware 144
accelerometer 230, 231
Advanced Research Projects Agency, ARPA 158
adware 144, 277
agile project methods 299
agile software development 27
Alan Turing 19, 32, 237
algorithm 91, 93, 105, 108, 109, 111, 114, 120, 147
alpha channel 63, 315
AlphaGo 238
AlphaGo Zero 238
analogue 43-45, 72, 90, 228, 315
anti-virus software 149, 277, 289
app 23, 97, 142, 315
application 23, 315
application software 97, 98, 121, 147, 148
architecture, computer 32
ARPANET 160
array 105, 115, 147
artificial general intelligence, AGI 235, 239
artificial intelligence, AI 234, 237, 239, 240, 242, 257
ASCII 50, 155, 315
assembler 102
assembly language 102
assignment 108
asymmetric cryptography 246, 248
atomic data type 115, 147
audio latency 227

B

backing storage 197
backing up 149, 207, 256
bandwidth 152, 315
barcode 78, 212, 214, 221, 256
barcode reader 222
barcodes, 2-D 216, 256
benefits 268, 289
binary 68, 69, 84, 87, 89, 90, 101, 147, 172
binary fractions 87
binary integers 90
binary prefixes 292
binary search 120
BIOS 96, 147
big data 273, 315
bit 71, 315
bitcoin 242, 248-252
bitmap 134, 137, 140, 315
bitmap graphics 134, 136, 140
bitwise complement 192
Black Box Model 23, 28, 36, 40
bloatware 144
blockchain 249-250, 252-253, 257
blog 315
Bluetooth 36, 187, 228, 315
BMP 64, 140
boolean 115, 147
booting up 96
bootstrap loader 96
bot, internet bot 284, 315
bubble sort 113
buffer 178, 184

bug	25, 96, 315	data normalisation	132
byte	71, 315	data packet	177, 191, 192

C

cache	179, 185	data protection	273
CD	50, 209	data structure	115, 147
CDMA	226	data type	115
cell	224, 225	data validation	132
cell phone	224	data verification	134
central processing unit	32	database	97, 129, 289
character	115, 147	database linking	272
check digit	76-78, 81, 90, 133	database management system, DBMS	130
circuit switching	223	debug	316
cloud (the)	315	decomposition	25, 42
cloud storage	206, 207	Deep Blue	238
cluster	203, 225	deep colour	83
CMYK	83	deep web	161
colour	171-172	defragging	98
compiler	102, 147, 315	deleting files	204
compression	54, 91, 315	denial of service attack	316
compression, lossless	54, 59, 315	desktop publisher, DTP	97, 127
compression, lossy	62, 63, 315	device tracking and disabling	279
computer	18	digital	43-45, 90, 228, 316
computer program	18, 91, 95	digital cliff effect	74
computer vision	239	digital device	17, 22, 42, 43, 68, 74, 97
cookies	271	digital footprint	269, 270, 274, 289
CPU	32, 34, 35, 42, 179, 316	digital immigrants	20
cryptocurrencies	242, 251, 252, 257	digital natives	20
		digital signal	72, 73
cylinder	203	digital signature	247
		digitise	45, 66, 90, 316

D

		digitising data	46
		digitising photographs	53
		digitising sound	49
		digitising text	50
DAB	316	disc fragmentation	98
dark web	161	domain name	158, 174, 316
data	17, 43, 64, 65, 72, 90, 316	Domain Name System, DNS	174
data backup	184	DOS	316
data compression	90	dry running	111, 112
data integrity	132		

E

EAN	78-81, 158, 212-215
EAN-13	212, 214
EAN-8	80, 81
EEPROM	194, 256, 316
email	155, 160, 184
encrypting devices	278
EPROM	194
error	80
error checking	74
error correction	81, 218
error detection	188
espionage	282, 290
Ethernet	153, 316
exchange sort	113
EXIF	66, 316
expansion slot	35
expert systems	234
exponent	89

F

failed IT projects	299
fake websites	284
FAT-32	203
field	115, 130, 131, 147
file	316
file compression	54, 98
file renaming	98
file server	150
File Transfer Protocol, FTP	155, 184
filename extension	316
filtering	278, 289
fire alarm system	24, 26
firewall	153, 276, 289
firmware	144
flash memory	96, 194, 195, 197, 292
flash memory drive	256
floating point	90
floating point representation	89
floppy disc	199, 200, 202
flowchart	93, 108, 147
FOR...NEXT	109
format	56
frame	127, 128
freeware	144
fuzzy data	240
fuzzy logic	235

G

GDPR	275
GIF	59, 140
GIF, animated	59
gigabyte	291
Global Navigation Satellite System, GNSS	233
gold standard	245
Google	180
Googlewhack	180
GPS	142, 228, 233, 234, 316
graphics software	134
graphics tablet	136
GS1	79, 158
GS1 prefix	79, 80
GSM	226, 227
GTIN	80

H

hacker	96
hacking	149, 281, 282, 317
handshaking	74, 187, 188, 192
hard disc drive	202, 205, 256
hardware	28, 42, 317
hash function	81, 247, 317
hash value	81

hazard matrix 267
hazards 266, 289
HDD 317
HDMI 34
heat sink 35
Hello World! 166, 173
Herman Hollerith 19
hexadecimal 171-173
high level programming language 102, 147
high level, logical or quick formatting 203
history 18, 158
html 175, 176
HTML 161, 165-167, 174, 184
HTTP 161
HTTPS 248
hub 152
hypertext 155, 167, 170
Hz 317

I

ICT 317
ICT capability 285
IF statement 93
information 64, 65, 90, 317
input 23, 24, 27-29, 33, 36
integer 116, 147
integers, negative 84
integers, positive 84
interface 36, 42, 95, 317
International Article Number 78
internet 141, 153, 154, 158, 160, 163, 184, 280
internet governance 158
Internet of Things 164
internet protocol 155
Internet Watch Foundation, IWF 278

interpreter 102, 147, 317
inverse square law 233
Investigatory Powers Act 2016 274
IP address 174
IT 317

J

jaggies 139
Java 141
John von Neumann 19, 32
Joint Photographic Experts Group 59
JPEG, JPG 59-63, 82, 91, 140

K

key field 130, 148
keyword 65, 317
kilobyte 292

L

LAN 151, 153, 184, 317
laptop 37, 279
layers 138
linear search 120
local area network 317
logging on 151
low level formatting 202
low level language 102
Luhn Algorithm 76, 77

M

machine code 101, 102, 147
magnetic storage 256
magnetic tape 199

mainframe 37
malware 145, 277, 317
MAN 151, 153
Manifesto for Agile Software Development 299, 303
Manifesto for Agile Software Development, Principles 304
mantissa 89
Marc Prensky 20
markup language 165
mathematical model 40
mathematical modelling 123
megabyte 291, 292
metadata 65, 66, 90, 170, 221, 318
metasearch engine 180
microblog 318
microblogging 164
microcomputer 37
microcontroller 17, 18, 22, 318
microelectromechanical systems, MEMS 230
microprocessor 101, 318
microwave oven 23
mini-computer 37
mining 249
mirror and magnify 262, 263, 265
mobile device 142
mobile telecommunications 224
module 95
money 243-245
monitor 318
most significant bit 85
motherboard 32, 35
MP3 91
multicasting 179
multi-tasking 97, 318

N

National Security Agency 281
natural language processing 234

network 141, 149, 184, 318
network configurations 150
network, client/server 149, 150
network, peer to peer 149
neural network 154, 235
NFC 36, 228
North Korea 281
NTFS 203

O

object code 102, 318
office suite 97, 121
online benefits 267, 268
online grooming 261
online hazards 266
online safety 261
online travel agent 28
open format 140, 318
open source 121, 318
operating system 96, 147, 318
optical media 209
orphanware 144
output 23, 24, 27-29, 33, 36

P

pace of technological change 259, 289
packet switching 160, 184
parity 74, 188
parity bit 75, 81
partition 202
peripheral 29, 30
personal vision 285, 287
petabyte 291
phishing 282
pixel 53, 81, 135, 318
platter 205
PNG 63, 140

pointer 116
power-on self-test, POST 96
presentation graphics 97, 125
print server 150
privacy 211, 289
process 23, 24
processor 32, 42
program 91, 318
programming languages 101
project failures 27
PROM 194
protocol 188, 318
proxy server 280
PS/2 34
pseudocode 109, 111, 114, 147
public key cryptography 246, 247, 257
PVR 318

Q

QR Code 216-218, 220, 221, 222, 256

R

RAM 32, 179, 193, 256
range check 133
ransomware 145, 277, 281
Raspberry Pi 39
raster image 134
real numbers 86, 89, 115, 147
re-booting 96
record 115, 116, 130, 147
redundancy 76
redundancy check 76
relational database 130
repetition 93, 147
resolution 53

RFID 210, 211, 256
RGB 82, 83, 171, 172, 176, 184
right to be forgotten 275
ROM 96, 193, 256
router 152
RSS 163, 318

S

sabotage 281-282, 290
sampling 46
sampling rate 48
satellite communications 232
satellite constellation 232
satellite navigation 233
scanner 66
scareware 145
scientific notation 89
Scratch 91, 102
SD card 256
search engine 179, 185
selection 93, 147
selection sort 105, 111
self-driving vehicles 239
sensor 38, 228, 230
sequence 93, 147
sexting 261
Seymour Cray 40
shareware 145
sharing of data 270
shelfware 145
SI prefixes 291
Silk Road 163
SIM 226, 227
Sir Tim Berners-Lee 161
smartphone 38, 142, 148, 227, 228, 270, 279
snooper's charter 274
social media 284
social networking 142-144, 164

software	23, 28, 95, 319
solid state memory	192, 193, 256
spam	319
spreadsheet	97, 123
spyware	145, 277
SSD	197, 256, 319
standard form, standard index form	89
storage	29, 33
storage media	29
streaming	177, 184
string	115, 147
Stuxnet virus	281
supercomputer	40
supermarket checkout	27
SVG	140, 175-176
switch	152
symmetric cryptography	246, 248
system on a chip	17
systems analysis	27

T

tablet	37, 38, 142, 279
tag	165, 175, 184, 319
technological change	21
technology issues	259
terabyte	291
The Cloud	153
The Information Revolution	19
The Internet Archive	273
TIFF	64, 140
touchpad	319
touchscreen	29
trackpad	136, 319
transistor	193
transposition error	80
Turing Test	237
two's complement	85

U

UEFI	96, 147
unicasting	179
United Nations	158
United States Cyber Command	282
Universal Serial Bus	33
UPC-A	214-215
URI	161
URL	155, 161, 319
US census	19
USB	33, 34, 189-191, 256
USB Implementers Forum, Inc.	189
user interface	96, 319
UTF-8	50
utility software	98, 147, 319

V

vacuum tubes	18
vapourware	145
variable	105, 109, 147
vector graphics	134, 136, 137, 140, 141
VGA	34
Virtual Private Network, VPN	279
virus	277, 319
virus scanner	98
vision systems	235
volume	202

W

WAN	151, 153, 184, 319
WannaCry virus	281
Wayback Machine	273
wear levelling	197
Web 2.0	163, 184

web browser	141, 174
web crawler	181, 185
web page	167, 184
website	174
wetware	145
wide area network	319
Wi-Fi	36, 152, 228
Wi-Fi Alliance	152
Windows	319
wipe	204, 205, 256
word	71
word cloud	16
word processor	97, 123
World Wide Web Consortium, W3C	140, 161
World Wide Web, WWW	141, 155, 161, 173, 175, 184

X

XML	175

Z

zero	67
ZIP	91, 319
zombies	277

www.ingramcontent.com/pod-product-compliance
Lightning Source LLC
Chambersburg PA
CBHW080007210526

45170CB00015B/1871